ESSE

W9-BDW-567

Chemical Dependency Counseling

SECOND EDITION

Gary W. Lawson, PhD
Professor
United States International University
Department of Psychology and Family Studies
San Diego, California

Ann W. Lawson, PhD
Associate Professor
United States International University
Department of Psychology and Family Studies
San Diego, California

P. Clayton Rivers, PhD
Professor
Department of Psychology
University of Nebraska-Lincoln
Lincoln, Nebraska

AN ASPEN PUBLICATION®
Aspen Publishers, Inc.
Gaithersburg, Maryland
1996

Library of Congress Cataloging-in-Publication Data

Lawson, Gary.
Essentials of chemical dependency counseling / Gary W. Lawson, Ann Lawson, P. Clayton
Rivers. — 2nd ed.
p.   cm.
"An Aspen publication."
Includes bibliographical references and index.
ISBN 0-8342-0683-8
1. Drug abuse counseling—United States.   2. Alcoholism counseling—United States.
I. Lawson, Ann W.   II. Rivers, P. Clayton.   III. Title.
HV5825.L38   1996
362.29'186—dc20

96-2427
CIP

Aspen Publishers, Inc., grants permission for photocopying for limited personal or
internal use. This consent does not extend to other kinds of copying, such as
copying for general distribution, for advertising or promotional purposes, for
creating new collective works, or for resale. For information, address Aspen
Publishers, Inc., Permissions Department, 200 Orchard Ridge Drive,
Gaithersburg, Maryland 20878.

Aspen Publishers, Inc., is not affiliated with the American Society of Parenteral
and Enteral Nutrition

The authors have made every effort to ensure the accuracy of the information
herein, particularly with regard to drug selection and dose. However, appropriate
information sources should be consulted, especially for new or unfamiliar drugs
or procedures. It is the responsibility of every practitioner to evaluate the
appropriateness of a particular opinion in the context of actual clinical situations
and with due consideration to new developments. Authors, editors, and the
publisher cannot be held responsible for any typographical or other errors found
in this book.

Editorial Resources: Ruth Bloom

Library of Congress Catalog Card Number: 96-2427
ISBN: 0-8342-0683-8

Printed in the United States of America

2 3 4 5

Table of Contents

Introduction

In the twelve years since we wrote the first edition of this book many things have changed in the chemical dependency counseling field. Many of the changes however have been political or economic, not clinical. Most of the basic procedures and approaches to chemical dependency counseling remain the same. What a client will respond to in counseling today is the same as it was 10 or even 20 years ago. The quality of the therapeutic relationship is still a key factor in treatment outcome. The clinical changes that have occurred in the past few years have been done for political and economic reasons, not because of some major research discovery that proves that one approach is significantly better than another. For example, brief therapy and dual diagnosis are both popular today because third-party payers (insurance companies) want the least costly treatment and are reluctant to support the traditional 30-day inpatient treatment programs, especially for addicts who have not tried outpatient therapy or those who do not have some other diagnosable mental disorder. This change in clinical procedure was not because we suddenly had an epidemic of mentally ill alcoholics or addicts that responded well to brief therapy. It was economically motivated.

We hope that the new additions to this book include relevant changes in the field and in the overall chemical dependency (CD) field knowledge base that will serve the counselor well. We believe they are important to the well-trained CD counselor.

Some of the major changes include new chapters on legal and ethical issues, family counseling, issues of diversity, and a chapter on relapse prevention and aftercare services. The Question-and-Answer Sections have been updated and all of the chapters contain new material. We hope the new addition meets the needs of those who want to work with chemically dependent individuals. We also hope that these changes are useful for those instructors who use this book as a text. We value their input and feedback. Many of the changes in the book are due to comments and suggestions from instructors who have used the first edition.

We encourage the reader to use this book as a starting point to begin a lifelong study of the therapeutic relationship and its use in the treatment of those people involved in chemical dependency. Be open to new answers as well as new questions. Please feel free to contact us with your comments regarding the book. We look forward to hearing from you.

Gary W. Lawson
Ann W. Lawson
P. Clayton Rivers

Note: The terms *patient* and *client* are used here interchangably. *Chemical dependency, addiction*, and *substance abuse* are also all used interchangably.

Chapter 1

Becoming a Chemical Dependency Counselor

CHAPTER OBJECTIVES

- Examine the qualities and characteristics of good counselors
- Examine the qualities and characteristics of good chemical dependency counselors
- Examine the role of values in counseling
- Examine common issues faced by chemical dependency counselors
- Encourage the reader to examine his or her reasons for wanting to become a chemical dependency counselor and to identify potential areas of conflict or difficulty
- Give examples of how chemical dependency counselors can avoid burnout and stay healthy, while helping others

The best place for a person who wants to become a chemical dependency counselor to start is with a thorough evaluation of why he or she wants to enter the field. It is not a field with high salary and earning potential. It is a difficult and demanding job. It is often hard to judge success, and appreciation and rewards are often few. It is a field where failure can come as suddenly as the death of a client. Counselor burnout is a frequent occurrence.

The outcome of this evaluation, for many people, is that they have a desire to help others and to do something meaningful in their work. Some people enter the field after making money in other professions that they found lacking in meaning. Others want to give back what they received in their own treatment and recovery. Most people who enter the field of chemical dependency counseling have some personal history with substance abuse or addiction. They may be recovering from their own personal struggles with chemical dependency or from the effects of living with someone with an addiction.

As the field has grown, it has accepted the idea that others rather than just the alcoholic or addict are affected by substance abuse, and these affected others can understand the addictive process and its treatment. As a result, spouses, children, parents, other relatives, and even friends of chemically dependent persons have become chemical dependency counselors. There are also those, without personal histories of substance abuse, who have genuine commitments to helping others and are particularly interested in chemical dependency. Some of these are mental health professionals, such as social workers, psychiatrists, nurses, psychologists, family therapists, and mental health counselors who are interested in specializing in chemical dependency treatment. Still others are people with no previous mental health training. The American society has become more interested, in general, in alcohol and other drug abuse and is more aware now of the problems it poses for individuals and the society as a whole. The drug wars, antidrinking and driving campaigns, programs for prevention of fetal alcohol syndrome, and drug prevention programs for children have all drawn attention to the problems. Hopefully, awareness of the problems will not lead to increased stigma for those with problems. Addicted celebrities have attempted to take away some of this stigma of alcoholism treatment with their public statements about their own alcoholism and drug abuse treatment. The debate still continues as to whether addiction should be punished, as in drunk driving, or treated, but at least, the problem is reaching a wider audience and more people are being drawn into the field.

Counselors who have personal experience with their own recovery have advantages and disadvantages over counselors without this experience. The biggest advantage is their own experience with addiction and the recovery process enabling them to empathize with their clients and to speak from experience. The disadvantages come in the "blind spots" they developed in the process. Substance abuse is a multigenerational problem. It is very probable that a chemical dependency counselor has one or more family members with substance abuse problems or with problems that resulted from living with an alcoholic/addict. They not only may have unresolved issues with these family members and/or spouses but also may have untreated interpersonal characteristics that can lead to projection of these dynamics onto their clients or excessive countertransference with some clients. For instance, if a counselor's mother was alcoholic, he or she may be particularly harsh with women alcoholics because they share similar attitudes or behaviors with his or her mother. The counselor may be totally unaware of this if he or she has not addressed this in some way, such as through personal therapy. This can lead to a vicious rescue-revenge cycle. Counselors who believe that they entered the field to help others who are suffering but have not resolved their own pain around their personal experiences with alcoholics/addicts can easily get caught in this trap.

Family members try for years to get alcoholics or addicts to stop drinking and using, often with little success. This can leave them angry and frustrated and feeling like failures. It is easy for a counselor to get caught up in the attempt to get his or her clients sober and thus take on too much responsibility for another person's sobriety. When this happens they are on the rescue side of the circle with thoughts like, "I didn't save my mother, but I'll save this woman (i.e., substitute mother)." If she fails at treatment or relapses, the circle shifts to the revenge side with all of the anger, hurt, and disappointment of the original failure. With some self-evaluation, however, people who have personal experiences with chemical dependency can become excellent counselors.

While there is some debate in the field as to whether recovering or nonrecovering counselors are better able to treat chemical dependency, a survey of administrators of treatment programs indicated that most administrators believe that the two groups do not differ in effectiveness. These administrators were evenly divided between preferring having a mix of recovering and nonrecovering counselors and having no preference at all (Anderson & Wiemer, 1992).

There is some evidence that, at least initially in counseling, chemically dependent clients see recovering counselors as having a more unconditional acceptance and level of regard—or possibly imagine that they do. When patients were asked to rate their counselors after the third counseling session, they rated recovering and generally older counselors higher than nonrecovering and younger counselors (Lawson, 1982).

CHARACTERISTICS OF GOOD COUNSELORS

There are three major areas of consideration for becoming a chemical dependency counselor: knowledge and skills, experience, and knowledge of self. This introductory chapter will consider the last area: the self as used in counseling. Although knowledge, skill, and experience are important for becoming a good counselor, people who are aware of their own values, belief systems, philosophies of life, strengths, weaknesses, and how they, as human beings, impact others will have valuable tools for the art of counseling. It is important for counselors to understand and accept their own selves and the self of the other person in order to create a counseling relationship that facilitates growth. Self-knowledge is also good prevention from burnout.

The field of counseling has tried to identify the personal characteristics of counselors that have made them successful for the last forty-five years. There has been speculation about what constitutes characteristics of good counselors; comparisons of effective and ineffective counselors; and research on personality traits, attitudes and beliefs, race, age, sex, attractiveness, expertness, and persuasiveness. Researchers have also evaluated the usefulness of other characteristics in counselors, such as tolerance for ambiguity, dogmatism, humor, profanity, transparency, self-concept, and awareness (Shertzer & Stone, 1980). The earliest list of characteristics of good counselors included the following: being interested in people, patience, sensitivity to others, emotional stability, objectiveness, respectfulness of facts, trustworthiness, and personal maturity (National Vocational Guidance Association, 1949). Later the following characteristics were considered: belief in each individual, commitment to individual human values, alertness to the world, open-mindedness, understanding of self, and professional commitment (Association for Counselor Education and Supervision, 1964).

In trying to distinguish effective and ineffective counselors, Combs (1986) summarized studies involving five different helping professions. He found that the differences involved what these helpers believed about empathy, self, human nature, and their own purposes. These effective counselors had positive beliefs about people and saw them as generally trustworthy, capable, dependable, and friendly. They also had a positive view of themselves and self-confidence in their ability as helpers.

Experience is another variable that distinguished effective and ineffective counselors. Regardless of the orientation of the therapists, the therapeutic relationship created by experts in one school of therapy more closely resembled experts in other schools than nonexperts in their own school (Fiedler, 1950). In many outcome studies comparing the effectiveness of treatment models this had been true. Experience is more predictive of a good outcome in counseling than the model of treatment used. Carl Rogers (1962) demonstrated that the more experienced counselors showed more congruence, empathy, and unconditional positive regard than less experienced counselors, and were more able to communicate these conditions to their clients.

Other studies looked at the relationship between counselor effectiveness and the personality of the counselor. Effective counselors were different from ineffective counselors in regard to self-concept, motivation, values, feelings about others, and perceptual organization. Further, effectiveness was associated with tolerance for ambiguity, understanding of the client, maturity, ability to maintain an appropriate emotional distance from the client, and ability to establish good social relationships with people who were not clients (Shertzer & Stone, 1980). In a study by Wicas and Mahan (1966), highly rated counselors were anxious, sensitive to the expectations of others and society, patient and nonaggressive in interpersonal relationships, and concerned about social progress but always with appropriate self-control.

Corey (1991) created a list of eighteen goals for counselors to strive for to become therapeutic persons and models of awareness and growth for their clients. He stated that counselors should see these characteristics as on a continuum and not consider them as all-or-nothing characteristics.

1. *Effective counselors have an identity.* These are people who are not just doing what they think other people want from them. They are people with a solid sense of self, values, life direction, and principles that they live by.

They can set goals and achieve them. They possess a certain sense of their own indivuation and separateness but are also willing to evaluate their ideas, beliefs, and values.

2. *Effective counselors respect and appreciate themselves.* These people have good self-esteem and consider themselves to be good people. They can give and receive love and caring and feel a connectedness to others.

3. *Effective counselors are able to recognize and accept their own power.* A counselor has power over his or her client by the nature of the relationship. A good counselor is aware of this power and uses it to help his or her client and does not abuse it. This is not a position of superiority, but the knowledge that there is potential for abuse. It is not used to diminish others.

4. *Effective counselors are open to change.* This is a sense of flexibility and openness to other possibilities and growth. It is the ability to risk new behaviors for the potential of learning or experiencing something new that could make them a better person.

5. *Effective counselors are expanding their awareness of self and others.* These people are aware that they are limited in their experiences and move toward growth and development in themselves and learning about other's experiences.

6. *Effective counselors are willing and able to tolerate ambiguity.* Black-and-white, polarized thinking is prevalent in clients with chemical dependency and people who have lived with them. The ability to tolerate ambiguity means becoming comfortable with not knowing as well as exploring the gray areas of life. It is more comforting to stick with absolutes and unbending rules. It takes courage to trust the process of life and to trust that intuitions and novel ideas can produce self-growth and growth in others.

7. *Effective counselors are developing their own counseling style.* This process comes with experience and being open to learning. Counselors who try to exactly imitate another counselor or apply a counseling theory without modification will be less successful than if they are able to pull from many sources, including self-knowledge, to develop their own unique theories.

8. *Effective counselors can experience and know the world of the client, yet their empathy is nonpossessive.* This is the ability of counselors to know themselves in a way that allows them to put their own needs aside long enough to truly understand the worlds of their clients. They, however, do not lose themselves in this process. They can clearly distinguish between the clients' issues and theirs.

9. *Effective counselors feel alive, and their choices are life oriented.* These are people who take an active stance in life. They are not passive but are proactive.

10. *Effective counselors are authentic, sincere, and honest.* These are people who have demonstrated congruence between what they think, feel, and do.

They do not play roles or hide behind masks. Their communication is straightforward and nondefensive.

11. *Effective counselors have a sense of humor.* These are people who use their sense of humor to put life in perspective. They can laugh at themselves and their mistakes. This is extremely important in treating substance abusing individuals and their families who have often forgotten, or never knew, how to laugh and play with one another. This is also the best antidote for burnout.

12. *Effective counselors make mistakes and are willing to admit them.* In a field where attempts at perfectionism abound, being able to admit and learn from mistakes is important to the chemical dependency counselor. They also become excellent role models for clients who hide their mistakes because of extreme guilt.

13. *Effective counselors generally live in the present.* Counselors who can live in the present are more available to their clients. Although the past may be interesting and useful in understanding their clients, they do not dwell on their own past or worry about the future.

14. *Effective counselors appreciate the influence of culture.* Counselors need to be aware of how their own cultures have affected them, and how they have integrated their cultures into themselves. They should also be aware of how culture, race, and gender create different experiences for others. They need to have respect for the differences of others.

15. *Effective counselors are able to reinvent themselves.* These are people who are always in the process of self-growth and can change themselves for the better. They have clear ideas of the person they would like to be, and they move in that direction.

16. *Effective counselors are making choices that shape their lives.* These people do not allow previous mistakes or incorrect decisions to make them victims. They learn from mistakes and make good choices based on continual self-evaluation.

17. *Effective counselors have a sincere interest in the welfare of others.* Their work is based on a genuine respect and desire to help others. They can respect and care for those they are helping.

18. *Effective counselors become deeply involved in their work and derive meaning from it.* These counselors enjoy the process of helping others and look forward to going to work. They recognize the ego needs that are met by helping others, yet they know how to balance their lives and are not workaholics.

CHARACTERISTICS OF GOOD CHEMICAL DEPENDENCY COUNSELORS

Unlike counseling in general, there is not a forty-five year body of research in the area of characteristics of good chemical dependency counselors. The field is in the beginning of this search and has mostly speculated about what these characteristics might be. A few studies have attempted to identify traits of effective chemical dependency counselors. One study surveyed residents in an addictions treatment program (Rohrer, Thomas, & Yasenchak, 1992). The first group of residents was asked to list traits that they felt were the most positive and negative in a counselor. These traits were then compiled into a list of 62 positive and 55 negative traits and given to a second group of residents who rated the top 10 positive and top 10 negative counselor traits. This second group of residents abused both alcohol (37) and other drugs (40). The most frequent drug abused was cocaine (36). The subjects ranged in age from 18 to over 43; they all had a history of previous treatment and legal involvement. The residents used colorful, profane, and imprecise language in their lists, and no attempt was made to define or change their words, in order to maintain the residents' true feelings.

The list of positive traits contains 11 items because there was a tie for 10th place. The following are lists of the ranked positive and negative addiction counselor traits (Rohrer, Thomas, & Yasenchak, 1992, p. 728).

Positive Traits	**Negative Traits**
1. understanding	1. asshole
2. concerned	2. can't relate
3. caring	3. dishonest
4. experienced	4. treat like children
5. honest	5. uneducated
6. certified	6. bullshitter
7. good listener	7. rude
8. streetwise	8. foul mouth
9. easy to talk to	9. show favorites
10. direct	10. unfair
11. open minded	

It appears that these residents want a well-balanced counselor who is able to be empathetic, genuinely caring, and nonjudgmental. This is interesting in the light of traditional confrontational addiction treatment approaches used to break down denial. A typical addiction counselor using the synanon approach, which was developed for therapeutic communities that treat drug addicts, is attacking, aggressive, and intolerant. The research of Rohrer et al. (1992), however, raised the question of whether the type of counselor the residents preferred would be the best counselor for these alcoholics and addicts or the easiest to manipulate.

A second study examined the characteristics of counselors who were successful in their treatment of clients in a methadone maintenance program (McLellan, Woody, Luborsky, & Goehl, 1988). Two counselors left the program at the same time and their clients were randomly assigned to four program counselors with at least eight years of experience. The counselors' performance was measured by their clients' urinalysis results, methadone dosage, prescriptions for psychotropic medications, employment, and arrest rates.

Two counselors were more successful than the other two. The most successful counselor significantly reduced the average methadone dose, number of medications, positive urine tests, and unemployment of the clients. In contrast, the least successful counselor significantly increased the average methadone dose, positive urine tests, and unemployment of the clients.

Performance differences were not totally due to background or education differences, but were affected by the content and process of counseling. More training, however, was associated with better counselor performance. The most successful counselors' charts reflected clearly formulated plans of rehabilitation that had been worked out in consultation with a treatment team and the patients. Their charts were thorough and accurate and indicated that initial plans were generally followed and progress was documented. Their patients followed program rules and were seen more frequently.

These patients were also more frequently referred to program resources such as physicians, nurses, and employment counselors. They were also helped through day-to-day problems with letters to legal authorities and public assistance agencies as well as through encouragement, support, and basic, sensible advice. The less successful counselors kept charts that were less organized in their treatment plans, and contained far less detail in the treatment notes. They were less likely to enforce program rules and use referrals to program resources.

The most successful counselor's notes indicated an approach of "*anticipating problems* in the patient and *discussing strategies* to deal with the anticipated situations" (McLellan, Woody, Luborsky, & Goehl, 1988, p. 429). The rehabilitation thus focused on new behaviors and new ways of thinking. This approach is consistent with other studies of successful professional psychotherapists. The researchers concluded that:

> the consistent and professional patient management practices shown by better drug counselors . . . enabled the patients to stabilize their lives and to use the other social/medical services available to address their problems. These patient management techniques appear to be the hallmark of the effective, professional counselor and may be the minimal conditions necessary for continued patient improvement, even with the powerful effects of methadone (McLellan, Woody, Luborsky, & Goehl, 1988, p. 429).

The addition of the psychotherapy techniques to these skills was the most effective approach to help patients reduce their need for mood-stabilizing medications, including methadone, psychotropic medications, and street drugs.

A recent attempt (April 1995) to describe effective chemical dependency counselors involved a meeting of the Task Force on the Characteristics of Effective Addictions Counselors, sponsored by the Center for Substance Abuse Treatment (CSAT) in Washington, D.C. The purpose of this task force was to generate ideas concerning (1) the characteristics of addictions counselors who work successfully with clients and (2) methods for assessing these counselor characteristics. The task force, made up of a diverse group of experts with experience in clinical practice, training, and research, came to consensus on the following counselor characteristics:

- good mental health and personal adjustment
- investment in personal and professional growth
- ability to create the core conditions of a therapeutic relationship, including empathy, respect, genuineness, and concreteness
- therapeutic optimism
- ability to be well-organized
- ability to recognize and maintain appropriate boundaries and balance between client and counselor needs
- experience with recovery, personal growth, and change
- understanding of professional and personal ethics and values
- sense of humor
- openness and a willingness to celebrate diversity

The task force was also asked to address the differences between generalist and addiction-specialized counselors. Task force members agreed that the changes that generalist counselors should make to become addiction-specialized counselors were:

- Develop appropriate conceptualizations of addiction.
- Examine the effects of alcohol and other drugs in their own lives and the lives of their families.
- Be prepared to deal with challenges around personal boundaries.
- View themselves as role models.
- Become familiar with 12-step work.
- Conceptualize the meaning of "powerlessness."
- Understand the effects of group processes on recovery.
- Learn to be direct if needed.

The task force suggested that addiction-specialized counselors working with broader issues would need to recognize the psychosocial context of addictions and learn to accept the use of medications when appropriate for specific clients. Also, they would need training in broader areas before moving beyond the counselor's scope of practice.

These characteristics are, of course, speculation based on task-force members' experiences in the field. The next step is to study these counselor traits in order to answer several research questions: (1) Which characteristics predict positive outcomes in addicted patients? (2) Are there universally desirable counselor characteristics, or does the set of characteristics vary based on treatment setting (e.g., inpatient vs. outpatient), patient characteristics (e.g., mandated treatment vs. voluntary; alcohol abuse vs. other drug abuse), stage of patient's recovery (early, middle, late), or modality (e.g., group vs. individual treatment)? (3) Can these counselor characteristics be taught? (4) To what extent do counselor characteristics vs. knowledge and skill predict the outcome of treatment? (5) To what extent do counselor characteristics vs. counselor background characteristics such as recovery or nonrecovery status, level of training, experience level, professional vs. nonprofessional, addictions specialist vs. nonspecialist predict treatment outcome?

Although there are no absolute answers about what personal characteristics are important for chemical dependency counselors, there are many commonalities and overlaps in the lists of characteristics generated from various sources. The more counselors are aware of their personal strengths, personality characteristics, and value and belief systems, the more valuable they will be in the counseling process.

THE ROLE OF VALUES IN COUNSELING

Part of the search of self that counselors should do is to examine their values and to see how the values are likely to affect their work as counselors. Although there is a certain amount of education presented in most chemical dependency treatment programs, counselors are not there to indoctrinate their clients about what is the right way to think, feel, and behave. They cannot answer all the questions or solve all the problems of their troubled clients. The counseling process is different from teaching or preaching.

The other extreme position that counselors take is to believe that they can remain valueless in their work. They think that they can check their values at the door so they do not judge their clients. The problem with this impossible position comes when the counselor tries too hard to suppress judgments and ends up unwittingly persecuting his or her clients because of unrecognized biases. Since it is impossible to keep values and beliefs out of the counseling process, counselors need to be completely aware of their own biases and beliefs. They need to recognize when their clients have values and beliefs that have caused them harm or are self-destructive, and challenge them. When counselors can acknowledge their values without imposing them on their clients, they are being honest and human. It is this real human connection that gives power to the therapeutic relationship.

It would be difficult for a counselor to set goals and move in a positive direction if he or she had no values concerning what a mentally healthy individual, marriage, or family might be. A national survey of mental health professionals discovered that there are a set of values that are used by therapists to guide their work (Jensen & Bergin, 1988). Ten values were listed by these professionals as contributing to a positive, mentally healthy lifestyle:

1. competent perception and expression of feelings
2. a sense of being a free and responsible agent
3. management of stress
4. self-awareness and growth
5. commitment to marriage, family, and other relationships
6. self-maintenance and physical fitness
7. have orienting goals and meaningful purpose
8. forgiveness
9. regulated sexual fulfillment, and
10. spirituality/religiosity.

It appears that it is difficult to separate out these values from the counselors' theory and practice. The important part of knowing values is the ability to allow clients to come to their own decisions about whether they want to pursue these same goals. It is not ethically responsible for counselors to make decisions for their clients. It may be clear to a counselor that his or her client should leave her husband who has been abusive to her, but she needs to come to that decision herself. There are many ramifications and consequences to important life decisions. There are many issues that clients bring to therapy that are value laden. Corey (1991) had listed some areas that frequently cause dilemmas for counselors whose values may clash with the beliefs, choices, and behaviors of their clients.

- **Religion**—A person's experience with religion forms an important part of his or her value system. There are many possibilities for client-therapist disagreements in religious belief. The therapist may be a fundamental Christian with certain strong beliefs. This may cause them difficulty in working with clients from other religions or other Christian denominations or with clients with no religious belief. Therapists who are atheists may also have difficulty with clients whose lives are strongly connected with their religion and church. A third problem arises when the therapist is unfamiliar with a client's religion and how this impacts their life—their thinking and behaving. The client's goals may be driven by their religious beliefs and be contrary to the therapist's values of mental health (i.e., self-sacrifice vs. independence).

- **Abortion**—There is no other issue that is as emotionally charged as this. People tend to become very polarized on one end of the continuum or the other and are unable to hear the opposite perspective. Counselors working with women, especially young women, will confront this issue in counseling. It may be difficult for a counselor who is strictly against abortion to be supportive of a woman who has chosen to end a pregnancy. It may be equally difficult for a counselor who emotionally supports women's rights to choose this option to support a 14-year-old girl's decision to give birth to her second child when she has abandoned the first one. Counselors with strong opinions on this issue need to decide if they can help their clients struggle with difficult abortion decisions or if they need to refer these clients to someone else.

- **Alternative lifestyles**—The gay and lesbian population is at high risk for chemical dependency. Counselors in this field may be treating gay and lesbian alcoholic or addicts, and they need to be clear with themselves what their feelings and beliefs are concerning this alternative lifestyle. Counselors should examine whether or not they can support these clients' goals, without trying to change them or impose their values on these goals. Counselors who find themselves with a high level of homophobia should either deal with this issue in supervision or refer their gay and lesbian clients to others.

- **Extramarital sex**—There are a number of myths that surround the issues of affairs. Couples have varying contracts concerning what constitutes an affair, from flirting with someone of the opposite sex to agreeing that men can have affairs but women cannot. This is a large issue in the treatment of chemical dependency. Both men and women may have infidelity as part of their history. Extramarital sex is an area deserving of attention and treatment in the recovery process, and counselors need to understand the damage that can be done by these infidelities. Pittman & Pittman (1995) have listed seven common myths that counselors have concerning affairs and counter these with truths.

  1. **Myth #1**—Everybody is unfaithful; it is normal, expected behavior.
     Truth—Infidelity is not normal behavior, but a symptom of some problem.
  2. **Myth #2**—Affairs are good for a marriage.
     Truth—Affairs are dangerous and can easily and inadvertently end marriages.
  3. **Myth #3**—Affairs prove that love has gone from a marriage.

Truth—Affairs can occur in marriages that, prior to the affair, were quite good.

4. **Myth #4**—The affairee was sexier than the spouse.
   Truth—Affairs involve sex, but sex is usually not the purpose of the affair.
5. **Myth #5**—The affair is the fault of the spouse not involved.
   Truth—No one can drive someone else to have an affair.
6. **Myth #6**—There is safety in ignorance of a spouse's affair.
   Truth—Affairs are fueled by secrecy and threatened by exposure.
7. **Myth #7**—After an affair, divorce is inevitable.
   Truth—Marriages can, with effort, survive affairs if the affairs are exposed (pp. 297–99).

There is a high posttreatment divorce rate in chemical dependency treatment. Many of these divorces can be avoided if infidelity is directly confronted in the recovery process. Counselors need to examine their values concerning extramarital sex and not be too quick to blame these affairs on the disease process. It may be useful for the alcoholic or addict to be absolved of guilt for having an affair while using or drinking, but at the same time this leaves the spouse with a feeling of guilt or shame for still being hurt and angry.

- **Divergence of cultural values**—Cultures differ with regard to many issues that relate to mental health, such as closeness and dependence on family. It would put clients in a dilemma if they had been raised to respect and follow their parent's wishes, and the counselor encourages them to make their own decisions and be independent because the counselor believes this is more healthy. Counselors need to listen to clients who are from other cultures and ethnic backgrounds to learn what values they bring with them. It will be more productive to work with their values than against them, even if they are not values held by the counselor.

- **Drugs**—This may seem like an issue that would not be a problem for a chemical dependency counselor. Yet, the subtle values of the counselor may get hidden as he or she enters the field wishing to help alcoholics, while at the same time being more condescending toward users of illegal drugs because they are breaking the law. Another area of conflict may come when counselors take a dogmatic stance against any drug or alcohol use. How will these counselors treat family members who use these substances in a "nonharmful" way? The field of chemical dependency treatment is filled with high emotion around the use of alcohol and other drugs. Counselors should be careful that their emotions do not cause value judgments that are harmful to their clients.

- **Right to die**—In the field of chemical dependency counseling it is possible for counselors to have clients in advanced stages of AIDS or other terminal diseases. These clients may want to evaluate suicide as an option to prolonged suffering and expense. Counselors may have very strong opinions against any type of suicide or against needless suffering. There are also legal issues that should be considered in this situation.

Counselors also have an ethical obligation not to treat clients for whom they have disdain. There may be certain qualities or characteristics of clients that counselors cannot get beyond, and certain problems that they bring to counseling that make it difficult to work with them in a helpful way. Counselors should be aware of problems that they are unable to work with or that cause more difficulty for them personally. When this occurs, counselors should refer these clients to other counselors who can be more helpful.

COMMON ISSUES FACED BY CHEMICAL DEPENDENCY COUNSELORS

Corey (1991) discusses issues that he believes are areas of difficulty for beginning therapists. Many of these issues are the same problems or concerns that chemical dependency counselors have. This section will briefly address these in the context of chemical dependency counseling.

Dealing with Anxieties

Most beginning counselors and some experienced counselors experience anxiety about what to do in a counseling session. They have fears that their clients will not like them, they will look foolish, or their clients' problems will be too overwhelming. These anxieties are normal and even desired. They indicate a genuine concern to do well. Wicas and Mahan (1966) identified anxiety as a characteristic of an effective counselor. However, too much anxiety can paralyze counselors and leave them unable to access their knowledge, resources, and strengths. A good way to deal with these anxieties is in supervision.

Being Genuine and Using Self-Disclosure Appropriately

The use of self in therapy is extremely powerful. "Therapy is a deeply intimate and vulnerable experience, requiring sensitivity to one's own state of being as well as to that of the other. It is the meeting of the deepest self of the therapist with the deepest self of the patient or client" (Satir, 1987, p. 17).

Beginning counselors may be concerned about what they should do or act like in a counseling session. This can lead to their wearing masks or hiding behind a front of insincere caring. If counselors rely too much on what they read about theories of counseling or focus too much on technique, they will miss the human connection and intuitions created by being in the here and now. When counselors can trust that they have integrated their learning and that it will come to them when they need it, they will be more available to their clients. Being genuine does not mean always being warm and caring. It means acknowledging what the counselor is really feeling at the time. Counselors' reactions to clients are probably similar to other peoples' reactions, and this is good information for clients. If a counselor is being bored or irritated by a client, that information may provide the client with good feedback about how he or she may be boring or irritating others.

Self-disclosure is a common concern with chemical dependency counselors who feel that they are role models for their clients. It can be very helpful for a client who is struggling with chemical dependency to know that his or her counselor has been through this same struggle and is doing well. The problem comes when self-disclosure is used too frequently or inappropriately. If the therapy session is dominated by the counselor's telling his or her recovery story, it may be more therapeutic for the counselor than for the client. A good question for counselors to ask themselves in deciding whether self-disclosure would be appropriate is: "Who will benefit from this self-disclosure?" If the answer is anything other than, "the client," then it is probably inappropriate. Issues that arise for the counselor during counseling sessions are best processed in supervision or in the counselor's own therapy.

Avoiding Perfectionism

It is easy for counselors to believe that they must be perfect: say the right thing, have the right feeling, know the right answer. These counselors have an exaggerated fear that making a mistake will ruin their clients' lives. These irrational thoughts will stifle the creative and intuitive process of counseling. In all honesty, it is often the mistakes that help counselors learn and grow. Just as it is true when learning to snow ski that the skier who never falls is neither learning nor improving, so it is with counseling. Taking risks in the therapy process can lead to greater changes for both the client and the counselor. Additionally, clients are rarely damaged by incorrect assumptions, statements, or reflections on the counselor's part. They will usually just correct the counselor and go on.

Counselors who are overly concerned with being perfect usually take too much responsibility for solving their clients' problems. This can be particularly problematic in the field of chemical dependency. Alcoholics and addicts are more than willing for someone else to take responsibility for their problems. The more difficult and the more therapeutic process is to get the alcoholic or addict to take responsibility for his or her problems. Counselors who believe that they have the power to change anyone other than themselves will be repeatedly disappointed.

Being Honest about Limitations

Counselors who believe that they can handle any problems that their clients bring to therapy may be actually doing their clients a disservice. It is important for counselors to know their limitations and not practice beyond their competencies. This is an ethical issue that is addressed in full in Chapter 2. Counselors should not enter into areas that they are not trained for, such as legal advice, medical advice, financial planning, or other areas where their clients might be having trouble. The clients should be referred to proper professionals.

It is especially important for chemical dependency counselors who are working with clients who have a multitude of life problems that coexist with their chemical dependency including mental illness, marital problems, parenting problems, and family dysfunction to refer them to other professionals. All of these problems do not need to be addressed by one counselor. A treatment team approach may be more helpful to these multiproblem clients.

There are also issues that clients bring to therapy that may cause counselors to be uncomfortable or that challenge their values and beliefs. Counselors who can recognize their limitations and refer clients to other specialists will be seen by their clients as more honest, trustworthy, and competent than counselors who try to fake it in areas they are either unfamiliar with or that cause them difficulties.

Avoiding Blurred Boundaries between Counselor and Client

A similar problem to taking too much responsibility for client change is blurred boundaries. Counselors who lose themselves in the therapy process become overwhelmed with their clients' problems. They ruminate over their cases and even lose sleep worrying about their clients. They become overly empathetic with their clients and lose their ability to help them. Counselors are responsible for being completely present with their clients in the process of counseling, but they need to let them take what they want from the interaction and live their own lives, including making mistakes. It is useful for counselors to remember that these people managed to live before they met them and will continue to do so after they terminate therapy. Counselors who cannot forget about a client when they terminate therapy are especially vulnerable to becoming lost in the helping process. They need to able to allow their clients to take charge of their own lives so that they can be completely present for their new clients. This is definitely true for chemical dependency counselors who are working with people who will be working on their recovery for the rest of their lives.

Countertransference, or what occurs when a counselor's own needs or past unresolved personal issues and conflicts arise in the therapy process and become entangled with the client's issues, can lead to the blurring of boundaries. This countertransference is often unrecognized at the time by the counselor, but an overinvolvement with a client should be brought to supervision so the counselor can sort out what his or her personal issue might be that is contributing to the loss of self.

Chemical dependency counselors who are recovering also need to make a clear distinction between their professional clients and the 12-step group members that they sponsor. There are different expectations for a sponsor than for a professional counselor. Chapter 2 elaborates on this issue.

Developing a Sense of Humor

Counseling is a serious commitment to helping others, yet counselors who take themselves too seriously are missing the healing tool of genuine laughter and the ability to laugh at themselves. Laughter can be used to avoid confronting painful issues or to cover up insecurities, but when a counselor can distinguish between humor that is distracting and humor that is helpful, he or she will have a powerful tool for genuine connection with others and an antidote for burnout.

Humor and fun are often sadly lacking in individuals and families in recovery. Families who associate the use of alcohol or other drugs with parties, celebrations, and having fun may believe that fun and laughter must be given up with the drugs. It is vitally important to help individuals and family members learn how to play, laugh, and have fun without the abuse of substances. Often these families have never experienced playing together, and they need help in discovering how to do this. Counselors should be good role models of how to appropriately laugh and play.

Establishing Realistic Goals

In working with chemical dependency recovery, counselors need to be realistic about what goals can be accomplished in the time they are often given by external sources like insurance companies, managed care organizations, program guidelines, and financial limitations. It is also unrealistic to set goals such as reestablishing intimacy with a spouse early in recovery when neither the pain and disappointment of the spouse nor more practical issues of how the recovering person will be integrated back into the daily running of the home and parenting have been addressed. Counselors who can see therapy and personal recovery as a long-term process are able to see that their encounter with the client is just one small part of this journey. They are not responsible for fixing all of the problems that they might see with their clients. In setting goals with their clients it may be useful to contract for short-term goals and discuss how these will lead to long-term goals.

Declining To Give Advice

It is very tempting for counselors to give advice to their clients. This may even seem necessary in chemical dependency counseling, where education and role modeling are part of the process. Education and advice giving, however, are two different things. Education involves giving out information to clients in a way that allows them to use what information is useful to them (i.e., teaching the 12 steps of Alcoholics Anonymous (A.A.) or recommending books to read). Advice giving is a no-win proposition for a counselor. If a counselor advises his or her client to do something and it turns out to be poor advice, the client loses respect for the counselor. If it is useful advice, the client does not get to experience the rewards because he or she did not think of it or because he or she feels inadequate for not thinking of it. This erodes the client's self-confidence.

There may be times when advice giving is necessary if the client is a danger to himself or herself or is in a state of confusion, but it should not be overused. The counselors' job is to empower their clients to discover their own solutions and not to deprive them of the freedom to chose their own path. This is also liberating for the counselors.

Avoiding Burnout

Burnout is common in chemical dependency counseling, but it is not inevitable. Counselors with a good burnout prevention program can be free of this problem throughout their careers. Burnout is caused by a combination of personal, interpersonal, and organization dynamics. These can include: monotonous work with little reward, work that is not meaningful and does not provide a sense of accomplishment, too much pressure and too many deadlines, nonsupportive supervisors, a lack of supportive colleagues, too many work hours, difficult clients who often drop out of therapy or have been mandated to therapy, a lack of opportunities for learning and growth, poor boundaries between self and clients, unrealistic expectations of self and clients, rigid family roles and unhealthy dynamics replayed in the workplace, ensnarement in the rescue-revenge cycle, and personal and family problems that spill over into work.

Therapists play an important role in their own burnout when they see the stress of their job and the problems they are having as coming entirely from outside sources. They believe that they are victims with no responsibility for their burnout and no control over it. The first step that they need to take in combating burnout is to take responsibility for what they can control: their behavior; their thoughts; and their feeling concerning their work, the work environment, their co-workers, administrators, and supervisors. The second step is that they need to take action and change what they can.

The best way to battle burnout is to follow a burnout prevention plan that might include the following:

- Continually evaluate whether you are learning and growing.
- Take regular vacations and do not take work along.
- Compartmentalize—be present in the activity you are doing. Don't worry about your client while you are on a date.
- Take mental health days off from work.
- Do not give your home phone number to your clients except in special circumstances.
- Regularly attend workshops and trainings to update your skills and get new energy.
- Take coffee and lunch breaks, but have juice instead of coffee.
- Follow an exercise program.
- Practice good nutrition.
- Read new books and journals in your field.
- Read novels and go to movies, concerts, and art museums.
- Learn to say no when you have reached your limits.
- Find a group of colleagues whom you admire and begin a supervision group if you are not getting regular supervision.
- Balance your time between personal growth, recovery and development, intimate or marital relationships, family connections, recreation, and work.
- Travel.
- Develop hobbies.
- Relax.
- Sleep.
- Find time for spiritual growth and evaluate meaning.
- Support your professional organizations.
- Volunteer.
- Seek professional help for your problems.
- Keep a journal.
- Be open to new experiences and potential for learning about others.
- Find ways to be creative in all areas of your life, including your job.
- Save all of the thank-you notes and special messages that you receive from clients and co-workers and read them regularly.
- Buy flowers for your office.

This is by no means an exhaustive list. What is important is for counselors to create a plan that works for them.

Becoming a chemical dependency counselor is a process. It is a process that requires continual self-examination and self-care. The field of chemical dependency can be addictive itself, and it holds great rewards and personal satisfaction for those who pursue it.

DISCUSSION QUESTIONS

1. Make a list of all of the effective counselor characteristics in this chapter. After each characteristic write either "strength" or "growth area." Then make a plan for improvement in the growth areas.
2. Consider the dilemmas concerning values or conflicting values that you may encounter in counseling. Make a list of issues or problems that you may not be able to work with and find resources in you community for referrals.
3. Review the section on issues that may be difficult for chemical dependency counselors and list all that apply to you. Make a plan for personal growth in each area.
4. List potential danger areas of burnout for you. Create a burnout prevention plan for yourself, and follow it.
5. Do some volunteer work in a chemical dependency treatment program, and keep a journal of your experiences and your emotional reactions to the process.

REFERENCES

Anderson, S., & Wiemer, L. (1992). Administrators' beliefs about the relative competence of recovering and nonrecovering chemical dependency counselors. *Families in Society: The Journal of Contemporary Human Services, 73* (10), 596–603.

Association for Counselor Education and Supervision (1964). The counselor: Professional preparation and role. *Personnel and Guidance Journal, 42,* 536–41.

Combs, A. W. (1986). What makes a good helper? A person-centered approach. *Person-Centered Review, 1,* 51–61.

Corey, G. (1991). *Theory and practice of counseling and psychotherapy* (4th ed.). Pacific Grove, CA: Brooks/Cole Publishing Co.

Fiedler, F. E. (1950). A comparison of therapeutic relationships in psychoanalytical, nondirective and adlerian therapy. *Journal of Consulting Psychology, 14,* 436–45.

Jensen, J. P., & Bergin, A. E. (1988). Mental health values of professional therapists: A national interdisciplinary survey. *Professional Psychology: Research and Practice, 14,* 290–97.

Lawson, G. (1982). Relation of counselor traits to evaluation of the counseling relationship of alcoholics. *Journal of Studies on Alcohol, 43* (7), 834–38.

McLellan, Woody, G. W., Luborsky, L., & Goehl, L. (1988). Is the counselor an "active ingredient" in substance abuse rehabilitation? An examination of treatment success among four counselors. *The Journal of Nervous and Mental Disease, 176* (7), 423–30.

National Vocational Guidance Association (1949). *Counselor preparation.* Washington, D.C.: The Association.

Pittman, F. S., & Pittman, T. W. (1995). Crises of infidelity. In N. S. Jacobson & A. S. Gurman (Eds.). *Clinical Handbook of Couple Therapy*. New York: Guilford.

Rogers, C. (1962). The interpersonal relationship: The core of guidance. *Harvard Educational Review, 32*, 416–29.

Roher, G. E., Thomas, M., & Yasenchak, M. S. (1992). Client perception of the ideal addictions counselor. *The International Journal of Addictions, 27* (6), 727–33.

Satir, V. (1987). The therapist story. In M. Baldwin & V. Satir (Eds.), *The use of self in therapy* (pp. 17–25). New York. The Haworth Press, Inc.

Shertzer, B., & Stone, S. (1980). *Fundamentals of Counseling* (3rd ed.). Boston: Houghton Mifflin Co.

Task Force on the Characteristics of Effective Addictions Counselors (April, 1995). Washington, D.C.: Center for Substance Abuse Treatment.

Wicas, E. A., & Mahan, T. W. (1966) Characteristics of counselors rated effective by supervisors and peers. *Counselor Education and Supervision, 6*, 50–56.

SUGGESTED READING

Corey, G., & Corey, M. (1990). *I never knew I had a choice* (4th ed.). Pacific Grove, CA: Brooks/Cole.

Corey, M., & Corey, G. (1989). *Becoming a helper*. Pacific Grove, CA: Brooks/Cole.

Bugental, J. F. T. (1987). *The art of the psychotherapist*. New York: Norton.

Baldwin, M., & Satir, V. (Eds.). (1987). *The use of self in therapy*. New York: Haworth Press.

Kottler, J. A., & Blau, D. (1989). *The imperfect therapist: Learning from failure in therapeutic practice*. San Francisco: Jossey-Bass.

Kottler, J. A. (1986). *On becoming a therapist*. San Francisco: Jossey-Bass.

Kilburg, R. R., Nathan, P. E., & Thoreson, R. W. (Eds.). (1986). *Professionals in distress: Issues, syndromes, and solutions in psychology*. Washington, DC: American Psychological Association.

Chapter 2

Legal and Ethical Issues in Chemical Dependency Counseling

CHAPTER OBJECTIVES

- Examine ethical issues in chemical dependency counseling
- Provide a model of ethical decision making
- Examine laws governing the practice of chemical dependency counseling
- Review current counselor certification regulations
- Provide examples of difficult ethical and legal questions for discussion and evaluation

As the field of chemical dependency counseling becomes recognized as a professional discipline, the need for self-regulation in the area of the ethical behavior of counselors is imperative. The recent history of ethics violations in the chemical dependency field has resulted in a tragic loss of trust on the part of the public (Dove, 1995). This tragedy included clients who were victimized by sexual contact with counselors; and programs and clinicians being punished by state review boards and the courts for the misrepresentation of "success rates," insurance fraud, and other unethical behaviors (Dove, 1995). Treatment programs were accused of holding patients against their wills, overdiagnosing addiction (especially in adolescents), and even offering prizes to hospital employees for increasing program statistics on admissions and days of treatment by recruiting patients and preventing them from leaving early. Inpatient placements were inappropriate for many adolescent substance abusers; large numbers of young people were deprived of their liberty under the guise of receiving medical treatment without the benefit of due process or procedural safeguards, and quality of care in many of these hospitals was poor and abusive (Schwartz, 1989). In the golden days of chemical dependency treatment the temptation for treatment providers was to overtreat the problem to increase income from third-party payers, such as medical insurance companies, however, in the current climate of managed care there are financial incentives for providing less treatment (Bissell &

Royce, 1987). Profit and financial gains are often at the root of unethical or questionable behavior.

Therefore, if the field of chemical dependency counseling is to thrive and grow as a professional discipline, counselors and other caregivers must follow a code of ethics and the laws governing this profession. Traditionally, chemical dependency counselors have been labelled paraprofessionals. If they are serious about being seen as professionals, they must build a tradition of acting as such, following a code of ethics, and being primarily concerned about rendering ethical service to clients (Bissell & Royce, 1987).

This chapter addresses ethical and legal concerns and dilemmas that arise in the field. There will not be absolute answers, which may be troubling to the reader, but there are very few absolute answers to the complicated questions of ethical treatment in the field. "True ethical dilemmas are those situations where two or more ethical principles must be weighed against one another, such as confidentiality against the public welfare in the case of a dangerous client" (Dove, 1995, p. 20). Ethics often deal with principles that "ought to" govern human behavior in gray areas and moral decisions. Ethical principles are guidelines for professionals that are designed to protect the consumers and the profession.

These principles are usually developed by professional organizations that certify the professionals who belong to them. Currently, there are many state and national organizations that have taken on the task of certifying chemical dependency counselors. Part of the reason for certification in the field is to test counselors on their knowledge of the law and the ethics that govern chemical dependency counseling in order to safeguard patients and to let the public know that this is a profession that will scrutinize its members and take a self-regulatory stance. Certification also lets the consumer know that the clinician has at least a basic knowledge and competence in the field of chemical dependency treatment. These codes of ethics are also helpful to the chemical dependency counselor in dealing with potential dangers. Codes not only protect the counselor from government interference and regulation by lawmakers and from internal discord among colleagues but also give some protection if the counselor is sued for malpractice (Van Hoose & Kottler, 1985).

This chapter is divided into two parts: ethical issues in chemical dependency counseling and legal issues. Some issues, such as confidentiality, will fall into both ethical and legal categories and are addressed in codes of ethics as well as being governed by federal law in the treatment of chemical dependency.

ETHICAL CONSIDERATIONS IN CHEMICAL DEPENDENCY COUNSELING

The field of chemical dependency counseling is unique in that it is multidisciplinary. Treatment is provided by physicians, psychiatrists, psychologists, social workers, clergy, family therapists, and chemical dependency counselors, often working as a team. Each of these disciplines has one or more professional organizations and a code of ethics that set guidelines for providing services and treatment. Professionals in each of these areas need to be familiar with their professional code of ethics. This chapter will not attempt to cover all of these guidelines but will address the special issues that arise in the treatment of substance abuse. Probably the most recent code of ethics to be adopted is the one put forth for chemical dependency counselors by the National Association of Alcoholism and Drug Abuse Counselors (NAADAC) (1993). While this is not the only national organization attempting to certify chemical dependency counselors, its code of ethics does address issues that are important for any professional who treats chemical dependency. It is not the intent of this chapter to promote NAADAC as the only professional organization for chemical dependency counselors nor to support its positions, but they have a code of ethics that addresses issues pertinent to chemical dependency counseling. Their code is used as an example. Other organizations may have different codes, but they will probably address similar ethical issues.

The National Association of Alcoholism and Drug Abuse Counselors has established a code of ethical standards for alcoholism and drug abuse counselors that includes twelve principles. The code begins with this preamble:

> The National Association of Alcoholism and Drug Abuse Counselors is comprised of professional alcoholism and drug abuse counselors who, as responsible health care professionals, believe in the dignity and worth of human beings. In the practice of their profession they assert that the ethical principles of autonomy, beneficence and justice must guide their professional conduct. As professionals dedicated to the treatment of alcohol and drug dependent clients and their families, they believe that they can effectively treat its individual and familial manifestations. Alcoholism and drug abuse counselors dedicate themselves to promote the best interests of their society, of their clients, of their profession and of their colleagues (National Association of Alcoholism and Drug Abuse Counselors, 1993, p. 1A).

The first principle is one of nondiscrimination and states that alcoholism and drug abuse counselors "must not discriminate against clients or professionals based on race, religion, age, handicaps, national ancestry, sexual orientation or economic condition" (NAADAC, 1993, p.1A). Although this seems fairly straightforward, it brings up questions about how to avoid discrimination in making decisions of who will receive service when there is a waiting list. Should a program assess people on the waiting list to see who would benefit most from services or who needs treatment the most? Should they take paying clients before those who cannot pay? Where should limited resources go? Does nondiscrimination mean that treatment programs must be able to serve all populations equally well when these populations have unique needs and often different languages? Is it equally unethical for treatment programs designed for white male adults to advertise that they can treat special groups such as adolescents, the elderly, Native Americans, or African-Americans, and then admit one or two of these people to their treatment centers without specialized programming for their unique needs (Bissell & Royce, 1987; Lawson & Lawson, 1989)? What about the hiring practices of treatment centers that will only hire people who are recovering from their own addiction? Although nondiscrimination is a good principle to guide decisions, it can be difficult to implement in all situations.

The second principle concerns responsibility as a teacher and a practitioner. It states:

> The alcoholism and drug counselor must espouse objectivity and integrity, and maintain the highest standards in the services the counselor offers.
>
> a. The alcoholism and drug abuse counselor, as teacher, must recognize the counselor's primary obligation to help others acquire knowledge and skill in dealing with the disease of chemical dependency.
>
> b. The alcoholism and drug abuse counselor, as practitioner, must accept the professional challenge and responsibility deriving from the counselor's work (NAADAC, 1993, p. 1A).

This principle is fairly self-explanatory. It describes the responsibility that chemical dependency counselors have when they represent themselves to the public and disperse information about the profession. This principle specifically mentions "the disease of chemical dependency." Some professionals in the field might have difficulty with promoting this concept in exclusion of other models.

The third principle addresses the issue of competence and the need for ongoing education and training. The issue of competence not only means having competence in the treatment of chemical dependency but also not treating problems outside of this competence, nor allowing others without this competence to treat alcohol and other drug abuse. This may be quite difficult, however, if the chemical dependency counselor is working with a treatment team and the hierarchy of command or politics of the situation makes it difficult to confront a person in an authority position. The other problem is what constitutes a qualified person and who should make this determination. The language of the principle indicates that it should be reported to the appropriate certifying authority who would then investigate if the therapist is practicing beyond his or her training and qualifications. This principle does imply that there is a body of knowledge that is unique to the treatment of chemical dependency, and therapists who are qualified to treat other types of problems may not be qualified simply by virtue of their training in psychology, mental health, or social work to provide chemical dependency treatment.

This third principle also requires counselors to seek help for themselves and their colleagues if they become impaired in any way. This is especially important for the substance abuse field where the possibility of relapse is a reality. This presents a dilemma for the treatment center that believes that relapses are to be expected in the recovery process, yet denies credibility as a role model to the chemical dependency counselor who relapses. Should the counselor be fired? What will happen to his or her patients and what will they be told? Is it fair to keep the counselor employed and treating patients with more sobriety than he or she has? Must this counselor achieve the required number of years (usually two or three) of sobriety before they can counsel others? Even more of a problem is the chemical dependency counselor with no previous addiction who develops a problem while working in the field. Even nonrecovering counselors with no problems with alcohol have created concern in others when they have been seen drinking alcoholic beverages in public. Should nonrecovering chemical dependency counselors drink any alcohol in public? These are questions that need to be considered by treatment programs in making personnel policy; thus making chemical dependency counselors aware of the policy concerning impaired therapists before they begin their jobs. Although this will not lead to easy solutions, it is a place to begin.

Principle 3 states:

> The alcoholism and drug abuse counselor must recognize that the profession is founded on national standards of competency which promote the best interests of society, of the client, of the counselor and of the profession as a whole. The counselor must recognize the need for ongoing education as a component of professional competency.
>
> a. The alcoholism and drug abuse counselor must prevent the practice of alcoholism and drug abuse counseling by unqualified and unauthorized persons.
>
> b. The alcoholism and drug counselor who is aware of unethical conduct or of unprofessional modes of practice must report such violations to the appropriate certifying authority.
>
> c. The alcoholism and drug abuse counselor must recognize boundaries and limitations of counselor's competencies and not offer services or use techniques outside of these professional competencies.
>
> d. The alcoholism and drug abuse counselor must recognize the effect of professional impairment on professional performance and must be willing to seek appropriate treatment for oneself or for a colleague. The counselor must support peer assistance programs in this respect (NAADAC, 1993, p.1A).

Competence is difficult to define, but it is an important issue in the treatment of chemical dependency counseling. The counselor can err in both directions: assuming too much or too little. When chemical dependency treatment specialists assume that they can provide everything their clients need to achieve recovery from addiction, they are taking on an enormous task and doing their clients a disservice by isolating them from professionals with unique skills that can aid in their client's recovery and treatment. Addiction is usually clustered with a number of other problems such as legal difficulties, financial problems, lack of job skills, medical problems, sexual dysfunction, marital problems, parenting problems, lack of transportation, educational deficits, inadequate social skills, and general living difficulties. The more of these problems that are attacked in the course of treatment, the better the potential for success. Rarely is one counselor trained to deal with this myriad of problems. What often interferes with professional crossreferral and networking treatment is the concept of patient ownership. The attitude, "My client is fragile, and I am the only one who understands and my client might relapse in having to deal with these problems," perpetuates this notion of ownership. Not only does this give clients a perception that they are weak, it is also a false assumption because these are the very problems, if left unsolved, that may set up a relapse. With the too often emphasis on addiction to alcohol and other drugs as the primary problem, the assumption by the therapist can be that the addiction is the only problem (Bissell & Royce, 1987). Removing the drug from the client or the family system does not relieve all the other associated problems. Working with other professionals also gives the chemical dependency counselor an opportunity to teach them about the treatment of addiction and get them interested in the field. In fact, Alcoholics Anonymous (A.A.) has a strong tradition of cooperation without affiliation with professionals (Alcoholics Anonymous World Services, Inc., 1972).

The issue of competency becomes even more of a problem if the chemical dependency counselor decides to set up a private practice. In many states there are no legal constraints preventing chemical dependency counselors, whether credentialed or not, from doing this (Bissell & Royce, 1987). This is a very different situation than working as part of a treatment team in a hospital or treatment clinic. Private practice requires far more competence and professional training. Bissell and Royce (1987) recommend that, "along with specialized training in chemical dependency counseling, a master's degree should be the minimum legal require-ment for private practice" (p. 12). Counselors working on their own may find themselves adequately trained in the early part of treatment where stabilization of sobriety is the goal. Different skills are required, however, as treatment moves into the related problems, for instance, sexual dysfunction, marital instability, and intergenerational family dysfunction. Although substance abuse is seen as a family problem, simply knowing the problems it causes to families and the "role behaviors" that family members play in the systems maintenance of the problem does not give the counselor the skills to treat these problems. Family therapy is a unique field of training with its own professional organizations and licensure processes. Too often the family members have been used by untrained counselors to confront patients about their behavior, while the therapeutic needs of the family as a whole and the problems of the individual members have been sacrificed. Counselors with an interest in treating families should get training and supervision in family systems therapy. The combination of chemical dependency counseling skills and family therapy training can be a very powerful tool in treating substance abuse that is often an intergenerational family problem effecting many members (Lawson, Peterson, & Lawson, 1983).

Equally as problematic is the giving of medical and/or legal advice by a counselor struggling with these co-existing problems of their clients. "It hardly needs saying that both a non-physician counselor and an A.A. member go beyond their competence when they advise an alcoholic not to take medicine prescribed by a physician. This is practicing medicine without a license and may amount to murder if the addict dies as a result" (Bissell & Royce, 1987, p. 14). The advice to discontinue prescriptions is often supported by the notion that "a drug is a drug is a drug." Certainly there are prescription drugs that are abused by alcoholics and addicts including amphetamines, barbiturates, opiates, and benzodiazepines (Valium, Xanax) and that abuse needs to be addressed in treatment. There are, however, prescription drugs that are needed to treat medical problems like heart conditions, diabetes, seizure disorders, and mental illnesses, such as manic-depression, that are not mood altering in the sense of the psychotropic medications that are abused. The current interest in dual-diagnosed patients is often fueled by insurance practices of refusing hospital admission for substance abuse diagnoses and approving admission for a mental health diagnosis, such as depression. This practice has led some counselors to question if dual-diagnosed patients are not just exhibiting symptoms caused by their alcohol and drug use. Again, this is an area of diagnosis that should be done by a medical professional. Psychotropic medications such as antidepressants and lithium can be lifesaving for properly diagnosed patients with coexisting mental illnesses. All nonmedical therapists working in the substance abuse field should develop a referral relationship with a psychiatrist, a pharmacologist, or an addictionologist who has special training in the field and is aware of the dangers of certain medications for alcoholics and drug addicts, yet can prescribe and monitor medications that may make recovery more successful and improve the quality of life for the patients.

As the legal system becomes more involved in incarcerating and treating prisoners who have committed drug-related crimes, employment opportunities are opening for chemical dependency counselors both in prison settings and in outpatient clinics. Many drug-addicted clients are on probation, which necessitates interfacing with the probation officers, writing reports, and doing urinalyses. The counselor's ignorance of legal implication of certain actions and court procedures can be of harm to the clients and can reflect poorly on the profession. Special training and consultation may be necessary to operate effectively with these legal agencies. It is important for the chemical dependency counselor not to enable or protect his or her clients from the legal consequences of their behavior or to generalize that every person arrested for drunk driving is an alcoholic (Bissell & Royce, 1987). It may be very tempting to spare a client a return to prison because of a relapse that the counselor believes is part of the recovery process, while probation sees it as a violation of parole. Collaboration with probation officers and close monitoring of the consequences of alcohol and other drug use can be very effective in the counseling process. The counselor who works with clients who have committed crimes while intoxicated or under the influence of drugs needs to reconcile society's need for protection from offenders with his or her own belief system concerning the disease process of addiction. If counselors believe that one's breaking the law under the influence is part of the disease process, they will be more vulnerable to enabling or protecting their clients from the consequences of their behavior.

One of the main ways of avoiding practicing beyond competence is the recognition of the need for ongoing training and learning. The counselors who recognize their deficiencies are much less likely to make poor ethical decisions than counselors who assume that once certified they know all there is to know. Continuing education requirements are a part of many certification processes. These can be opportunities to learn skills and theories in areas outside chemical dependency treatment that will allow the counselor to expand his or her competency.

The fourth principle discusses legal standards and moral standards. It reads:

> The alcoholism counselor must uphold the legal and accepted moral codes which pertain to professional conduct.
>
> a. The alcoholism and drug abuse counselor must not claim either directly or by implication, professional qualifications/affiliations that the counselor does not possess.
>
> b. The alcoholism and drug abuse counselor must not use the affiliation with the National Association of Alcoholism and Drug Abuse Counselors for purposes that are not consistent with the stated purposes of the Association.
>
> c. The alcoholism and drug abuse counselor must not associate with or permit the counselor's name to be used in connection with any services or products in a way that is incorrect or misleading.
>
> d. The alcoholism and drug abuse counselor associated with the development or promotion of books or other products offered for commercial sale must be responsible for ensuring that such books or

products are presented in a professional and factual way (NAADAC, 1993, p. 2A).

This fourth principle is concerned with protecting the consumer and the association. A chief reason for certification is to let consumers of chemical dependency treatment know that this counselor has certain basic skills in the treatment of chemical dependency. Counselors who claim to be psychologists, family therapists, social workers, marriage counselors, or sex therapists but do not have the appropriate training and certification or license are misrepresenting their qualifications to the public. Similarly, if members of NAADAC make claims about their certification that goes beyond what the certification means, they are not being truthful to the public.

The last two sections of the principle deal with services, products, or books that are sold by chemical dependency counselors. With the significant amount of pain and suffering that addiction causes to millions of people in this society, the opportunity to make money at their expense is always present. People looking for quick fixes and miracle cures can be easy targets for those who are more interested in making money than in helping people. Not only do these unprofessional practices mislead the public, they tarnish the field of chemical dependency treatment.

The fifth principle is also concerned with public statements that might mislead the public or present inaccurate information. It reads:

> The alcoholism and drug abuse counselor must respect the limits of present knowledge in public statements concerning alcoholism and other forms of drug addiction.
>
> a. The alcoholism and drug abuse counselor who represents the field of alcoholism counseling to clients, other professionals, or to the general public must report fairly and accurately the appropriate information.
>
> b. The alcoholism and drug abuse counselor must acknowledge and document materials and techniques used.
>
> c. The alcoholism and drug abuse counselor who conducts training in alcoholism or drug abuse counseling skills or techniques must indicate to the audience the requisite training/qualifications required to properly perform these skills and techniques (NAADAC, 1993, p. 2A).

One problem of consumer fraud that this principle is addressing is the inflated or false claims of treatment success made by treatment programs to entice clients to enter their programs. Success rates are difficult, at best, to measure. Programs that eliminate people who do not finish the program for any reason from their statistics and that measure success at the end of an inpatient stay are not being honest with the public about the life-long nature of recovery or about their treatment failures. This kind of advertising of inflated success rates or quick cures also misleads the public about the nature and treatment of addictions.

The last section of this principle is a guideline for counselors who are also educators. Substance abuse is a complicated, multicausal problem. Consumers who enroll in training should be told what their skill level will be upon finishing the training and what competencies and deficiencies they will have. Most certification boards and associations have set minimum education standards that counselors need before they can be certified.

The sixth principle concerns giving credit to authors and contributers to published materials, such as books, articles, and pamphlets. It is not an acceptable practice to plagiarize another person's writings or to present another person's theories, techniques, or work as the author's original ideas. Written credit must be given to the originator of the work. The principle specifically reads:

> The alcoholism and drug abuse counselor must assign credit to all who have contributed to the published material and for the work upon which the publication is based.
>
> a. The alcoholism and drug abuse counselor must recognize joint authorship, major contributions of a professional character, made by several persons to a common project. The author who has made the principle contributions to a publication must be identified as a first listed.
>
> b. The alcoholism and drug abuse counselor must acknowledge in footnotes or an introductory statement minor contributions of a professional character, extensive clerical or similar assistance, and other minor contributions.
>
> c. The alcoholism and drug abuse counselor must acknowledge, through specific citations, unpublished, as well as published material, that has directly influenced the research or writing.
>
> d. The alcoholism and drug abuse counselor who compiles and edits for publication the contributions of others must list oneself as editor, along with the names of those others who have contributed (NAADAC, 1993, p. 2A).

The seventh principle moves away from the protection of the public and the profession to outlining the doctrine of client welfare. Following the adage of first do no harm, this principle clearly states that the client's welfare must come first. Treatment decisions, termination of treatment, and referrals must be made in the client's best interest. On the other hand this may seem like common sense and may seem to be easy to follow, but it may not seem so clear when terminating or referring a client means lost income, especially if the program is struggling to keep its door open. On the other hand, premature termination can be as damaging. If a counselor cannot work with a particular client due to value conflicts, personality conflicts, or excessive countertransference, he or she must refer the client to someone who can work with him or her. This also brings up the issues of currently using or relapsing clients. Is it in the best interest of clients to refuse to work with them if they are not sober or have had a relapse? Should relapsers be kicked out of treatment programs when they are being treated for an illness that has loss of control as part of its definition? These clients are certainly in need of treatment, but are counselors enabling them to continue using if they continue to see them or refer them to someone who will work with them? Often this depends on the content and goal of the therapy. If the use or relapse is ignored, it is probably not helping; if confronted it can be helpful in focusing on the main goal of therapy. Counselors need to examine their own belief systems concerning this treatment dilemma while keeping the principle of client welfare in mind.

This guideline for protecting client welfare can be useful to the counselor in making difficult decisions. At times, however, it can be difficult to determine who the client is. For example, a supervisor who discovers that a counselor has been unethical during a supervision session may have a conflict between reporting this behavior to the program director and/or certification board and feeling that the counselor may have believed he or she was revealing this to the supervisor in confidence. This confusion can be eliminated if the counselor who is in supervision understands from the beginning that the supervisor is being paid by the program director to make certain that good and ethical treatment is being provided to the program clients and that confidentiality will not be guaranteed to the supervisees. The principle gives examples of when client welfare should be protected:

> The alcoholism and drug abuse counselor must respect the integrity and protect the welfare of the person or group with whom the counselor is working.
>
> a. The alcoholism and drug abuse counselor must define for self and others the nature and direction of loyalties and responsibilities and keep all parties concerned informed of these commitments.
>
> b. The alcoholism and drug abuse counselor, in the presence of professional conflict must be concerned primarily with the welfare of the client.
>
> c. The alcoholism and drug abuse counselor must terminate a counseling or consulting relationship when it is reasonably clear to the counselor that the client is not benefiting from it.
>
> d. The alcoholism and drug abuse counselor, in referral cases, must assume the responsibility for the client's welfare either by termination by mutual agreement and/or by the client becoming engaged with another professional. In situations when a client refuses treatment, referral or recommendations, the alcoholism and drug abuse counselor must care-

fully consider the welfare of the client by weighing the benefits of continued treatment or termination and must act in the best interest of the client.

e. The alcoholism and drug abuse counselor who asks a client to reveal personal information from other professionals or allows information to be divulged must inform the client of the nature of such transactions. The information released or obtained with informed consent must be used for expressed purposes only.

f. The alcoholism and drug abuse counselor must not use a client in a demonstration role in a workshop setting where such participation would potentially harm the client.

g. The alcoholism and drug abuse counselor must ensure the presence of an appropriate setting for clinical work to protect the client from harm and the counselor and the profession from censure.

h. The alcoholism and drug abuse counselor must collaborate with other health care professionals in providing a supportive environment for the client who is receiving prescribed medications (NAADAC. 1993, p. 3A).

The eighth principle concerns the ethical principle of confidentiality. In the field of chemical dependency counseling this is also covered by a federal law, which will be reviewed in the next section of this chapter. Confidentiality is extremely important in providing any type of counseling or mental health treatment. It is linked to the concept of trust and sets the counseling session apart from a talk with a good friend. Confidentiality is simply defined as the guarantee that a counselor gives a client that what is said in a counseling session will be held in confidence and the client's privacy will be protected by the counselor. People need to believe that they will not be discriminated against or suffer from social stigma associated with therapy and addiction and that harm will not come to them from the act of seeking treatment. Otherwise, they will resist pursuing the help they need. Confidentiality protects the client from unauthorized disclosures without their consent. There are, however, certain exceptions to confidentiality that will be discussed in the legal section regarding exceptions to privileged communications—the legal version of confidentiality.

The ethical principle of confidentiality is presented by NAADAC in the following way:

The alcoholism and drug abuse counselor must embrace, as a primary obligation, the duty of protecting the privacy of clients and must not disclose confidential information acquired, in teaching, practice or investigation.

a. The alcoholism and drug abuse counselor must inform the client and obtain agreement in areas likely to affect the client's participation including the recording of an interview, the use of interview material for training purposes, and observation of an interview by another person.

b. The alcoholism and drug abuse counselor must make provisions for the maintenance of confidentiality and the ultimate disposition of confidential records.

c. The alcoholism and drug abuse counselor must reveal information received in confidence only when there is clear and imminent danger to the client or to other persons, and then only to appropriate professional workers or public authorities.

d. The alcoholism and drug abuse counselor must discuss the information obtained in clinical or consulting relationships only in appropriate settings, and only for professional purposes clearly concerned with the case. Written and oral reports must present only data germane to the purpose of the evaluation and every effort must be made to avoid undue invasion of privacy.

e. The alcoholism and drug abuse counselor must use clinical and other material in classroom teaching and writing only when the identity of the persons involved is adequately disguised (NAADAC, 1993, p. 3A).

This guideline gives some practical ways that the principle of confidentiality is applied in clinical work. For instance, counselors must get permission to video or audio tape a counseling session or to allow others to observe the session. Records are also covered by confidentiality and, therefore, should not be left on a desk or even in an unlocked file cabinet. A temptation for counselors who are working in a treatment program that requires many forms and unending recording and paperwork is to take the records home with them to complete. Since this allows the records to be accessed by others not working for the treatment program or sets up the possibility of the loss of records, this practice can lead to unauthorized disclosures and cause great concern for program administrators and licensing boards.

Confidentiality can be more difficult to guard when the counselor is working in an Employee Assistance Program (EAP). Managers can be more concerned about employee productivity, profit margins, and the total organization than about one individual's confidentiality (Vesper & Brock, 1991). Supervisors may pressure EAP counselors to divulge confidential information that they believe may affect employee performance, or pass over employees who have used the EAP services. Although EAPs have increased productivity and morale and decreased tardiness and absenteeism, some managers and supervisors may not understand the benefit of these services and penalize employees who use them (Vesper & Brock, 1991).

Thus, the EAP counselor must fiercely guard confidentiality and inform clients of the limitations and nature of the guarantee of confidentiality. If the referral to the EAP is a supervisory referral and an adjunct to disciplinary measures, an employee's right to confidentiality should be maintained unless an illegal act is uncovered such as embezzlement (Vesper & Brock, 1991). Usually, the employee will be allowed to keep his or her job if they comply with the recommendations of the EAP counselor, including treatment for substance abuse, and refusal to comply is grounds for probation or dismissal. The EAP counselor should be very clear about his or her role in working for a business and about how this may impact decisions of client welfare. EAP counselors have national organizations, codes of ethics, and certification processes that frame this work as a special area of expertise. Chemical dependency counselors who are interested in working in this area should pursue special training and certification.

The ninth principle describes factors that would interfere with the counselor-client relationship or compromise the client or the therapy process. These problems have been referred to as dual relationships and are discouraged because of the erosion that takes place in the therapy process as well as the potential harm to the client. Dual relationships exist whenever a counselor has any other relationship with a person who is their client, and they become unethical if there is any harm or potential for harm to the client or benefit to the counselor (Dove, 1995).

Dual-relationship dilemmas are very common, particularly in the treatment of chemical dependency, and include sexual exploitation of clients, which is considered to be one of the most harmful, yet most common, violations (Vasquez, 1988). Sexual contact with clients and former clients is not only strongly discouraged by ethical codes, but it is also a felony in some states, punishable by prison terms up to ten years with fines up to $20,000 (Corey, 1991). Professional liability insurance has also limited coverage pertaining to sexual intimacies or has eliminated the coverage all together.

So, why is sexual contact still so prevalent? The potential for sexual exploitation has several roots. First, whether counselors believe it or not, clients see them as being in a powerful position. Clients have come for help and have surrendered to the counselor, which puts them in a humble one-down position. The power of the helping relationship also comes from the transference that occurs when clients work out their past issues with others through the counselor. Clients are often confused about strong feelings that occur in this process. Countertransference on the part of counselors may also cloud the picture, and they may be very flattered by the client's adoration that they have created. The counseling process is a very intimate encounter between two people that may remind both parties of sexually intimate relationships they have had. Counselors can have false beliefs that the way to show total acceptance of their clients is to validate them through sexual behavior, and they delude themselves that this would somehow be therapeutic.

Another problem is counselors who need to be validated by their clients in order to boost their self-esteem. In addition, women who suffer from substance abuse frequently have a history of sexual molestation, rape, and/or promiscuous sexual behavior coupled with a false belief that they can only get love or acceptance through sex. Counselors who are having sexual thoughts about their clients should seek help through supervision and consultation with other counselors and/or refer the clients to another therapist.

Yet another complicating factor lies with the number of recovering alcoholic/addict counselors who are employed in the treatment field. While this makes sense clinically, it sets up unique circumstances that encourage dual relationships. Often these counselors come from alcoholic and drug-addicted families where personal boundaries were not recognized, and they may have problems setting appropriate professional boundaries with their clients. Alcoholics Anonymous and other self-help group attendance can also present some difficult situations. Counselors may find themselves sharing group attendance with their current or former clients. This leads to the dilemma of whether to be in the counselor role, which may block their own self-disclosure, or the A.A. member role, which puts them in a peer relationship that may feel awkward for the counselor and the client. If members of the meeting go for coffee afterward, this could create another uncomfortable situation. Differentiating the role of a sponsor and a counselor can be very difficult, as well. It seems important to keep these two roles separated since a counselor usually has firmer boundaries concerning client contact and accessibility. Counselors who try to be both counselor and sponsor to their clients may find themselves with very little time for the rest of their life and family, which is not good role modeling. Treatment programs that encourage their counselors to sponsor their clients should reconsider this policy. Bissell and Royce (1987) offer two measures to avoid some of these traps: (1) Schedule no appointments with former patients, although it may be awkward to try and avoid casual contact. (2) Avoid situations in which the counselor would be alone with former patients, particularly those of the opposite sex. Some additional advice and common sense in differentiating between being a chemical dependency professional and an A.A. member can be found in the *A.A. Guidelines for Members Employed in the Alcoholism Field* (Alcoholics Anonymous World Services, Inc., 1987).

In a field where hugging is viewed as a therapeutic tool, problems surface when counselors become confused about when touching in therapy is appropriate and when it might be construed as erotic or sexual contact. Some clients may even expect to be hugged by their therapists. This can be a tricky issue, especially between opposite-sex client and counselor. It is possible that nonerotic contact in therapy can be beneficial in some circumstances. In a survey, psychologists gave the following examples of where hugging might be appropriate: (1) with socially and emotionally immature clients with a history of maternal deprivation, (2) with people in crisis who are suffering from grief or trauma, (3) in providing general emotional support, and (4) as a greeting or ending of a session (Holroyd & Brodsky, 1977). Other things should be considered such as age differences, gender differences, history of the client, transference and countertransference issues, and the meaning of physical contact to the client. For instance, clients with a history of incest or sexual molestation may be frightened by the contact, and clients with certain cultural backgrounds may be uncomfortable with physical closeness. Counselors also need to evaluate their part in the interchange. If it is not genuine or authentic, the client will become suspicious or not trust the sincerity of the contact or the counselor. Timing is also important. "Counselors may reach out physically, not to meet the needs of their clients but to comfort themselves, because they are uncomfortable with the pain their clients are expressing" (Corey, 1991, p. 65). Clients need to be allowed to experience and struggle with their pain, not be rescued from it. A good test of when to touch is to evaluate who's needs are really being met by the touching (Corey, 1991). A second question should be, "What meaning will this have for the client?"

A further caution in Principle 9 is against treating family members or close associates or intimate friends. Doing so is a certain formula for failure. Family members and friends have a certain image of the counselor that blocks their ability to see them in the counseling role. They will also be more guarded and less able to share difficult issues with someone whom they will be interacting with in other situations. Usually counselors cannot counsel members of their own families because they are too close to them, and their own needs interlock with the other family members' problems (Corey, 1991). A good solution is to go with family members to another therapist.

Chemical dependency counselors in training sometimes have difficulty in knowing how to distinguish between training and therapy. Teachers of these students need to be careful not to get themselves into dual relationships with their students by allowing didactic training to become personal therapy. Teachers need to keep themselves in the role of trainer and must not slide into the role of therapist to their students. Students will often identify themselves as in recovery and may use their own experiences in class discussions. Although this is appropriate, it can easily slide over into therapy when it becomes evident that these are unresolved problems and the students are fishing for advice or treatment. Role playing in class is also a potential problem area if the students are not really role playing but are using their own current problems. It would be appropriate for teachers who are faced with these situations to discreetly refer these students for personal therapy.

Principle 9 also covers informing clients, or guardians of minor clients, about the potential impact of their participation in therapy that is recorded, observed, or used for demonstrations and how this information will be used. In working with minors, the parents or legal guardians have the legal right to privileged communication and can request information about the therapy of a minor. Usually, it is in the best interest of the minor client for the parents or guardians to agree to the confidentiality of the therapy content. Specifically, Principle 9 states:

> The alcoholism and drug abuse counselor must inform the prospective client of the important aspects of the potential relationship.
>
> a. The alcoholism and drug abuse counselor must inform the client and obtain the client's agreement in areas likely to affect the client's participation including the recording of an interview, the use of the interview material for training purposes, and/or observation of an interview by another person.
>
> b. The alcoholism and drug abuse counselor must inform the designated guardian or responsible person of the circumstances which may influence the relationship, when the client is a minor or incompetent.
>
> c. The alcoholism and drug abuse counselor must not enter into a professional relationship with members of one's own family, intimate friends or close associates, or others whose welfare might be jeopardized by such a dual relationship.
>
> d. The alcoholism and drug abuse counselor must not engage in any type of sexual activity with a client (NAADAC, 1993, pp. 3A–4A).

The tenth principle concerns interprofessional relationships. Professional therapists need to respect other professions and cooperate with them in the provision of services. It is not useful to the client or the profession of chemical dependency counseling to discredit another therapist or type of therapy. Although there has been a history of professional bashing in the chemical dependency field, most of this was born out of an early history of the treatment failure of psychoanalysts who were treating alcoholism or out of the insecurity of untrained chemical dependency counselors who feared that trained professionals might take their jobs. It may be tempting for chemical dependency counselors to believe their clients when they tell stories of the incompetencies of their previous therapists, and it may make them feel more competent themselves. However, counselors need to remember that they will soon be these client's previous counselors, and may have stories told about them to the next therapist. Clients may do this for several reasons: (1) They may truly have had a bad experience. (2) They may be trying to flatter the counselor to gain a more powerful or manipulative position in therapy, or they may be trying to triangulate in a third person to reduce the intensity of the dyadic interaction. (3) They are warning their counselor that the previous therapist made them uncomfortable and they do not want that to happen again. Unfortunately, the previous therapist may have been right on target and the client was not ready to change. The best policy is to obtain a signed release of information from the client to talk directly to any previous therapists. Client reports are often clouded. A special area of concern, however, is when a client reports that he or she was sexually exploited by a previous therapist. Counselors cannot report this information to certification boards, licensing boards, or the authorities without a signed consent from the client, who should be informed of the consequences of this disclosure for the previous therapist as well as their potential involvement in an investigation. Another way to handle this information is to have the client make the report to the proper professional agencies and authorities. In either case, the client should be completely informed of any ramifications they may face in making the report.

This principle also discourages counselors from treating clients who are already in treatment with another professional. When clients are in therapy with more than one person, they can become very confused if they are working on different, and sometimes even conflicting, goals. Another danger is the client who believes that just attending therapy sessions is sufficient. This idea leads to therapist hopping, triangulating one therapist against the other, and generally not taking responsibility for change. In chemical dependency treatment it is easy for a client to get two therapists angry by simply saying, "My other counselor doesn't think abstinence is a good goal for me." Most likely this is what the client thinks, and the other counselor would never say this or even think it. This tactic also allows the client to not take responsibility for his or her own ambivalence about sobriety and misdirects the therapist's focus.

Principle 10 says specifically:

> The alcoholism and drug abuse counselor must treat colleagues with respect, courtesy and fairness, and must afford the same professional courtesy to other professionals.
>
> a. The alcoholism and drug abuse counselor must not offer professional services to a client in counseling with another professional except with the knowledge of the other professional or after the termination of the client's relationship with the other professional.
>
> b. The alcoholism and drug abuse counselor must cooperate with duly constituted professional ethics committees and promptly supply necessary information unless constrained by the demands of confidentiality (NAADAC, 1993, p. 4A).

The eleventh principle is concerned with policies of remuneration or fees for service. It states:

> The alcoholism and drug abuse counselor must establish financial arrangements in professional practice and in accord with the professional standards that safeguard the best interests of the client, of the counselor and of the profession.

a. The alcoholism and drug abuse counselor must consider carefully the ability of the client to meet the financial cost in establishing rates for professional services.

b. The alcoholism and drug abuse counselor must not send or receive any commission or rebate or any other from of remuneration for referral of clients for professional services. The counselor must not engage in fee splitting.

c. The alcoholism and drug abuse counselor in a clinical or counseling practice must not use one's relationship with clients to promote personal gain or the profit of an agency or commercial enterprise of any kind.

d. The alcoholism and drug abuse counselor must not accept a private fee or any other gift or gratuity for professional work with a person who is entitled to such services through an institution or agency. The policy of a particular agency may make explicit provisions for private work with its clients by members of it staff, and in such instances the client must be fully apprised of all policies affecting the client (NAADAC, 1993, p. 4A).

This principle discourages both "bounty hunting," or paying people for referrals, and exploitation of patients. In spite of all good intentions, treatment centers are still businesses with bottom lines. When money is involved in anything, the potential for corruption, bribery, and exploitation is rampant. With hospital fees in the hundreds-of-dollars-a-day range, a 28-day hospital chemical dependency stay brings in thousands of dollars in revenues. Past hospital program boom days, where most insurance companies paid for long hospital stays, often led to insurance fraud, double dipping by consultants (being paid by the hospital and the insurance company), exaggerated success rates, and overdiagnosing. The chemical dependency treatment field has paid a terrible price with reduced credibility, closed treatment programs, and diminished resources for alcoholics and addicts.

A second issue of this principle concerns the exploitation of patients newly in the recovery process. It may be tempting to public-relations departments and hospital administrators to solicit newly released patients for donations or to entice them to go public with their substance abuse treatment. For patients who are newly sober this can be an exploitation of their mental state for the profit of the treatment program. Although it is true that celebrities and famous people who speak openly about their addictions and recovery help reduce social stigma and encourage others to seek help, if this disclosure is done prematurely without proper thought to all of its ramifications on the client's family and career, it may feel like the exploitation of the client to benefit the treatment center (Bissell & Royce, 1987). This can be avoided by allowing plenty of time, even two years after discharge from the program, for the client to be clear about his or her desire to donate money to the program or be a public figure that promotes it.

The twelfth principle describes the social obligations for the chemical dependency counselor. Alcoholism and other drug abuse is not only a medical or psychological problem, it is very much a social concern. The public atmosphere concerning this problem has shifted over the course of United States history. Alcoholism has been seen as a moral weakness, something to be attacked through prohibition; an untreatable problem; a disease; an illness; a psychiatric disorder; a family problem; and a social menace when it involves drunk driving. When alcoholism is coupled with other drugs of abuse, it is also seen as criminal behavior. Public hysteria over illegal drug abuse puts an additional stigma on drug addicts, but also allows for public and institutional denial of the huge problems that legal drugs cause society, the tremendous health care costs associated with them, and the lack of treatment and prevention programs. Public policy is often determined by society's view of the problem at the time, and money is shifted from one attempted solution to another. There is usually the debate between treating the person with the disease vs. incarcerating the law breaker. Principle 12 addresses the need for the alcoholism and drug abuse counselor to have a wider view of chemical dependency treatment that also takes in his or her responsibility to social policy. It states:

> The alcoholism and drug abuse counselor must advocate changes in public policy and legislation to afford opportunity and choice for all persons whose lives are impaired by the disease of alcoholism and other forms of drug addictions. The counselors must inform the public through active civic and professional participation in community affairs of the effects of alcoholism and drug addiction and must act to guarantee that all persons, especially the needy and disadvantaged, have access to the necessary resources and services. The alcoholism and drug abuse counselor must adopt a personal and professional stance which promotes the well-being of all human beings (NAADAC, 1993, p. 4A).

ETHICAL DECISION MAKING

Although the above principles can be used as guidelines in making difficult ethical decisions, a process for weighing both sides of ethical dilemmas to arrive at the best possible response is useful. Kitchener (1986) proposed four processes in applying ethics in psychotherapy.

1. **Interpreting a Situation as Requiring an Ethical Decision**—Huber and Baruth (1987) list four assets needed to see a situation as requiring an ethical decision. First, counselors need to be able to perceive how their actions affect the welfare of others. Counseling has the ability to harm as well as help others. They need to be able to see the consequences of their behavior

and not be self-absorbed. The second quality needed is the ability to be sensitive to other people's needs; to have an empathic understanding of how other people feel. Third, counselors need the ability to infer the effects their actions have on others as well as to infer others' needs. This skill develops with age. Fourth, social situations may arouse strong emotions that erupt without a person's having time to reflect or think about these situations. In order to interpret these situations, counselors need to understand their feelings about them. Good choices in ethical decisions may not produce good feelings. When counselors have to choose between two negatives such as breaking confidentiality vs. preventing harm to another, either choice may cause a sense of regret. Yet, counselors must make decisions that involve deciding which action causes less harm.

2. **Formulating an Ethical Course of Action**—Once an interpretation has been made that an ethical decision is needed in a situation, the counselor must then have a process for formulating a course of action. Kitchener (1984, 1985) presents a two-level model of justification of an ethical course of action. The first level is the intuitive level that provides a basis for immediate action in situations that call for a quick judgment, such as a client's threat of or attempt at suicide. This level is based on a set of beliefs, knowledge, and assumptions about what a counselor ought to do or what is right. Intuition, however, is not a good basis for making decisions that are contrary to ethical guidelines, such as sexual contact with a client, or that involve more complicated situations. In these cases it is more appropriate to use the second, or critical-evaluative, level of justification. Often the professional code of ethics spells out clearly what behavior is unethical. If the answer is not clear in the code, counselors should then consider more general ethical principles, such as respect for others' rights. The third level of evaluation is ethical theory, which dictates that counselors who are in an ethical dilemma should consider what they would want for themselves or their loved ones or what would cause the least harm.

   General ethical principles of client welfare can be a guide in making decisions where there are no clear guidelines. Beauchamp and Childress (1983) recommended five principles of biomedical ethics that are relevant to issues of client welfare in psychotherapy. (1) Autonomy is the right of all human beings to make decisions and act on them in an independent way. (2) Beneficence is the expectation that a person must actively attempt to benefit another in a positive way. (3) Nonmaleficence is the principle of avoiding harm to another person. (4) Justice is the belief that all individuals should be treated fairly. (5) Fidelity is the commitment to keep promises; be truthful and loyal.

3. **Integrating Competing Personal and Professional Values**—Counselors sometimes may know what the ethical course of action is but decide not to

make the ethical choice. This can be influenced by money, ambition, or other self-serving reasons. The counselor can be tempted to keep clients in therapy long after it is useful to them because of the income it produces. If the counselor is working in a treatment agency, they may be pressured by the program administrator to keep clients in therapy as long as their insurance will pay. Counselors may also have difficulty reporting impaired colleagues or others who are behaving in an unethical way because of loyalty or friendship. Although this may temporarily help the colleague, it will, most likely, tarnish the profession in some way.

4. **Implementing an Action Plan**—It is not enough for counselors to be aware of the ethical code of their profession and to be concerned about ethical issues. Counselors can become overwhelmed with the ambiguity of ethical dilemmas and the lack of absolute answers. This is especially true in the field of chemical dependency counseling where complicated issues have been too quickly resolved with absolute rules. Clients are told not to make any major decisions for the first year of sobriety or to not focus on family issues for at least one year or they will relapse. The "rules" are created without the benefit of any scientific research, but they do reduce the counselor's anxiety about difficult issues in therapy. Ethical decisions often require tolerating the uncertainty of the situation and making the best possible decision based on ethical guidelines and consultation with supervisors and colleagues. The final process, however, is to act on the decision.

LAWS GOVERNING THE PRACTICE OF CHEMICAL DEPENDENCY COUNSELING

There are many different types of laws that govern the practice of chemical dependency counseling. They can be federal, state, county, or city laws. Because of the overlap between counseling and law enforcement in the field of addictions, due to the illegality of some drug use and the criminal behavior associated with addiction, it is important for chemical dependency counselors to be aware of the laws concerning treatment and the rights of their clients. It is also important for their own benefit in protecting themselves against malpractice suits. Five distinctions in types of laws are of particular concern for the counselor (Huber & Baruth, 1987).

1. **Common Law**—This is the fundamental law of the United States. Common Law demonstrates the belief that law does not have to come from written sources. Common Law is derived from the tradition and usage of English Common Law. Many of our laws and practices are based in beliefs and attitudes of our English ancestors. Many of these ideas, however, have been modified by current legislation.

2. **Statutory Law**—These laws are passed by a state legislature or Congress and signed into law. These statutes are binding only in the jurisdiction where they are passed. For example, a law passed in California cannot be applied in Oregon, but federal laws are in effect in all 50 states.
3. **Administrative or Regulatory Law**—These are laws made by agencies that have areas of specialized knowledge. Congress or state governments can determine areas that are beyond the scope of the average legislator and delegate rule-making authority to agencies that can then regulate specific areas.
4. **Case Law or Court Decisions**—These are a body of legal decisions and interpretations of laws. Courts consider statutes and legislative history and decide what the legislators meant when they wrote the law. These decisions are based on federal as well as state laws and decide what law has precedence over the other if they are in conflict. Many legal decisions are taken collectively to make rules for deciding other cases. There are various levels of courts that make these decisions. Trial courts determine the facts and make decisions. The losing party in the trial may appeal to an appellate court that decides if the law was properly applied. A higher court is usually available for further appeals.
5. **Criminal vs. Civil Law**—Civil law pertains to offenses to individuals, while criminal law applies to offenses to society. Criminal violations result in punishment to the perpetrator, and civil violations result in compensation to the victim.

Confidentiality—A Federal Law

The field of chemical dependency counseling is unique in that it is governed by a federal regulation concerning the confidentiality of alcohol and drug abuse patient records. The two statutes are the Comprehensive Alcohol Abuse and Alcoholism Prevention, Treatment and Rehabilitation Act of 1970 (42 U.S. C. 290 dd-3) and the Drug Abuse Office and Treatment Act of 1972 (21 U.S. C. 290 ee-3). These statutes set a general rule that records of alcohol and drug abuse patients must be kept confidential, except in certain limited circumstances. Congress also gave federal agencies the power to adopt rules and regulations to further define certain issues of the law (Weger & Diehl, 1986). The additional regulations are in the Code of Federal Regulations (42 CFR Part 2).

The reason for these statutes and regulations was to increase the likelihood that people with alcohol and other drug addiction would seek treatment because their privacy would be protected. These regulations apply only to programs specializing in alcohol or drug abuse diagnosis, treatment, or referral and that are provided with any direct or indirect federal assistance in the form of federal grants, contracts, revenue-sharing funds, or state block grants. These programs must give patients written notice of these confidentiality regulations upon admission or as soon as they exhibit rational communication. Although the regulations use the term *records,* they refer to any information, whether it is recorded or not, that relates to a patient that was received or acquired in connection with alcohol or drug abuse treatment or prevention. These records can include general medical records if the patient is identified as an alcohol or drug abuser, pretreatment records, records of former patients in aftercare or follow-up treatment, and oral records.

Disclosure of this information may only be with patient consent in certain circumstances and without patient consent in even more limited circumstances (Weger & Diehl, 1986). Some disclosures can be made that do not come under this regulation. These are communications that do not identify the patient, like reporting statistics to a central registry; communications within a treatment program among counselors, supervisors, administrators, and other personnel; and communications between a program and a qualified service organization with whom the program has an agreement to share information. It is generally accepted that disclosures concerning clients' treatments are permitted between treatment team members who fall under the umbrella of the treatment program. There are also occasions where patients have been released by the criminal justice system and granted probation or parole on the condition that they will enter a treatment program. The patient, in this circumstance, may consent to unrestricted communication between the program and the court and between the parole board and probation officers. This does not include communication to the police.

Disclosures of information other than the above exceptions can only be made with the patient's consent, with a court order, or in certain limited situations where neither consent nor a court order is required (Weger & Diehl, 1986). If the disclosure is made with the patient's consent, it must be written consent that includes the following eight items of information:

1. name of the program that is to make the disclosure
2. name of the person to which the disclosure is to be made
3. name of the patient
4. purpose or need for the disclosure
5. extent and nature of the information
6. statement to the effect that consent can be revoked at any time and a date, event, or condition when the consent will expire
7. date signed
8. signature of the patient and signature of a parent or guardian or other authorized person in the case of a minor, incompetent, or deceased person (Weger & Diehl, 1986)

Disclosures can be made without patient consent in the case of medical emergencies; for research, audit, or evaluation purposes; when authorized by court order; or when the patient poses a threat to a third party or has committed an extremely serious crime, including causing serious bodily harm, child abuse, or neglect. In medical emergency cases, the information about the patient must be conveyed directly to the medical personnel and not the police or others. Although the regulations permit disclosures for conducting scientific research, management audits, financial audits, or program evaluations, programs must ensure that an independent group of three or more individuals has reviewed the research protocol and determined that the patients' rights would be protected and that the benefits of the research would outweigh any possible risk to the patients' confidentiality. The federal regulations were changed in 1987 to allow for additional situations for disclosure without obtaining a court order. One change allowed information to be provided to law-enforcement officers without restriction regarding the individual's name, address, patient status, and last known whereabouts of patients who had committed crimes on program premises or against program personnel. Another important change concerned the reporting of child abuse. Because of the narrow limitations of disclosures without consent, this federal regulation was in conflict with state mandatory child abuse reporting laws. The statute has been changed to exempt child abuse and neglect reporting from the confidentiality requirements. The confidentiality protection, however, still applies if the state authorities attempt to gain the original records for related civil or criminal prosecution.

A further change in the regulation allows patients to access their own records. The regulation does not grant patients a right of access, but it states that the regulation will not interfere with any right of access to records that patients may have under state laws or court decisions.

This discussion of the statutes and regulations governing patient confidentiality is a brief summary and is not a legal interpretation. Counselors should be familiar with the details of these regulations and responsible for staying abreast of the inevitable changes and interpretations of these statutes and regulations. They also need to inform their clients of their rights under the law and the exceptions to these rights prior to treatment.

OTHER LEGAL AND ETHICAL ISSUES IN CHEMICAL DEPENDENCY TREATMENT

Duty to Warn

One of the most difficult decisions to make in counseling is whether to maintain a client's confidentiality or break confidentiality to warn a potential victim. In 1976, the California Supreme Court handed down a decision in *Tarasoff v. Board of Regents of the University of California* that set a trend toward protection of the public's safety over the right of the client's confidentiality in psychotherapy (Huber & Baruth, 1987). This case involved a client who threatened during therapy to kill his girlfriend and proceeded to follow through with the threat two months later. The court found that if a therapist has a "special relationship" with a person whose conduct needs to be controlled and can "reasonably" predict that he or she poses a threat to a third party who is a "foreseeable victim," the therapist must warn the third party and the police. These legal terms can be difficult to determine at times, and this is not a clear mandate to warn in contrast to mandated child abuse reporting laws.

Counselors should have a process for determining if they should break confidentiality and warn intended victims. First, they should decide if this is a vague threat or a clear threat. If it is a clear threat, does it pose serious danger or marginal danger, which should be considered with a supervisor or colleague. If the counselor does not have enough information to identify and warn the victim, he or she should attempt to get a name and phone number. Next, the counselor should determine if there is imminent danger that requires action, or if there is no real immediate danger. If the counselor suspects that there is imminent danger to a family member, he or she may be able to deal with the problem if the client is amenable to family therapy. If the client is not amenable to family therapy or the intended victim is a public official or figure or any other person, the counselor needs to consider involuntary commitment, warning the police, and warning the victim. All of these decisions in this process should be done in conjunction with a supervisor, program director, and other colleagues and be documented completely in treatment records. In these difficult situations, it is advisable to consult an attorney for advice.

Confidentiality in Treating Clients with AIDS

Duty to warn becomes an even more difficult issue in treating clients with the AIDS virus. AIDS is a problem that chemical dependency counselors cannot deny because the same groups that are at high risk for AIDS are also at high risk for substance abuse: sexually active homosexual or bisexual men and present or past intravenous drug users. Professional literature, ethics codes, and the legal system have not defined the limits of confidentiality raised by the life-threatening activities of clients who have the AIDS virus and who continue to be sexually active without telling their partners (Corey, 1991). The dilemma lies with protecting the confidentiality of the client vs. protecting the safety of the unsuspecting partner. This could be a sex partner or someone with whom they share needles. Does this constitute a duty to warn? Is this imminent danger? What damage could result from the disclosure?

Gray and Harding (1988) take the side of the unsuspecting partner and believe there are no limits to confidentiality in such cases. They suggest that counselors use a process of helping clients take responsibility for telling their sex partners. This process includes educating, consulting, and actively supporting clients while building a trusting relationship. If this process does not work, Gray and Harding suggest that counselors inform their clients of their intent to break confidentiality and inform known sex partners. If the sex partners are unknown, counselors should inform the state public-health officer. On the other side of the dilemma is the damage done to the client when the stigma of AIDS is so great. Kain (1988) brings up the question of why the client is not telling sex partners. He recommends addressing potential problems such as issues of rejection, abandonment, loneliness, homophobia, and infidelity. With a mandate from federal regulations for the protection of confidentiality, the chemical dependency counselor needs to take this responsibility seriously. Each case should be carefully considered and decisions to break confidentiality should be made only after consultation with supervisors, colleagues, and legal advisors. At some point in the future, case law will provide better guidelines with regard to warning potential victims of clients with AIDS. Until that time, counselors have the best possibility of resolving this dilemma by using the therapeutic relationship to help the client act in a responsible way for the safety of others.

Child Abuse Reporting

Since child abuse is not a federal crime, federal law only makes money available to the states that meet the reporting guidelines and agree to set reporting standards (Huber & Baruth, 1987). In order for states to be eligible for federal funds granted by the Child Abuse and Treatment Act, states must agree to grant immunity to reporters, acting in good faith, from civil and criminal suits. All of the states have complied with these requests and have adopted definitions of child abuse that vary from state to state. None of the states require that a reporter be certain of the abuse. Usually the wording of the state laws is that the reporter has "reason to believe" or a "reasonable suspicion" of the abuse or neglect. Laws do vary from state to state with regard to the definition of child abuse and what types of child abuse are mandated to report. Types of abuse that are usually reportable include physical injury, mental or emotional injury, and sexual molestation or exploitation. Neglect is often included in the reporting laws, but it is more difficult to prove. The counselor's duty, however, is not to determine if the abuse or neglect falls into the state definition. Counselors are mandated to report their suspicions to the proper authorities, usually a child protective agency or the police. The authority in charge of investigating child abuse makes the determination and decides on a course of action. Reports are often made by telephone immediately and followed up with a written report. Since physical abuse, sexual abuse, and incest are coexisting problems in many substance abusing families, it is quite likely that substance abuse counselors will encounter these problems. Thus, chemical dependency counselors should be familiar with the child abuse reporting laws of their states. Consultation with supervisors and colleagues is also a good idea before breaking confidentiality and reporting child abuse. The changes in the federal regulation that exempt child abuse and neglect reporting from the confidentiality requirements make it clear that chemical dependency counselors are bound by their state laws and may be breaking the law by not reporting suspected child abuse. Failure to report is a misdemeanor in most states that could carry a jail sentence and a fine, although this is rare. This may put the counselor in an ethical dilemma of deciding between the welfare of their client or the safety of a child. The state laws usually make it quite clear that this is not a choice the counselor can make; he or she must report the child abuse.

A related area that affects chemical dependency counselors is the use and abuse of drugs by a pregnant woman. There is certainly evidence that drinking and using other drugs during pregnancy can create fetal alcohol syndrome or drug addiction in these women's babies. There is, however, no absolute data concerning the amount and frequency of use that creates these problems for children. It is hard to define what could be considered abuse. The other issue for counselors who are fairly certain that a pregnant woman is abusing enough drugs to create problems, is whether the fetus is protected by in the child-abuse laws. This is a difficult area that requires legal advice and a knowledge of the state definition of child abuse. Test cases in the courts will also be adding clarity to this issue.

Danger to Self—Suicide Threats

Alcoholics and drug abusers have a high risk for suicide, and within that population, adolescents and the elderly with alcohol and other drug problems have an even higher risk (Lawson & Lawson, 1989). One of the more difficult situations for chemical dependency counselors is the treatment of suicidal patients. The stakes are high in making the decision whether or not to break confidentiality to potentially save a patient's life. The decision must be based on the counselor's assessment of the seriousness of the threat. However, if there is any indication that the patient is depressed, has a history of suicide attempts, or a family history of suicide attempts, the counselor should do a suicide-potential evaluation immediately, using direct questioning. It is a myth that asking about suicidal thoughts will put the idea into a person's head. It may be a relief for someone to talk about these thoughts and associated fears. In determining the level of danger to self, the counselor should ask questions such as: "Are you thinking about hurting yourself?" "Have you been feeling suicidal?" "For how long have you been feeling that way?" Next the counselor should assess the patient's impulsivity. Can the patient guarantee that for a period of time or until the next counseling session that he or she will not attempt suicide? An assessment of the plan and the means to carry it out is important. The more specific the plan for the suicide attempt, the more the danger. Patients who just wish that they were not alive are in less immediate danger than those who have a loaded gun at home and live by themselves. Other factors that increase the risk of suicide are a history of destructive or self-destructive behavior, a family history of suicide, and current alcohol and other drug use, all of which can lower destructive inhibitions. Factors that decrease the risk are a strong relationship with the therapist and a current strong level of support from family, friends, and the community. Other areas for assessment are the person's affective state, stress level, and level of reality testing. A person who is very depressed might not have the energy to commit suicide. Risk, however, increases as a person's energy level begins increasing. A shift from a crisis state to becoming at peace also may indicate that a person has made a decision to take his or her own life.

Management of a suicide threat should begin with the least restrictive alternative. The first level of intervention should be negotiating a contract between the counselor and the patient that has clear guidelines regarding communication, contacting the counselor if the suicidal idea becomes stronger, asking for extra sessions, and being in situations where hospitalization might be necessary. It would also be helpful for the counselor to ask the patient for written consent to alert family members of the suicide risk and to have them remove lethal weapons from the house. If there is a more immediate need for intervention, the patient should be evaluated by a psychiatrist for medication or hospitalization. If the patient is not willing to voluntarily enter the hospital, the psychiatrist or other health professional can have the patient held on an involuntary commitment, usually for 72 hours for further evaluation. If the suicide threat comes over the phone, the counselor can have the line traced and ask the police or a mental health crisis team to pick that person up and take him or her to an emergency room.

Sometimes these interventions do not work or only work temporarily. Counselors need to realize that they can only do so much to prevent suicide. If they lose a patient to suicide, they may need to process this with a supervisor or colleague so they can go on with their work and help others.

Professional Liability—Malpractice Suits

Legally, therapists have a responsibility to give their clients an honest representation of their skills, methods, conditions of treatment, fees, appointment schedules, and any other special obligations of either the client or therapist, and the client's informed consent should always be obtained (Huber & Baruth, 1987). This understanding and agreement constitute a contract between the counselor and the client, and each party has a responsibility to abide by the agreement.

Counselors' legal liability involves civil liability, including contract law, unintentional torts or malpractice, and intentional torts (Schultz, 1982). If the counselor's practice is a fee-for-service arrangement, it has implied contractual elements and legal responsibility that make the counselor liable through contract law (Huber & Baruth, 1987). Tort liability, however, is a civil wrong that is not part of contractual liability. A tort is a harm done to an individual in a manner that allows the law to order the person who inflicts the harm to pay damages to the injured party, whether the harm was intentional or unintentional (Huber & Baruth, 1987).

Unintentional torts are referred to as malpractice wherein a counselor caused injury to a client, through ignorance or negligence, by not providing an acceptable standard of care. Intentional torts can include causing willful harm through the acts of battery, defamation, invasion of privacy, infliction of mental distress, and malicious prosecution and false imprisonment (Huber & Baruth, 1987).

Counselors can minimize their chance of being sued by practicing in a responsible and ethical manner. These practices include:

- providing clients with a professional disclosure statement that covers the counselor's qualifications, guarantees and limits of confidentiality, fee structures, and therapy cancellation and termination policies
- getting ongoing supervision or forming peer supervision groups
- belonging to professional organizations and knowing and following their codes of ethics
- using legal consultants in making difficult ethical decisions
- practicing ongoing continuing education
- keeping excellent and accurate records of all treatment sessions, other client contact, supervision suggestions, consultations with consultants and colleagues, and updated treatment plans and progress

Special Issues for Counselors Who Are A.A. Members

Although some of these issues were discussed previously in the context of dual relationship and A.A. members who work in the chemical dependency counseling field, further differentiation may be necessary to avoid confusion. Counselors sometimes confuse the ethical and legal concept of confidentiality with the A.A. tradition of anonymity. Although there is overlap, they are not the same. Both of these principles protect the alcoholic or addict and the profession, and confidentiality allows people to seek treatment without fear of being stigmatized. The public, however, might see the tradition of anonymity as further perpetuating the stigma of substance abuse and see members of A.A. as hiding behind this tradition. "The A.A. tradition of anonymity is not intended to perpetuate the stigma of alcoholism, but instead to prevent ego-trips among its members, to reassure newcomers who might fear for their reputations, and to protect the fellowship both from adverse publicity if a member relapses, and from individuals appointing themselves spokespersons" (Bissell & Royce, 1987, p. 46). The main purpose of the tradition is the protection of the fellowship. There is a fine balance between protecting A.A. and educating the public about the organization so others can benefit from the program. The tradition allows a person to identify as an alcoholic but not as a member of A.A. through the public media. Traditions eleven and twelve also prohibit any unauthorized disclosure of another member's identity as an A.A. member but allow members to identify them below the level of public media (Bissell & Royce, 1987). It is not required that members use only first names in meetings. While some groups practice this, the majority of groups use full names (Bissell & Royce, 1987).

Another area of concern is court-mandated attendance at A.A. meetings. While some people may get exposed to the program and go on to a life of sobriety, many will not. People who are only at a meeting to avoid jail usually do not participate in the meeting and may hinder others from getting maximum benefit. They also have no stake in keeping information that is shared at the meeting confidential or keeping other members' anonymity. Even worse, they may associate A.A. as an extension of a coercive system that spies on them and reports back to the authorities (Bissell & Royce, 1987). This negative experience may rule out A.A. as an option for people when they are truly ready for its help. This is especially true for adolescents, who feel overcontrolled by the world. If they are forced to attend, it may rule out this option for the rest of their lives.

Counselors who are also members of A.A. need to help their clients understand the difference between therapy and A.A. and being a counselor and a sponsor. They should also protect the A.A. program from social pressures to use it as mandatory treatment.

COUNSELOR CERTIFICATION

Royce (1989) believed that the estabishment of chemical dependency counseling as an independent profession began with the incorporation of recovering alcoholics into the treatment team at the Yale Plan Clinic in 1944. Soon, many programs included recovering counselors as part of a multidisiplanary treatment team. One of these programs was Willmar State Hospital where the Minnesota Treatment Model was originally developed. This model was subsequently refined at Hazelden in Minnesota. Anderson (1981) considers the designation of the alcoholism worker, in 1954 by the state of Minnesota Civil Service Commision, as a formal employment category to be a significant step in the acceptance of alcoholism counseling as a legitimate activity.

During the fifties and the sixties, recovering alcoholic paraprofessional counselors dominated the treatment scene. There were those who had reservations about the use of these nonprofessional counselors. In a debate that appeared in the *Quarterly Journal on the Studies of Alcohol,* Krystal argued that only trained professionals could treat the underlying emotional problems of the alcoholic. Moore on the other hand believed that alcoholics did not respond to traditional individual psychotherapy and that an approach using the skills of all mental health disciplines, including alcoholism counselors, would be more effective (Krystal & Moore, 1963). It was the historical failure of existing health care professionals, especially mental health professionals, to provide adequate care for persons with alcoholism that resulted in the large number of recovering alcoholics who became counselors. They were believed to bring commitment and natural counseling gifts to the care of other alcoholics (Banken and McGovern, 1992).

In defense of the psychiatrists, psychologists, social workers, and other mental health counselors who worked with alcoholics in the early days of treatment, little was known about alcoholism and addiction. Now that much more is known about the addiction process, and it is understood that denial is a common defense in addictive disorders, it is easy, for two reasons, to see why there was little early success for those doing individual therapy with alcoholics. First, many alcoholics seeking help for "their problems" would not mention their drinking or they would lie about its impact to the therapist. Second, mental health workers were not trained to ask about such personal matters. In fact, it might have seemed like an invasion of privacy to do so. Most alcoholics were seen by mental health workers who had no understanding of, or training in, addictions. However, the recovering counselor had two advantages. One, if an individual went to see an "alcoholism counselor" it is very likely that they were worried about their use of alcohol. This was not true for the general mental health worker. Two, having gone through the addiction and a recovery process, the recovering counselor would be aware of the tendency for the alcoholic to deny or minimize alcohol-related problems. They could therefore confront them about the real role of alcohol. The fact is, when they have the appropriate training there are many effective chemical dependency counselors drawn from a variety of disciplines including, physicians, social workers, psychologists, and nurses. The problem is that many of these disciplines still do not include chemical dependency training as part of their requirments for practice. Those who do generally only include a brief overview. For example, most physicians only receive a few hours of lecture on chemical dependency during the entire four years of medical school. Some psychology programs have no course work at all on addictions. There are organizations, however, that are working to improve the training for members of their particular professions. For example, division 50 (Psychologist in Addictive Behaviors) of the American Psychological Association (APA) and the American Society of Addiction Medicine are two such groups. And some states such as California have included training in chemical dependency as a licensure requirement for mental health professionals. Also the government has recognized the need to improve training in this area and the Center for Substance Abuse Treatment (CSAT) has recently funded eleven Addiction Training Centers (ATC) across the United States. These centers are all involved in the upgrading of addiction counselor competencies in all disciplines, including medicine, mental health, social work, as well as for chemical dependency counselors in all settings at all levels. Some of the work funded by CSAT has been included in this text. These include a list of addiction counselor competencies and a list of prerequisites, including foundational knowledge and attitudes for addiction professionals. These were developed by the Addiction Training Center Curriculum Review Committee, chaired by Dr. David Deitch. The government has also funded counselor training through the Project for Addiction Counselor Training program (PACT).

Earlier in this chapter under Principle 4, the need to protect the consumers of chemical dependency treatment through certification of those working in the field was discussed. Certification is also important to promote the field of chemical dependency counseling as a profession. As long as there is no minimum standard of skill or training for CD counselors the pay and respect for such work will be minimal. The trend in the eighties and nineties is toward higher levels of education for those working in the field. As the number of inpatient programs decreases and managed health care organizations become more involved in the treatment of addictions this trend will continue. If chemical dependency counselors are not required to be certified and to have a minimum level of education and training, they will be replaced with mental health workers who have advanced degrees and training in addictions.

Each state has its own laws regarding the certification of CD counselors. Some states have certification controlled by the state, and other states appoint organizations to be in charge of the process. Still other states, California for example, do not have a state-mandated certification process. When that happens, various organizations representing different groups often offer their own certification. California has seven different organizations that give some type of certification in the addictions field, but requirements for education and experience vary from state to state. Just as in medicine or psychology there are no national laws regarding licensing or certification. There are, however, national organizations that provide certification. Two such organizations are the National Association of Alcohol and Drug Abuse Counselors (NAADAC) and the American Academy of Health Care Providers in Addictive Disorders (AAHCPAD).

NAADAC has different levels of counselor certification depending on training and experience. They require a written exam at each level. AAHCPAD gives the Certified Addiction Specialist (CAS) credential to degreed persons with two years of supervised experience and to nondegreed persons with five years of experience. No written exam is currently required, although one is planned for the future. They also give special certifications in gambling addiction, eating disorders, and sexual addiction. At this time, there are no states that require a license to practice chemical dependency counseling. There are also very few if any insurance companies who will pay a chemical dependency counselor in independent practice unless they are licensed as a mental health professional. There are also organizations that certify training programs. The California Drug and Alcohol Educators Association is an example of such an organization. There is also a national organization comprised of addiction educators, the International Coalition of Addiction Studies Educators (INCASE). Perhaps in the future they will offer a certification for those who teach in the addictions field. In the meantime it would appear that the presence of so many systems of credentialing is confusing to the public and damaging to the field. It will be difficult to change this, however, due to the different political agendas of each group treating those who are chemically dependent.

DISCUSSION QUESTIONS

Read the following vignettes and use ethical decision-making strategies, the NAADAC code of ethics, and laws governing counseling to make the best decision.

1. A new client comes for an evaluation to a treatment program. In the process of the evaluation she states that she has been experiencing nightmares since she began to have a sexual relationship with her previous therapist. Should the counselor call the police? The therapist? The therapist's licensing board or professional organization?
2. During an outpatient session with an intravenous drug user, the client reveals to the counselor that he has been diagnosed with AIDS and that he is having unprotected sex with several women. Should the counselor warn these women?
3. A client with a history of illegal drug use is concerned about his wife's getting sole custody of their children in a divorce settlement because of his previous drug history and some legal involvement. He says in a counseling session that the next time he has visitation with his children he is going to take them to another state where his wife cannot find him or the children. Should the counselor warn the wife or call the police?
4. A male chemical dependency counselor attends an A.A. meeting and a new member who is a woman he treated for alcoholism three months ago attends that night. After the meeting she asks him to go for coffee. Should he go? After the next meeting she asks him to go to a dance. Is this OK?
5. A chemical dependency counselor is putting together a booklet for a women's treatment program that she is designing. She photocopies ar-

ticles, charts, and diagrams from some books she has about women and alcoholism to put in the booklet. The original authors' names are not on the material, and she has put her name on the cover of the booklet. Since she is not technically publishing this booklet, is this ethical? Legal?

6. During a supervision session a chemical dependency counselor reports to the supervisor that a client he has been treating on an outpatient basis for six months is doing very well and using support groups and other family and social supports, and he thinks he should end therapy. The supervisor tells the counselor that he needs to continue to see this client, because the client census is low and there is talk of closing the outpatient program. What should the counselor do?

7. A counselor with a bachelor's degree in psychology is hired at an inpatient chemical dependency treatment program to do group therapy and education with the patients. A few weeks later he receives a box of business cards with the word *psychologist* printed under his name. Since he is not in private practice and is working as part of a treatment team of various professionals, is this title OK?

8. A male patient who has been in treatment in an outpatient program for chemical dependency reports to his counselor in an individual counseling session that he had a relapse because he feels very guilty about his sexual behavior with his ten year old daughter during the last two years while he was drinking heavily. His wife is not aware of this behavior and the patient begs his therapist not to tell her. Can the counselor guarantee this? What should the counselor do with this information?

9. A counselor at a treatment facility that is partially funded by federal money given to the state in a block grant receives a request for information on one of her former patients. The release of information is for treatment plans, progress notes, and a termination summary. It is being requested by a psychologist in private practice. The form has the psychologist's name and the signature of the former client, but there is no stated purpose for how the information will be used and no expiration date of the release. Can the counselor send her former patient's records to the psychologist?

10. During a counseling session a client tells his counselor that his wife has left him because he got drunk; they got into a fight, and he hit her. He swears that she will never leave him and live. He states that he knows that she is at her sister's house, and he plans to go get her after the session. Earlier he had mentioned that he keeps a loaded gun in his car for security. Should the counselor call the man's wife and warn her?

11. On the first visit to a counselor a woman mentions that she has two other therapists she is seeing for drug problems. She says that she wants to try several therapists so she can get lots of help. Should the counselor continue to see her? What could be the problems if she does?

12. After several sessions with an attractive woman, her male counselor begins to fantasize about becoming sexually intimate with her. He has noticed that she asks for his last appointment of the day and tends to stay and talk with him after the session has finished. This week she comes to the session dressed in a transparent blouse and shorts, complaining of the heat. The counselor is having difficulty concentrating on the therapy. What should he do?

REFERENCES

Alcoholics Anonymous World Services, Inc. (1972). *If you are a professional, A.A. wants to work with you.* New York: AA World Services, Inc.

Alcoholics Anonymous World Services, Inc. (1987). *For A.A. members employed in the alcoholism field,* formerly subtitled *For those who wear two hats* (A.A. Guidelines). New York: AA World Services, Inc.

Anderson, D. J. (1981). *Perspectives on treatment: The Minnesota experience.* Minneapolis: Hazelden Foundation.

Banken, J. A., & McGovern, T. F. (1992). Alcoholism and drug abusing counseling: State of the art considerations. *Alcohol Treatment Quarterly, 9* (2), 29–53.

Beauchamp, T. L., & Childress, J. F. (1983). *Principles of biomedical ethics.* London: Oxford University Press.

Bissell, L., & Royce, J. (1987). *Ethics for addiction professionals.* Minneapolis, MN: Hazelden Foundation.

Corey, G. (1991). *Theory and practice of counseling and psychotherapy.* Pacific Grove, CA: Brooks/Cole Publishing Co.

Dove, W. R. (1995). Ethics training for the alcohol/drug abuse professional. *Alcoholism Treatment Quarterly, 12* (4), 19–30.

Gray, L. A., & Harding, A. I. (1988). Confidentiality limits with clients who have the AIDS virus. *Journal of Counseling and Development, 66,* 219–23.

Holroyd, J. C., & Brodsky, A. (1977). Psychologists' attitudes and practices regarding erotic and nonerotic physical contact with patients. *American Psychologist, 32,* 843–49.

Huber, C. H., & Baruth, L. G. (1987). *Ethical, legal and professional issues in the practice of marriage and family therapy.* Columbus, OH: Merrill Publishing Co.

Kain, C. D. (1988). To breach or not to breach: Is that the question? A response to Gray and Harding. *Journal of Counseling and Development, 66,* 224–25.

Kitchener, K. S. (1984). Ethics in counseling psychology: Distinctions and directions. *Counseling Psychologist, 12,* 15–18.

Kitchener, K. S. (1985). Ethical principles and ethical decisions in student affairs. In H. J. Cannon & R. D. Brown (Eds.), *Applied ethics: Tools for practitioners.* San Francisco: Jossey-Bass, Inc. Publishers.

Kitchener, K. S. (1986). Teaching applied ethics in counselor education: An integration of psychological processes and philosophical analysis. *Journal of Counseling and Development, 64,* 306–10.

Krystal, H. and Moore, R. A. (1963). Who is qualified to treat the alcoholic: A discussion. *Quarterly Journal of Studies on Alcoholism, 24,* 705–18.

Lawson, G., & Lawson, A. (Eds.). (1989). *Alcoholism and Substance Abuse in Special Populations.* Gaithersburg, MD: Aspen Publishers.

Lawson, G., Peterson, J., & Lawson, A. (1983). *Alcoholism and the family: A guide to treatment and prevention.* Gaithersburg, MD: Aspen Publishers.

National Association of Alcoholism and Drug Abuse Counselors (NAADAC) (1993, June 6). The certified alcohol and other drug abuse counselor in health care (A joint task force report by The National Association of Alcohol and Drug Abuse Counselors and The International Certification Reciprocity Consortium/Alcohol and Other Drug Abuse).

Royce, S. C. (1989). *Alcohol problems and alcoholism* (rev. ed.) New York: Collier-Macmillan.

Schultz, B. (1982). *Legal liability in psychotherapy.* San Francisco: Jossey-Bass, Inc., Publishers.

Schwartz, I. M. (1989). Hospitalization of adolescents for psychiatric and substance abuse treatment. *Journal of Adolescent Health Care, 10,* 473–78.

Van Hoose, W. H., & Kottler, J. A. (1985). *Ethical and legal issues in counseling and psychotherapy.* San Francisco: Jossey-Bass, Inc., Publishers.

Vasquez, M. (1988). Counselor-client sexual contact: Implications for ethics training. *Journal of Counseling and Development, 67,* 238–41.

Vesper, J. H., & Brock, G. W. (1991). *Ethics, legalities, and professional practice issues in marriage and family therapy.* Boston: Allyn & Bacon.

Weger, C. D., & Diehl, R. J. (1986). *The counselor's guide to confidentiality.* Honolulu, HI: Program Information Associates.

Chapter 3

The Counseling Process

CHAPTER OBJECTIVES

- Understand the clinical evaluation skills of screening and assessment, treatment planning, and referral
- Understand the case management skills of treatment plan implementation, consulting, and continuing assessment and treatment planning
- Understand the core elements of individual counseling: empathy, genuineness or congruence, attentiveness, respect, immediacy, concreteness, and warmth
- Understand the counseling skills of reflecting, questioning, confrontation, self-disclosing, interpreting, and clarifying
- Seek and select a personal approach to counseling
- Understand clinical practices of documentation, supervision, and client and community education

In the field of chemical dependency counseling, the counseling process is more than making friends with clients, giving information, and referring them to self-help groups. Knowledge, skills, and attitudes all play important parts in the competent practice of substance abuse counseling and the treatment of addictions. Chapter 1 discussed the use of self in the counseling process, which is a very powerful skill. It is, however, one thing for a counselor to know what attitudes, beliefs, and behaviors are therapeutic and another thing to be able to implement them to create change in others. This requires learning the skills that allow you to use yourself in the counseling process to create change. Chemical dependency counselor skills and competencies have been described by various certification groups.

This chapter will describe the clinical evaluation skills of screening and assessment, treatment planning, and referral, and the case management skills of implementation of a treatment plan, consulting, and continuing assessment and treatment planning. Other competencies that are covered in this chapter are individual counseling, including rapport building, empathy, genuineness, attentiveness, respect, immediacy, concreteness, and warmth; and developing core relationship abilities, such as listening, reflecting, questioning, confronting, self-disclosing, interpreting, and clarifying; selecting a treatment approach; documentation and charting; using supervision, and client and community education.

CHEMICAL DEPENDENCY COUNSELOR SKILLS

Basic chemical dependency counseling skills have been defined by several certification and accreditation organizations to help educators develop a curriculum for training chemical dependency counselors and a criteria for evaluating these trainees for certification. A recent set of skills was developed by the Curriculum Review Committee of the federally funded Addiction Training Centers Program (Curriculum Review Committee, 1995). These centers are funded by the national Center for Substance Abuse Treatment. Committee members included representatives from the Addiction Training Centers, the Center for Substance Abuse Treatment, and the Project for Addiction Counselor Training. They have attempted to describe the knowledge, skills, and attitudes essential to the competent practice of chemical dependency counseling in today's health care environment.

Clinical Evaluation

Evaluation is a crucial part of the counseling process. It involves screening and assessment. Without a good assessment the counselor does not have a roadmap of how to proceed. This process is so important that an entire chapter (Chapter 4) has been devoted to it. Clinical evaluation involves a multitude of skills, from testing to diagnosing, that precede treatment planning or goal setting.

Screening

Screening is defined as the process through which counselor, client, and available significant others determine the most appropriate initial course of action, given the client's needs, characteristics, and available resources within the community. The counselor should first establish rapport with the client and assess if there is a crisis situation and if there is a need for additional professional assistance. This might include law enforcement, medical assistance, or care for dependent children. Counselors should then systematically gather information from the client and other available sources, using screening instruments and other methods that are sensitive to culture and gender. Age should also be a factor in choosing assessment instruments. Screening instruments such as the Michigan Alcohol Screening Test (MAST) were designed for adults with a history of alcohol abuse. A number of questions on the MAST are irrelevant for adolescents. Questions concerning being arrested for driving while intoxicated or being hospitalized for alcohol-related physical problems do not apply to adolescents without driver's licenses and who have not been drinking long enough to develop major physical problems.

A screening interview should include current and historic substance use and abuse, a health history, previous or current mental health problems, a history of mental health or substance abuse treatment, mental status—an orientation to time and place—a social and family history including who might be available for conjoint treatment (marital or family counseling), and any current social, environmental, and/or economic constraints on the client's ability to successfully follow through with an action plan. These constraints might be a lack of insurance or financial resources to pay for treatment, inability or unwillingness to enter inpatient treatment for fear of loss of job or income, or lack of childcare. The scope of this history taking should involve only the information that will be necessary for crisis intervention and to make an appropriate diagnosis and referral for treatment. More in-depth history taking will be done during the treatment process.

The first consideration for a plan of action is for the safety of the client and others. Alcohol and other drug toxicity and withdrawal symptoms should be evaluated for the need of detoxification under medical supervision. The danger for harm to others—homicide, and harm to self—suicide must be evaluated to determine the need to warn potential victims or to intervene in a possible suicide attempt.

Once these issues of danger are eliminated or resolved, counselors need to help clients identify the role of substance use in their current life problems. During the history taking, counselors can make note of the problem areas that the client is self-identifying, such as arrests, loss of employment, divorce, abuse, and physical problems. They can then return to these problem areas and inquire about the connection of substance abuse to these problems.

One technique that can be used to help clients see this connection is a life-history graph. Clients are asked to make a graph of the ups and downs of their lives, labeling each peak and valley. They then take a different color marker or pen and draw a drinking history line on the same graph, indicating amount of alcohol and other drugs used during their lifetimes. Often this graphic display of substance use increase during the same time period that problems increased helps clients make the connection.

When the client has decided that substance abuse has created problems in his or her life, the counselor can assess the client's readiness for treatment or change and can suggest the treatment options that are relevant to the client's needs, characteristics, and goals. Recommendations for treatment should be made on the basis of the evaluation process that applied criteria for diagnosis and differentiated treatment and that included ethnic, gender, and age considerations; financial resources; employment issues; severity of the problem; social supports; needs of family members for treatment; and available resources.

The next step is to construct with the client and appropriate others an initial plan of action. Once the plan has been agreed upon, specific steps should be taken to initiate an admission to a treatment program or a referral to other types of treatment. The final part of the screening process is to follow up on the admission or referral to ensure that the client successfully began an appropriate course of treatment.

Assessment

Assessment is defined as an ongoing process through which the counselor collaborates with the client and others to gather and interpret information that is necessary for planning treatment and evaluating client progress. In this process, counselors select and use comprehensive assessment instruments that are sensitive to age, gender, and culture. Although there are some good evaluation instruments for many areas of assessment, some areas have to be covered in structured assessment interviews. The following is a list of areas of assessment and suggestions of possible evaluation instruments:

- **Alcohol and other drug use history**—Health, mental health, and substance abuse-related treatment history. After taking a treatment history, counselors should obtain releases of information to request treatment records from previous physicians, therapists, and drug treatment programs. These reports can be invaluable in learning from previous treatment what worked and what failed with this client. It can save valuable treatment time.

- **Family issues and dynamics**—A family genogram (see Chapter 6) to chart intergenerational addiction, alliances, coalitions, coexisting problems, and adaptive consequences; the Family Adaptability and Cohesion Scale (FACES) created by David Olson; and the Family Environment Scale (FES) created by Rudolph Moos are all helpful.

- **Work history and career issues**—For clients who need career counseling, there are several instruments that can assess interest and potential success in various careers, such as the Strong-Campbell Interest Inventory. A referral to a career counseling center or a vocational rehabilitation program may also be appropriate.

- **Psychological concerns**—The Minnesota Multiphasic Personality Inventory (MMPI) or other personality tests may be useful in assessing mental disorders. A referral to a psychologist or a psychiatrist may be useful if there is a history of previous mental illness or a current report of symptoms of depression or other mood disorders, such as a change in sleeping and eating habits and a depressed or manic mood that do not subside 30 days after detoxification; symptoms of thought disorders, such as hallucinations or delusions not associated with withdrawal; symptoms of anxiety disorder and phobias; or other mental illness symptoms. Usually it is difficult to make a mental illness diagnosis while a person is under the influence of substances or is in the process of detoxification.

- **Physical and mental health status**—A physical examination by a health care professional and a mental heath status exam determine if the client is reality based and is oriented with respect to current time and place.
- **Educational and basic life skills**—This may involve an intelligence test, such as the Wescheller Adult Intelligence Scale (WAIS), or various aptitude tests to evaluate reading and mathematical skills. A general evaluation of self-care ability and mobility may also be needed.
- **Socioeconomic characteristics, lifestyle, current legal status**—This data can be compiled from an interview that questions financial resources; employment status; resources for shelter, food, and clothing; family supports; relationships with significant others; any pending criminal or civil court actions; and probation or parole status.
- **Use of community resources**—The evaluation interview may include questions about current use of resources, such as shelters, food programs, health care programs, support groups, churches, mental health centers, aid for dependent children, welfare, or other community agencies or programs.
- **Behavioral indicators of problems in the domains listed above**—One of the best tools a counselor has is his or her observation skills. Assessment has two parts: what the client reports through written or oral modalities and what the counselor observes. These two parts may contradict each other and indicate the need for further evaluation.

Once the data have been gathered, the counselor analyzes and interprets the data to determine treatment recommendations. This is often done in consultation with other professionals, other treatment team members, and with supervision. Assessment findings should be completely documented in the client's file along with treatment recommendations that can lead to an individualized treatment plan.

Treatment Planning

The treatment plan is equally as important as a good evaluation, and it should follow directly from the information that was gathered and interpreted in the clinical evaluation process. *Treatment planning* is defined as a collaborative process through which the counselor and client develop desired treatment outcomes and identify the strategies for achieving them. At minimum, the treatment plan addresses the identified substance-related disorder(s) plus issues related to the treatment progress, including relationships with family or friends, employment, education, spirituality, health concerns, and legal needs. It is important to note the word *collaborative*. In the past, treatment programs have been guilty of using the same treatment plan for everyone and presenting it to the client, instead of coevolving the treatment plan. Chemical dependency is complicated and does not affect everyone in the same way. Counselors should not expect a universal treatment plan that is done prior to the evaluation process to work for very many of their clients or to address individual problems.

In cocreating a treatment plan the counselor needs to assemble and interpret all of the evaluation data and explain this information to the client. The counselor should clarify any areas of misunderstanding or confusion, gather any further information needed, and explain the implications of treatment with the client. The counselor should then confirm the client's readiness to participate in treatment and make certain that the client is aware of what the commitment entails.

Once the counselor gets a commitment from the client, he or she can then begin to prioritize the client's problems and needs that were outlined in the evaluation. Using the prioritized list, the client and counselor need to agree upon what will be the treatment outcomes for each need; decide what strategy will be applied to meet the outcomes; match treatment activities and community resources to the needs; and develop a mutually acceptable plan of action and method for monitoring and evaluating progress. Strategies for change should be measurable, so the counselor and the client can see progress. Vague treatment goals like becoming happy or learning about myself are very difficult to measure. Treatment goals like getting my driver's license back or daily journal writing for self-evaluation are more easily measured. Sometimes goals need to be divided into small achievable steps.

Once a treatment plan has been created, it is a good time to inform clients of their confidentiality rights, the program procedures that safeguard them, and the exceptions to these rights that are imposed by law, such as child abuse reporting and danger to self and others. (See Chapter 2 for a complete discussion on disclosures.) Some programs have their own rules for conduct concerning outside contact, visitation, and what is expected of them while in the treatment program. These should be explained to the client, and he or she should be given a written statement about patient's rights, limitations to the rights, and program rules.

The treatment plan should not be a document that is "written in stone." It should be a flexible document that can be evaluated and changed at regular intervals or when circumstances change. For instance, it may be necessary to change a health need to a higher priority, or it may become evident that marital or family work may need to be done earlier than was planned because of the family system's involvement with the addiction. Counselors may be overwhelmed with the list of needs generated by the evaluation and the length of time the client's insurance allows for treatment or the constraints of their treatment program. Given these limitations, the treatment plan may need to differentiate between short-term goals and long-term goals. The counselor may only be able to meet the first few priorities that will probably involve intervening with the substance abuse and stabilizing the client. However, if the treatment plan is for long-term recovery in many areas of the client's life, the counselor can provide referrals to community resources that will help the client continue with the treatment plan after they are discharged from the program.

Referral

Familiarity with community resources and a willingness to refer clients to these resources are essential for the chemical dependency counselor who wants long-term success for his or her clients. *Referral* is defined as the process of facilitating the client's utilization of available support systems and community resources to meet needs identified in clinical evaluation and/or treatment planning.

The first step in becoming skilled at the referral process is to identify and establish relationships with civic groups, agencies, other professionals, government entities, and the community at large to ensure appropriate referrals, identify service gaps, expand community resources, and help address unmet needs. This process takes time, but it is worth the effort and time involved. Many communities have already compiled referral books that are regularly updated. The United Way in many cities publishes a directory of services. If there are not any current directories, counselors can create their own referral books by collecting business cards, brochures, and information about community resources and professionals. The Yellow Pages of the phone book can be a starting place to find out what is available in a community. Professional associations can also provide information about their members in cities across the country if referrals are to professionals outside the community where the treatment was provided.

Because many resources are funded by shifting tax bases or grants, these referral sources should be continually evaluated to determine their appropriateness. When these resources are identified, counselors can then make referrals for their clients in order to meet the needs that were identified in the treatment plan. Counselors should explain in clear and specific language the necessity for and process of referral to increase the likelihood of client understanding and follow through. It may even be necessary for the counselor initially to accompany the client to the referral source.

Part of the referral process is obtaining appropriate releases of information from the client prior to making the referral so that relevant information can be exchanged between the counselor and the agency or professionals to whom the referral is being made. The amount and type of information that is shared with the referral source by the counselor should be consistent with confidentiality regulations and generally accepted professional standards of care (see Chapter 2). The release to disclose information is also important, because it allows the counselor to follow up on the referral and to evaluate the outcome. If a referral did not meet the client's need, then a different referral can be made.

Case Management

Once the treatment plan has been established and referrals are made to outside resources, the process of treatment can begin. Case management is similar to quarterbacking a football team. The case manager does not do all the work, but takes direction from the coach or program director, utilizes a team treatment approach, gets consultation from various sources, and implements the game plan. *Case management* is defined as the administrative, clinical, and evaluative activities that bring the client, treatment services, community agencies, and other resources together to focus on the issues and needs that were identified in the treatment plan. Case management establishes a framework of action for the achievement of specified goals. It involves collaboration with the client, coordination of treatment and referral services, liaison activities with community resources and managed care systems, and ongoing evaluation of treatment progress and client needs.

Implementing the Treatment Plan

Implementing the treatment plan is the core of the case management process. Counselor activities associated with this process include: (1) initiating collaboration with referral sources; (2) obtaining and interpreting all relevant screening, assessment, and initial treatment planning information; (3) confirming the client's eligibility for admission and continued readiness for treatment and change; (4) completing necessary administrative procedures for admission to treatment; and (5) establishing accurate client expectations for treatment, including the nature of services, program goals, program procedures, rules regarding client conduct, schedule of treatment activities, costs of treatment, factors affecting duration of care, and the client's rights and responsibilities.

Once all of the administrative duties have been completed, there is an ongoing expectation of the case manager to coordinate all treatment activities with services that are provided to the client by other resources. This may include doing individual therapy with the client; referring the client to appropriate group therapy, marital therapy or family therapy; referring the client to educational presentations; monitoring progress in all of the program modalities with external resources; and evaluating the readiness of the client to move to higher levels in the program or to terminate treatment.

Consulting

Another part of case management is *consulting* with other treatment providers. Counselors' skills in this area include: being able to summarize a client's background, treatment plan, recovery progress, and problems inhibiting progress for the purpose of assuring quality of care, gaining feedback from the client and other treatment providers, and planning changes in the course of treatment. In this process, counselors are working with professionals in many specialized fields, and they need to be aware of the terminology used by them and the roles that they play in the treatment of chemical dependency.

Case managers are also a part of a multidisciplinary treatment team and make significant contributions to this process. They are also the contact person between the treatment program and the outside community. As such, they must be responsible for guarding the client's right to confidentiality and to demonstrate respect and nonjudgmental attitudes toward their clients in all contacts with professional and other agencies.

Continuing Assessment and Treatment Planning

Case management is an ongoing process that includes *continuing assessment and treatment planning.* Counselors maintain ongoing contact with clients to ensure that they are adhering to the action plan. They need to watch for stages of change and signs of treatment progress. If progress is stalled or it appears that the treatment plan that was initially created at intake is no longer appropriate, counselor and client need to renegotiate a new plan. Although relapse prevention should begin at the initial treatment planning stage, this is a good time to evaluate this part of the program. It is a mistake to wait until the last therapy session to develop a relapse prevention plan (see Chapter 8). Any treatment plan change or addition to the treatment needs to be well documented in the client's chart so the rest of the treatment team is aware of the changes.

INDIVIDUAL COUNSELING

There are many different theories of counseling including: cognitive-behavioral theories, such as rational-emotive therapy; psychoanalytic theories; existential therapy; person-centered therapy; Gestalt therapy; transactional analysis; behavioral therapy; reality therapy; and many integrated theories. It is beyond the scope of this book to describe each of these theories, and the reader should consult a counseling-theories book (Corey, 1991) for the details of each of them. All of these counseling theories, however, agree that the establishment of a quality relationship between counselor and client is of utmost importance. Other common elements of counseling theories are the skills that create change. This section will discuss the core elements that facilitate counseling: rapport, empathy, genuineness, attentiveness, respect, immediacy, concreteness, and warmth, and the skills of: listening, reflecting, questioning, confronting, self-disclosing, interpreting, and clarifying.

Core Elements

The core elements of counseling are the qualities of the counseling process that make the counselor-client relationship unique. They involve behaviors and attitudes and set the stage for the counseling process to begin.

Rapport

"Rapport is described most simply as a condition essential to a comfortable and unconditional relationship between counselor and counselee. It is established and maintained through the counselor's genuine interest in and acceptance of the client. It cannot be forced or contrived. It is a bond characterized by interest, responsiveness, and a sensitive emotional involvement" (Shertzer & Stone, 1980, p. 261).

Rapport needs to be established from the beginning of the client contact and carried through to the last minute of contact. It is the counselor's behavior, tone, choice of words, and topics that say to the client, "I care about you, and you are safe here." The therapeutic relationship is not like any other. The fifty-minute hour has different rules and expectations than time spent in general life activities. It is a safe place for people to be vulnerable, to be in pain, to try new behaviors, and to find solutions to their problems. Initially, many clients are unsure about coming to therapy, and they need reassurance. Counselors should not overwhelm clients in the beginning by jumping into problem solving too soon, yet they need to establish what will happen during their time together. Counselors can be too casual, talking about the weather or sports, which gives clients the impression that counseling is merely a social visit.

Opening introductions should be brief, with the counselor being attentive and demonstrating interest in the client, while moving to the purpose of the therapy. Counselors can ask, "How can I help you?" or "What brings you here?" The counselor develops rapport by being interested, attentive, and understanding of the client. The time it takes to establish rapport varies with clients and is dependent on the counselor's skills and experience as well as the motivation of the client.

Clients who are mandated to counseling may be more resistant to developing a trusting relationship with counselors.

Empathy

Empathy is a counselor's putting himself or herself in the client's shoes (Shertzer & Stone, 1980). It is different from sympathy. Empathy is comprehending the emotions of another, not feeling the same emotions as in sympathy. Empathy is also the counselor's communicating back to the client what the counselor perceives that the client is describing. It is an interrelationship between two who understand the experience being shared.

Empathy requires good listening skills that involve not only listening to what is being said but to how it is being said. Counselors listen to the process as well as to the content of communication. Nonverbal behavior can be equally as important as verbal behavior. When reflecting these observations back to the client, the counselor can summarize what is being said and what he or she is observing the client doing, for example:

Client: (Wringing her hands.) "Every time I try to tell my husband what's bothering me he just shuts down and leaves the room."

Counselor: "I hear that you are very upset with your husband, and I can see you wringing your hands in concern."

Client: "Yes. I don't know what else to do."

Even if the counselor is wrong or misses the point, he or she is still creating a healing environment by becoming intensely involved with the client. "The communication that is important is taking place on a subterranean, therapeutic level" (Small, 1990, p. 29).

In addition, empathy is the counselor's ability to not lose him- or herself in the process. Rogers (1961) believed that empathy was one of the six necessary conditions of counseling. He described it as a sensing of the client's world "as if it were your own, but without ever losing the 'as if' quality" (p. 284). It is not possible to completely understand or experience another person's position. Counselors who become overidentified with their clients lose the perspective they need to help them. If they become overwhelmed with emotion or hopelessness, they cannot communicate hope and the possibility of change.

Small (1990) describes some roadblocks to empathy that counselors need to guard against. First, clients will not feel heard if counselors reflect back their own perceptions or projections and insist that they belong to clients. Second, empathy does not include counselors' analyzing clients and assuming they are experts on how clients are feeling. Third, when counselors are preoccupied with their own issues or life problems they are unavailable to be truly with their clients. Although it may be useful for a counselor to share his or her addiction and recovery story with clients, real empathy is hearing the uniqueness of each client's path of addiction. The areas of similarity will give the counselor a good picture of what the client has experienced. Counselors, however, need to be flexible enough to discard their ideas, tactics, or goals if they do not fit the client's situation.

Genuineness or Congruence

Genuineness is also referred to as congruence. Rogers (1967) described it as the counselor's being himself or herself and not denying himself or herself. He further defined congruence with the following statement. "By this we mean that the feelings the counselor is experiencing are available to him, available to his awareness, that he is able to live these feelings, be them in the relationship, and to communicate them if appropriate" (p. 90). When counselors are congruent and genuine, they are free to be themselves without phoniness. They are not playing a role or wearing a mask. "Congruence implies honesty and candor with oneself while functioning as a counselor." It "demands authenticity and transparency of the counselor" (Shertzer & Stone, 1980, p. 265).

There are times when the genuineness concept can be distorted. It does not mean that counselors communicate everything they are thinking or feeling. For example, boredom or hostile feelings toward the client may not facilitate a therapeutic environment for clients and may come from projections or the countertransference of the counselor. If these feelings are real and persistent, however, the counselor should refer the client to another therapist. Genuineness is also not total self-disclosure, but if counselors use self-disclosure, it should be honest. Genuineness and congruence allow counselors to help their clients put down their masks and face their difficult or defended feelings. It is easier for clients to acknowledge their genuineness if counselors are modeling this quality.

Genuineness is especially important in chemical dependency counseling. Alcoholics and addicts are masters at masking feelings and playing games. They are experts at spotting phoniness and are sensitive to nonverbal messages and unauthentic behavior. They expect to be misunderstood and despised (Small, 1990). Counselors who can risk being real in every way with these clients can have a major impact and create real contact.

Attentiveness

A fundamental part of the counseling process is attentiveness, which implies maximum involvement by the counselor in the client's communication (Shertzer & Stone, 1980). Attentiveness requires counselors to listen and observe in order to try and understand the client's feelings and perspectives that are being presented. Hackney, Ivey, and Oetting (1970) describe attending behaviors as the counselor's emitting both verbal and nonverbal behaviors that communicate to the client that the message emitted by the client has been heard. The counselor is not dividing his or her attention between the client and other extraneous variables. Nonattending behaviors include frequent breaks in eye contact, intonation, and vocal pitch, or topic-jumping verbal behavior.

When counselors are truly listening to their clients they can pick up subtle nuances of the conversation and will be more accurate in their observations and reflections, which will foster the counseling relationship. Attentiveness is communicated through facial expressions, body positions and movement, and verbal response (Ivey, 1971). When clients experience these positive responses to what they are saying, they will feel acceptance and their feelings of vulnerability, uncertainty, or lack of trust will begin to dissipate (Hackney & Cormier, 1979).

Facial expressions communicate messages that are meaningful to the client. These include: eye contact, head nods, and manipulation of facial muscles to produce positive connotations of smiles or negative responses of frowns, as well as puzzled or indifferent looks (Hackney & Cormier, 1979). Eye contact has different meanings for different cultures. Some cultures such as Native American find it rude, but other cultures see it as a sign of attentiveness. This does not mean staring at the client. A counselor's eyes can move slightly away from the client's and then return. Head nodding can be an affirmation of the client but should not be overdone, and facial expressions provide a mirror for the client and communicate that the counselor is alert and interested. Body position also gives messages to the client. Tension and an upright position may imply a working state, while a relaxed posture may communicate comfort with the counseling process.

Verbal behaviors can also reflect an attentive state. Counselors who stay with the topic and help the client develop the theme they are exploring will be more facilitative to the counseling process than those who interrupt their clients or jump from topic to topic. The tone and pitch of the counselor's voice also communicates a sense of comfort and acceptance. The use of minimal responses such as, "mm-hmm" or "ah" can be used to let clients know that they are being heard, but much like the head nod they can be overused.

Attentiveness is important in developing rapport, communicating empathy, and emitting a genuine presence in counseling. It involves listening attentively and communicating this attentiveness to clients through the use of eye contact, intermittent head nods, a variety of facial expressions, a relaxed posture, a modulated voice, minimal verbal responses, and following the client's topics (Hackney & Cormier, 1979).

Respect

Unconditional positive regard is one of the conditions that Rogers (1957) believed was necessary to bring about personality change. Change means surface or deep changes in a person's personality structure, change from immature behavior or change in the sense of utilizing more energy for effective living (Shertzer & Stone, 1980). This positive regard is seen as unconditional because it does not depend on the behavior of the client. In the face of the client's imperfections the counselor is nonjudgmental and accepts the client for who he or she is, assuming the client has done the best they could with the circumstances they were given. The counselor needs to communicate sincere belief that the client has inherent strength and capacity to make it in life, and that the client has the right to choose alternatives and make decisions (Small, 1990).

Respect has also been defined as care and concern for another person, as well as trust and sharing (Wrenn, 1973). Truax and Carkhuff (1967) developed a scale to measure positive regard, called nonpossessive warmth, which was later labeled respect. They describe the highest level of respect as, "the helper communicates the very deepest respect for the helpee's worth as a person and his potentials as a free individual" (Carkhuff, 1969, p. 179).

To communicate respect to clients, counselors need to believe that clients have the capacity to solve their own problems. It is the counselors' responsibility to help clients find their own inner strengths and solutions. Acting like the expert and giving clients advice about how to solve difficult life problems robs them of the growth experience of coming to their own decisions. For instance, if a client is struggling with a decision about whether or not to leave his wife, a counselor who respects his client will allow him to struggle with the decision and support his struggle, not give him the answer. For example:

Client: "I just don't think I can live with Judy any longer. All we do is fight and there never seems to be any good times between us. But I keep remembering how good our marriage used to be before we got caught up with drugs. What should I do? Stay or go?"
Counselor: "Why do you think it is so difficult for you to make this decision?"
Client: "I keep thinking that maybe the drugs have caused the problems. If we can both get clean and sober, we might be able to go back to the way it used to be."
Counselor: "It sounds like you still have hope for your marriage."
Client: "I guess I do."
Counselor: "What can you do to make it better?"
Client: "Well, first I need to work on my own recovery."

An important part of chemical dependency counseling is helping addicted clients take responsibility for themselves. Often they have cognitive distortions about their real strengths and weaknesses; jumping from a position of powerlessness to omnipotence. Counselors who can demonstrate respect can help their clients find their real strengths and weaknesses and support their clients in taking responsibility for both. This respect gives alcoholics and addicts hope that they may actually be worthwhile people with the ability to make choices and govern their lives (Small, 1990).

Immediacy

Immediacy is a term that describes the counselor's ability to communicate feelings and experiences that are happening between the counselor and the client in the here and now. It is sharing with the client what the counselor believes is happening on many levels at the moment. This helps the client clarify what he or she may be feeling about the counselor or the counseling process. Immediacy takes the focus off of the content of the communication and brings it to the process of what is happening between the counselor and the client, i.e., talking about their relationship. By doing this the counselor helps the client better understand what is happening.

By being aware of the multiple levels of communication in counseling, counselors can listen to both the content of their client's speech and to the way it is spoken. For example, if a client brings up how angry he is about what is happening at work and rambles on for some time, the counselor might suspect that he is filling up time with this complaint to avoid something else. The dialogue might go like this:

Client: "I just don't think my boss understands how hard I work. He's always on my back."

Counselor: "You seem quite upset about work, but I have a feeling you might be avoiding me with these complaints and afraid that I might bring up something you don't want to deal with."

Client: "You may be right. I was afraid you would be disappointed in me because I didn't show up for the group meeting last night."

Counselor: "I think we need to clear the air about that."

It might have been easier for this counselor to empathize with the client about his work situation and ignore the uncomfortable feeling he was experiencing. By taking the risk of confronting the lack of here-and-now communication, the counselor was able to really connect with the client and allow him to be honest about his fear. In the field of chemical dependency counseling this is an important skill. Alcoholics and addicts are experts at verbal manipulation. They use denial and projection as defense mechanisms to avoid pain, which deprives them of genuine human connection. These clients can learn to deal with the immediate reality of their lives when their counselors take the risk to model this honest, direct communication.

The here and now is the focus of several theories of counseling, such as person-centered counseling and Gestalt therapy. There are techniques for staying in the present and bringing clients back to the here and now, but the best resource is the counselor's knowledge of self. Chapter 1 describes the use of self and the knowledge of self as it applies to counselors. When counselors know themselves and understand what issues are difficult for them or where their blind spots are, they are better able to identify what they bring to the counseling relationship and what belongs to their clients—a very useful skill for developing immediacy in the counseling process.

Concreteness

Concreteness refers to the accuracy and specificity of the counselor's response to the client (Shertzer & Stone, 1980). Counselors' responses to their clients need to be specific about the feelings, experiences, and behaviors that the clients are describing. This allows the counselor to stay close to the client's level of feeling and experience, eliminates misunderstandings, and helps the client attend to specific problems (Carkhuff & Berenson, 1967). Carkhuff (1969) described a high level of concreteness as, "the helper appears always helpful in guiding the discussion so that the helpee(s) may discuss fluently, directly, and completely specific feelings and experiences" (p. 183).

Counselors should avoid going off on tangents or allowing clients to get into abstract discussions, to gossip, or to speculate about others. They need to direct clients who do this back to relevant issues and the process of the moment. For example:

Counselor: "Last time we met you were very angry at your wife."

Client: "Well, John was saying in group last night that all men have trouble understanding women. Women don't even know what they want most of the time."

Counselor: "Well, that's all well and good, but I am interested in what is happening between you and your wife."

This client is avoiding the painful subject of his marital problems by reporting someone else's opinions and making global statements about men and women. The counselor pulls the client back to the original question about the client's relationship with his wife. This may be sufficient for the client to then get to the avoided subject, or he may again avoid it by bringing up something else or by dismissing it as not important. The client may not be ready to deal with the painful issue, and the counselor should then respect his wishes for the time being. The counselor can also be concrete by bringing the topic of conversation to the here and now of what is happening between the counselor and the client. For example:

Counselor: "I think you need to talk to your wife about your feelings."

Client: "Yes, but she doesn't listen."

Counselor: "Maybe if you picked a good time and told her it was important to you . . ."

Client: "Oh, she doesn't care about anything important to me."

Counselor: "I'm feeling frustrated right now, and I don't know how to help you. It seems like you're very upset with your wife, yet you seem to reject all of my suggestions of how to work this out."

By returning the content of the conversation to what is happening for the counselor at that moment, it puts the responsibility of change back on the client. It is an acknowledgement by the counselor that he cannot change the client.

Chemical dependency counselors may find that their clients are very astute at intellectualization and generalization. This keeps the focus off them and helps them avoid taking responsibility for themselves. Many alcoholics/addicts have used mind-altering substances to avoid the real world and all of the responsibilities that come with being an adult. They will resist taking responsibility for themselves in the here and now in favor of talking about the idea of taking responsibility. These alcoholics and addicts may also take more time than other clients to trust counselors, and they may test the waters with irrelevant or safe topics in counseling sessions. As counselors stay concrete and connected to these clients, the clients will begin to take responsibility for their thoughts, beliefs, and actions.

Warmth

Warmth is a characteristic of a counselor that is similar to respect. It is one way of showing respect for a client. The opposite of a counselor with warmth is one who is cold, aloof, and too businesslike. Particularly in the beginning of counseling, clients like to have a counselor who they perceive as friendly and warm.

Warmth is generally communicated through nonverbal behavior, such as smiles, gestures, tone of voice, touches, and posture. Warmth, however, can be overused, which can make clients feel uncomfortable. The counseling relationship is not a real friendship. It is a unique relationship with special rules and there must be clear boundaries between the counselor and client. An overuse of touching, for instance, may make the client uncomfortable and feel that his or her personal space is being invaded. On the other hand, a counselor who has a strict rule of never touching a client may miss an opportunity to make a human connection with his or her client.

Being genuine is also a part of appropriate warmth. If a counselor is genuinely a warm person, this will be communicated through the use of genuineness and immediacy. If the counselor is not naturally a warm person, he or she should not try to be falsely warm toward the client. It is more important to be genuine. Clients differ in the amount of warmth they need from their counselors. Counselors should gear the amount of warmth expressed to the need of the client, not to their own need to be seen as warm.

Counselor Skills

Counselor skills are learned behaviors that promote client self-exploration, understanding, and change. They go hand in hand with the core elements of counseling and guide the counselor in the therapy process.

Listening

"Listening is the means by which counselors sustain, extend, and deepen their knowledge of the client" (Shertzer & Stone, 1980, p. 267). It is a different kind of listening than listening to a speech or lecture or social listening in a conversation. In these instances people are listening with only part of their minds. They may be processing what they are hearing or formulating a response to the speaker. In counseling, the client requires the counselor's complete attention. This is called active listening. This requires the counselor to be present psychologically, socially, and emotionally (Egan, 1990). Egan further defines complete listening as having four parts: "first, observing and reading the client's nonverbal behavior— posture, facial expressions, movement, tone of voice, and the like; second, listening to and understanding the client's verbal messages; third, listening to the whole person in the context of the social setting of life; fourth, tough-minded listening" (p. 112).

Nonverbal behavior is important because it can give the counselor another avenue of gaining information about the client. By observing posture; body movements; facial expressions; physical characteristics; physiological responses, such as facial flushing or pupil dilation or listening for changes in the tone, pitch, or level of voice; pauses; silences; and inflections or spacing of words, the counselor can gain information about the congruence of verbal and nonverbal behavior. Chemical dependency clients, who are experts at manipulating words, may be more truthful with their nonverbal behaviors or, at least, may not be able to conceal their nonverbal communication.

Listening to the client's verbal messages requires full attention to the client and hearing the verbal descriptions of his or her experiences, behaviors, and affect (Egan, 1990). The counselor's job is to help the client be specific about experiences: the specific behaviors, observations, and emotions. Most verbal expression has a cognitive part and an affective part. The cognitive part is the fact of the experience or the thought process connected with the experience, i.e., what the client thought about the experience. The affective part is the feeling or emotion that was evoked by the event or the thought about the event. Counselors should listen to both parts of the verbal message and begin to sort out the core messages or the themes that keep recurring in the verbal part of the communication.

Communication may be made up of verbal and nonverbal processes, but clients are more than their words and behaviors. They do not live in a vacuum. They live in contexts, surrounded by other people who have influences on their lives, and, thus, the context of their experiences is part of who they are and what they say. Counselors can develop empathy for their clients when they begin to understand what life is like for them and how it may be different from what the counselors have experienced. When counselors can listen in such a way that they see the world as their clients do, they have a better understanding of the clients' struggles, support systems, and values than they get from their families and friends.

Tough-minded listening is defined by Egan (1990) as including: "detecting the gaps, distortions, and dissonance that are part of the client's experienced reality" (p. 116). Sometimes clients have a false perception of themselves. They think that they are ugly, when they are not; helpless, when they are not; or they may even overestimate their abilities, when they should not. Part of listening is evaluating the content of the verbal communications and comparing the content with the observable reality. It may not be appropriate to challenge clients the moment they say something that is distorted. The counselor can make a mental note of the distortion for use at a time when it will be most useful to the client.

Another type of listening is listening to self or what might be called intuitive listening. This process can happen in several ways. When counselors are intently listening, they will have a sensation that the rest of the world has disappeared. This is like having tunnel vision that is focused on the client, with the rest of the world out of focus. This intense process often creates a physiological reaction in the counselor, such as muscle tension, or an emotional reaction. When counselors can listen to clients' verbal and nonverbal behavior, they can get other clues about the client and how others may experience the client. Intuitive flashes may also occur that seem unrelated to the content of the conversation, and it is difficult for counselors to trust these intuitions because they seem to come from nowhere, but they may contain the most real information. When counselors can step back and check their own reactions to clients, they may also find that they are mimicking their clients' postures and voice intonations. This is a process that may be automatic, but it is also a way to give feedback to clients, telling them that you are trying to get into their world.

Reflecting

The skill that is coupled with active listening is reflecting or restating. Counselors can restate the content of what they think they heard the client say, or they can reflect the feelings that the client is emoting. The restatement is a verbatim repetition of the main thought or feeling expressed by the client's preceding communication (Hackney & Cormier, 1979). For example:

Client: "I don't know whether I can go back to the stress of my job after completing this treatment program. It's a pretty demanding job, but I don't know what other kind of job I could get."

Counselor: "You don't know whether to go back to your job, but you don't know what else you might do."

In this example, the client had two thoughts: concern about returning to his or her stressful job and not knowing about other options. It is tempting for counselors to reflect the last thing said by clients, but this may not represent the theme of the conversation. The counselor in the example tried to reflect both parts of the client's dilemma. Although this may let the client know that the counselor is listening, if it is overused, it can sound like the counselor is simply parroting back the client's words.

Counselors can also reflect the affective content of the communication. "Reflection of feeling is a paraphrased response to a feeling communicated by the client, either verbally or nonverbally" (Hackney & Cormier, 1979, p. 50). For example:

Client: "I don't know whether I can go back to the stress of my job after completing this treatment program. It's a pretty demanding job, but I don't know what other kind of job I could get."

Counselor: "You're afraid to return to a stressful job, but you're worried about what else you might do."

In this case the counselor did not restate the content of the client's communication, but reflected the feelings that he thought the client had about the content. This is useful when working with an alcoholic or addict who has difficulty talking about feelings or who may be unaware of these feelings.

Rogers (1951) defined reflection of feeling as an attempt "to understand from the client's point of view and to communicate that understanding" (p. 452). Reflection is an attempt to communicate the core of what the client is feeling or experiencing. When this is done in a nonthreatening way, clients can then see their feelings as a part of themselves. This can be done by reflecting a feeling immediately after it is expressed or alluded to or can be done by summarizing in one statement several feelings that the client has expressed (Shertzer & Stone, 1980). Often an accurate reflection of feelings comes from the intuitive level of listening, when a counselor can sense a feeling or have an emotional reaction to the client's feelings. Even if the counselor does not accurately reflect the client's feelings, the client has to focus on real feelings. The counselor can then ask for a clarification from the client to get a clearer picture of what the client is feeling.

Questioning

Questioning is a technique used by counselors to obtain information from clients. Ideally this is done with open-ended questions that allow clients to fully describe their experiences. Questioning can be overused and can become problematic. Inexperienced counselors ask many more questions than do those with experience.

If questions are stated in a way that the client can answer them with a "yes" or a "no," the counselor will learn little about the client and the client will feel like the counseling process is an interrogation. This also limits the responsibility of the client to work in the session and exaggerates the work done by the counselor. It is the job of the counselor to structure the rhythm of the counseling process. A good way for counselors to check this is to listen to an audio tape of a counseling session and note the amount of time the counselor is speaking and the amount of time the client is speaking. Counselors who are questioning excessively will also feel drained at the end of the session. "The counselor's safeguard in the use of questions is true interest in understanding and aiding the individual" (Shertzer & Stone, 1980, p. 275). Questions are useful in obtaining specific information or in directing the client's conversation to more fruitful channels (Shertzer & Stone, 1980). Questions that redirect should be open ended but target relevant areas that the client may be avoiding or that may be difficult to explore.

Questions that say to the client that the counselor is interested are empathetic types of questions. They are often tentative statements of reflection that happen to be in the form of a question. When the counselor is ahead of the client and is groping for understanding, a request for clarification will tell the client that the counselor is trying to understand. For example:

Client: "I'm looking forward to graduating from the drug treatment program, but I feel nervous about it."

Counselor: "Are you frightened about having to return to your old environment where your friends that you used to hang out with and use drugs with live?"

The counselor is anticipating that this is why the client might be nervous about completing the program, and leads the client to talk about the fear of returning home. This could help clients understand their feelings and direct them to discuss relapse prevention skills.

Confronting

Confrontation is often associated with drug and alcohol counseling. The use of heavy confrontation techniques was thought to be necessary to confront the denial of alcoholics and addicts. This led to a type of group therapy for addiction dubbed "the hot seat" therapy. Group members would take turns being on the hot seat while other group members would confront them with their behavior. Although this may have been effective for some, particularly those who were reluctant to recover, it was damaging to the self-esteem of others. This practice has led to a misunderstanding in the field of chemical dependency treatment that confrontation must be of the hot seat type. Confrontation, however, can come in many forms and not only helps clients come more directly in contact with their own experience but also creates a situation where they can grow (Small, 1990).

Confrontation is used to help clients face reality when the counselor perceives denial or false ideas in his or her client. Confrontation occurs when the counselor observes a discrepancy between (1) what the client is saying and what the counselor perceives they are experiencing; (2) what the client is saying and what the counselor heard him or her say before; and (3) what the client is saying to the counselor in the moment and what the client's actions are in everyday life (Small, 1990).

Confrontation is often thought of as tearing down a person by attacking his or her defenses, but it can be used to reveal assets as well as deficits, strengths as well as weaknesses (Shertzer & Stone, 1980). For example:

Client: "I've never been successful at anything in my life."
Counselor: "Wait a minute. You told me that you got a college degree in business, and you started your own consulting firm."
Client: "Yeah, but I lost that business last year."
Counselor: "Do you think that might have had something to do with your drinking?"
Client: "I suppose you're right."
Counselor: "It seems to me that you can be quite successful when you're not preoccupied with drinking."

Egan (1990) has listed some areas where clients might need to be challenged or invited to challenge themselves:

- failure to own problems
- failure to define problems in solvable terms
- faulty interpretations of critical experiences, behaviors, and feelings
- evasions, distortions, and game playing
- failure to identify or understand the consequences of behavior
- hesitancy or unwillingness to act on new perspectives (p. 187)

It is not suprising that confrontation is frequently used in chemical dependency treatment. Alcoholics and addicts often have distorted senses of themselves due to years of living in a fog and using the defense mechanisms of denial, rationalization, minimization, intellectualization, and manipulation of others in order to maintain their addiction. One of the main goals of chemical dependency treatment is to help clients take responsibility for their own behavior and stop blaming others. These defensive behaviors have also pulled distorted responses from family members and friends who are angry, upset, and confused about the alcoholic's or addict's behaviors and blaming statements. These significant others often resort to distorted accusations to try to get the alcoholic or addict to wake up and stop abusing alcohol and other drugs. These accusations are often internalized, creating even more of a sense of failure in the alcoholic and addict, even though it is not accurate and perpetuates the addiction.

Cognitive distortions are also common to alcoholics and addicts. They may have developed a faulty belief system about themselves, the world, and how life should or should not be. These ways of thinking keep them blocked and unable to make changes. Ellis (1985), in his rational-emotive therapy, described the need to challenge inner thoughts that sustain self-defeating behavior. He believed that people have some common self-defeating thoughts about how life should be.

When reality does not match up with these shoulds they get depressed and give up. A common theme of these irrational thoughts is absolutism, i.e., always, never, should, and must statements. Counselors who hear these self-defeating, irrational ideas need to confront this type of thinking and help their clients modify their thoughts to more closely resemble reality.

Self-Disclosing

Chemical dependency counselors frequently have concerns about how much of their own recovery process or their personal connections with addiction to share with their clients. In some ways it may be helpful to the client to know that the counselor has successfully struggled with the same problem they are facing, but this also presents a danger of the counselor's relying on that connection as being enough.

Self-disclosure is the act of the counselor's sharing feelings, attitudes, and experiences with the client in order to help that person. Such sharing should be meaningful and pertinent in context and content in order to be therapeutic (Small, 1990). Self-disclosure can be very effective if it is used sparingly and with a good sense of timing and appropriateness. It works well when the counselor is aware of how to use a sense of self as a therapeutic tool, and it can come in several forms. These include disclosures about:

- the counselor's own problems
- the facts about the counselor's role
- the counselor's reactions to the client (feedback)
- the counselor's reactions to the counselor-client relationship (Hackney & Cormier, 1979, p. 14)

When the counselor gives clients feedback or discusses their reactions to the relationship, self-disclosure is usually very helpful so that the clients can know about how they are perceived by others. Self-disclosures about the counselor's own problems are more difficult to evaluate as to their helpfulness.

A general rule about self-disclosure is to ask, "Who is really benefiting from this self-disclosure—the counselor or the client?" The answer to this question must be "the client." Counselors should not disclose personal problems that they need help with. These issues should be discussed in the counselor's personal therapy. Disclosures, by the counselor, of personal success, however, may be helpful in both connecting with the client on a human level and also providing role modeling for a client who is struggling with a similar problem. Caution should be used, however, in the overreliance on self-disclosure. The client needs to see the counselor as a relatively healthy and successful human being.

Counselors who overuse self-disclosure may be seen by their clients as un-healthy and unable to help.

Clients are often interested in their counselors and may ask about their personal lives or their training. These questions can be answered briefly to satisfy casual curiosity, but if the client shifts the focus of the counseling process to an interrogation of the counselor, they may be avoiding being the focus of the therapy. When this happens the counselor can shift the focus back to the client with questions such as, "You're asking a lot of questions today."

Interpreting

"Interpretative techniques are those that identify and conceptualize patterns of relationships and explain meanings behind client statements" (Shertzer & Stone, 1980). Interpretations point out the underlying feelings or attitudes of the client and attempt to integrate feelings, thoughts, and actions. It is the counselor's attempt to imply meaning or cause-and-effect reasoning to the client's description of self—to create insight.

Interpretation is a technique used after the counselor has gotten to know the client and has spent time listening to his or her view of self and the world. If the counselor is correct in his or her interpretation and the client is ready to accept the interpretation, it may speed the client to insight. Insight, however, does not always lead to a change in behavior. Clients also reject interpretations if they believe that they are incorrect or if they are not ready to accept the interpretation of their behavior.

Client-centered therapies do not put much emphasis on interpretations because it puts the responsibility for change more with the counselor than with the client. Interpretation is also seen as a cognitive process that ignores the affective component. Rogers (1942) listed some issues for counselors concerning interpre-tation: (1) counselors should avoid interpretation if they are unsure of themselves; (2) counselors should use the client's symbols and terms in the interpretation; (3) interpretations should deal with attitudes that have already been expressed; (4) it is not useful to argue about the correctness of the interpretation with the client; (5) if genuine insight has been gained by the client, he or she will be able to spontaneously apply it in new areas; and (6) after the client has achieved a new insight, he or she may temporarily relapse to old behaviors.

Clarifying

Clarifying techniques are related to reflection and interpretation. Clarifying is an attempt by the counselor to place the client's feelings or attitudes in a clearer or more recognizable form for the benefit of both (Shertzer & Stone, 1980). Clarifications are more than just mere reflections of the content of the client's speech. It is a statement that elicits more information so that the client's meaning can be understood. Clarifications can also be attempts at interpretation where statements are designed to crystallize the thoughts and feelings of clients around a particular subject or focus on a subject that needs further thought or attention (Shertzer & Stone, 1980).

Clients from cultures other than the counselor's may use unique words or speech patterns to explain themselves. Clarifications can be very helpful in allowing clients to teach counselors about how they see the world and how they think.

SEEKING AND SELECTING A PERSONAL APPROACH TO COUNSELING

Counselors must choose a style or approach to counseling that fits their own personality. This should involve their own models or theories of why people change addictive behaviors and how they can best use their skills to enhance this change in their clients. If counselors do not have a solid belief in what they are doing during the counseling process and what their role is in that process, a positive outcome for the client will be a matter of luck, or the client's motivation, rather than what the counselor does.

New or beginning counselors are limited by their lack of education and experience. They do not always know what the options are, and they are often limited to what their supervisors or instructors do or tell them to do. Counseling is a skill that involves the beliefs, values, motivation, education, and personalities of counselors. The more experience counselors have, the more they should be able to use their personal attributes to enhance their ability to assist clients with a positive change. As new counselors combine experience with additional education, counseling will become more natural and will begin to involve all of their personal attributes to make the most out of their relationship with the client.

The most important beginning step is for counselors to take an inventory of their values, beliefs, skills, and personalities and to ask themselves what theory or model best fits these attributes. For example, some counselors are very confrontational with clients, and they believe that it is necessary to provide this confrontation to motivate clients to change. Other counselors are more supportive and believe that clients are more likely to change in a supportive environment. Counselors should choose a style that they believe in and that they believe will be useful to their clients. Clients can usually sense that their counselors are not operating out of belief systems that support what they are doing. Some counselors may be comfortable being both confrontive and supportive in different situations. That is effective as long as the counselor is able to wisely choose which client will respond best to which approach. That is also a skill that takes experience.

The more options for treatment and counseling approaches that counselors have to choose from, the more likely it is that they will chose one that maximizes their abilities and enhances treatment for their clients. It may take several years before a new counselor is completely comfortable with his or her approach. This process is shortened if the new counselor continues to learn new skills and receives regular supervision.

There are many approaches to counseling and to the treatment of chemical dependency. Some of them have been briefly presented in this text. It is up to the individual counselor to learn about the many approaches to treating chemical dependency. Training through workshops and other continuing-education events will give the new counselor additional information regarding what is available. As counselors gain experience and receive supervision, they can make adjustments to their approaches in order to find the one that is comfortable.

DOCUMENTATION

Documentation is the recording of the screening and intake process and the assessment and treatment plan as well as the preparation of written reports, clinical progress notes, discharge summaries, and other client-related data. This is often the least liked part of the counseling process, but it can be the most important. The purpose of keeping accurate and complete records is to clearly document the entire treatment process, which begins with written screening and assessment data, treatment plan, releases of information, and any previous records from prior admissions or prior treatment. The documentation continues with treatment plan updates, progress notes concerning the client's progress on the treatment plan, reports from adjunctive therapies or referral sources, and any other written documents that are relevant to the therapy. The file is completed with an accurate, concise, and informative discharge summary, aftercare plan, and any referrals made to other professionals or programs.

Each facility has its own set of forms for documentation, but there are some generally agreed upon materials that should be placed in a client's file. Documentation serves an important function as a written record of the client's treatment. It is a record of what was done in treatment, what failed, and what succeeded. If the client is readmitted at a later date, the new counselor has a wealth of information about the previous treatment and does not have to start from the beginning.

A client's records can also be used in nontherapeutic ways that can be damaging to the client and the treatment process. Records are protected by confidentiality regulations and should not be available to anyone other than members of the treatment staff who need access to the file in order to maintain a consistent treatment plan and to document progress. Requests by third parties for copies of records must follow the confidentiality guidelines of having appropriate, signed releases of information that conform to the regulations. Even with the appropriate procedures, client records often fall into the hands of people who are not governed by the confidentiality regulations or who are unaware of them. That is why it is especially important to carefully write evaluations, treatment plans, and progress notes in a professional style that clearly indicates what are observed behaviors, client communication, and counselor interpretations or hunches. Progress notes should directly reflect a client's progress in relation to treatment goals and objectives. Client files are not a place for keeping secrets or elaborating on the opinions of the counselor.

Clients should be involved in all parts of their treatment. This includes under-standing their evaluation results, cocreating and signing their treatment plan, clearly understanding the progress they are making in treatment, and being aware of any referrals or third-party involvements. Thus, there should not be anything in a client's record that he or she is not aware of. Clients do have a right to know what is in their records. It may not be in their best interest for counselors to give the clients the actual records to read, but counselors should be able to explain everything in the chart to the client.

Counselors should be timely and accurate in charting a client's progress. A study of successful chemical dependency counselors indicated that counselors who performed their duties in a concerned and organized manner had better success rates in enabling clients to stabilize their lives and to use the other social and medical services available to them (McLellan, Woody, Luborsky, & Goehl, 1988). They described the charts from the most successful counselors as, "notable for the thorough and accurate charting of all pertinent aspects of patient contact" (p. 429). The charts indicated clearly formulated plans of rehabilitation created through consultation with the treatment team and client. The plans were followed and documented at all points.

SUPERVISION

Supervision is a very important part of counselor education and training. However, it is not always easy to find a good supervisor in a chemical dependency treatment setting. Some counselors are supervisors because they have worked in an agency longer than anyone else. Longevity does not necessarily make them good supervisors. In fact, in some cases these individuals may not even meet current requirements to be a counselor, because they were grandfathered in when chemical dependency counselor certification was just beginning. Some of these individuals may be outstanding supervisors, but many are not.

In other situations agencies that are underfunded and understaffed take on trainees to help with the work load. In these cases there are usually not enough staff to provide the necessary therapy, much less adequate supervision. Trainees may be put into counseling situations with little or no supervision. Clients may suffer as a result.

Supervision is often approached in the chemical dependency field from an apprenticeship model. That is, the supervisor gives the message, "Do just like I do, and don't question my approach." This is contrasted with the scientific model that encourages individuals to seek what is best for themselves and their clients. The scientific model also encourages all questions, even if the supervisor is being questioned about his or her approach. Supervision should be a tutorial process where principles are transformed into practical skills. The supervisor should monitor and assist the supervisee in a minimum of these areas:

- record keeping, including all agency requirements
- counseling activity via audio, video, or direct observation
- referral
- assessment and diagnosis
- ethics and professional issues
- presentations in case conferences
- client evaluation of performance
- issues of diversity among clients

The supervisor should talk to the counselor-in-training about such issues as client motivation, covert sexual issues, transference and countertransference issues, termination procedures, unconscious material that may be interfering with counseling, and other issues related to the process of counseling.

There are several different models or combinations of supervision, some of which include:

- Lecturer
- Teacher
- Case Reviewer
- Collegial-Peer
- Monitor
- Therapist

Each approach has its advantages and disadvantages. It is important that the supervisor choose an approach that the counselor being supervised is comfortable with and a process that he or she will gain from. The supervisor will need to choose the modality of supervision, emphasis and focus of supervision, style of supervision, and form of evaluation of the supervisee. These things should be decided in consultation with the supervisee.

In some cases a trainee might be in supervision with someone who is not providing good quality supervision. The supervisor may have an entirely different idea about a treatment approach than the trainee. The trainee may even have more formal education than the supervisor, in which case the trainee should keep an open mind. It is best for the trainee to deal with issues like these directly with the supervisor. If the problems cannot be worked out directly with the supervisor, the situation will dictate the appropriate course of action. The trainees may have no choice other than to accept the poor supervision until they have reached their goal in training (i.e., number of hours for certification, or a certificate). One option for trainees in this situation is to arrange for some supplemental supervision with someone who can provide appropriate training. One hour of good supervision may be better than 100 hours of bad supervision. The trainee needs to acknowledge that the supervisor has an authoritative position, and it would not be in the trainee's best interest to undermine that position. To avoid a negative training situation, trainees should choose training sites and supervisors carefully. It is a good idea for trainees to visit the prospective training site, talk to the staff, find out who the supervisor will be, and speak directly to him or her. Trainees need to interview the staff and supervisors to determine if the site will be able to provide the training and experiences that they want. If the site or the supervisor is not what the trainees need, they should try other agencies.

Taking courses, reading, and role playing are all necessary and valuable learning experiences for the counselor-to-be. However, working as a counselor with real clients and with good supervision is the only way that one becomes an accomplished counselor. It is the responsibility of the counseling student to seek out good supervision in a treatment setting that meets his or her training needs.

CLIENT AND COMMUNITY EDUCATION

This is the process of providing clients, individuals, and community groups with information on the risks related to alcohol and other drug use, as well as available prevention, treatment, and recovery resources. Education is often an important component in drug and alcohol treatment programs. It is also essential in combating the stigma of addiction by informing the public about prevention strategies, warning signals, symptoms, the course of recovery, and treatment opportunities and successes. Chemical dependency counselors will be expected to design and provide culturally relevant formal and informal education programs that raise the awareness and support substance abuse prevention and/or the recovery process. These presentations may include factors that increase the likelihood for an individual, community, or group to be at risk for alcohol and other drug problems. Further, there is a need to sensitize others to issues of cultural identity, ethnic background, age, and gender role or identity in prevention, treatment, and recovery.

Counselors will need information about the many subjects that are related to chemical dependency and that affect the individual, the family, and the community. These include how addiction affects the family and concerned others; the principles and philosophies of prevention, treatment, and recovery; and the related health and behavioral problems of HIV/AIDS, tuberculosis, sexually transmitted diseases, and other communicable diseases. Counselors should also be able to teach basic life skills to their clients, such as stress management, relaxation, communication, assertiveness, and refusal skills.

It is frequently difficult to separate counseling and education. While counseling is focused on helping the client find his or her own solution, education is the process of giving others didactic information. In chemical dependency treatment, counselors may have to learn to blend these two processes to maximize their treatment success. Clients who want to remain sober will be more successful if they are taught stress management and refusal skills. Family education programs are usually part of a treatment process as well. These can be very helpful to families in breaking the blame-and-revenge cycle; but when family education is augmented with systemic family therapy, the outcome is even better.

DISCUSSION QUESTIONS

1. What are the key components of screening and assessment when working with substance abusers? Design an assessment protocol for assessing substance abuse including all the areas that need to be reviewed and create questions that would elicit information in those areas.
2. Define the role of a case manager working with a treatment plan. What are the case manager's primary duties? How does a case manager interact with other resources and the community?
3. Make a list of the core elements in individual counseling. Describe what words and body language would communicate each element to a client.
4. Define confrontation as it is used in substance abuse treatment. When would heavy confrontation be useful? When would heavy confrontation be harmful?
5. How is self-disclosure useful in counseling? When would it be harmful?
6. Make a list of your strengths and weaknesses as a substance abuse counselor. What type of counseling theory and process would be best suited to you?
7. Design a set of forms for documenting substance abuse treatment. What information would be necessary for providing quality substance abuse treatment?

REFERENCES

Carkhuff, R. R. (1969). *Helping and human relations: Vol. 1. Selection and training.* New York: Holt, Rinehart & Winston.

Carkhuff, R. R., & Berenson, B. G. (1967). *Beyond counseling and therapy*. New York: Holt, Rinehart & Winston.

Corey, G. (1991). *Theory and practice of counseling and psychotherapy* (4th ed.). Pacific Grove, CA: Brooks/Cole Publishing Co.

Curriculum Review Committee, Addiction Training Center Program (Sept. 1995). *Addiction counselor competencies*. Albany, NY: State University of New York.

Egan, G. (1990). *The skilled helper: A systemic approach to effective helping*. Pacific Grove, CA: Brooks/Cole Publishing Co.

Ellis, A. (1985). Expanding the ABCs of rational-emotive therapy. In M. Mahoney & A. Freeman (Eds.), *Cognition and psychotherapy*. New York: Plenum Publishing Corporation.

Hackney, H., & Cormier, L. S. (1979). *Counseling strategies and objectives*. Englewood Cliffs, NJ: Prentice-Hall.

Hackney, H., Ivey, A. E., & Oetting, E. R. (1970). Attending, island and hiatus behavior: A process conception of counselor and client interaction. *Journal of Counseling Psychology, 17,* 343–44.

Ivey, A. E. (1971). *Microcounseling: Innovations in interviewing training*. Springfield, IL: Charles C Thomas, Publisher.

McLellan, A. T., Woody, G. E., Luborsky, L., & Goehl, L. (1988). Is the counselor an "active ingredient" in substance abuse rehabilitation? An examination of treatment success among four counselors. *Journal of Nervous and Mental Disease, 176* (7) 423–30.

Rogers, C. (1951). *Client-centered therapy*. Boston: Houghton Mifflin Co.

Rogers, C. (1942). *Counseling and psychotherapy*. Boston: Houghton Mifflin Co.

Rogers, C. (1957). The necessary and sufficient conditions of therapeutic personality change. *Journal of Consulting Psychology, 21,* 95–103.

Rogers, C. (1961). *On becoming a person*. Boston: Houghton Mifflin Co.

Rogers, C. (1967). The interpersonal relationship: The core of guidance. In C. Rogers & B. Stevens (Eds.), *Person to person* (pp. 89–98). Lafayette, CA: Real People Press.

Shertzer, B., & Stone, S. C. (1980). *Fundamentals of counseling* (3rd ed.). Boston: Houghton Mifflin Co.

Small, J. (1990). *Becoming naturally therapeutic* (Rev. ed.). New York: Bantam Books, Inc..

Truax, C. B., & Carkhuff, R. R. (1967). *Toward effective counseling and psychotherapy*. Chicago: Aldine.

Wrenn, C. G. (1973). *The world of the contemporary counselor*. Boston: Houghton Mifflin Co.

Chapter 4

❧～✦✦❧～✦

Characterizing Clients and Assessing Their Needs

The eyes believe themselves; The ears believe other people.
Old Chinese Proverb

CHAPTER OBJECTIVES

- Examine the rationale for a diagnosis
- Examine the options for diagnosing chemical dependency
- Examine areas that should be included in a diagnosis
- Encourage the reader to match patient diagnoses to appropriate treatment plans
- Examine different classification approaches
- Review the DSM-IV approach to diagnosis

There is no so-called typical chemically dependent person; they are as different as fingerprints (see Chapter 7 on diversity). There is no specific personality type, family history, socioeconomic situation, or stressful experience that has been found to categorically predict the development of chemical dependency, although all of these play a part. Chemically dependent persons include doctors, ministers, chemical dependency counselors, lawyers, truck drivers, teachers, housewives, and members of virtually every profession known. In some cases, treatment programs are designed for certain professions. For example, medical doctors and Catholic priests both have inpatient treatment programs designed just for those in those professions. Chemical dependency transcends race, religion, social class, intelligence, and ethnic affiliation. Chemical dependency is a complex behavioral disorder, and attitudes and concepts about chemical dependency are changing for those who work in the field (Peele & Brodsky, 1991). As more objective information concerning chemical dependency accumulates, the total picture will become clearer. The issues of use, misuse, and abuse are now being examined from many perspectives: legal, clinical, professional, personal, social, and cultural, among others. Chemical dependency is now seen as a series of complex interactions among people, their environment, and the chemical they choose to use. Chemical dependency problems should be seen on a continuum. For example, alcohol problems are not limited just to alcoholics: They also include problem drinkers, prealcoholics, and families of alcoholics. Not only are there different types of people who have chemical dependency problems, there are many types of chemical dependency problems. There are also a variety of treatment choices available to the chemically dependent person. The type of person, their environment, the chemical involved, and the use pattern should all be considered in the diagnosis and treatment plan for the chemically dependent person, which often falls to the CD counselor. This information should be used to match the patient to an appropriate treatment setting. Simple definitions and simple methods of diagnosis sacrifice important scientific and clinical distinctions. Quality treatment is preceded by quality diagnosis. Counselors must know their clients and be able to assess their needs with accuracy.

DIAGNOSIS

The therapeutic relationship that a counselor establishes with a client is usually called counseling or therapy. This process is discussed in detail in Chapter 3. The importance of this relationship should be self-evident. The relationship may be therapeutic to a greater or lesser degree depending on its quality; however, in most instances, therapy does not end with the counseling relationship. Therapy can include many things, for example, relaxation training, assertiveness training, group counseling, recreation therapy, or a bibliotherapy (reading) program. The counseling session, besides providing some direct therapeutic value, is the appropriate place for the counselor to assess the client's diverse therapeutic needs. During the initial counseling sessions the counselor should evaluate the client and his therapeutic needs. The direction of this initial interview is likely to be determined by the setting in which it is done.

Treatment Settings

Addictions counselors work in a variety of settings. These include but are not limited to:

- inpatient drug or alcohol treatment programs (usually 30 days or less)
- long-term residential programs

- outpatient drug and alcohol treatment programs
- a private practice setting
- family clinics
- mental health programs
- corrections settings
- therapeutic communities
- methadone maintenance programs
- high-school and college settings
- military addictions programs (inpatient and outpatient)

Counselors have different backgrounds and training experiences depending on what is required by the program (Winick, 1991) and the regulatory agency in the state where the treatment program is located. Decisions regarding which program patients are sent to are sometimes predetermined by the setting. For example, an inmate in a corrections setting will stay in the available program because there is no choice. However, treatment plans and specific goals can be individualized and this is usually done by the counselor. In other situations the counselor may choose among several program options for each individual. An example of this is a drug counselor who works in an outpatient mental health center. The choice might be to send a patient to a therapeutic community, a methadone maintenance outpatient program, or just to see them in outpatient counseling. In whichever situation, the assessment and diagnosis is very important in relation to the eventual outcome.

Diagnosis

The quality of this assessment, or diagnosis, will be based on the quality and depth of the counseling relationship, and the outcome of treatment, or therapy, will have a direct relationship to the accuracy of the diagnosis and how it has been reflected in the treatment plan. Therefore, diagnosis becomes an integral part of the outcome, or prognosis. Counselors who know how to diagnose and how to translate this diagnosis into an individualized treatment plan are maximizing the benefits from their efforts.

George (1990) recommends that the diagnosis process include these areas:

- physical symptoms
- behavioral symptoms
- emotional symptoms
- social symptoms
- spiritual symptoms

Many of these areas are discussed in detail in Chapter 7, "Dealing with Diversity," particularly the emotional, social, and spiritual areas.

The physicial symptoms usually involve the changes in physical health one experiences after using a toxic substance for a period of time. A medical examination is recommended in most cases. The primary issues a counselor should ask about include physical health related to vital organs; physical damage acquired while drinking or using; and poor overall health due to an inadequate diet, lack of exercise, and the possibility of AIDS. Additional important physical symptoms include blackouts, an increased or decreased tolerance for the drugs they use, a change in sex drive, and physical signs like ataxia or tremors. Advanced physical problems can be used to help motivate the patient to stop using if there are no other complicating factors. However, the counselor should be leery of using statements like, "If you continue to use like this you're going to die!" In some cases that may be just what the patient wants to do. The counselor's reminder might give cause for the patient to use even more.

CHEMICAL DEPENDENCY BEHAVIOR CLASSIFICATION AND SYMPTOMS

There are two major ways to classify deviant behavior such as chemical dependency: the first is as immoral or sinful, the second is as amoral and beyond the control of the individual. In turn, this deviant behavior is either addressed through the social institutions of the judicial system or the social institutions of the health care system. If the judicial system is involved, this often means jail versus a hospital treatment program. Alcoholism and the abuse of medically prescribed drugs are now viewed less as immoral, sinful behavior (legal diagnosis) and more as personal sickness (medical diagnosis). The use or abuse of illegal drugs, however, has not made this transition. Alcoholism Is a Disease is a slogan that has a great deal of public acceptance. Heroin Addiction Is a Disease or Drug Addiction Is a Disease have less chance for such acceptance because of the legal status of the substance involved. Addiction may be addiction; however, the social context of use has special meaning when legal and political aspects of diagnosis are considered.

Diagnosis as a Social Process

Diagnosis may be viewed as a social process: At issue is how a specific society or segment of society creates and uses social rules to define chemical use versus abuse. These rules may be narrow or broad, depending on the drug and the particular society. The abuse of alcohol, for example, is seen rather consistently in

American culture as a pattern of repetitive, heavy drinking with obvious personal deterioration; consequently, almost anyone can make an accurate "social" diagnosis of alcoholism. However, this process of collective identification of alcoholics or of seeing all alcoholics as only those who have shown obvious deterioration, such as "skid-row" alcoholics, has probably done more to deter progressive treatment and rehabilitation of the individual alcoholic than any other single variable, for two reasons. First, as part of the alcoholic's denial system, problem drinkers or prealcoholics must see the alcoholic from a skid-row perspective. In the process they can deny the existence of their own alcohol problems for as many years as it takes for them to reach their own skid row (Forrest, 1978). Second, persons may resist being labeled as alcoholic because they view alcoholics as down-and-outers. They may refuse treatment with that label, though they might accept treatment without the label.

Diagnosis as a Clinical Process

The counselor is primarily involved with diagnosis from a clinical or treatment perspective. The first aspect of this diagnosis is to establish that chemical dependency problems are present. This screening diagnosis is conducted to establish whether or not the client is appropriate for the counselor and his treatment agency. Some agencies have intake specialists to make these evaluations. But many other agencies place this responsibility on the person who will be the client's individual counselor. A key question here is: Are mood-altering chemicals involved? or Does this person ingest drugs? (McAuliffe & McAuliffe, 1975). After this has been established, the counselor can proceed to the second phase of diagnosis.

Diagnostic Classifications

The precise detail of this in-depth diagnosis is closely related to precision treatment. Where treatment is general and imprecise, there is little need for detailed diagnosis. This has, in the past, been the case in the field of alcoholism and drug abuse. Until recently most treatment approaches for alcoholism and drug abuse have been global and imprecise. Each person would go through the same treatment program, regardless of diagnosis. However, as significantly different treatment methods and treatment goals are established, the need for more detailed and precise diagnostic methods increases (Pattison & Kaufman, 1982).

There are two major types of diagnosis: binary diagnosis and multivariate diagnosis. The binary type of diagnosis is an either/or method: One is either chemically dependent or one is not. The multivariate approach considers many factors and degrees of addiction. The binary approach may be based on either a unitary or a multivariate framework. When the assumption is that there is a discrete entity termed *chemical dependency* or *drug addiction* or *alcoholism,* the diagnostic goal is simply to find an effective way to distinguish those who are dependent on chemicals from those who are not. However, even though many still believe such entities exist, the research data of the past 20 years clearly demonstrate that the unitary concept is incorrect. The adverse effects of chemical use depend on many factors, and the binary diagnosis of chemically dependent persons leaves much to be desired.

Conjunctive and Disjunctive Classifications

Concepts or categories can either be conjunctive or disjunctive. A conjunctive classification is one in which all the defining attributes must be present for any individual to be classified in that category. For example, one must be over 18 and registered to be classified as a voter. This does not occur in the classification of alcoholism: Alcoholism is disjunctively categorized. That is, a person classified as alcoholic can have a number of different defining attributes: blackouts, legal problems, family problems, physical problems, or any of the many other problems related to alcohol use. The alcoholic may have experienced any one or any combination of these problems (Wallace, 1977).

As might be expected, the alcoholic or drug addict in treatment denies alcoholism or drug abuse and focuses on the areas where no problems exist. The focus for the counselor is on the addictive problems. The following exchange is typical:

Counselor: "You appear to have an alcohol problem, because you were picked up twice for drinking and driving."
Client: "Yes, but I still have a good job and my family life is fine; besides, many of my friends have been picked up for drinking and driving."

These encounters often end with the counselor's concluding that the client is in denial and that nothing can be done until the client drinks some more and "hits bottom." The client is left feeling that "the counselor does not understand the situation and has only one goal, and that is, to diagnose me as an alcoholic." These sessions often end without resolution, with both counselor and client feeling frustrated. Too often, the binary method of either/or diagnosis identifies only those in the late stages of alcoholism. Early stage alcoholics and problem drinkers typically are not treated but are sent on their way until they hit bottom. Those who do enter treatment are likely to drop out or exhibit resistance. This approach is no longer acceptable, given the different types of treatment interventions available for all types of alcohol and drug problems (Hester & Miller, 1989; L'Abate, L.,

Farriar, J. E., & Serritella, D. A., 1992; Ellis, A., McInerney, J. F., DiGiuseppe, R., & Yeager, R. J., 1991; Lawson, G., Peterson, J., & Lawson, A., 1983).

Multivariate Syndromes

Most scientific authorities in the field of chemical dependency now agree that the factors involved in chemical dependency, drug addiction, and alcoholism are most accurately viewed as multivariate syndromes (that is, multiple patterns of dysfunctional chemical use that occur in many different types of personalities, with multiple combinations of adverse consequences and multiple outcomes, that may require different treatment interventions). Pattison and Kaufman (1982) list six implications of multivariate syndromes that apply to alcoholism. (They are presented here in adapted form to show their relevance to chemical dependency.)

1. There are multiple patterns of use, misuse, and abuse that may be denoted as a pattern of chemical dependency.
2. There are multiple interactional etiological variables that combine to produce a pattern of chemical dependency.
3. All persons are vulnerable to the development of some type of chemical dependency problem.
4. Treatment interventions must be multimodal to correspond to the particular pattern of alcoholism or chemical dependency in a specific person.
5. Treatment outcomes will vary in accord with specific chemical-use patterns, persons, and social contexts.
6. Preventive interventions must be multiple and diverse in order to address diverse etiological factors.

The future of the chemical dependency field will, no doubt, include the description of consistently interrelated sets of symptoms with implications for etiology, prognosis, treatment, and prevention. The chemical dependency counselor will contribute to this by providing a multivariate diagnosis that is free of imprecise and ambiguous definitions that binarily impose a diagnosis of chemical dependency. The chemical dependency counselor will be expected to identify and treat all manner of people on all points of the chemical dependency continuum.

DEFINING THE PROBLEM

How is "the problem" defined? There are many terms that are used in the field of chemical dependency. Some have clear meanings, others are confusing and less well-defined. It is difficult for counselors to talk to one another (or to clients or other professionals) if they are using similar words but these words have different meanings to each person.

To begin with, what is chemical dependency? Does it refer only to physical dependency, or does it also include psychological dependency? What is considered a chemical? Alcohol? Nicotine? Caffeine? For the purpose of this book, and as a general guide for the counselor, the following definition is offered: Chemical dependency is a condition where there are perceivable signs or indications that the ingestion of a psychoactive or mood-altering chemical is causing the individual continuous life problems, yet this individual continues to use psychoactive chemicals. Although this is a rather broad definition, it does not fully encompass the range of clients that a chemical dependency counselor is likely to see.

The important aspects of this definition of chemical dependency are the phrases *life problems* and *continued use*. What are these life problems and what treatment approach is best suited to assist the client in dealing with them? What role does chemical use play in these problems and what is the payoff because of continued use? Note that the rationale behind this definition is not to seek an either/or diagnosis but to determine at what level these problems exist. For the individual who is beginning to experience problems related to chemical use, the counselor may only want to point out the relationship between the problems and the chemical use. The counselor may imply that the use must change, or the problems will likely remain or get worse. It can no longer be assumed, however, that the only choice available to the client is to give up chemical use or progressively develop more and more problems. Chemical dependency problems are similar to other chronic medical disorders in that the condition may improve, remain stable, or become worse. As is also the case with most behavioral disorders, the client's economic, intellectual, and personal resources are often a major determinant of outcomes, with or without therapeutic intervention (Mendelson & Mello, 1979). The prognosis for problem drinkers, for example, is far more encouraging than once believed. Rapid, spontaneous remission or gradual disappearance of alcohol-related problems may occur in a relatively high number of people. Cahalan (1978) reported that approximately 20 percent of those surveyed who reported alcohol-related problems no longer had these problems three years following the onset of the problem even though they had not sought help or treatment (p. 202).

Others have reported on those who "cure" themselves of addictions, on alcoholics who reduce their alcohol intake to nonproblem levels, and on former heroin addicts who returned from Vietnam to a drug-free life without treatment (Peele, 1982). It is true that many factors are now clear regarding chemical dependency; however, other pertinent issues remain unclear. One reason for this is the use of circular definitions. The counselor should avoid these semantic traps. For example, if, by definition, an alcoholic is a person who cannot drink alcohol without experiencing problems, it is impossible for an alcoholic to return to nonproblem drinking, and the only acceptable treatment goal for an alcoholic is total abstinence. If an alcoholic should, by chance, return to nonproblem drinking, then by definition they were not really an alcoholic. This definition eliminates the possibility of scientific inquiry and is called circular thinking.

Denial

Denial is a concept that can be used to distort issues. If alcoholism is a "disease of denial," as many contend, then the only logical diagnosis that can be made of the problem drinker is alcoholism. If a problem drinker or a prealcoholic, diagnosed as alcoholic, rightfully denies his alcoholism, the denial is seen as the first stage of alcoholism (denial). If the problem drinker does not deny alcoholism the only alternative is to accept it. These "yes-you-are-no-I'm-not" games only cloud the issues with regard to a specific diagnosis. They also detract from the counselor-client relationship. Definitions should be for the benefit of the counselor and the client, and they should not detract from the therapeutic process. They should be flexible, yet understandable to both the counselor and the client.

Defining Terms

Some of the words that counselors should examine for themselves are *use, misuse, abuse, addiction, habituation,* and *dependence.* The following brief definitions are offered to assist counselors in developing their own meanings for these words relative to their own personal, social, and physical criteria:

- **Use**—The intake of a chemical substance into the body with the goal of somehow altering one's state of consciousness. (Use may or may not cause problems.)
- **Misuse**—Using a chemical with some physically, psychologically, socially, or legally adverse consequence (often carries unnecessary moral implications).
- **Abuse**—Chronic, recurrent misuse of chemicals. (This term should, perhaps, be left for such situations as child abuse, animal abuse, and self-abuse. The term *chemical abuse* tends to anthropomorphize chemicals by making them the object of the abuse.)
- **Addiction**—A cellular change that occurs with the increased use of most depressant drugs. The primary clinical features are the development of tolerance and the development of withdrawal symptoms upon removal of the drug.

- **Habituation**—The repetition of behavior. (This behavior is often anxiety reducing for the individual.)
- **Dependence**—Physical dependency is much the same as addiction. Psychological dependence is a state that occurs when there is a strong urge to alter one's state of consciousness through the use of a chemical. These two types of dependence may occur independently or in combination with each other.

These are not the only terms that the chemical dependency counselor needs to clarify; there are many others. The point is that the counselor cannot be too clear or too specific about a client's problems and how these problems relate to a treatment plan.

DEFINITIONS AND DIAGNOSES

Even though alcoholism and drug abuse have many commonalities, and it can no longer be assumed that alcoholics abuse alcohol to the exclusion of other drugs, alcoholism and drug abuse are still regarded as distinct and separate disorders. Therefore, separate diagnostic and evaluation methods will be presented for each.

Diagnosing Alcoholism

Many approaches have been presented in the literature for evaluating and diagnosing alcoholism. There are biological methods, but these are indirect because they reflect consequences of alcohol use, and many persons may have alcoholism syndromes without biological damage.

There are psychological methods of diagnosis that include indirect psychometric measures, such as the McAndrews Scale of the Minnesota Multiphasic Personality Inventory (MMPI). There are also direct psychometric methods, such as the Michigan Alcoholism Screening Test (MAST). The National Council on Alcoholism's list of major and minor criteria for the diagnosis of alcoholism is presented here as an example.

- **Diagnostic Level 1**—Classical, definite, obligatory. A person who fits this criterion must be diagnosed as alcoholic.
- **Diagnostic Level 2**—Probable, frequent, indicative. A person who satisfies this criterion is under strong suspicion of alcoholism; other corroborative evidence should be obtained.
- **Diagnostic Level 3**—Potential, possible, incidental. These manifestations are common in people with alcoholism but do not by themselves give a

strong indication of its existence. Other significant evidence is needed before the diagnosis is made.

Tables 4–1 and 4–2 delineate these diagnostic levels in more detail.

Criteria such as these are helpful but are not foolproof in diagnosing alcoholism. One of the problems is false positives; while some of these measures have a 99 percent accuracy rate for identifying those in an alcoholic population, they diagnose almost 50 percent of those who are not alcoholics as alcoholics. Often, the results from measures such as these do not translate well into treatment plans. Each of these measures has shown some degree of success in diagnosing a certain type of alcoholic, but often this is to the exclusion of many other types. Several authors have made an attempt to differentiate between these types of alcoholics. One such differentiation was reported by Greenblatt and Shader (1978). They suggested that alcoholism be divided into three distinct conceptual entities:

1. A pathologic psychosocial behavior pattern, characterized by deteriorating function in occupation, family, and citizenship, resulting from excessive alcohol ingestion.
2. A drug addiction of the classic type. Cessation of alcohol ingestion is followed by withdrawal.
3. A medical disease with certain characteristic sequelae, such as cirrhosis, nutritional disorders, and neurological damage.

They suggest that for those alcoholics who have all three characteristics, a diagnosis of alcoholism is easy. However, the alcoholic may have only one of these disorders or perhaps a combination of two. (For example, the heavy-drinking executive may have characteristic two but not one or three; the skid-row alcoholic may have one and two but not three, and so on.) These classifications are most useful for physicians.

Kuanert (1979) has divided alcoholism into three somewhat different categories. He classifies alcoholism as either reactive, secondary, or primary. Reactive alcoholics are those who become preoccupied with alcohol only after being overwhelmed by some external stress. Secondary alcoholics are those who are suffering from a major psychiatric illness such as schizophrenia, and they medicate for this illness with alcohol. Primary alcoholics are those who find, from their first drinking experience, that their relationship with alcohol is extremely positive and highly desirable. They choose to involve themselves with alcohol and to capture the feelings evoked from this special relationship time and time again, and they disregard any negative consequences of their drinking. What is fundamentally useful about Kuanert's approach is that he supplies a different and varied treatment plan for the underlying psychiatric illness than the alcoholism.

Table 4–1   Major Criteria for the Diagnosis of Alcoholism

Criterion	Diagnostic Level

TRACK I. PHYSIOLOGICAL AND CLINICAL

A.   Physiological Dependency

   1. Physiological dependence as manifested by evidence of a *withdrawal syndrome* when the intake of alcohol is interrupted or decreased without substitution of other sedation. It must be remembered that overuse of other sedative drugs can produce a similar withdrawal state, which should be differentiated from withdrawal from alcohol.

a. Gross tremor (differentiated from other causes of tremor)	1
b. Hallucinosis (differentiated from schizophrenic hallucinations or other psychoses)	1
c. Withdrawal seizures (differentiated from epilepsy and other seizure disorders)	1
d. Delirium tremens. Usually starts between the first and third day after withdrawal and minimally includes tremors, disorientation, and hallucinations.	1

   2. Evidence of *tolerance* to the effects of alcohol. (There may be a decrease in previously high levels of tolerance late in the course.) Although the degree of tolerance to alcohol in no way matches the degree of tolerance to other drugs, the behavioral effects of a given amount of alcohol vary greatly between alcoholic and nonalcoholic subjects.

a. A blood alcohol level of more than 150 mg. without gross evidence of intoxication.	1
b. The consumption of one-fifth of a gallon of whiskey or an equivalent amount of wine or beer daily, for more than one day, by a 180-lb individual.	1

   3. Alcoholic "blackout" periods. (Differential diagnosis from purely psychological fugue states and psychomotor seizures.)   2

B.   Clinical: Major Alcohol-Associated Illnesses. Alcoholism can be assumed to exist if major alcohol-associated illnesses develop in a person who drinks regularly. In such individuals, evidence of physiological and psychological dependence should be searched for.

Fatty degeneration in absence of other known cause	2
Alcohol hepatitis	1
Laennec's cirrhosis	2
Pancreatitis in the absence of cholelithiasis	2
Chronic gastritis	3
Hematological disorders:	
Anemia: hypochromic, normocytic, macrocytic, hemolytic with stomatocytosis, low folic acid	3
Clotting disorders:	
prothrombin elevation, thrombocytopenia	3
Wernicke-Korsakoff syndrome	2

continues

Table 4–1   continued

Criterion		Diagnostic Level
Alcoholic cerebellar degeneration		1
Celebral degeneration in absence of Alzheimer's disease or arteriosclerosis		2
Central pontine myelinoylis	} diagnosis only	2
Marchiafava-Bignami's disease	} possible postmorterm	2
Peripheral neuropathy (see also beriberi)		2
Toxic amblyopia		3
Alcoholic myopathy		2
Alcoholic cardiomyopathy		2
Beriberi		3
Pellagra		3

TRACK II. BEHAVIORAL, PSYCHOLOGICAL, AND ATTITUDINAL

All chronic conditions of psychological dependence occur in dynamic equilibrium with intrapsychic and interpersonal consequences. In alcoholism, similarly, there are varied effects on character and family. Like other chronic relapsing diseases, alcoholism produces vocational, social, and physical impairments. Therefore, the implications of these disruptions must be evaluated and related to the individual and his pattern of alcoholism. The following behavior patterns show psychological dependence on alcohol in alcoholism:

1. Drinking despite strong medical contraindication known to patient   1

2. Drinking despite strong, identified, social contraindication (job loss for intoxication, marriage disruption because of drinking, arrest for intoxication, driving while intoxicated)   1

3. Patient's subjective complaint of loss of control of alcohol consumption   2

Chemical Dependency Diagnosis

Wright (1982) has presented a useful profile of the chemically dependent person. Each of the areas in the profile (below) could be addressed in a diagnostic interview and could also be included in a treatment plan:

- **Risk factors**
  1. alcoholic relatives
  2. disorder in family of origin
  3. unusual early life history
- **Physical symptoms**
  1. diseases related to substance usage

Table 4–2 Minor Criteria for the Diagnosis of Alcoholism

Criterion	Diagnostic Level
TRACK I. PHYSIOLOGICAL AND CLINICAL	
A. Direct Effects (ascertained by examination)	
1. Early	
Odor of alcohol on breath at time of medical appointment	2
2. Middle	
Alcoholic Facies	2
Vascular engorgement of face	2
Toxic amblyopia	3
Increased incidence of infections	3
Cardiac arrhythmias	3
Peripheral neuropathy (see also Major Criteria, Track 1, B)	2
3. Late (see Major Criteria, Track 1, B)	
B. Indirect Effects	
1. Early	
Tachycardia	3
Flushed face	3
Nocturnal diaphoresis	3
2. Middle	
Ecchymoses on lower extremities, arms, or chest.	3
Cigarette or other burns on hands or chest	3
Hyperreflexia, or in drinking heavily, hyporeflexia (may be a residuum of alcoholic polyneuritis)	3
3. Late	
Decreased tolerance	3
C. Laboratory Tests	
1. Major—Direct	
Blood alcohol level at any time of more than 300 mg/100 ml	1
Level of more than 100 mg/100 ml in routine examination	1
2. Major—Indirect	
Serum osmolality (reflects blood alcohol levels) every 224 increase over 200 mOsm/liter reflects 50 mg/100 ml alcohol	2
3. Minor—Indirect	
Results of alcohol ingestion	
Hypoglycemia	3
Hypochloremic alkalosis	3
Low magnesium level	2
Lactic acid elevation	3
Transient uric acid elevation	3
Potassium depletion	3
Indications of liver abnormality:	
SGPT elevation	2
SGOT elevation	3

continues

Table 4–2   continued

Criterion	Diagnostic Level
BSP elevation	2
Bilirubin elevation	2
Urinary urobilinogen elevation	2
Serum A/G ration reversal	2
Blood and blood clotting	
Anemia: hypochromic, normocytic, macrocytic, hemolytic with	
stomatocytosis, low folic acid	3
Clotting disorders: prothrombin elevation, thrombocytopenia	3
ECG abnormalities	
Cardiac arrhythmias, tachycardia: T waves dimpled, cloven,	
or spinous; atrial fibrillation; venticular premature contractions;	
abnormal P waves	2
EEG abnormalities	
Decreased or increased REM sleep, depending on phase	3
Loss of delta sleep	3
Other reported findings	3
Decreased immune response	
Decreased response to Synachthen test	3
Chromosomal damage from alcoholism	3

TRACK II. BEHAVIORAL, PSYCHOLOGICAL, AND ATTITUDINAL

A.   Behavioral

1.   Direct effects

Early

Gulping drinks	3
Surreptitious drinking	2
Morning drinking (assess nature of peer group behavior)	2

Middle

Repeated conscious attempts at abstinence	2

Late

Blatant indiscriminate use of alcohol	1
Skid row or equivalent social level	2

2.   Indirect effects

Early

Medical excuses from work for variety of reasons	2
Shifting from one alcoholic beverage to another	2
Preference for drinking companions, bars, and taverns	2
Loss of interest in activities not directly associated with drinking	2

Late

Chooses employment that facilitates drinking	3
Frequent automobile accidents	3
History of family members undergoing psychiatric treatment:	
school and behavioral problems in children	3
Frequent change of residence for poorly defined reasons	3

continues

Table 4–2 continued

Criterion	Diagnostic Level
Anxiety-relieving mechanisms, such as telephone calls inappropriate in time, distance, person, or motive (telephonitis)	2
Outbursts of rage and suicidal gestures while drinking	2

B. Psychological and Attitudinal

    1. Direct effects

        Early

Criterion	Diagnostic Level
When talking freely, makes frequent reference to drinking alcohol, people being "bombed," "stoned," etc., or admits drinking more than peer group	2

        Middle

Criterion	Diagnostic Level
Drinking to relieve anger, insomnia, fatigue, depression, social discomfort	2

        Late

Criterion	Diagnostic Level
Psychological symptoms consistent with permanent organic brain syndrome (see also Major Criteria, Track 1, B)	2

    2. Indirect effects

        Early

Criterion	Diagnostic Level
Unexplained changes in family, social and business relationships, complaints about wife, job, and friends	3
Spouse makes complaints about drinking behavior, reported by patient or spouse	2
Major family disruptions, separation, divorce, threats of divorce	2
Job loss (due to increasing interpersonal difficulties), frequent job changes, in financial difficulties	3

        Late

Criterion	Diagnostic Level
Overt expression of more regressive defense mechanisms: denial, protection, etc.	3
Resentment, jealousy, paranoid attitudes	3
Symptoms of depression, isolation, crying, suicidal preoccupation	3
Feelings that he is "losing his mind"	3

    2. physical signs of usage

    3. tolerance

    4. withdrawal

    5. stress-related or obscure illnesses

- **Mental symptoms**

    1. decreased cognitive ability

    2. memory failure

    3. psychological dependency

    4. obsession
    5. defensiveness
    6. delusioned denial
- **Emotional symptoms**
    1. compulsive use
    2. unstable moods
    3. powerlessness
- **Social symptoms**
    1. job
    2. relationships
    3. legal
    4. financial
    5. psychiatric
- **Spiritual symptoms**
    1. rigid negative attitudes
    2. low self-image
    3. negative God concept
    4. unusual religious observances
    5. failure of humility
    6. failure of love

Wright's list does not delineate all the potential problem areas of the chemically dependent person, but it does provide an excellent starting place. To provide more detail, each area would need to be expanded; for example, under relationships might be spouse and under that sexual, recreational, and so on.

The most extensive set of criteria for chemical dependency diagnosis that has been published to date is the diagnostic manual of McAuliffe and McAuliffe (1975). It is much too detailed to present here; however, the major areas covered are:

- symptoms of mental obsession
- symptoms of emotional compulsion
- symptoms of low self-image
- symptoms of rigid, negative attitudes
- symptoms of a rigid defense system
- symptoms of delusion
- symptoms of powerlessness
- physical symptoms

Although this manual is quite thorough, it might not translate as well into a specific treatment plan as other, less complicated approaches to diagnosis. However, the beginning counselor as well as the more advanced counselor could find this manual very useful with some adaptation to their own situation.

Other Diagnostic Manuals

Another diagnostic manual should be mentioned here, if only because of its wide acceptance by the mental health field and by insurance companies who need a specific diagnosis to evaluate claim payments. This is the Diagnostic and Statistical Manual of the American Psychiatric Association (DSM-IV). This manual bases diagnosis on a description of the clinical features of the dysfunction. The chapter entitled "Substance Abuse Disorders" lists the specific criteria for addiction and related problems.

DSM-IV divides substance-related disorders into two categories, substance dependence and substance abuse.

The criteria for substance dependence are listed in Exhibit 4–1 and the criteria for substance abuse are listed in Exhibit 4–2.

The DSM-IV also lists the criteria for substance intoxication and for substance withdrawal. They are included in Exhibits 4–3 and 4–4.

The DSM-IV separates drugs by class and diagnosis associated with class of substance is listed in Table 4–3. As one can see in this table, not all drugs involve addiction or abuse. Spend some time reviewing this table and learn the differences among the drugs.

Exhibit 4–1   Criteria for Substance Dependence

A maladaptive pattern of substance use, leading to clinically significant impairment or distress, as manifested by three (or more) of the following, occurring at any time in the same 12-month period:

1. tolerance, as defined by either of the following:
   — a need for markedly increased amounts of the substance to achieve intoxication or desired effect
   — markedly diminished effect with continued use of the same amount of the substance
2. withdrawal, as manifested by either of the following:
   — the characteristic withdrawal syndrome for the substance (refer to Criteria A and B of the criteria sets for Withdrawal from the specific substances)
   — the same (or a closely related) substance is taken to relieve or avoid withdrawal symptoms
3. the substance is often taken in larger amounts or over a longer period than was intended
4. there is a persistent desire or unsuccessful efforts to cut down or control substance use
5. a great deal of time is spent in activities necessary to obtain the substance (e.g., visiting multiple doctors or driving long distances), use the substance (e.g., chain-smoking), or recover from its effects

continues

Exhibit 4–1   continued

> 6. important social, occupational, or recreational activities are given up or reduced because of substance use
> 7. the substance use is continued despite knowledge of having a persistent or recurrent physical or psychological problem that is likely to have been caused or exacerbated by the substance (e.g., current cocaine use despite recognition of cocaine-induced depression, or continued drinking despite recognition that an ulcer was made worse by alcohol consumption)
>
> *Specify if*:
> **With Physiological Dependence:** evidence of tolerance or withdrawal (i.e., either Item 1 or 2 is present)
> **Without Physiological Dependence:** no evidence of tolerance or withdrawal (i.e., neither Item 1 nor 2 is present)

Exhibit 4–2   Criteria for Substance Abuse

> - A maladaptive pattern of substance use leading to clinically significant impairment or distress, as manifested by one (or more) of the following occurring within a 12-month period:
>   1. recurrent substance use resulting in a failure to fulfill major role obligations at work, school, or home (e.g., repeated absences or poor work performance related to substance use; substance-related absences, suspensions, or expulsions from school; neglect of children or household)
>   2. recurrent substance use in situations in which it is physically hazardous (e.g., driving an automobile or operating a machine when impaired by substance use)
>   3. recurrent substance-related legal problems (e.g., arrests for substance-related disorderly conduct)
>   4. continued substance use despite having persistent or recurrent social or interpersonal problems caused or exacerbated by the effects of the substance (e.g., arguments with spouse about consequences of intoxication, physical fights)
> - The symptoms have never met the criteria for Substance Dependence for this class of substance.

Exhibit 4–3   Criteria for Substance Intoxication

> - The development of a reversible substance-specific syndrome due to recent ingestion of (or exposure to) a substance. **Note:** Different substances may produce similar or identical syndromes.
> - Clinically significant maladaptive behavioral or psychological changes that are due to the effect of the substance on the central nervous system (e.g., belligerence, mood lability, cognitive impairment, impaired judgment, impaired social or occupational functioning) and develop during or shortly after use of the substance.
> - The symptoms are not due to a general medical condition and are not better accounted for by another mental disorder.

Exhibit 4–4   Criteria for Substance Withdrawal

- The development of a substance-specific syndrome due to the cessation of (or reduction in) substance use that has been heavy and prolonged.
- The substance-specific syndrome causes clinically significant distress or impairment in social, occupational, or other important areas of functioning.
- The symptoms are not due to a general medical condition and are not better accounted for by another mental disorder.

A local psychologist or mental health counselor would probably be happy to provide some training on the DSM-IV for the chemical dependency counselor.

Each of the diagnostic criteria presented here is accurate from the perspective of the person who established it. Chemically dependent persons' symptoms can be evaluated, split up, divided, and diagnosed in hundreds of ways: all of these ways could conceivably be correct. Most likely, chemical dependency counselors will be expected to follow the DSM-IV or the rules that their agency has established with regard to diagnosis. However, the beginning counselor will soon be the experienced counselor and, in that regard, can have an effect on the agency's policies, including how diagnosis is used and what criteria are followed. There is one simple rule to follow when making these decisions: Make sure the diagnosis is helpful to the client and leads to an appropriate treatment plan.

CASE EXAMPLES

To best illustrate the type of in-depth diagnosis that we encourage, we will present two case examples. The first example has been taken directly from the case file of a very traditional alcoholism treatment program: Note that almost anyone would fit into this treatment plan and that the treatment recommended does not necessarily relate to the patient as presented in the history. It is not at all unusual to see this traditional kind of diagnosis and treatment plan. Specific data have been changed to protect the individual and the agency.

Case Number One

Date of Admission: 3/14/95
Date of Discharge: 4/10/95
Data Base: Patient is a twenty-five-year-old male from San Diego, California; height, 75 inches; weight, 200 pounds.

Patient came in voluntarily on 3/14/95.

Chief Complaint: Patient was pushed by authorities, after second DWI, to seek treatment at the present time. Went through detoxification.

Table 4-3 Diagnoses Associated with Class of Substances

	Dependence	Abuse	Intoxication	Withdrawal	Intoxication Delirium	Withdrawal Delirium	Dementia	Amnestic Disorder	Psychotic Disorders*	Mood Disorders	Anxiety Disorders	Sexual Dysfunctions	Sleep Disorders
Alcohol	X	X	X	X	1	W	P	P	1W	1W	1W	1	1W
Amphetamines	X	X	X	X	1				1	1W	1	1	1W
Caffeine			X								1		1
Cannabis	X	X	X		1				1		1		
Cocaine	X	X	X	X	1				1	1W	1W	1	1W
Hallucinogens	X	X	X		1				1	1	1		
Inhalants	X	X	X		1		P		1	1	1		
Nicotine	X			X									
Opioids	X	X	X	X	1				1	1		1	1W
Phencyclidine	X	X	X		1				1	1	1		
Sedatives, hypnotics, or anxiolytics	X	X	X	X	1	W	P	P	1W	1W	W	1	1W
Polysubstance	X												
Other	X	X	X	X	1	W	P	P	1W	1W	1W	1	1W

*Also Hallucinogen Persisting Perception Disorder (Flashbacks).

Note: X, 1, W, 1W, or P indicates that the category is recognized in DSM-IV. In addition, *1* indicates that the specifier With Onset During Intoxication may be noted for the category (except for Intoxication Delirium): *W* indicates that the specifier With Onset During Withdrawal may be noted for the category (except for Withdrawal Delirium); and *1W* indicates that either With Onset During Intoxication or With Onset During Withdrawal may be noted for the category. *P* indicates that the disorder is Persisting.

History of Illness: Patient drinks only scotch, a pint per day. Drinks three or four days a week at a bar and at home. Some hangovers. Blackouts denied. No delirium tremens. Had one period of sobriety for three months.

Physical Examination: Liver was not enlarged.

Laboratory Report: SGOT, 19; GGT, 18; Hemoglobin, 18; MCV, 84; Ua, negative; VDRL, negative.

Chest X-Ray: 3/14/95, normal.

Psychological: Assessment on 3/16/95. I.Q. was 110. Test readministered on 4/1/95, and I.Q. was 121. A total of two hours with psychology department.

Observations: On entry, patient was cooperative, detoxification was not needed, no withdrawal symptoms.

Medications: 500 mg. Antabuse, three times a week; Unicap T, two daily; Tennes lotion to back (patient's own medication), as needed.

Medication on Discharge: 250 mg. Antabuse daily; B-complex daily; Tennes lotion to back (patient's own medication).

Ward: Patient was alert and compliant and cooperated reasonably well. Well aware of problems. Self-esteem improved. Patient was definitely serious about program. Family contacts—active girlfriend who picked him up after discharge.

Social Worker: Mr. Smith entered treatment as the result of a DWI. He was verbally skilled throughout his stay. Felt he has gained maximum benefit. His recovery plans include Alcoholics Anonymous (A.A.), Antabuse, and continued individual counseling. Did have three consents that were signed.

Counselor: Mr. Smith completed program, including A.A. steps one through five. During the third week, he continued to play with the idea that a cured alcoholic could return to social drinking. His intellectualization and avoidance of responsibility for his recovery are a strong defense against accepting alcoholism. He made statements that his girlfriend and mother would keep him sober. No visible change in behavior or attitude was observed; unless he follows a supervised recovery plan, his prognosis is poor.

Medical: Patient was present when the medical goal was set to confront legal problems ensuing from alcohol ingestion. Patient needs very closely supervised follow-up or he will not do well. Was very compliant, a junior at the university, and used intellectualization as a defense. Would plan to return to school. Only mildly involved in program.

Final Diagnosis: Alcohol dependence

Problems and/or Solutions:

Alcohol dependence—Patient was educated on alcoholism and completed the routine program. Patient was compliant throughout.

Legal problems ensuing from abnormal alcohol use and/or illegal drug use—Patient was educated on alcoholism and completed routine program. Patient was compliant throughout.

Anxiety—Patient reduced anxiety level slightly through participation in individual and group therapy.

Lacks understanding in the dynamics of addiction—He was urged to follow recovery plan but was never able to work on a feeling level.

Intellectualization—Patient was always wondering whether he would be able to drink socially further. This attitude remained unchanged. Patient needs a supervised environment to stay sober.

Treatment Modalities:

Lectures, 21 hours; Group, 12½ hours; Movies, 8½ hours; Religious therapy, 8½ hours; A.A. orientation, 6 hours; Reading and tapes, 25 hours; Social skills, 5 hours; Counselor, 2½ hours; Social Worker, 1½ hours; Team, completed fifth step; Testing, 2 hours; and Medical exam, ½ hour.

Aftercare Plan:

Date of Discharge: 4/10/95

Placement: San Diego; Family, contact; Own finances; Student at university

Legal: Second DWI in county; Follow-up A.A. in city of residence

Staff Recommendations:

A.A. meetings twice weekly; Antabuse daily for two years with supervision; outpatient counseling; seek sponsorship in A.A. and become active in A.A. or patient will not make it.

Summary of the Case:

Participation good. Problems identified and treatment plan completed. Patient received moderate detoxification benefit from treatment.

Awareness of problems related to drinking were poor on entry—good on discharge. Plans for dealing with problems related to drinking were poor on entry—good on discharge. Changes in self (attitude, behavior, feelings) related to drinking were moderate.

Prognosis: Poor, unless follow-up is closely supervised.

Case Number One Discussion

Note that the presentation omits a great deal of information relating to this individual (for example, his feeling of self-worth, his sexuality, his family, his work history, his development, etc.). The treatment plan was not specific and did nothing or very little to meet the patient's specific needs.

The diagnosis was alcohol dependence, yet there was nothing to indicate that the patient was physically addicted. (Detoxification was noted as unnecessary, though he did go through a detoxification procedure. It is not uncommon for inpatient programs to require all new patients to go through detoxification as a medical precaution.) Psychological addiction, if it existed, was not mentioned.

Drinking did not occur daily but three to four times weekly. Very little was mentioned regarding his family. Anxiety was mentioned but with no specifics. (It is not unusual for a person to be anxious because of being in a treatment program.)

Treatment consisted mainly of lectures, group therapy (which some people respond to and others do not), movies, and A.A. orientation. Aftercare was simply "A.A. in city of residence."

Although the patient seemed poorly motivated, nothing was done to improve his motivation. Little wonder, then, that his prognosis is listed as poor; however, the poor prognosis is made to look as if it is the patient's fault. Statements such as, "patient was always wondering whether he would be able to drink socially," "lacks understanding in the dynamics of addiction," and "never able to work on a feeling level" were used to focus on the patient's deficiencies, but these issues were apparently never dealt with in treatment.

It is also interesting to note the counselor's conclusion, that "no visible change in behavior or attitude was observed." What did happen in treatment to change anything in the life of this patient? One would suspect very little by reading his records. A more appropriate statement to sum up what happened in treatment would be the following: A thorough diagnosis was never completed, and the patient was run through the standard treatment program.

To illustrate a more thorough approach that relates diagnosis to treatment, we will present this case again, with a narrative of what diagnosis and treatment could have been like.

Case Number Two

Upon admission a complete personal history was taken to determine basic demographic data; educational, vocational, health, treatment, social, and judicial histories; relationships with family and friends; recreational and community involvement; personality and emotional development; sexual functioning; and motivation for treatment.

A behavioral assessment of alcohol abuse was completed that included, in detail, what goes on before, during, and after the client consumes alcohol. This also includes the people he is with, when and where he drinks, the amount and type of available alcohol, concurrent activities, and any emotional state that could have influenced his drinking. The specific reinforcers for drinking were also identified.

Personal Data

Joe is an unmarried 25-year-old white male, third-year university student majoring in business. Joe presented March 14, 1995, for treatment of alcohol abuse, motivated by authorities due to a second DWI. At time of presenting, Joe had been drinking over a pint of scotch daily, three to four times per week. This pattern had existed for over a year.

Personal History

Joe is the oldest of three children. He has two brothers, five and seven years younger than he. He was born in Yuba City, California. His attitude toward his parents and siblings, on the surface, appears positive. However, he reports that as a child he found it difficult to approach his father and that he never seemed able to please him. Most of his communications in the family were through his mother. He did report some resentment toward his brothers because he had to help his father, a farmer, with the chores, and his brothers did not because they were too young. This often involved getting up at 4:30 in the morning while his brothers slept in.

The youngest brother is a senior in high school, and the middle brother is a junior in college preparing to go to medical school.

His father, now 69, continues to farm but at a reduced level. His mother is a retired school teacher. Neither parent drinks because of religious beliefs.

Joe does have a girlfriend whom he plans to marry sometime after college. Their relationship seems tenuous due to his drinking behavior. He is often verbally abusive to her when he drinks heavily.

Joe is in the third year of college as a business major. However, his grades have been falling because of his drinking and sleeping through class. He is unsure about his business major and reports that he majored in business because he thought his father wanted him to. He has never seen a guidance counselor about his career plans, nor has he spoken to his parents or teachers. He has worked as a sales clerk in a clothing store for the past two years to help pay his way through school. He hates the job but needs the money.

Joe spent two years in the Army, stationed in Europe as a tank gunner during most of that time. He receives some military benefits to assist him through school. He loved Europe and hated the Army.

Joe's only encounters with the police are the two DWIs, which were approximately two years apart.

Joe has some interest in music, sports, reading, and movies. He seems to have led a fairly normal, middle-class, small-town existence.

Joe seems reluctant to adopt a treatment goal of total abstinence. However, he does seem anxious to attend to the other aspects of his life (i.e., vocation, sexual relationships, personal satisfaction in social relationships, and family relationships).

Joe attended A.A. after his first DWI, but he "didn't like it or the people in it." "A bunch of burned-out drunks" was the way he described it. The religious aspects reminded him of his Baptist upbringing, which he has rejected.

Behavioral Assessment

Joe's problems are:

- alcohol abuse
- vocational dissatisfaction
- relationship problems with girlfriend and family
- skill defect in expression of positive and confrontational statements to peers and family
- anxiety in presence of strangers and crowds

Etiological Description

Alcohol Use—Joe's immediate concern is his inappropriate use of alcohol, the DWIs, and the problems that drinking causes between him and his girlfriend. He first drank alcohol while in basic training in the Army seven years ago. He found that alcohol made him feel at ease around other people. He drank nearly every day during his two years in the Army. Although he reported some hangovers, he had no blackouts or other alcohol-related problems. He has smoked marijuana but did not find it enjoyable. He reports no other drug use.

His beverage of choice is scotch, which accounts for 90 percent of his alcohol intake. Seventy-five percent of his drinking is done at bars, with friends. He reports that he often drinks, with no related problems. He has had no suicide attempts, no psychiatric treatment, and no formal treatment for his alcohol abuse.

Vocational Potential

Joe is also very concerned about his vocational future. He is afraid that a degree in business will limit him in his career choices. He is not sure what he wants to do. He does not particularly like school, and he did not like the Army. He does not feel that he is capable of much more in school than he is already doing. He does not see himself as bright; "close to average intelligence" is how he described himself. His teachers in high school always told him that he was not working up to his potential, but he thought he was.

Interpersonal Relationships

Joe does not seem to have much insight into the nature of relationships. Often he does not see the cause-and-effect relationship between his behavior and the way other people treat him. He also has given little thought to the relationship between how he feels about himself now, his personal needs, and his early family life. He feels that others just "don't understand him." In this way, he seems to externalize his problems, placing the responsibility for his happiness on those around him. He appears to have many unverbalized expectations of others, and he is hurt when these others do not live up to these expectations. This hurt is also hard to verbalize and is often expressed inappropriately as anger during a drunken episode. He later regrets this behavior and feels guilty about it. This, in turn, makes him feel unworthy of any positive regard from others.

Joe indicated that while his home life as a child was mostly satisfactory, little, if any, real communication existed. He believes that strong emotions of any type were discouraged. His mother and father never fought; there was never a raised voice in the household. The only time his father showed any emotion was when his mother (Joe's grandmother) died. Even then there was very little; just one short crying episode then things were back to "normal."

Joe has indicated that he has felt ill at ease with other people most of his life. As a child, he was physically smaller than most of his classmates and, as such, was not invited to participate in competitive sports; in adolescence he felt that his size led to his frustrated attempts at dating.

More recently, Joe has expressed skill deficit and anxiety in speaking with strangers and expressing himself in crowds. Joe is also unassertive in various social situations.

Treatment Techniques

Joe is a candidate for Motivational Enhancement Therapy (MET) (Miller et al., 1989) during which he will be asked to undergo an extensive assessment battery requiring approximately seven to eight hours. This battery is designed to access his drinking compared to others, his normal level of intoxication, his risk factors, his negative consequences, hidden liver functioning via a blood test, and any neuropsychological damage he may have sustained as a result of his drinking. Motivational Enhancement Therapy is based on principles of motivational psychology and is designed to produce rapid, internally motivated change. This treatment does not attempt to guide and train the client step by step through recovery, but instead it employs motivational strategies to mobilize the client's own resources. MET consists of four carefully planned and individualized treatment sessions. The first two sessions focus on structured feedback from the initial assessment, future plans, and motivation for change. The final two sessions allow the therapist to reinforce progress, encourage reassessment, and provide an objective perspective on the process of change.

As it happens, Joe meets all the criteria of those people who have been successful on a controlled drinking program:

- He has, at times, practiced social drinking.
- He is under 40 years of age.
- He was never physically addicted to alcohol.
- He has few life problems related to alcohol (in comparison to most alcoholics).
- He has a relatively short problem-drinking history (less than ten years).
- He does not see himself as an alcoholic.
- He does not subscribe to the disease concept of alcoholism.
- He prefers the controlled drinking option to abstinence.
- He has no family history of alcoholism.
- He has environmental support (girlfriend, peers) for controlled drinking.

He will be offered a controlled-drinking program on an outpatient basis, but he must remain abstinent for 30 days before beginning the program. If he is unsuccessful at controlled drinking, he has agreed to accept total abstinence as an alternative goal.

The following program will be adopted to deal with Joe's abuse of alcohol wherein Joe will:

- Investigate situations, feelings, or thoughts that occur before, during, and after excessive drinking.
- Arrange effective alternative responses to excessive drinking.
- Learn how controlled drinking differs from alcoholic drinking.

- Practice drink refusal.
- Establish contract with the outpatient counselor, girlfriend, and family to reward period of controlled drinking and to levy penalties (e.g., loss of attention and monetary fines) for excessive drinking.
- Set up a reading program on controlled drinking including *How to Control Your Drinking,* Miller and Muro, 1976.
- Complete Continuous Data Questionnaire at outset of program with counselor and once every three months thereafter. (See Appendix 4–A.)
- See a vocational counselor for testing and evaluation to set career and educational goals that he feels good about based upon the test results and vocational counseling.
- Seen a family therapist in family therapy with his parents and brothers as well as his girlfriend.
- Modify through assertiveness training his skill deficit in interpersonal relationships.

In this example, the treatment plan is directly related to the diagnostic information. All of a person's problems cannot be dealt with in a short time period, so the client in consultation with his counselor must decide which problems should be selected for treatment to achieve the best overall results. This decision will depend, in part, on the resources of the treatment agency. Some treatments might include educational and vocational counseling; marital counseling; family counseling; sexual dysfunction, obesity, exercise, nutrition, or recreational counseling; and education as to nonalcoholic ways of getting "high."

GOAL SETTING

Alcohol and drug and nonuse-related treatment goals must be established as part of the treatment plan. The following six steps for goal setting are suggested by Poley, Lea, and Vibe (1979):

1. Define each goal in terms of identifiable behaviors.
2. Define the goal in such a way that it is measurable in terms of frequency, quantity, or length of time.
3. Define the situations in which the desired behavior is to occur: the time, the place, with whom, how, and the client's emotional state. Some examples of behavioral goals are: to drink a maximum of two twelve-ounce bottles of beer per 24-hour period, at a rate of no more than one bottle of beer per hour; to spend one hour per evening with the television off, speaking with one's spouse without arguing; to make the acquaintance of three new people every

week (greet them, find out their names, phone numbers, and two of their interests); and to complete five applications for employment by 2:00 P.M. each weekday.

4. Determine with the client the relative importance of the treatment goals. Some clients may have five to seven treatment goals: In order to determine the order in which the goals are to be addressed, it is helpful to write each of the treatment goals on an index card and have the client do a card sort, identifying the priority of goals as he sees it. This is often an excellent, yet simple, way of determining those goals that the client feels most motivated to work on. Counselor reservations about the ordering of the treatment goals should be aired and revisions of the priorities sought out with the client when indicated.

5. Determine baseline data, using a questionnaire (Appendix 4–A).

6. Determine intermediate goals once the final treatment goals are defined and baseline data are collected. Intermediate goals may be determined. For instance, if the goal of a client who currently weighs 185 pounds is to weigh 145 in six months, an intermediate goal would be to weigh 175 in one month.

Once goals have been set, treatment may begin as outlined. Continue to gather data on the client's progress. Some behavior patterns, interventions, and goals are offered as examples in Table 4–4.

CLIENT MOTIVATION

It is useful to divide clients into one of these two categories: motivated to change or not motivated. It is true that there are degrees of motivation; but, basically, clients either come to the counselor's office willingly or they do not. There are two types of motivation: intrinsic (motivation from within the individual) and extrinsic (motivation from outside sources such as the courts and family members). Clients who seek treatment because they will be fired if they do not are usually extrinsically motivated; clients who are just sick and tired of their lifestyles are intrinsically motivated.

The counselor can have a great deal of influence on both kinds of motivation. First, it is important to establish what motivation is already there. Then, build on that and expand to the other area of motivation. Counselors who tell clients, "You're the only one who can motivate yourself to stay straight" do not know much about motivation or their clients. Counselors can motivate their clients, and clients cannot do it all by themselves. (If they could, they would not need to see a counselor.) The counselor can motivate in many ways: by example, by providing hope where there is none, and by providing information and education where

Table 4–4 Behavior Patterns, Interventions, and Goals

Behavior Pattern	Intervention	Goals
Low self-esteem, anxiety, high verbal hostility	Relationship therapy, client-centered model	Increase self-seteem, reduce verbal hostility and anxiety
Defective personal construct system, ignorance of interpersonal means	Cognitive restructuring using therapies that are directive, such as Ellis, Glasser, group therapy	Insight
Focal anxiety (i.e., fear of crowds)	Desensitization	Change response to same cues
Undesirable behaviors, lacking appropriate behaviors	Aversive conditioning, operant shaping, counter-conditioning	Eliminate or replace behavior
Lack of information	Information giving	Give information, have client act on it
Client complaint indicates that social situation is causing difficulty	Organization intervention, environmental manipulation, family therapy	Remove cause of complaint, modify environment
Interpersonal rigidity, poor functioning in social situations	Sensitivity training, communication training, group therapy	Increase interpersonal repertoire, desensitization to group functioning
Grossly bizzare behavior	Medical referral	Medication or hospitalization to protect client from society, ready client for further treatment

myths and misconceptions exist. The counselor can also aid in motivation by doing family therapy, working with the client's employer, or helping to find the client an employer.

MOTIVATIONAL TECHNIQUES

Some motivational techniques mentioned by Poley, et al. (1979) include treatment deposit contracts (in which patients put up money that they will lose if they do not complete treatment or other goals); Antabuse treatment; bibliotherapy (reading assignments); essay assignments (e.g., write an essay on why and what you would like to change); involvement of significant others (e.g., family, employer); and audio-visual feedback that includes video replays of drunken and sober behavior. The counselor must not rely totally on the chemically dependent person to be self-motivated. Without outside assistance, some people will never succeed.*

SUMMARY

Chemically dependent persons come in all ages, shapes, and sizes, and they have various physical, psychological, and sociological problems. They use various chemicals, and their chemical use interferes with their life in various ways. It is the counselor's job to assess these many conditions and symptoms and put them into a useable diagnosis that will translate into an effective treatment plan. The counselor uses his or her knowledge of the treatment approaches available and their assessment of the client to match the client to the treatment approach that will result in the best outcome for the client. Whether a twelve-step program, cognitive therapy, motivational counseling, or some other approach is chosen, the client's best interest is the counselor's goal.

In the past, this was rarely done. Simplistic definitions led to general, nonspecific treatment programs. The alcoholic was diagnosed as either alcoholic or not alcoholic. Alcoholics were sent to A.A. or entered treatment where they learned about A.A.; nonalcoholics went back to drinking as did many alcoholics that would not admit to being powerless or alcoholic. Drug addicts were sent to Narcotics Anonymous (N.A.), or Cocaine Anonymous (C.A.), or inpatient drug programs. There was only one goal for all of these programs—total abstinence through living the 12 steps. It was assumed that if abstinence was maintained, the other problems would go away. This did not happen. Many patients could not maintain abstinence, and for many who did, the real problems were just beginning.

Can a person diagnosed as chemically dependent ever return to nonproblem drug or alcohol use? The answer to this question and others are being researched

---

*For an excellent presentation on motivation see Miller, W. R., Zewben, A., DiClemente, C., & Rychtarik, R.G. (1989), *Motivational Enhancement Therapy Manual,* Rockville MD, U.S. Department of Health and Human Services. National Institute on Alcohol Abuse and Alcoholism Project MATCH Monograph Series Vol. 2. There is also a video tape demonstrating this type of interview that is available by sending $25.00 plus 10 percent for postage to:

Dee Ann Quintana
Department of Psychology
University of New Mexico
Albuquerque, NM 87131–1161
Ask for tape T-001 and make checks out to Research Division-CASSA.

everyday, and answers are being found. In some cases they may not be the answers everyone would like to have. But counselors who want to accurately assess their clients must have all the information that is available—and they must be able to adjust to the complex problems of each client with an individualized treatment plan. A thorough diagnosis is the key to that treatment plan.

DISCUSSION QUESTIONS

1. How can I use diagnosis to develop an individualized treatment plan?
2. Am I willing to treat someone who refuses to stop drinking?
3. How can I improve the diagnosis and treatment planning in my agency?
4. Do I consider alcoholics different than drug abusers? How?
5. What does that mean in terms of treatment?

REFERENCES

American Psychiatric Association. (1994). *Diagnostic and statistical manual of mental disorders* (4th ed.), Washington, D.C.

Cahalan, D. (1978). *Problem drinkers*. San Francisco: Jossey-Bass, Inc. Publishers.

Ellis, A., McInerney, J. F., DiGiuseppe, R., & Yeager, R. J. (1991). *Rational-Emotive Therapy with alcoholics and substance abusers*. New York: Pergamon Press.

Forrest, G. (1978). *The diagnosis and treatment of alcoholism* (2nd ed). Springfield, IL: Charles C Thomas, Publisher.

George, R. L. (1990). *Counseling the chemically dependent: Theory and practice*. Boston: Allyn & Bacon, Inc.

Greenblatt, D. I., & Shader, R. I. (1978). Treatment of alcohol withdrawal syndrome. In Shader, R. (Ed.), *Manual of psychiatric therapeutics* (pp. 50–59). Boston: Little, Brown and Co.

Hester, R. K., & Miller, W. R. (1989). *Handbook of alcoholism treatment approaches: Effective alternations*. New York: Pergamon Press.

Kuanert, A. P. (1979). Perspectives from a private practice: The differential diagnosis of alcoholism. *Family and Community Health—Alcoholism and Health, Part II, 2* (2), 1–11.

L'Abate, L., Farrar, J. E., & Serritella, D. A. (Eds.). (1992). *Handbook of differential treatments for addictions*. Boston: Allyn & Bacon, Inc.

Lawson, G., Peterson, J., & Lawson, A. (1983). *Alcoholism and the family: A guide to treatment and prevention*. Gaithersburg, Md.: Aspen Publishers, Inc.

McAuliffe, R. M., & McAuliffe, M. B. (1975). *Essentials for the diagnosis of chemical dependency*. Minneapolis: The American Chemical Dependency Society.

Mendelson, I., & Mello, N. K. (Eds.) (1979). *The diagnosis and treatment of alcoholism*. New York: McGraw-Hill Publishing Co.

Miller, W. R., Zeweñ, A., DiClemente, C., & Rychtarik, R. G. (1989). *Motivational Enhancement Therapy manual*. (National Institute on Alcohol Abuse and Alcoholism Project MATCH Monograph Series Vol. 2). Rockville, MD, U.S. Department of Health and Human Services.

Pattison, M. E., & Kaufman, E. (Eds.). (1982). *Encyclopedic handbook of alcoholism*. New York: Gardner Press.

Peele, S. (1982). The human side of addiction: People who cure themselves of addictions. *The U.S. Journal,* August, p. 7.

Peele, S, & Brodsky, A. (1991). *The truth about addiction and recovery*. New York: Simon and Schuster.

Poley, W., Lea, G., & Vibe, G. (1979). *Alcoholism: A treatment manual*. New York: Gardner Press.

Wallace, J. (1977). Alcoholism from the inside out: A phenomonological analysis. In Estes, N., & Heineman, E. (Eds.), *Alcoholism, development, consequences, and interventions*. St. Louis: C. V. Mosby Co.

Winick, C. (1991). The counselor in drug user treatment. *The International Journal of the Addictions, 25* (12A), 1479–1502.

Wright, C. (1982, August 29–September 1). *New patterns in alcohol and drug addiction: The physician as a pusher*. Paper presented at the 33rd Alcohol and Drug Problems Association of North America (ADPA) Annual Meeting, Washington, D.C.

Appendix 4–A

※

Continuous Data Questionnaire

To be completed by therapist in interview with the client. To be given: (1) during assessment, (2) at the start of treatment, and following that, (3) at regular three month intervals, and lastly, (4) at treatment completion (or termination). Following treatment completion, the CDQ will be given as a follow-up at three, six, and twelve month periods in post completion (or termination) of therapy. Report periods are defined as follows:

The first time the questionnaire is given is during the Assessment period. In all interviews, the questions are asked with respect to the previous three months of the client's life (or the period since the last CDQ, if that is less than three months). Thus the words "report period" in this questionnaire refer to the previous three months of the client's life.

Please give responses to all questions, even if the answer is zero.

Name of Client _____

1.   Stage of Treatment:
      1.   Assessment
      2.   Treatment initiation
      3.   Treatment
      4.   Treatment completion
      5.   Follow-up (not in treatment, not yet discharged)
      6.   Completed program (discharged)
      7.   Terminated, explain
      8.   Readmitted

2.   Date administered _____
      Administered by _____

I.   ALCOHOL USE
      Regardless of treatment goal (abstinence or controlled drinking), answer the following as completely and as accurately as you can:

126

1. Over the past three months you have consumed alcohol on the average as follows:
    a. how much per week?
    b. how many days per week?
    c. how many days abstinent per week?
    d. amount per day?
    e. preference of beverage a) _____ b) _____ c) _____
    f. who with?
    g. where?
    h. note all other drugs taken whether licit or illicit and include prescription and over the counter medications

2. Most of my friends are _____. My spouse (including common-law) is _____ (place correct number in blank space).
    1) abstainers
    2) occasional users
    3) moderate or average users
    4) frequent or heavy users
    5) alcoholics
    6) not applicable

3. During the past report period what is the longest period of time over which you did not drink?

    Days _____ Weeks _____ Months _____ Always drank _____

4. How difficult is it for you to control the amount of alcohol that you consume?
    1) extremely easy
    2) moderately easy
    3) neither difficult or easy
    4) moderately difficult
    5) extremely difficult

5. During the past report period your alcohol urges have been:
    1) nil or almost none
    2) quite weak
    3) average
    4) moderately strong
    5) very strong

6. When do you drink?
    A.   B.
    1) weekends only   1) morning mostly
    2) during week   2) afternoon mostly
    3) both   3) evening mostly
    4) N/A   4) at any time
                               5) N/A

7. General comment on drug-alcohol use (thoughts, feelings, attitudes, performance)

II.   WORK-EDUCATION

1. Are you employed _____ Not employed _____

2. Has your place of employment changed since last report period? Yes _____
No _____. If yes, how many times? _____ If not employed proceed to #9.

Name of employer (if changed since last report) _____

Name and address of firm or company _____

_____

Telephone _____

3. Average monthly income from this job (indicate to nearest dollar)

$ _____ None _____

4. Length of time in present job.

Years _____ Months _____ Weeks _____

5. How many days have you missed from work during this report period?
a.   Alcohol-related _____
b.   Illness _____
c.   Leave of absence _____

6. How many times were you late for work in the last month? _____

7. How satisfied are you with your job?
1)   Very satisified
2)   Moderately satisfied
3)   Neither satisfied nor unsatisfied
4)   Moderately unsatisfied
5)   Very unsatisfied
6)   N/A

8. How would you rate yourself on your performance at work?
1)   Excellent
2)   Quite good
3)   Average
4)   Moderately poor
5)   Very poor
6)   N/A

9. Length of time unemployed. Yrs. _____ Months _____ Weeks _____

10. Usual occupational status.
1)   Full-time (more than six hours per day)
2)   Part-time (less than six hours per day)
3)   Temporarily unemployed
4)   Permanently unemployed
5)   Welfare

11. Usual occupational category.
    1) Professional, executive, or managerial
    2) White collar (secretary, clerk, etc.)
    3) Skilled laborer, tradesman (chef, electrician)
    4) Unskilled laborer
    5) Semi-professional (nurse, skilled technician)
    6) Houseperson
    7) Unemployed
    8) Student
    9) Other
    Also, please indicate the specific job title _____

12. Additional income other than job if employed (during report period) 1) welfare, 2) unemployment, 3) donations, 4) loans, 5) illegal sources, 6) personal wealth, 7) spouse/common-law partner, 8) family, 9) other, specify.

    Source _____ Amount _____

    Source _____ Amount _____

    Source _____ Amount _____

13. How much money do you presently owe?

    mortgage _____

    car debts _____

    credit cards _____

    family _____

    friends _____

    others _____

14. How much money have you repaid on loans, etc. (during this report period)?

    mortage _____

    car debts _____

    credit cards _____

    family _____

    friends _____

    others _____

15. Have you been meeting required payments? Yes _____ No _____

16. Do you plan to continue your education or training?
    1) am currently doing so
    2) yes, most definitely
    3) yes, want to
    4) maybe, thinking about it

　　　5) undecided
　　　6) no plans
　　　7) never
　　　If #1 or #2, specify _____

17. General comments on work-education-income areas (thoughts, feelings, attitudes, etc.)

III. FAMILY INVOLVEMENT

1. Who do you live with? (use up to three categories)

		Now	*Usually*
1)	Spouse/common-law partner	_____	_____
2)	Parents	_____	_____
3)	Grandparents	_____	_____
4)	Brother or sister	_____	_____
5)	Other relatives	_____	_____
6)	Friends	_____	_____
7)	By yourself	_____	_____
8)	Institution or at a residence	_____	_____
9)	Members of the same commune	_____	_____

2. Main type of place that you live in:
　　1) no regular place (street, abandoned bldg., etc.)
　　2) hostel, rooming or boarding house
　　3) hotel
　　4) apartment or other family dwelling
　　5) jail, prison, or other correctional institution
　　6) therapeutic community or other rehabilitation facility
　　7) hospital
　　8) school, college, or university residence
　　9) employer's housing, including armed forces
　　10) own house
　　11) other, specify _____

3. How well do you get along with your

　　_____ family? (other than spouse)

　　_____ friends?

　　_____ spouse (incl. common-law)?
　　1) very well
　　2) moderately well
　　3) neither well nor poorly
　　4) moderately poor
　　5) very poor
　　6) N/A

4.   How often do you do things with your

_____ family? (other than spouse)

_____ friends?

_____ spouse (incl. common-law)?

_____ alone?
1)   very often (every day)
2)   quite often (several times/week)
3)   sometimes (several times/month)
4)   rarely (several times/year)
5)   never
6)   N/A

5.   How important are your friends to you? _____

_____ family? (other than spouse)

_____ spouse (incl. common-law)?
1)   very important
2)   moderately important
3)   neither important nor unimportant
4)   moderately unimportant
5)   very unimportant
6)   N/A

6.   How important do you feel that you are to your

_____ spouse? (incl. common-law)

_____ friends?

_____ family? (other than spouse)
1)   very important
2)   moderately important
3)   neither important nor unimportant
4)   moderately unimportant
5)   very unimportant
6)   N/A

7.   How well do you handle arguments with your

_____ spouse? (incl. common-law)

_____ family? (other than spouse)

_____ friends?
1)   very constructively
2)   moderately well
3)   neither well nor poorly
4)   moderately poorly
5)   very poorly

     6)   ignore the problem
     7)   don't argue (probe)
     8)   N/A

8.   Do you usually keep appointments, dates and obligations to your

    _____ friends?

    _____ family? (other than spouse)

    _____ spouse? (incl. common-law)
    1)   yes, always
    2)   usually
    3)   sometimes
    4)   rarely
    5)   almost never
    6)   N/A

9.   General comments on family involvement (thoughts, feelings, attitudes, performance, etc.)

IV. SOCIAL-RECREATIONAL-COMMUNITY INVOLVEMENT

1.   What were your social/recreational activities during the past report period? (Include informal activities like drinking with friends.) (Indicate if any of these were new.)

Activities   *New(Yes, No)*

2.   About how many times a week do you participate in these social/recreational activities?
    1)   four or more
    2)   two to three times
    3)   once a week
    4)   less than once
    5)   rarely or never

3.   During the past report period, how many new friends have you met by participating in these events?
    1)   none
    2)   one friend
    3)   two friends
    4)   three friends
    5)   four friends
    6)   five or more friends

4. General comments on social-recreational-community involvement (thoughts, feelings, attitudes, performance).

V. JUDICIAL INVOLVEMENT

1. During this report period, has there been any change (less or more involvement) in your status with the criminal justice system?

Yes _____ No _____

**If "yes," complete judicial section, if "no," skip to Personality & Emotional Development.

2. Reasons for arrests during report period. Record number of arrests in each category (use zero where appropriate).

Number

1) Crimes against person, e.g., assault, rape, homicide _____
2) Crimes for profit, e.g., robbery, burglary, forgery, theft _____
3) Prostitution, pimping, or soliciting _____
4) Gambling _____
5) Motor vehicle driving offenses (excluding minor offenses) _____
6) Other, specify _____

3. If arrested during report period please indicate charge, conviction, and sentence.

charge _____

conviction _____

sentence _____

charge _____

conviction _____

sentence _____

charge _____

conviction _____

sentence _____

charge _____

conviction _____

sentence _____

4. Do you have any oustanding bench warrents?

Yes _____ No _____

If yes, specify

5. Is there a presentence report outstanding?

Yes _____ No _____

6. Has there been a change toward less involvement with the criminal justice system (i.e., off parole, off probation, cleared bench warrant?)

Yes _____ No _____

If yes, specify

7. General comments (thoughts, attitudes, feelings, performance, etc.).

VI.   PERSONALITY AND EMOTIONAL DEVELOPMENT

1.   Please rate the following characteristics as you feel they may apply to you.
   1) very low
   2) moderately low
   3) neither high nor low
   4) moderately high
   5) very high

   1) Responsibility to self _____.
   2) Responsibility to others _____.
   3) Self-esteem (self-worth) _____.
   4) Initiative (motivation) _____.
   5) Anxiety _____.
   6) Sociability _____.
   7) Assertiveness _____.
   8) General feeling of well-being _____.
   9) Hostility-aggression-punishment toward others _____.
   10) Depression _____.

2.   Please indicate on each of these scales, how you felt during the report period.
   (circle correct number)

1) tense	1	2	3	4	5	relaxed
2) tolerant	1	2	3	4	5	critical
3) depressed	1	2	3	4	5	happy
4) hard (tough)	1	2	3	4	5	soft (tender)
5) calm	1	2	3	4	5	nervous
6) sickly	1	2	3	4	5	healthy
7) forgiving	1	2	3	4	5	unforgiving
8) sociable	1	2	3	4	5	unsociable
9) unfriendly	1	2	3	4	5	friendly

3.   Comments or reflections on personality and moods.

VII.   HEALTH

1.   Your overall physical health has been: _____. Your overall mental health has been: _____.

   1) excellent
   2) very good
   3) average
   4) poor
   5) very poor

2.   During the past report period, have you had any major diseases or illnesses?

   Yes _____ No _____

   If yes, specify _____

3. Have you been eating regular meals?
   1) all of the time
   2) most of the time
   3) occasionally
   4) rarely or never

4. Have you been eating reasonably balanced or nutritious meals? (Probe what they have eaten over the last few days.) Answer to be rated by therapist.
   1) all of the time
   2) most of the time
   3) occasionally
   4) rarely or never

5. On the average, how many hours of sleep do you get each night?
   1) more than 10 hours
   2) 9–10 hours
   3) 7–8 hours
   4) 5–6 hours
   5) less than 5 hours

6. Is that enough? Yes _____ No _____

7. Do you use drugs/alcohol to help get to sleep? Yes _____ No _____

8. How much time do you spend doing physical exercise? (sports, work, bicycling, etc.)
   1) more than fifteen hours per week
   2) ten to fifteen hours per week
   3) five to ten hours per week
   4) one to five hours per week
   5) less than one hour a week

9. Have you had any difficulties with menstruation?

   Yes _____ No _____ N/A _____

10. During the past report period how many times did you see a medical doctor? _____ psychiatrist? _____

11. How much time have you spent (during this report period) in the hospital for physical reasons? _____ mental reasons? _____
    1) no time
    2) less than one day (not overnite)
    3) one day to less than one week
    4) one week to two weeks
    5) two weeks to less than a month
    6) one month to three months
    7) three to six months
    8) more than six months

12. Have you attempted to harm yourself during the report period?

No _____ Yes _____

(During Assessment, check for anytime in client history.) If yes, how many times have you attempted to harm yourself (including attempted suicide) and by what method. Please indicate approximate date(s).

SEXUAL HEALTH

1. Your sexual drive or urges are:
   1) strong
   2) average
   3) weak
   4) very weak
   5) no urges

2. Can you reach orgasm through intercourse, masturbation, or other means?
   1) all of the time
   2) most of the time
   3) occasionally
   4) seldom
   5) never

3. How satisfied are you with your sex life?
   1) very satisfied
   2) moderately satisfied
   3) neither satisfied nor unsatisfied
   4) moderately unsatisfied
   5) very unsatisfied

4. General comments, thoughts, attitudes, etc. on general or sexual health.

VIII. MOTIVATION

1. What do you see as the most desirable goals of treatment for you? And, giving your honest opinion, how well do you feel that you have achieved (i.e., your present success) or will achieve these goals (i.e., your expected success)?
   1) very successful
   2) moderately successful
   3) no indication (haven't attempted, no indication of success yet, etc.)
   4) moderately unsuccessful
   5) very unsuccessful
   6) N/A (no goals)

Goals	Present Success	Expected Success
1. _____	_____	_____
2. _____	_____	_____
3. _____	_____	_____
4. _____	_____	_____

2. How important is it for you to stop abusing alcohol or abstain?
    1) very important
    2) moderately important
    3) undecided
    4) moderately unimportant
    5) very unimportant

3. What do you feel would be your most desirable use of alcohol?
    1) never use
    2) use rarely
    3) use socially
    4) occasional heavy use (i.e., binge drinking)

4. Rate your responses to the following items:
    1) strongly agree
    2) agree
    3) undecided
    4) disagree
    5) strongly disagree
        A. My alcohol problem is something I can get over soon. _____
        B. No one I know is really interested in my problem. _____
        C. Nowadays a person has to live pretty much for today and let tomorrow take care of itself. _____
        D. I have a good relationship with all my family. _____
        E. It's hardly fair to bring children into the world with the way things look for the future. _____

To be completed by interviewer

5. Interviewer's rating of person's overall motivation.
    1) very motivated
    2) moderately motivated
    3) neither motivated nor unmotivated
    4) moderately unmotivated
    5) very unmotivated

6. Interviewer's expectancy of client success at decreasing/eliminating alcohol abuse.
    1) very successful
    2) moderately successful
    3) neither successful nor unsuccessful
    4) moderately unsuccessful
    5) very unsuccessful

7. General comments, attitudes, feelings, thoughts, performance, etc. on motivation.

IX.   THERAPIST'S SECTION

To be completed on second and subsequent administration of the Follow Up Questionnaire

1.   Problems experienced during the Report Period which involved any of the following (circle yes or no)

1)	Family	Yes	No
2)	Friends	Yes	No.
3)	Drugs	Yes	No
4)	Alcohol	Yes	No
5)	Legal Authorities	Yes	No
6)	School	Yes	No
7)	Work	Yes	No
8)	Finances	Yes	No
9)	Health (include pregnancy)	Yes	No

If yes, explain briefly _____

_____

_____

_____

2.   Treatment facilities to which client was referred during Report Period, in order of occurrence
1)   Inpatient (hospital)
2)   Therapeutic community or other residence for group living (Initiation)
3)   Partial hospitalization (day or night hospital)
4)   Outpatient
5)   Other; specify _____
6)   None

3.   Number of days client received therapeutic or support contacts at clinic

_____

4.   Where did therapeutic or support contacts occur? (List category numbers in order of frequency with *most frequent* first.)
1)   Hospital
2)   Therapeutic community or other residence for group living
3)   Day or night hospital
4)   Outpatient clinic
5)   Pharmacy
6)   Vocational counseling or training center
7)   Social rehabilitation center
8)   Religious organization
9)   Patient's home
10) Community meeting place
11) Social or community agency

12) Other, specify _____

Category	Agency Name
1)	_____
2)	_____
3)	_____
4)	_____
5)	_____

5. Drugs prescribed or administered to the client during the Report Period. Specify drugs used within each category. Check whether drugs used for withdrawal, maintenance, or support.

	Withdrawal	*Support*	*Maintenance*
1) Antabuse	_____	_____	_____
2) Antidepressants	_____	_____	_____
3) Barbiturates or sedatives	_____	_____	_____
4) Tranquilizers	_____	_____	_____
5) Others, including those for medical conditions specify: _____	_____	_____	_____

_____

_____

6. Types of therapy or support received (circle Yes or No)

1) Vocational counseling		Yes	No
2) Vocational training		Yes	No
3) Educational training		Yes	No
4) Individual counseling		Yes	No
5) Group counseling		Yes	No
6) Family counseling		Yes	No
7) Recreational therapy		Yes	No
8) Therapeutic community or other living group		Yes	No
9) Religious activities		Yes	No
10) Other: specify _____		Yes	No

7. Contacts with therapeutic or support personnel during Report Period.

1) Medical practitioner, western trained		Yes	No
2) Medical practitioner, indigenous		Yes	No
3) Specialist in psychiatry		Yes	No
4) Psychologist		Yes	No
5) Social worker or sociologist		Yes	No
6) Vocational counselor or trainer		Yes	No
7) Ex-addict counselor		Yes	No
8) Nurse		Yes	No
9) Clergy or religious leader		Yes	No
10) Agency counselor		Yes	No
11) Other counselor: specify _____		Yes	No

General Assessment by Therapist

8. Social Functioning (within treatment setting)

1)	Well-adjusted socially	Yes	No
2)	Co-operative with staff	Yes	No
3)	Conforms to treatment regulations	Yes	No
4)	Disrupts therapeutic milieu	Yes	No
5)	Requires excessive therapeutic attention	Yes	No
6)	Physically violent or threatening	Yes	No
7)	Other problems: specify _____	Yes	No

9. Diagnosis of medical problems requiring treatment.

10. Source(s) of information for completing report.

1)	Personal interview with client	Yes	No
2)	Staff members involved in treatment	Yes	No
3)	Medical records	Yes	No
4)	Client's family	Yes	No
5)	Friends of client	Yes	No
6)	Other: specify _____	Yes	No

11. Where was the questionnaire completed:
    1) At home
    2) At clinic in interview
    3) At clinic by client alone

12. If questionnaire done by client alone was it later reviewed in a client/therapist session?

    Yes _____ No _____

Source: Reprinted from *Alcoholism: A Treatment Manual* by Wayne Poley, Gary Lea, and Gail Vibe with permission of Gardner Press, © 1979.

Chapter 5

❦

Group Counseling in the Treatment of Chemical Dependency

CHAPTER OBJECTIVES

- Examine reasons to use group therapy
- Examine advantages and limitations of groups
- Review different types of groups
- Examine therapeutic nature of groups
- Review goals and objectives for groups
- Examine attributes of good group leaders
- Examine issues in choosing group members
- Examine stages of group process

INTRODUCTION

Perhaps the best way to begin this chapter is with a statement of what it is not: It is not all you have ever wanted to know, or will ever need to know, about groups. It would be impossible, in one short chapter, to provide the reader with the knowledge and skill to be an effective group leader (that is, a group leader who consistently produces therapeutic results when leading a group). It takes study and practice to develop into a first-rate group facilitator. There have been hundreds of books and articles written about groups; so why should a chemical dependency counselor read this particular chapter about groups?

First, this chapter is being written specifically with the beginning chemical dependency counselor in mind. Second, it provides a structure for your future study and practice of group counseling in the treatment of chemical dependency. This chapter should be viewed as a map for chemical dependency counselors to use to help themselves along toward a greater understanding of group process and, in turn, toward improved skills as group leaders. The point is to encourage you, as

Portions of this chapter have been adapted from *Group Process and Practice*, by G. Corey and M. S. Corey, with permission from Brooks/Cole Publishing, © 1992.

a chemical dependency counselor, to continue your study of group counseling far beyond the scope of this chapter—and to have you recognize that group counseling is not just individual counseling done with more than one person. The dynamics and usefulness of group counseling go far beyond those of individual therapy in the treatment of the chemically dependent client. Medicare has even approved the use of group and individual counseling by the same therapists, even offered the same day, as a specific treatment "modality" rather than one approach being just an augmentation of the other (Medicare, 1994). The clinical pros and cons of this will be discussed later in this chapter. However like all forms of therapy, groups that are used inappropriately can be harmful to the group member and can detract from rather than add to movement toward the individual group member's treatment goals. This negative effect will be discussed in more detail later.

WHY USE GROUPS?

The first question that should be addressed is one of major concern for all chemical dependency counselors, and that is, why use groups at all? This leads to many other questions, for example:

- How is group therapy different from individual therapy?
- What are some advantages of groups?
- What are some limitations of groups?
- What kinds of groups are there?
- What makes a group therapeutic?
- What is group process?
- Are there stages that groups go through?
- What are the stages?
- Are there general rules and goals for a group?
- How much should a group leader structure the group session?
- What are the qualities of a good group leader?
- Who are appropriate group members?
- What are some specific models for alcohol or drug groups?
- What are some group dynamics that can make a member feel worse rather than better?
- What are the ethical issues involved in groups?

These and other questions will be discussed in the following pages. Read these pages not from the perspective of, "at last I have found the answers" but rather, "at last I have begun to understand the questions!"

So why should the chemical dependency counselor use groups as a treatment approach? This can be answered from many different perspectives. First and foremost in the heart of the program administrator is the fact that groups make sense economically. A counselor who can see six individual clients per day can run three groups instead and see over 20 clients. In a field such as chemical dependency, where there are many more clients than counselors, group counseling may be the only way for counselors to effectively handle their caseloads. This would not be an acceptable solution to the time bind if there was evidence that those attending groups received significantly less therapy than those who attended only individual sessions. This, however, is not the case, and group psychotherapy is the treatment of choice for addicts (Rogers, 1992). Although most treatment programs include both group and individual therapy, often it is in the group that the client or patient makes the most progress toward significant therapeutic movement. Why is this? The reason is because essentially humanity is an indivisible, social, decision-making being whose actions have a social purpose (Dreikurs & Sonstegard, 1968). As social beings we are influenced more by a group of people than by just one person. (That is unless that person is very special to us such as a child, a parent, or a spouse. See Chapter 6 on family counseling.) This group effect is also true for chemically dependent clients; however, they have often had very poor experiences in social relationships and desperately need positive social interaction to enable them to give up the self-destructive patterns of chemical use that have developed over a lifetime. Substance abusers often feel socially isolated, and they lack interpersonal skills. They are also often dependent and manipulative and use defenses such as denying, blaming, and rationalizing as ways to avoid accepting personal responsibility for their problems (Corey & Corey, 1992). Groups, particularly ones including savvy peers, are the ideal place to provide the therapeutic impact to confront and change these traits while providing support and structure (Rogers, 1992).

Fulfilling Individual Needs through the Group

To be more specific, individual needs that can potentially be fulfilled in the group include:

- the need to belong, to find a place, and to be accepted as one is
- the need for affection, to be loved, to be able to provide love, and to have the opportunity to have a therapeutic effect on others
- the need for the opportunity to engage in the give-and-take that is required for the maturing of social interest and altruistic feelings
- the need to see that one's problem is not unique but perhaps is universally experienced in the group

- the need to have the opportunity to develop feelings of equality, to be part of a group regardless of what one brings to it in terms of intellect or affect
- the need to develop one's identity and work out an approach to the various social tasks of life (Dinkmeyer & Muro, 1979)

Each theoretical approach to group counseling (e.g., transactional analysis, rational emotive therapy, behavioral therapy) provides its own rationale for using groups as a therapeutic technique. Each type of group (e.g., Adult Children of Alcoholics [ACOA] groups, encounter groups, t-groups, educational groups) has separate reasons why it should be used. It is not appropriate in this chapter to detail when, and why, each different type of group or theoretical model should be used; however, it is important to note that the reason a counselor chooses to use groups as part of a treatment plan should be congruent with the type of group chosen. For example, if one of the major individual treatment goals is to build self-esteem, a group that involves a great deal of personal confrontation might not be the most appropriate type of group to reach this goal—a more supportive group would be more appropriate.

The answer to the original question becomes this: The chemical dependency counselor should consider the use of group therapy as part of an overall treatment plan because it is economically the best use of time, and groups are often the best method for reaching many of the social goals of a complete treatment plan for the chemically dependent client.

ADVANTAGES OF GROUPS

Therapeutic groups have certain distinct advantages over other intervention strategies. Corey and Corey (1992) list these advantages:

- Participants are able to explore their style of relating to others and to learn more effective social skills.
- The group setting offers support for new behavior and encourages experimentation.
- There is a recreation of the everyday world in some groups, particularly if the membership is diverse with respect to age, interests, background, socioeconomic status, and type of problem. When this occurs, a member has the unique advantage of being in contact with a wide range of personalities, and the feedback received can be richer and more diverse than that available in a one-to-one setting.
- Certain factors that facilitate personal growth are more likely to exist in groups. For instance, in groups, members have the opportunity to learn

about themselves through the experience of others, to experience emotional closeness and caring that encourage meaningful disclosure of self, and to identify with the struggles of other members.

LIMITATIONS OF GROUPS

While there are some distinct advantages to group methods, there are some limitations to the effectiveness of therapeutic groups.

- Groups are not cure-alls. Unfortunately, some practitioners and participants view groups as the exclusive means of changing people's behavior. Worse yet, some hope that a brief and intense group experience can remake people's lives. Counseling and therapy are difficult forms of work, and we believe that shortcuts are not necessarily fruitful.
- There is often a subtle pressure to conform to group norms, values, and expectations. Group participants sometimes unquestioningly substitute group values and norms for norms and values that they had unquestioningly acquired in the first place. This is mindlessness. Rigid adherence to values without careful consideration of why is not healthy, no matter what values a person has selected.
- Some people become hooked and make the group experience an end in itself. Instead of using the group as a laboratory for human learning and as a place where they can learn behavior that will facilitate their day-to-day living, they stop short, savoring the delights of the group for its own sake.
- Not all people are suited to groups. The idea that groups are for everybody has done serious harm to the reputation of the group movement. Some people are too suspicious, or too hostile, or too fragile to benefit from a group experience. Some individuals are psychologically damaged by attending certain groups. Before a person is accepted into a group, all the factors need to be carefully weighed by both the counselor and the client to increase the likelihood that the person will benefit from such an experience.
- Some people have made the group a place to ventilate their miseries and be rewarded for "baring the soul." Unfortunately, some use groups as a vehicle for expressing their woes, in the hope that they will be understood and totally accepted, and make no attempt to do what is necessary to affect substantial change in their lives (Corey & Corey, 1977).

The chemical dependency counselor who knows the most about the different types of groups and the different theoretical approaches will be the most effective at helping chemically dependent persons reach their treatment goals.

TYPES OF GROUPS

There are many different types of groups, as well as many different theoretical approaches to groups. Among the many varieties of group psychotherapy, there is enormous diversity of format, goals, and role of the leader (McKay & Paleg, 1992). There are also many ways to select the members of a group. They could be homogeneous and have the same problem, for example cocaine addiction. They could be selected by age as in children's or adolescents' groups. They might be a combination of both as in elderly, prescription-drug abuser groups. They could be the same sex or unisex groups. Members could be heterogeneous with regard to problems and have several different problems like depression, drug abuse, and phobias. The make-up of the group should be decided by the leader based on the goals of the group. There are advantages and disadvantages to every combination. (For more on this see Chapter 7.)

It would go beyond our purpose here to list and describe every type of group, but we will mention a few that are often used in chemical dependency treatment. One of the major types of groups that the chemical dependency counselor is likely to become involved with is the treatment group, sometimes called the focal group, that is often used during an inpatient treatment program in conjunction with individual therapy. Sometimes these groups are used mostly to "break the denial" of the patient, using heavy confrontation by the group leader and other group members: Sometimes this is called the hot seat method. Often this simply leads to compliance rather than to the individual's actually getting in touch with the reality of his or her chemical dependency; it becomes easier for the patient to falsely admit to a belief that they are alcohol or drug dependent than to be confronted by the group. This might be one reason for a high dropout or recidivism rate among chemically dependent clients in treatment. An alternative to the hot seat model might be a less threatening, more supportive group that would allow patients to explore their life situations with honest and open feedback. Certainly not all therapy groups that use confrontation conclude with high dropout rates and recidivism; the majority are supportive as well as confrontational and end with a positive result. It is important, however, to remember that groups can be harmful as well as helpful and that extremes, whether in confrontation or support, are subject to negative results.

Educational Groups

The second type of group often used in the treatment of chemical dependency is the educational group. This is a modified lecture format, where patients learn about new ways to look at old problems. For example, a group topic might be sex and recovery. The facilitator or group leader might make several remarks about the importance of sex and its relationship to the recovery process and then lead a discussion among group members about the topic. These groups are often very meaningful to the members, both from the perspective of the information they provide and from the feeling of having shared problems with other group members. Members often find that they are not, as they thought, the only ones with a particular problem. In addition, these groups are often used in the addiction field with co-dependents rather than the actual addict. The motto of many treatment programs seems to be, "treat the addict and educate the family." This approach is better than not involving that family at all. However, we suggested some time ago that the family is in as much need of treatment as the addict, and both should receive education and therapy (Lawson, G., & Lawson, A., 1984; Lawson, Peterson, & Lawson, 1983).

Multifamily Groups

A relatively new type of group is being offered at treatment centers across the country. It involves getting several families together for a group session. These groups have been used for the treatment of adolescent substance abuse, and in the treatment of families of alcoholics or drug addicts. Although there is little research on their effectiveness, the clinical reports of the outcomes of these groups have been very positive. In one study comparing multifamily therapy groups with multifamily education groups both groups showed improvement in family functioning and overall mental health of the family members (Valentine, D., Lawson, A., & Lawson, G., 1995).

Self-Help Groups

Another type of group that helps members not to feel alone with their problem is the self-help group. The self-help group has a long and successful history in the field of chemical dependency. Many people around the world are sober and leading productive lives as a result of groups such as Alcoholics Anonymous (A.A.), Narcotics Anonymous (N.A.), and Rational Recovery. If these groups are so successful, why should the chemical dependency counselor bother with any other type of group? Why not just see that clients or patients attend a self-help group? There are several reasons. First, it is unclear just how many people respond to the self-help group. It would be safe to assume that there are people who attend one or more of these groups but who do not get sober or lead productive lives. It would also be safe to assume that some members of these groups are sober, yet not happy or fully functioning. The group members themselves have coined a name for such people—"the dry drunk." Second, self-help groups are self-selective; that is to say, the membership is made up of people who *want* to be members and who are willing to follow the guidelines of the group. Those who are not successful at doing either of these usually do not maintain attendance or membership. There-fore, only those who are successful remain members, which accounts for the high degree of success reported among members. Third, the reality is that in the United States there are over 20 million people with drug (including alcohol) problems, and, thus far, only about 2 million of those have been successful in self-help groups. In most cases, self-help groups should be an adjunct to, not a substitute for, therapy groups. For a discussion of why self-help groups work for some and fail to work for others, see Lawson, et al., *Alcoholism and the Family: A Guide to Treatment and Prevention*, Aspen Publishers, Inc., 1983. For further information see Ward, *Alcoholism: Introduction to Theory and Treatment,* Chapter 9, Kendall/Hunt, 1990. There are some exciting new self-help groups. Chemical dependency counselors should become knowledgeable about all of them.

Aftercare Groups

Perhaps a blend of the qualities of the self-help group and the therapy group has been reached in the aftercare group. These groups are used to support the chemically dependent person after inpatient treatment and are sometimes offered in conjunction with individual outpatient counseling. Unlike the self-help groups, they usually have a trained group leader and an identified goal, possibly stated in the client treatment plan. The aftercare group can be run using any number of theoretical models. For example, social therapy as conceptualized by Rudolf Dreikurs would seem an excellent approach. A brochure from the Dreikurs Institute for Social Equality* lists these goals of social therapy:

- to develop a sense of belonging, not isolation
- to learn to consider alternative solutions to problems
- to learn to function as a decision-making person
- to learn to express frustration or annoyance without blaming someone else
- to rediscover your strengths, learn to build upon them, and help others do the same
- to learn to take feedback about yourself
- to gain perspective on your own lifestyle
- to rediscover your sense of humor

---

*Authors' Note: *Beginning counselors should take an entire course on group therapy and get several hundred hours of co-therapy supervision before leading a group on their own.*

This brochure is available from the Rudolf Dreikurs Institute for Social Equality, 725 Emerson Ave. South, Minneapolis, MN 55403.

The Behavioral Approach to Groups

Some good reasons have also been presented to use a behavioral approach in groups. According to Varenhorst (1969, p. 131), the behaviorist use of learning principles in group process makes groups more effective than individual therapy because:

- there is a greater variety of models within a group
- there are greater numbers of sources of reinforcement within the group
- there are more opportunities for creating realistic social enactments whereby role rehearsal can be practiced, changed, and strengthened
- there is an immediate situation in which generalization as well as discrimination can be learned with greater efficiency
- membership in the group itself can be utilized as a powerful reinforcing agency

The behaviorists suggest that persons in groups need to perform certain specific behaviors. They are:

- share feelings openly
- suggest ideas and actions
- reinforce others as the need occurs
- give feedback
- participate in demonstrations or role playing of alternative actions
- be willing to accompany group members on assignments outside the group
- make a commitment to one's goals and the purposes of the group

These are only a few of the many possible theoretical approaches to groups. Whether the chemical dependency counselor leads a treatment group, an educational group, an aftercare group, or another type of group, several theoretical approaches should be explored in an attempt to find the one most compatible with the group goals and the skills and style of the facilitator. Besides the ones mentioned above, a chemical dependency counselor might consider these additional theoretical models:

- transactional analysis (TA) groups
- group-centered or humanistic groups

- gestalt groups
- rationale emotive therapy groups
- t-groups
- reality therapy groups
- focal groups

For a detailed description on how to run a beginning group with addicted populations see Chapter 13 by Rogers, in *Focal Group Psychotherapy*, edited by McKay and Paleg, New Harbinger Publications, 1992.

WHAT IS THERAPEUTIC ABOUT GROUPS?

In one of the most widely read and quoted books ever written about groups, Yalom (1986) has identified 11 curative factors of groups: They are presented here with regard to the chemically dependent client. The first of these is the instillation of hope. This is a crucial factor in the treatment of chemically dependent clients because, so often, they have given up all hope. They have tried many things to deal with their condition, without success. The family doctor, their minister or priest, self-control, and all manner of internal and external assistance for the problem have been sought and tried. Hope is important because it keeps the patient in therapy, and fosters high expectations, which have been shown to correlate highly with success. In other words, the more a person believes in a treatment approach the more likely it is to work. By observing the improvement of other group members, each member draws hope from the other members; thus, hope can be enhanced in chemical dependency groups by including beginning patients in groups that also include patients more advanced in treatment.

The second curative factor is universality, that is to say, a sense of shared problems. Often chemically dependent persons enter therapy with the disturbing thought that they are the only ones alive with their particular problem; they are plagued with the thought that what they have experienced is unacceptable. Usually, just realizing that they are not unique in their problems is a powerful source of relief. After hearing others disclose problems similar to their own, group members report feeling more in touch with the world and, simply put, the feeling that "we are all in the same boat" is very comforting. Statements reinforcing this by the group leader are effective in chemical dependency groups.

The third curative factor is the imparting of information. This includes information about chemical dependency (the dynamics involved in the chemical dependency condition as well as advice to clients about how to cope with their problems) offered by the group facilitator or other group members. It is important for the group leader to be aware of the group member who seeks advice from other group members, only to reject their advice: This should be pointed out to that member. Other dynamics include making a bid for attention and nurturance by constantly asking for group suggestions for a problem that is insoluble or that has already been solved. Other types of groups give advice and guidance directly through slogans (for example, "one day at a time," asking that the person remain sober for only the next 24 hours). There is much misinformation and myth regarding chemical dependency; the counselor should have accurate facts in this area.

The fourth curative factor is altruism. Simply put, you receive through giving. When a group member is able to help another group member, it is hard to distinguish who receives the most benefit from the exchange. There is nothing that does more to build self-esteem than the act of unselfishly giving help to another. This wisdom has long been shared and proven by A.A., with the twelfth step—"We try to carry this message to alcoholics." Many an alcoholic has maintained a high level of sobriety by helping others. In short, people need to feel needed; the group can fulfill this need.

The fifth curative factor is described as the corrective recapitulation of the primary family group. Without exception, chemically dependent persons enter group therapy with a history of a highly unsatisfactory experience in their first and most important group—their family of origin. Over half of those who enter treatment have parents who themselves are chemically dependent. For many patients, working out problems with therapists and other group members means also working through unfinished business from long ago. The role of the family is explained in more detail in Chapter 6.

The sixth curative factor is the development of a socializing technique that includes the development of basic social skills. Many chemically dependent persons either never learned basic social skills or lost them sometime during their period of chemical abuse. For these people, the group often represents the first opportunity for accurate interpersonal feedback. The changes gained in the level of social skills are not an end in themselves, but they are often exceedingly instrumental in the initial phases of therapeutic change.

It is often apparent that senior members of a group have acquired some highly sophisticated social skills. They are aware of group process and have learned how to be helpfully responsive to others. They have acquired methods of conflict resolution and are less prone to be judgmental. They are also more capable of experiencing and expressing accurate empathy. These skills cannot but help to improve their future social interactions; these senior members should be pointed out and offered as models of behavior for newer group members.

The seventh curative factor, imitating behavior, is an important therapeutic force. The healthy behavior of the group leader often becomes the model for the rest of the group. Imitating another group member, even if it turns out that the role does not fit, is a therapeutic process. Learning what one is not is often progress toward learning what one is.

The eighth and ninth curative factors as listed by Yalom are interpersonal learning and group cohesiveness. He includes an entire chapter on each of these concepts. Interpersonal learning involves the corrective emotional experience involved in a group as well as the therapeutic value of experiencing the group as a social microcosm. Group cohesiveness includes the source of stability that one feels from being a part of a cohesive group. This has been described as a "oneness" with the group.

The tenth curative factor, catharsis, has assumed the role of a therapeutic process from the early time of Freud. This is the purging of oneself to cleanse away excessive emotions. But this expulsion alone is not enough; it is the process of "learning how to express feelings" that is the most therapeutic aspect of catharsis, not the expulsion itself.

Finally, the eleventh curative factor, the existential factors of group therapy, are considered. This is basically a compilation of factors not included in the categories above. There are five of them, and they seem particularly important for the chemically dependent client. They are:

1. recognizing that life is at times unfair and unjust
2. recognizing that ultimately there is no escape from some of life's pain and from death
3. recognizing that no matter how close I get to other people, I still face life alone
4. facing the basic issues of my life and death, and thus living my life more honestly and being less caught up in trivialities
5. learning that I must take ultimate responsibility for the way I live my life, no matter how much guidance and support I get from others

It is highly recommended that the chemical dependency counselor read Yalom's book in its entirety.

The ideas of Corey and Corey (1992), who have also addressed the issue of therapeutic factors that operate in groups, bear mentioning here. Although there is some overlap among these factors and the ones listed above, they are worth listing again:

- **Hope**—This is a belief that change is possible—that one is not a victim of the past and that new decisions can be made. Hope is therapeutic in itself, for it gives members confidence that they have the power to choose to be different.
- **Commitment to change**—A resolve to change is also therapeutic in itself. If one is motivated to the point of becoming an active group participant, the chances are good that change will occur. This commitment to change involves a willingness to specify what changes are desired and to make use

of the tools offered by group process to explore ways of modifying one's behavior.

- **Willingness to risk and trust**—Risking involves opening oneself to others, being vulnerable, and actively doing in a group that which is necessary for change. The willingness to reveal oneself is largely a function of how much one trusts the other group members and the group leader. Trust is therapeutic, for it allows persons to show the many facets of themselves, encourages experimental behavior, and allows persons to look at themselves in new ways.

- **Caring**—Caring is demonstrated by the listening and involvement of others. It can be expressed by tenderness, compassion, support, and even confrontation. If members sense a lack of caring from either group members or the group leader, their willingness to lower their masks will be reduced. Clients are able to risk being vulnerable if they sense that their concerns are important to others and that they are valued as persons.

- **Acceptance**—This involves a genuine support from others that says, in effect, "We will accept all of your feelings. You do count here. It's OK to be yourself—you don't have to strive to please everyone." Acceptance involves affirming a person's right to have his own feelings and values and to express them.

- **Empathy**—A true sense of empathy involves a deep understanding of another's struggles. In groups, commonalities emerge that unite the members. The realization that certain problems—such as loneliness, the need for acceptance, fear of rejection, fear of intimacy, and hurt over past experiences—are universal, lessens the feeling that one is alone. And, through identification with others, one is able to see oneself more clearly.

- **Intimacy**—People are able to experience closeness in a group, and from this intimacy develops a new sense of trust in others. Participants may become aware, after experiencing this feeling of closeness with others, that there are barriers in their outside lives that prevent intimacy.

- **Power**—This feeling emerges from the recognition that one has untapped reserves of spontaneity, creativity, courage, and strength. In groups, personal power may be experienced in ways that were formerly denied, and persons can discover ways in which they block their strengths. This power is not a power over others; rather, it is the sense that one has the internal resources necessary to direct the course of one's life.

- **Freedom to experiment**—The group situation provides a safe place for experimentation with new behavior. After trying new behavior, persons can gauge how much they want to change their existing behavior.

- **Feedback**—Members determine the effects of their behavior on others from the feedback they receive. If feedback is given honestly and with care, members are able to understand more clearly the impact they have on others. Then it is up to them to decide what to do with this feedback.

- **Catharsis**—The expression of pent-up feelings can be therapeutic in that energy can be released that has been tied up in withholding certain threatening feelings. Catharsis may allow a person to realize that negative and positive feelings toward others may coexist. A woman may be suppressing a great deal of resentment toward her mother, and, by releasing it, may discover a need for her mother's affection and a feeling of love for her mother.
- **The cognitive component**—Catharsis is even more useful if a person attempts to find words to explain the feelings that are expressed. Some conceptualization of the meaning of intense feelings associated with certain experiences can give one the tools to make significant changes.
- **Learning interpersonal skills**—Participants in groups can discover ways of enhancing their interpersonal relationships. Thus, a woman who feels isolated from others may come to understand the concrete things she does that lead to these feelings and may learn to lessen this isolation by asking others for what she needs.
- **Humor**—Laughing at oneself can be extremely therapeutic. This requires seeing one's problems in a different perspective. Thus, a man who sees himself as stupid may eventually be able to laugh at the stupidity of continually convincing himself that he is stupid. People who are able to laugh at themselves are better able to cope with seeing themselves clearly.
- **Group cohesion**—A group is characterized by a high degree of "togetherness" at times, providing a climate in which participants feel free to share problems, try new behaviors, and in other ways reveal the many dimensions of themselves. Group cohesion is influenced by many variables, a few of which are the attraction of the group for its members, the enthusiasm of the leaders, the trust level of the group, and the extent to which the members identify with one another.

To further conceptualize what is therapeutic about group therapy, Corey and Corey have asked group members what they had learned through the group process. Their responses were:

- Others will care for me if I allow them to.
- I am not alone in my pain.
- I am not helpless, as I had convinced myself I was.
- I do not need to be liked by everyone.
- It is not too late to change if I want to.

- The choice is mine if I want more from others.
- Experiencing intense feelings will not make me crazy.
- There are others close to me, and I need not feel isolated.
- I alone am responsible for my misery.
- I can trust people, and this trust can be freeing.
- I do have options.
- Whether I change or not depends on my decisions.
- Being spontaneous is fun.
- I am a lot more attractive than I gave myself credit for.
- I will never be truly accepted unless I am willing to risk rejection.
- I get from a group what I put into it.
- My greatest fears did not come true when I revealed myself.
- I am more lovable than I thought I was.
- I need to ask others for what I want and need.
- I am hopeful about the future, even though it may involve struggle.
- Some degree of risk and uncertainty is necessary—there are no guarantees.
- I am able to identify with the emotions of others; regardless of age, there is a common bond linking humanity.
- Intimacy is frightening, but it is worth it.
- Decisions about my behavior must come from within and not from the group members or leaders.
- Making changes takes sustained effort.
- People can be beautiful and creative when they shed their masks.
- It takes a great deal of effort to maintain a facade.

It can be concluded that the goal of a group is to provide its members with the therapeutic factors discussed above. But, to maximize the use of these therapeutic forces, it is wise to be even more specific about group goals.

FAILURES IN GROUPS

With all that groups have to offer they can fail to provide the necessary conditions for a member to improve. In some instances they can even be harmful. Failures in group therapy are well known by those who are practitioners in the field. Harpaz (1994) contends that the unresolved, irrational fears of the group leader, in particular the fear of abandonment and the fear of engulfment, are the major contributors to failures in group psychotherapy. This position is only supported by clinical vignettes, and there are those who disagree with his premise. He does make several important points, however. First, therapists should not be so quick to blame treatment failures on the patients. Second, therapists should examine their role when patients fail in group. And finally, group leaders profit by having ongoing supervision regardless of how much experience they have had.

GROUP GOALS AND OBJECTIVES

For the chemically dependent client, the group provides a chance for self-exploration that can lead to a reassessment of one's values and behaviors. This process should be an invitation to examine seriously a segment of one's selfhood or behavior. It is up to the group member to decide what, how much, and when he wishes to explore and change; if this invitation becomes a command, the likelihood of real self-exploration is diminished. Far too many chemical dependency counselors believe that clients need to be coerced or forced to look at themselves before they will avail themselves of this opportunity. Chemically dependent clients are in a great deal of pain emotionally, physically, and spiritually. Given the opportunity of self-exploration and change by a group leader who is accepting and permissive, and at the same time confronting and encountering, the chemically dependent person will most often welcome the opportunity to change.

Goals for Group Members

Some general types of goals that are appropriate for any type of group and are universal to all group members have been listed by Corey and Corey (1992). They include:

- to increase self-esteem
- to accept the reality of one's limitations
- to reduce behavior that prevents intimacy
- to learn how to trust oneself and others
- to become freer and less bound by external "shoulds" and "musts"
- to increase self-awareness and thereby increase the possibilities for choice and action
- to learn the distinction between having feelings and acting on them
- to free oneself from the inappropriate early decisions that keep one less than the person one would like to be
- to recognize that others struggle too

- to clarify the values one has and decide whether and how to modify them
- to learn to make choices in a world where nothing is guaranteed
- to find ways to solve personal problems
- to increase one's capacity to care for others
- to become more open and honest with selected others
- to deal with other members in a direct manner in the here-and-now group situation
- to support and challenge others
- to confront others with care and concern
- to learn how to ask others for what one wants
- to become sensitive to the needs and feelings of others
- to provide others with useful feedback

All of these are appropriate goals for the chemically dependent person. Additional goals for a substance-abuse group listed by Corey and Corey (1992) are to help the abuser confront difficult issues and learn to cope with life stresses more effectively, to provide a supportive network, and to learn more appropriate social skills.

Goals for Group Leaders

Dinkmeyer and Muro (1979) have listed ten specific goals for group leaders. They are:

1. to help each member of the group know and understand himself and to assist with the identity-seeking process
2. to help individuals develop increased self-acceptance and feelings of personal worth, as a result of coming to understand self
3. to develop social skills and interpersonal abilities that enable members to cope with the developmental tasks in their personal and social areas
4. to develop increased self-direction, problem-solving, and decision-making abilities, and to help members transfer these abilities to use in regular work and social contacts
5. to develop sensitivity to the needs of others, resulting in increased recognition of responsibility for one's behavior and helping members become able to identify with the feelings of significant others as well as to develop a greater capacity for empathy
6. to help members learn to be empathic listeners who not only hear what is said but also recognize the feelings that accompany what has been said

7. to help members develop the ability to be congruent with self, able to offer accurately what they think and believe

8. to help members formulate specific goals that can be measured and observed behaviorally, and to help them make a commitment to move toward those goals

9. to help members develop a feeling of belonging and acceptance by others that provides security in meeting the challenges of life

10. to help members develop courage and the ability to take rational social risks, and to show them that it is rewarding to risk and grow through sharing

Guidelines for Group Leaders

At this point it will be helpful to list some guidelines for chemical dependency counselors to follow when leading a group. Corey and Corey (1992) have also listed these.

- It is important to teach group process to the members. This need not involve giving a lecture; rather, issues can be discussed as they arise in the course of a group discussion.

- The issue of confidentiality should be emphasized in the group. The dangers of inappropriate sharing of what occurs during a session need to be highlighted, and members need to have an opportunity to express their fears or reservations concerning the respect of the rest of the group for the disclosures that are made.

- Instead of talking about a group member, the leader and other members should speak directly to the person in question.

- Each member is free to decide for himself what issues to work on in the group, and each person may decide how to explore a problem. A person's right to say, "I pass," should be respected. It is the member who is responsible for the decision to disclose or not to disclose.

- Confrontation is an essential ingredient in most groups, but members must learn how to confront others in a responsible manner. Essentially, confrontation is a challenge to look at the discrepancy between what one says and what one does, or to examine the degree to which one is being honest.

- Questioning is more often a distraction than a help in group process, and members should be warned of this. Generally, questions of a probing nature have the effect of pulling the questioned participant away from the experience of feeling. Asking questions can generate a never-ending series of "whys" and "becauses." Questioning is an impersonal way of relating that keeps the questioner at a safe distance.

- If members are to engage in any personal work, it is imperative that a climate of trust and support be established. If people feel that they can be themselves and be respected for what they feel, they are far more inclined to take the risk of sharing intimate aspects of themselves than if they expect to be harshly judged.
- Members need to learn how to listen without thinking of a quick rebuttal and without becoming overly defensive. We do not encourage people to accept everything they hear, but we do ask them to really hear what others say to them and to seriously consider those messages—particularly those messages that are repeated consistently.
- The issue of how what is learned in a group can be translated into out-of-group behavior should be given priority. Contracts and homework assignments can help members carry the new behaviors that they develop in a group into their daily lives.

By following these guidelines, the counselor should achieve the group's goals. It is worth mentioning here that just reading this material will not make a person an excellent group counselor; practice and experience, along with the supervision of a well-trained supervisor, are essential. However, there are certain individuals who learn group counseling more readily than others (those who are almost naturally therapeutic and who have very little problem learning the group model). There are also those who find it difficult to lead a successful group.

THE GROUP LEADER

It is overly simplistic to say that a good group leader is one who has good leadership skills. But the fact remains that this is true. That which separates those who are therapeutic from those who are not is their leadership-skills level. This discussion, then, becomes one of what are good leadership skills, not what is a good leader. In terms of such factors as client satisfaction, smooth group operation, and positive client change, the following skills are offered by Dinkmeyer and Muro (1979). They are discussed here in terms of the chemical dependency counselor.

- Effective group counselors are able to develop trust in the group. Without a sense of trust, no group can be successful. A trusting counselor invites trust in the group members. If the counselor does not trust the group members to make decisions in their own best interest, they will not do so. Trust also means that the counselor and group will not use the results of their interaction to hurt each other. The cohesion that develops in a group is not a license for manipulating others to fit the mores of a culture or subculture. The counselor who earns the confidence of the group can, in turn, help each member gain the self-confidence necessary for positive growth.

- Effective group counselors are skilled listeners. The term *active listeners* can be applied here. This means that the counselor hears not only the words but also the emotional tone in which the words are spoken; this is more than what happens in a day-to-day conversation. Counselors who listen actively are interested in group members and are willing to give of themselves to those who need help.

- Effective group counselors are able to develop mutual group and idiosyncratic goals. If a group member has as a goal the exploration of the possibility of controlled drinking in the future, and a major goal of the group leader is total abstinence for all members, neither the group leader nor the group member is likely to meet his goals. In group counseling, as in individual counseling, the goal is not necessarily first and foremost to change behavior; this is difficult for chemical dependency counselors to accept. When it is obvious to all but a particular group member that chemical use is causing that group member continued problems, it is easy for the group leader and members to insist on abstinence as the primary goal for this individual. However, unless the individual has accepted this goal, it is likely that he will leave the group feeling out of place and identified by other group members as not ready to work on his problem, even when this person may have been ready to work on his problem as he saw it. In this instance the group might have been able to influence an attitude change and thus a change of goals and behavior. But if the original goals are not accepted by the group and the member does not return to the group, there will be no continued group influence. It is essential for the group leader and the group members to be flexible and to come to mutually agreeable goals.

- Effective group counselors are spontaneous and responsive. Responses should be natural and direct, yet they must not harm any member of the group. In individual counseling, the counselor can take time to ponder and speculate about a comment or technique; the group rarely allows time for this. The group counselor must rely on an immediate, intuitive, honest reaction. Those who lack spontaneity will likely find group counseling difficult.

- Effective group counselors can be firm. The counselor's firmness lies in encouraging the group to recognize him as the leader and the central figure in the group. As such, the leader must minister to the needs of all members, challenging some, encouraging others, and blocking or reducing the potential impact of harmful interaction. The counselor must not use the group to meet personal needs but must be willing to change, grow, and learn. By combining firmness with spontaneity, humor, and empathy, the group leader becomes a real person rather than a manipulator of desired behavioral norms.

- Effective group counselors have a sense of humor. The treatment of the chemically dependent person is often perceived as a somber, serious business. Indeed, at times it is, but there are other times in the life of the client that call for appropriate laughter. The counselor's ability to laugh shows a genuine individual who is capable of expressing a full range of emotions. This is an appropriate model for group members.

- Effective group counselors are perceived by group members as being with them and for them as individuals. Successful group counselors are able to convey an attitude of care and concern for each group member. Group members should not see the counselor as ranking them as better or worse along any given continuum. For example, group members cannot be told that they have complete freedom to discuss whatever they wish and then find that the counselor is more interested in Helen's sex problem than in Bob's drinking problem. Success in group counseling is a product of strong, mutual liking and respect between the counselor and each group member and among the various members. No counselor who cares little for the group members will earn their respect or care.

EVALUATING GROUP COUNSELING SKILLS

The skills mentioned above (and, in fact, all the group counseling skills) should be thought of as existing in various degrees rather than on an all-or-none basis (that is, they may be highly, or only minimally, developed). Corey and Corey (1992) have developed rating scales for counselors to rate themselves and for group members to rate group leaders. These scales are most beneficial for counselors who wish to improve their skills and are included here with that purpose in mind.

Self-Rating Scale

Rate yourself from 1 to 7 on the following items:
1 = I am very poor at this. **7** = I am very good at this.
  1. **Active listening:** I am able to hear and understand both direct and subtle messages.
  2. **Reflecting:** I can mirror what another says, without being mechanical.
  3. **Clarifying:** I can focus on underlying issues and assist others to get a clear picture of some of their conflicting feelings.

4. **Summarizing:** When I function as a group leader, I am able to identify key elements of a session and to present them as a summary of the proceedings.
5. **Interpreting:** I can present a hunch to someone concerning the reason for his behavior without dogmatically stating what the behavior was.
6. **Questioning:** I avoid bombarding people with questions about their behavior.
7. **Linking:** I find ways of relating what one person is doing or saying to the concerns of other members.
8. **Confronting:** When I confront another, the confrontation usually has the effect of getting the person to look at his behavior in a nondefensive manner.
9. **Supporting:** I am usually able to tell when supporting another will be productive and when it will be counterproductive.
10. **Blocking:** I am able to intervene successfully, without seeming to be attacking, to stop counterproductive behaviors (such as gossiping, story-telling, and intellectualizing) in the group.
11. **Diagnosing:** I can generally get a sense of what specific problems people have, without feeling the need to label people.
12. **Evaluating:** I appraise outcomes when I am in a group, and I make some comments concerning the ongoing process of any group I am in.
13. **Facilitating:** In a group, I am able to help others openly express themselves and work through barriers to communication.
14. **Empathizing:** I can intuitively sense the subjective world of others in a group, and I have the capacity to understand much of what others are experiencing.
15. **Terminating:** At the end of group sessions, I am able to create a climate that will foster a willingness in others to continue working after the session.

Rating Scale for Group Counselors

The following evaluation form can be used in several ways. Group leaders can use it as a self-evaluation device, supervisors can use it to evaluate group leaders in training, group leaders can use it to evaluate their coleaders, and group members can use it to evaluate their leader.

Rate the leader from 1 to 7 on the following items:

1 = to an extremely low degree. **7** = to an extremely high degree.

1. **Support:** To what degree does the group leader allow clients to express their feelings?
2. **Interpretation:** To what degree is the group leader able to explain the meaning of behavior patterns within the framework of the theoretical system?

3. **Confrontation:** To what degree is the group leader able to actively and directly confront clients when the clients engage in behavior that is inconsistent with what they say?
4. **Modeling:** To what degree is the group leader able to demonstrate to members behaviors to emulate and practice both during and after the session?
5. **Assignment:** To what degree is the group leader able to direct clients to improve on existing behavior patterns or to develop new behaviors before the next group session?
6. **Referral:** To what degree is the group leader able to make available to clients persons capable of further assisting clients with personal concerns?
7. **Role direction:** To what degree is the group leader able to direct clients to enact specific roles in role-playing situations?
8. **Empathy:** To what degree does the group leader demonstrate the ability to adopt the internal frame of reference of a client and communicate to the client that he is understood?
9. **Self-disclosure:** To what degree does the group leader demonstrate a willingness and ability to reveal his own present feelings and thoughts to clients when it is appropriate to the group counseling situation?
10. **Initiation:** To what degree is the group leader able to initiate interaction among members or between leader and members?
11. **Facilitation:** To what degree is the group leader able to help clients clarify their own goals and take steps to reach these goals?
12. **Diagnosis:** To what degree is the group leader able to identify specific areas of struggle and conflict within each client?
13. **Follow-through:** To what degree is the group leader able to implement (and follow through to a reasonable completion) work with a client in an area that the client has expressed a desire to explore?
14. **Active listening:** To what degree does the group leader actively and fully listen to and hear the subtle messages communicated by clients?
15. **Knowledge of theory:** To what degree does the group leader demonstrate a theoretical understanding of group dynamics, interpersonal dynamics, and behavior in general?
16. **Application of theory to practice:** To what degree is the group leader able to appropriately apply a given theory to an actual group situation?
17. **Perceptivity and insight:** To what degree is the group leader able to sensitively and accurately extract the core meanings from verbal and nonverbal communications?
18. **Risk taking:** To what degree is the group leader able to risk making mistakes and to profit from mistakes?
19. **Expression:** To what degree is the group leader able to express thoughts and feelings directly and clearly to clients?

20. **Originality:** To what degree does the group leader seem to have synthesized a personal approach from a variety of approaches to group leadership?
21. **Group dynamics:** To what degree is the group leader able to assist a group of people to work effectively together?
22. **Cooperation as a coleader:** To what degree is the group leader able to work cooperatively with a coleader?
23. **Content orientation:** To what degree is the group leader able to help group members focus on specific themes in a structured type of group experience?
24. **Values awareness:** To what degree are group leaders aware of their own value systems and of the client's value system, and to what degree are they able to avoid imposing their values on the client?
25. **Flexibility:** To what degree is the group leader able to change approaches—to modify style and technique—to adapt to each unique working situation?
26. **Awareness of self:** To what degree is the group leader aware of his own needs, motivations, and problems, and to what degree does the leader avoid exploiting or manipulating clients to satisfy these needs?
27. **Respect:** To what degree does the group leader communicate an attitude of respect for the dignity and autonomy of the client?
28. **Care:** To what degree does the group leader communicate an attitude of genuine caring for the client?
29. **Techniques:** To what degree is the group leader knowledgeable of techniques and able to use them well and appropriately to help clients work through conflicts and concerns?
30. **Ethical awareness:** To what degree does the group leader demonstrate awareness of, and sensitivity to, the demands of professional responsibility?

CHOOSING GROUP MEMBERS

In reality, the chemical dependency counselor often has very little choice about which clients or patients become group members. Inpatient drug and alcohol treatment programs routinely include patients in group therapy as a part of the total treatment program. All of those in treatment attend groups. Whenever possible, however, the chemical dependency counselor can maximize the group's effectiveness by carefully selecting group members. Referrals to self-help groups after, or in conjunction with, treatment should also be done in a selective manner.

For example, despite the widespread recognition that A.A. has enjoyed an exceedingly fine success rate (and A.A. itself has spread widely throughout the world), it must also be recognized that the traditional precepts of A.A. as spelled out in the 12 steps have no appeal for, and may even antagonize, the patient in some populations. More specifically, the traditional A.A. group may be problematic for some people. Heath, et al. (1981) has reported that some years ago a

Navajo Indian made the simple but eloquent point that "it's not right to tell all them personal things, about what I did to my wife and how I argued with her father, and all that." And by contrast, in a Costa Rican community many problem drinkers were willing, even eager, to publicly confess the injuries they had caused others but could not accept the principle of surrender. As one Costa Rican put it, "Damn, I'm not about to admit that alcohol is stronger than I am. What kind of a man would say that? . . . One's purpose should be again to be strong like a man, to overcome this alcohol with one's own forces."

In instances such as these, routine referrals to a specific self-help group might be unwise. Offering a choice of groups like A.A., N.A., Rational Recovery, Women for Sobriety, and so on, would be a much better idea. Who belongs in what group? How does one determine which combinations of individuals produce optimal conditions for maximum effectiveness?

The first approach one might take is to decide whom to exclude from the group. All manner of individuals have been recommended for exclusion from the group: these include psychotics or prepsychotics; those who are brain damaged, paranoid, extremely narcissistic, hypochondriacal, or suicidal; and even those addicted to drugs or alcohol. For obvious reasons it would be impossible for the chemical dependency counselor to exclude all of these as group members.

The best approach might be to include individuals who meet the following four criteria:

1. They have a sense of reality.
2. They can be related to interpersonally.
3. They have sufficient flexibility to help reduce, or to heighten, intragroup tensions.
4. They can serve, at times, as a catalyst for the group.

Motivation is another factor to consider; however, many seemingly unmotivated persons have become motivated as a result of their group experience. It would be a mistake to assume that because people do not admit to being alcoholic or drug dependent they do not desire or value personal change. (It may be that they are unwilling to pay the price of admitting to chemical dependency.) They may also view themselves as deficient in understanding their own feelings or the feelings of others. Admitting one's problems is a step toward solving those problems, but it is not the only step or necessarily the first step. The first step may be examining those problems, and this can be effectively done in a group. It is important for group members to express satisfaction with their group if they are to continue membership. Members continue membership if:

• they view the group as meeting their personal needs
• they derive satisfaction from their relationship with group members

- they derive satisfaction from their participation in the group task
- they derive satisfaction from group membership vis-à-vis the outside world

There is yet another factor that should be considered here: Should the group be homogeneous or heterogeneous in makeup? That is, should groups be made up of members with similar problems and backgrounds or different problems and backgrounds? With regard to the chemically dependent client there are some definite advantages to homogeneous groups.

- Group identification takes place rapidly.
- Reeducation takes place rapidly, and insight develops quickly.
- Psychodynamics are laid bare more rapidly.
- Duration of treatment is lessened.
- Attendance is more regular.
- Interferences, resistances, and interactions of a destructive nature are lessened.
- Intragroup cliques are uncommon.
- Recovery from symptoms is more rapid.

There are advantages to heterogeneity within groups as well, but for the chemically dependent client the advantages of a homogeneous group are far greater. Yalom (1986) has cited alcoholics as an example of a population that does poorly in mixed, intensive outpatient group settings. This is not because of their drinking but because of their interpersonal behavior; he cites excessive nurturant needs and a low tolerance for frustration as possible reasons for this.

Yalom (1986) also sees the selection of group therapy members with specialized goals such as obesity, alcoholism, or addiction as relatively uncomplicated. The admission criterion, he states, may simply be the existence of the target symptom—chemical dependency.

We would again remind chemical dependency counselors that there are many different reasons why people become chemically dependent and that chemical dependency manifests itself in numerous behaviors. The counselor who remains constantly aware of this and who meets each client's needs on an individual basis (including what group to refer a client to) will have the most success. The point is, some kind of screening and selection process is necessary; counselors who do not pay attention to this phase of group work unnecessarily increase the psychological risk for the group members.

GROUP PROCESS

What is group process? Group process refers to the stages of development of a group and the interactions that go on during each stage of the group (Corey & Corey, 1992).

All groups are different. The leadership styles and personalities of the leader or coleaders and the make-up of the group members affect the direction in which the group will go. However, a typical group goes through four stages. These are:

1. the initial stage
2. the transition stage
3. the working stage
4. the ending or final stage

Each of the stages has certain characteristics that a leader can observe to determine if the group is progressing at an appropriate rate. In order to help members get the most from a group experience the leader should know and understand these stages and assist the group in its journey through them.

The Initial Stage

The initial stage is perhaps the most important because it will establish the future direction that will ultimately lead to the success or failure of the group. The initial stage could last for several sessions or just one session depending on the make-up of members and the skill of the leaders. During this period the leader should help establish the goals of the group; but, the first item on the agenda is to establish the rules of the group. Most leaders offer only a few rules at the beginning and add others if it is necessary. The fewer the rules at the beginning the better. Some examples are:

• No physical violence during group.
• What goes on in group is not discussed outside of group.
• Do not talk over someone else; wait until they are finished.
• Do not be late for group.

During this stage the leader wants to establish the structure of the group, set guidelines for opening and closing the session, help establish goals, foster group cohesion and trust, and deal with resistance and hidden agendas. It is also important to encourage members to be active participants and not just observers. One way to begin this process is by having each member tell a little about themselves and then have the group talk about their reservations about being in the group.

The characteristics of the initial stage as listed by Corey and Corey (1992) are:

• Members test the atmosphere and get acquainted.
• Members learn what is expected, how the group functions, and how to participate in the group.

- Risk taking is relatively low, and exploration is tentative.
- Group cohesion and trust are gradually established if members are willing to express what they are thinking and feeling.
- Members are concerned with whether they are included or excluded, and they are beginning to define their place in the group.
- Negative feelings may surface as members test to determine if all feelings are acceptable.
- A central issue is trust versus mistrust.
- There are periods of silence and awkwardness; members may look for direction and wonder what the group is about. Members are deciding whom they can trust and how much they will disclose, how safe the group is, whom they like and dislike, and how much to get involved.
- Members are learning the basic attitudes of respect, empathy, acceptance, caring, and responding—all attitudes that facilitate the building of trust.

For details on all of the stages see Corey and Corey (1992), *Group Process and Practice*.

Transition Stage of a Group

The transition stage of a group is perhaps the most difficult for the leader or leaders of the group. They must deal with increasing anxiety in the group as more and more personal issues are discussed. They must deal with defensiveness and resistance as group members become threatened by the material or the process of the group. As members begin to trust each other and begin to share, there are always members who are fearful of rejection, of making a fool of oneself, of losing control, of disclosing too much as well as other such fears. There are always struggles for the control of the group. There is conflict, there are challenges to the group leader, and there is confrontation. Some other problem behaviors and difficult behaviors among group members that often occur during the transition stage according to Corey and Corey (1992) include:

- silence and lack of participation
- members who monopolize the group
- members who tell long stories
- members who are always asking questions as if they were interrogating someone
- members who always have advice to give

- members who soothe over everything because they cannot stand conflict or stress
- members who are hostile
- members who are dependent
- members who act superior
- members who are seductive
- members who socialize outside of group as a form of resistance
- members who intellectualize everything
- members who are too often emotional in group

These issues can be dealt with in group or outside of group by speaking directly with the member involved. If they are not dealt with appropriately, the group will have a difficult time moving to the working stage.

During the transition stage, the members of the group are sizing up the leader. There are several inappropriate ways that group members may see the leader, and these must be dealt with as well. Members may view leaders as experts who have all the answers. They may see them as authority figures, which may get in the way of establishing trust. They may see them as superpersons, infallible or perfect, which makes it hard on their own self-esteem. They may view them as friends, which is unrealistic. Finally, group leaders may be seen as lovers. Even if the leader has given no evidence of wanting a relationship with the member other than as group leader, some members may want to convert the therapeutic relationship into a romantic one. "Sexual intimacies between group counselors and members are unethical" (Association for Specialists in Group Work, 1990, p. 9, c.) and in many states illegal.

These issues need to be dealt with by the group leader, achieving an appropriate balance between support and confrontation. Too much of either may be destructive to the group member. Too much support leaves the member unchallenged, and aggressive confrontation has been shown to be directly related to negative outcomes in groups (Lieberman, M., Yalom, I., & Miles, M., 1973; Corey & Corey, 1992).

The transitional stage of a group's development is marked by feelings of anxiety and defenses in the form of various resistances. Corey and Corey (1992) list member resistances and stage characteristics as:

- concerned about what they will think of themselves if they increase their self-awareness, and concerned about others' acceptance or rejection of them
- testing the leader and other members to determine how safe the environment is

- struggling between wanting to play it safe and wanting to risk getting involved
- experiencing some struggle for control and power and some conflict with other members
- observing the leader to determine if he or she is trustworthy
- learning how to express themselves so that others will listen to them

Working Stage of a Group

Earlier in this chapter the therapeutic factors that operate in a group were presented. There are similar factors in play during the working stage of a group. The factors involved in the working phase of a group as listed in Corey and Corey (1992) working groups are:

- have members who trust the leaders and other group members
- have members who take risks
- have clear goals and move toward those goals
- have members who feel included
- have an accurate expression of what is being experienced
- focus on the here and now
- share leadership functions
- have members who initiate activities
- have members willing to share threatening material
- have high cohesion
- have members who can resolve conflict in the group
- have members who accept responsibility for solving their problems
- have members who give feedback freely
- have members who deal with needed confrontation without an attack
- have members whose communication is clear and direct
- have members who use each other as resources
- have members who encourage diversity
- have members who have cooperatively developed norms
- have members who use out-of-group time to work on problems raised in group
- have members who emphasize thinking as well as feeling

The Final Stage: Ending a Group

The end of a group can be as meaningful an experience as the working phase. A wise leader will take advantage of this phase to consolidate the learning by clearing up unfinished business, by giving an opportunity for members to say good-bye, by reviewing, and by making referrals where necessary. Termination of the group experience more specifically includes: dealing with feelings of separation, dealing with unfinished business, reviewing the group experience, helping other members to practice for behavioral change, and giving and receiving final feedback. To assist in transferring the group experience to real life the leader may want to make a contract with each member on how they will use the information they have gained in group in their lives. Finally, leaving the members with the following information may be helpful.

- Realize that the group is a means to an end.
- Realize that change may be slow and subtle.
- Do not expect one group alone to renovate your life.
- Decide what to do with what you learned.
- Think for yourself!

Corey and Corey (1992) include in their book the final-stage characteristics of a group as:

- There may be some sadness and anxiety over the reality of separation.
- Members are likely to pull back and participate in less intense ways, in anticipation of the ending of the group.
- Members are deciding what courses of action they are likely to take.
- There may be some fears of separation as well as fears about being able to carry over into daily life some of what was experienced in the group.
- Members may express their fears, hopes, and concerns for one another.
- Group sessions may be devoted partly to preparing members to meet significant others in everyday life. Role playing and behavioral rehearsal for relating more effectively to others are common.
- Members may be involved in evaluations of the group experience.
- There may be some talk about follow-up meetings or some plan for accountability so that members will be encouraged to carry out their plans for change.

ETHICAL AND PROFESSIONAL ISSUES

The group leader is the one who is primarily responsible for the direction that the group takes with regard to ethics. The group leader sets the tone and models behaviors for group members. Some issues and responsibilities that a group leader should consider are these:

- What does a group leader need to tell potential members about the group?
- Were members screened? How?
- Is group membership voluntary or involuntary?
- What does a group member need to do if he wishes to leave the group?
- Arc there any consequences attached to leaving the group?

Confidentiality

Confidentiality is a major issue for the group leader. It is not only that the group leader must keep confidences but also that he must get the group members to do so as well. Group leaders should emphasize the importance of confidentiality at various stages of the group's development. If, at any time, any member gives an indication that confidences have been broken, the group leader should explore this matter with the group.

Group leaders owe it to their clients to specify at the beginning of a group the limits on confidentiality. For example, group leaders should let the members know that they may be required to testify against them in court unless the leader is entitled to privileged communication. In general, licensed psychologists, psychiatrists, and licensed clinical social workers are legally entitled to privileged communications. This means that these people cannot break the confidence of a client unless in their judgment, the client (1) is a danger to himself or others; or (2) may do serious harm to someone else (Corey & Corey, 1992). Many an A.A. meeting place has a sign that sums up confidentiality. It says: Let what is said here stay here. That is generally good advice for group members in any group.

Psychological Risk

Another ethical and professional issue is that of psychological risk to the group members. The therapeutic forces at work in a group are powerful ones, and their unleashing involves a certain amount of risk. These forces have the potential to be just as harmful as they are helpful. The leader must not assume that the members of a group are aware of them. Members of a group may be subject to scapegoating, group pressure, breaches of confidence, inappropriate reassurance, and hostile confrontation; the group process may even precipitate a crisis in the group member's life. These hazards should be discussed and examined during the initial session, focusing on ways that these hazards can be avoided. For more information on ethics see Chapter 2.

Evaluating Oneself as Group Leader

Another issue that the group leader must confront is that of his own competence as a group leader. Counselors should ask themselves questions such as: What kind of clients am I capable of dealing with? What are my areas of expertise? What techniques do I handle well? How far can I safely go with clients? When should I refer? Truly competent group leaders have answers for why they do what they do in a group. They can explain the theory behind their group work. They can express the goals of their group. They can provide a relationship between the way they lead a group and the goals that they hope to achieve. And, finally, they know how to evaluate how well these goals are being met.

As you might imagine, one does not become an effective group leader without extensive training and experience; that is the idea that we began this chapter with and the one we will end it with. The group experience can be one of the most therapeutic tools that the chemical dependency counselor has to work with. But it takes time and effort for the counselor to learn to maximize the group experience for the therapeutic benefit of its members. However, it will be time and effort well spent especially considering that group therapy is evolving into the treatment of choice as consumers and insurers continue to look for proven, affordable treatments (Sleek, 1995).

SEVEN COMMON QUESTIONS FROM NEW GROUP LEADERS

Since there are no real right or wrong answers to most of these questions you may want to discuss them in class or with your colleagues.

1. **When should you use a co-therapist?**
    One of the best ways to learn to do group therapy is to colead a group with a trained, experienced group leader. New counselors should have several hundred hours of time coleading a group before attempting a group on their own. Then that leader should have a year or more experience before they attempt to train another person as a coleader.

    From a therapeutic standpoint it is usually a good idea to have a coleader. In most cases two heads are better than one. That is, one person may see something the other does not or each person may offer a different but equally valuable prospective. The exception to this is if the coleaders have unresolved personal issues. In this case, group process is usually more productive if there is only one leader. For mixed-sex groups, male and female coleaders are ideal.

    The other consideration is always economics. Can the agency afford to put two counselors in one group? Are you willing to split your fees if you are in private practice? It would be nice to believe that everyone makes the coleader decision based on what is best for the patients or clients; however, cost will always be a factor. For a detailed description of the advantages and disadvantages of coleadership see Corey and Corey (1992).

2. **Should my group be open or closed?**

    Open groups have a constantly changing membership, while closed groups have the same members and are usually time limited in some way. Do not confuse this with A.A.'s open and closed meetings. The group setting usually is the determining factor in the open or closed group decision. Some settings lend themselves to open groups and others to closed groups. The group leader often has no say in the decision.

    Adding new members and having some members leaving a group is disruptive to the group process. There are, however, some advantages to this. For example, the older members can help newer members progress quickly to the working stage of group. Also the departing members can model appropriate separation for those who will follow them. As members come and go, the dynamics of the group will change—sometimes for the better, sometimes for the worse.

    If a treatment program has patients at different phases of treatment, that is people coming to and leaving the program all the time, it is difficult to have anything other than an open-ended group. If, as a leader, you have a choice, try to decide which would be more therapeutic based on the goals of the group.

3. **Should I mix drug addicts with alcoholics in a group?**

    Some in the field feel that an addict is an addict and the issues are the same. As you will learn in Chapter 7, diversity of any kind should be considered. Again there are positive and negative aspects to both sides. Alcoholics sometimes do not like to be compared to drug addicts because they have not broken the law like most drug abusers have. Some drug abusers do not like alcoholics because they seem self-righteous. Other times, members have both drug and alcohol problems. If there is a problem mixing the two, it is a prime issue that can be dealt with during group. An experienced group leader will use group friction as a tool in therapy and as a learning experience for group members.

4. **What about mixing sexes, races, codependents and addicts, or ethnic groups?**

    The chapter on diversity addresses this question and the answer to the question above also applies. Determine the setting and the goals for the group and then decide on the type of membership that will be best to meet those goals.

5. **Should I see a group member in individual therapy as well?**

    As mentioned earlier Medicare (1994) sees this as a specific therapeutic approach. They believe that "the one-to-one doctor-patient relationship enables a deep examination of the transference reaction for some patients, for others it may not provide the corrective emotional experiences necessary for the therapeutic change. The group therapy gives patients a variety of persons with whom they can develop transferential reactions." (p. 4). However, Medicare is a conservative organization and a bit in the dark ages as evidenced by their using psychoanalytic terms such as transference. It is also clear that a nonclinical individual wrote this regulation.

If you do see group members in individual therapy, you should see all of them to avoid the feeling of special status about the ones you do see. There are also issues regarding bringing up things you talked about individually in the group setting. Is that alright with the client? If not, you could damage your relationship by revealing something of a personal nature in group. If you choose to see group members in individual therapy, be sure to consider the clinical ramifications both for the individual and the other group members as well as what it might do for group process.

6. **What about simultaneous membership in groups, like A.A. and a therapy group?**
   It is common for substance abusers, family members, and ACOAs to be members of 12-step or other self-help groups when they enter group therapy. It is good to encourage such contact as helpful support, but it is also important to underscore the ways in which the ground rules of group therapy differ. During the initial stage of the group this should be explained to everyone in the group since the likelihood is that there are several members who have self-help group experience. Issues of attendance, the difference between a group leader and an A.A. speaker, and the differences in the group focus should be discussed (Vannicelli, 1992).

   Finally, if patients feel that there is a conflict between their A.A. or other self-help experience and group therapy because the formats are so different, the leader should make it clear that the two are not in any way mutually exclusive but, rather, serve different functions (Vannicelli, 1992).

7. **What training do I need before I can ethically lead a group on my own?**
   When the field of chemical dependency treatment was emerging and groups were becoming a popular method of treatment, many people ran groups with little if any training or experience. This author is aware of a newly sober individual in treatment who was a group member one week and working in the same treatment center as a group leader the next week. His total training and experience consisted of group membership for a total of 16 sessions during a twenty-eight-day inpatient treatment program. The reality is that this individual turned out to be a very good group leader, and he helped many addicts recover over the years. But that was some time ago when hardly anyone had training in any aspect of chemical dependency treatment. Someone had to fly the first plane without the benefit of instruction. Someone performed the first liver transplant without instruction. Because of those who went before, it is no longer necessary to fly, do a liver transplant, or do group therapy without instruction.

Because the potential for harm is equal or greater to the potential for positive therapeutic movement in a group, only those who know what they are doing should lead therapy groups. Some people like the one mentioned above can be naturally therapeutic, just as some people are naturally harmful to be around. Training will weed out harmful individuals and sharpen the skills of those who are naturally therapeutic.

There are those who believe only someone with a graduate degree should be allowed to do group therapy. But many people, with the right motivation (see Chapter 1), a course in group counseling, and several hundred hours of supervision with a coleader, have become outstanding group leaders. As they begin to lead groups on their own they should continue to be supervised during a probationary period. Anything less than this would be unadvisable. The section on credentials and certifications has additional information on this topic.

With regard to group therapy, the Curriculum Review Committee of the Addiction Training Centers Program, funded by the Center for Substance Abuse Treatment (CSAT), recommends that a CD counselor be able to:

1. describe, select, and appropriately use strategies from accepted models for group counseling with addicted or substance abusing clients
2. perform the actions necessary to start a group, including: determining group type, purpose, size, and leadership; recruiting and selecting members; establishing group goals and clarifying behavioral ground rules for participating; identifying outcomes; and determining methods for termination or graduation from the group
3. facilitate the entry of new members and the transition of exiting members
4. facilitate group growth within the established ground rules and precipitate movement toward group and individual goals by using methods consistent with group type
5. understand the concepts of "process" and "content" and shift the focus of the group when such an intervention will help the group move toward its goals
6. describe and summarize client behavior within the group for the purpose of documenting the client's progress and identifying needs and issues that may require a modification in the treatment plan.

DISCUSSION QUESTIONS

1. How do I feel in a group situation?
2. What are my group skills?

3. What are my personal group experiences?
4. How would my personal group experiences affect my group leadership style?
5. What type of group would be best for my clients?

REFERENCES

Association for Specialists in Group Work. (1990, May). *Ethical guidelines for group counselors* (vol 15 No. 2, pp. 119–26), Author.

Corey, G., & Corey, M. S. (1977). *Group process and practice.* Pacific Grove, CA: Brooks/Cole Publishing Co..

Corey, G., & Corey, M. S. (1992). *Group process and practice.* (4th ed.) Pacific Grove, CA: Brooks/Cole Publishing Co.

Dinkmeyer, D., & Muro, I. (1979). *Group counseling: Theory and practice.* Itaska, IL: F. E. Peacock Publishers, Inc.

Dreikurs, R., & Sonstegard, M. (1968). Rationale for group counseling. In D. C. Dinkmeyer (Ed.), *Guidance and counseling in the elementary school: Readings in theory and practice.* New York: Holt, Rinehart & Winston, Inc.

Harpaz, N. (1994). Failures in group psychotherapy: The therapist variable. *International Journal of Group Psychotherapy, 44* (1), 3–19.

Heath, D. B., Waddell, J. D., & Topper, M. D. (Special Eds.). (1981). Cultural factors in alcohol research and treatment of drinking problems. *Journal of Studies on Alcohol.* (Suppl. 9).

Lawson, G., & Lawson, A. (1984). Treating the whole family: When intervention and education aren't enough. *Focus on the Family and Chemical Dependency, 7* (1), 14–16.

Lawson, G., Peterson, J., & Lawson, A. (1983). *Alcoholism and the family.* Gaithersburg, MD: Aspen Publishers, Inc.

Lieberman, M., Yalom, I., & Miles, M. (1973). *Encounter groups: First facts.* New York: Basic Books, Inc..

McKay, M., & Paleg, K. (Eds.). (1992). *Focal group psychotherapy.* Oakland, CA: New Harbinger Publications.

(Your) Medicare Newsletter (1994 September). Transamerica Life Companies. Los Angeles, 79, 4.

Rogers, P. D. (1992). Beginning group therapy with addicted populations. In McKay, M., & Paleg, K. (Eds.). (1992) *Focal Group Psychotherapy.* Oakland, CA: New Harbinger Publications.

Sleek, S. (1995, July). Group therapy: Tapping the power of teamwork. *APA Monitor.* 1, 38.

Vannicelli, M. (1992). *Removing the roadblocks: Group psychotherapy with substance abusers and family members.* New York: Guilford Press.

Valentine, D., Lawson, A., & Lawson, G. (1995, May). *A comparison of family education and family therapy in treatment of spouses of alcoholics.* Seventh International Congress on Treatment of Addictive Behaviors, Leevenhorst, Netherlands.

Varenhorst, B. (1969). Behavioral group counseling. In G. M. Gazda (Ed.), *Theories and methods of group counseling in the schools.* Springfield, IL, Charles C Thomas Publisher.

Yalom, I. D. (1986). *The theory and practice of group psychotherapy.* (3rd ed.) New York: Basic Books, Inc.

Chapter 6

❦ ❧

Family Counseling: Seeing the Family As the Client

CHAPTER OBJECTIVES

- Provide counselors with an introduction to systems thinking
- Provide a history of systems thinking
- Help counselors apply this thinking to family dynamics that foster or maintain addictive behaviors
- Define family therapy terminology as it applies to substance abusing families
- Provide a brief overview of several family therapy theories
- Describe typical patterns of alcoholic and addict family systems

It is beyond the scope of this book to give counselors all the knowledge that they need to know in order to become family therapists. It takes years of training and supervision to become a competent family therapist. Counselors, however, may find themselves in a treatment setting that does not employ a family therapist or in a geographical area where referral to a family therapist is not possible, and they will need to be able to provide help to the families of their clients. Whether counselors are in these situations or not they should know as much as possible about family systems and how they are affected by chemical dependency. People do not develop an addiction in a vacuum. They are influenced by their families, peers, and the society as a whole, which have an impact on addicts as well.

Counselors who can understand the systemic, intergenerational process of chemical dependency are more likely to intervene in factors that keep families stuck in repeated patterns and can reduce the risk of relapse, especially if the substance abuser is treated in a program that is separate from the family to which he or she will return. Family therapy does not always mean that the entire family must come in for treatment. Counselors can work with individual clients on family issues and change the way one person interacts with a family, which will produce changes in others.

It is the goal of this chapter to provide counselors with an introduction to systemic thinking and to help them apply this thinking to family dynamics that foster addictive behaviors or maintain them. In contrast to linear thinking that states A causes B, systems thinking involves A causing B that causes C that affects D and interacts with E that affects A and B and so on. There is no real beginning and no real ending; just a constant state of interaction among the parts of the system. Systems thinkers also see symptoms or problems as not existing within an individual but among individuals. They are interested in understanding peoples' behavior in a context. These ideas grew out of several sources that came from various fields of study.

ROOTS OF FAMILY THERAPY

Family therapists took from the anthropological approach of functionalism the notion that deviant behavior may serve a protective function for a social group and applied this to the symptoms of family members (Nichols & Schwartz, 1995). Functionalists believed that families needed to adapt to their environment. Symptoms in family members meant that the family was not adapting to the environment and was unable to meet its needs.

Ludwig von Bertalanffy, a biologist, developed a model of General Systems Theory that related to any system whether physical (a machine), biological (a dog), psychological (a personality), or sociological (a labor union or set of laws). A system could be made up of smaller systems or be a part of a larger system (Davidson, 1983). These systems also had properties or rules, such as a system is more that the sum of its parts. In other words, when the parts of a system come together, they create something like a watch's telling time when all of its parts are assembled. Thus, therapists should not concentrate on just the people in a family but should observe the interaction and process of these family parts. Bertalanffy espoused that living systems, people, were not machines and had special properties. *Equifinality* was a principle that organisms had the ability to reach final goals from different initial conditions and in different ways and had the ability to protect and restore their wholeness (Davidson, 1983). Bertalanffy also promoted a belief in the importance of values and the ecological protection of the environment.

Cybernetics, another major influence on family therapy, was developed by a mathematician studying machines, Norbert Weiner. The core of this theory is the *feedback loop,* which is a process of a system's getting information for self-correction to maintain a balance or progress toward a goal (Nichols & Schwartz, 1995). These can be *positive feedback loops,* which amplify deviation from a course or state, or *negative feedback loops,* which reduce deviation. An example of how this works is the effect of rising temperature outside a house, which creates a negative feedback loop that activates the thermostat and starts the air conditioner to bring the temperature back to the original state. Gregory Bateson, an anthropologist, brought cybernetics to family therapy with the notion of *circular causality:* Psychopathology is not caused by events in the past but it is part of ongoing circular feedback loops (Nichols & Schwartz, 1995). These ideas are applied to families by studying: (1) their rules that govern behavior; (2) negative feedback loops or the process families use to enforce the rules; (3) the sequence of events around the problem or how the family reacts and in what order to a problem; and (4) what happens if the negative feedback does not solve the problem or positive feedback loops do not push for new solutions. This is evident in alcoholic families when the family has a set pattern in reaction to the intoxication of the alcoholic member. Rules are established to attempt to solve the problem: "Don't make noise. It will disturb your father." The nonalcoholic spouse takes on most of the responsibility for running the family. All family members learn not to talk about the alcoholic behavior. Secrets are kept and role behaviors develop in an attempt to fix the problem. All of this leads to a balance or status quo in the family in an attempt to keep the family together, but the sequences of family behavior become part of the problem. Instead of the drinking behavior being the deviation from that stable state, it becomes part of the status quo of the family. Family members learn how to adapt to it, thus, keeping it stuck. This usually results when negative feedback about the drinking behavior (nagging or complaining) has failed to correct the deviation. An example of a negative feedback loop that does not work is the classic communication pattern: "I drink because you nag." "I nag because you drink." This usually leads to increased or at least a continued pattern of drinking.

Murray Bowen, a psychiatrist, was strongly influenced by biological sciences because he wanted to draw his concepts from a science that concerned living organisms. His concept of *differentiation of self* (or how one is differentiated from his or her family of origin), which is the core of this theory, was taken from the process by which cells differentiate from each other or are fused together. He saw this process in families with schizophrenic children who appeared highly emotionally reactive to each other and formed what Bowen called an *undifferentiated family ego mass,* like one undifferentiated cell (Nichols & Schwartz, 1995). Bowen was also influenced by the theory of evolution in adopting his premise of the *multigenerational transmission process* whereby low levels of differentiation were passed down through the generations, creating symptoms in family members. This concept is relevant to chemical dependency that has become part of a multigenerational process in families. Bowen describes the transmission of alcoholism across generations in the only paper he wrote about a specific symptom or problem (Bowen, 1974).

These early explorations of various fields of study led to the development of key concepts that are common to many of the theoretical models of family therapy. Each theory has special concepts of its own to explain problems in families and to explain how these key concepts fit into their theories.

KEY CONCEPTS IN VIEWING THE FAMILY AS THE CLIENT

The following are some definitions of commonly used family therapy terms. It is important for counselors to understand this terminology, which may be new to them, before moving on to the various theoretical models and techniques of family therapy.

Homeostasis

A common bond or thread runs through family members. Jackson (1957) coined the term *family homeostasis* to define a balancing behavior in families. "This balance or equilibrium shifts in response to changes which occur within the family (illness, aging, death, unemployment) and influential forces from without (economic, political, social)" (Meeks & Kelly, 1970, p. 400). Ewing and Fox (1988) adopted theoretical concepts from Jackson's theory of homeostasis in families. They viewed the alcoholic marriage as a "homeostatic mechanism" that is "established . . . to resist change over long periods of time. The behavior of each spouse is rigidly controlled by the other. As a result, an effort by one person to alter typical role behavior threatens the family equilibrium and provokes renewed efforts by the spouse to maintain status quo" (p. 87). Alcohol is often a key part in the balance of the alcoholic family. Wegscheider (1981a) drew a parallel between the alcoholic family and an art form, the mobile, that is made up of rods and strings upon which are hung the parts. There is balance and flexibility, and when influenced by an outside force, such as the wind, it shifts position but remains in a balance. In families where there is stress, the whole family shifts to bring a balance for stability and survival. This balance can be a healthy or unhealthy one. Wegscheider explains that in the chemically dependent family each person is affected by the chemical abuse of one member and says that "in an attempt to maintain balance, members compulsively repress their feelings and develop survival behaviors and walls of defense to protect them from pain" (p. 37).

Family balance is often achieved in the alcoholic or addict family with drinking or other drug use as a central point. When this drinking or other drug use is removed through treatment, the family is thrown into turmoil as if it were a mobile in a windstorm. Mother is not needed as the overly responsible martyr when Dad returns to take over running the household. Brother has no reason to stay away from home and must reevaluate his relationship with Dad. The family suddenly notices little sister's hyperactive mannerisms. The emotional distance of the marriage may still exist, and the precipitating environment that encouraged the drinking may remain. Without family intervention, relapses may occur, the family may separate, or a new family member may become symptomatic.

Family Roles

The basic principles of homeostasis include predictable roles for family members to act out and a set of rules, both overt and covert, for interaction of these roles. Family roles include: husband, wife, father, mother, daughter, son, grandmother, grandfather, aunt, uncle, cousin, step-father, step-mother, step-brother, step-sister, and many more. Each of these roles comes with a set of expectations, depending on the cultural and ethnic backgrounds of the families and the current societal parameters of appropriate behavior.

Other roles played by family members are more subtle and derive from a person's birth order and the requirements of the family. Many firstborns, for instance, are high achievers. They are born into a family of adults who have high expectations of the first child. A son may be groomed to take over the family business or follow in his father's footsteps. Oldest daughters are often encouraged to be responsible and help parent younger siblings. They become little adults who make the family proud and give stability to the system. The second-born children come along and dethrone the firstborn, and competition is set up. This can be a healthy or unhealthy competition. If the oldest is academically good in school, the second may excel in sports or music. If the family needs a focus for its problems, the second born can fill a need for a scapegoat and be the family's worst child. Youngest children are born into a system that has established rules and patterns of operation. They are often left out of family matters because they are too young, and they usually have many bosses. They may tend to act out to get attention from this established family. If the youngest is the third child, the second born becomes a middle child. Middle children can be concerned with finding their place and making certain they are treated fairly. These birth position roles shift with the demands of the family. Middle children become like the oldest when the oldest leaves home. Families with large gaps between children's ages have two oldest children.

In all families, members take on role behaviors; however, in alcoholic and addict families, normal role behavior becomes rigid in response to the family's alcoholism, which helps the family members cope (Black, 1979; Wegscheider, 1981a, 1981b; Nardi, 1981; Booz-Allen & Hamilton, 1974). This does not mean that they are pathological role behaviors, they are simply attempts to rigidly play out expected role behaviors to protect the family in a time of stress. Virginia Satir, a pioneer in family therapy, identified role behaviors that family members play when they are under stress (Bandler, Grender, & Satir, 1976). She labeled people in these roles the blamer, the placater, the irrelevant, and the superreasonable. Family members work hard at these roles to save the family system at the expense of their own emotional and physical health. The roles hide the true feelings of these people and interfere with clear, congruent communication. When these role behaviors fail and the stress continues, family members change roles in a desperate attempt to cope.

Wegscheider (1981a, 1981b), a student of Satir, identified role behaviors specific to an alcoholic family. These are seen as defenses that cover the true feelings of the person and make communication difficult. The roles include: the dependent or alcoholic, the enabler or spouse, the family hero who is usually the oldest or most responsible and a high achiever, the scapegoat or problem child, the lost child who is a loner and lives in a fantasy world, and the mascot or clown who pretends to be carefree.

These theories emphasize the negative aspects of these roles in children of alcoholics—self-denial, repression of feelings, and denial of needs. But a number of investigators (Wilson & Orford, 1978; Thornton & Nardi, 1975; Nardi, 1981) have asserted that there is a positive component to this role acquisition. These roles may help children of alcoholics develop important life skills like responsibility, initiative and independence, and insight into peoples' problems.

Black (1979, 1981a, 1981b) places the roles that children of alcoholics assume in two categories: (1) the misbehaving, obviously troubled children, and (2) the mature, stable, overachieving, behaving children that Black believed were in the majority. They have also been called the responsible ones, the adjusters, and the placaters. Black (1979) stated that the roles adopted by children of alcoholics may appear to be functional, but they really serve to cover up problems that may emerge in adulthood when these roles are no longer sufficient for coping. She stated, "These adults often find themselves depressed, and they do not understand why life seems to lack meaning. They feel loneliness, though many are not alone. Many find great difficulty in maintaining intimate relationships. And many become alcoholic and/or marry alcoholics" (Black, 1979, p. 25).

Of all of the theories of the family movement in substance abuse, the idea of "role behaviors" has been the most popular. The idea that a child of an alcoholic was a family hero or a scapegoat or any of the other roles gave meaning to the Adult Children of Alcoholic's (ACOAs) struggle. If the clinical notion that ACOAs have an identity problem is correct, then these ACOAs without identity can claim one from the list of role behaviors. However, identifying each child with a role behavior does not help the counselor or the family to understand the family dynamics that helped set the stage for alcoholism or drug abuse in a family member or the dynamics that maintain the symptom or the problems of recovery.

The field of chemical dependency has stopped short in the understanding of alcoholism and addiction as a family system problem by identifying each member as diseased and in need of individual treatment. This is counterproductive to healing the system and halting the intergenerational transmission of addiction, and it is harmful to the individuals in the system who are searching for an identity. They do not need a diagnosis of pathology.

It is this emphasis on role behaviors that often leads to a lifelong search for recovery from what is a natural birth-order role. The current emphasis on individual recovery and inpatient treatment of ACOAs is often based on these individual pathology theories. These theories usually lump all ACOAs together and imply that they all have the same types and severity of problems. Recent research studies have dispelled this uniformity myth and have found may variables that distinguish them: gender of alcoholic parent; number of alcoholic parents; age of child at the onset of parental addiction; birth order; coexisting problems of poverty, sexual abuse, and violence; number of siblings; availability of mentors or family members with resources; maintenance of family rituals during active alcoholism; and levels of individual resiliencies (Barry & Blane, 1977; Bennett, Wolin, Reiss, & Teitelbaum, 1987; Bennett, Wolin, & Reiss, 1988; Booz-Allen & Hamilton, 1974; O'Sullivan, 1991; Simmons, 1991; Wolin, Bennett, & Noonan, 1979, 1980; Wolin & Bennett, 1984). Newly married ACOAs are also not predisposed to marry heavy drinkers, and their marriages are no less intimate than those of children of nonalcoholics (Boye-Beaman, Leonard, & Senchak, 1991).

Role behaviors are a natural part of living in a family. They become harmful only when they are acted out in a rigid manner with little or no other option for problem solving. Roles are only one of several parts of systems theory. It is equally important to understand family rules, family values, cultural issues, alliances, coalitions, homeostatic mechanisms, and intergenerational transmissions and projections.

Family Rules

Decisions are made or not made according to the rules, boundaries, and alliances of family members. Families have rules about the expression of feelings such as love, hurt, or anger. Some rules are spoken about and others are not, but everyone knows them. These rules include who can express feelings, how they are expressed, and how they are received. In an alcoholic family, the unspoken rule may be that anger can only be expressed during intoxication or that affection and intimacy can occur only when one or both spouses are drinking. Barnard (1981) believes other areas where rules are formulated for family functioning are: (1) what, when, and how family members may comment on what the see, feel, and think; (2) who can speak to whom and about what; (3) how a member can be different; (4) how sexuality can be expressed; (5) what it means to be male or female; and (6) how a person can acquire self-worth and how much is appropriate to possess. Typical rules that govern alcoholic and addict families concern the best way to deal with the intoxicated or high person, secret keeping, and family preservation. Black (1981b) lists three rules that children of alcoholics often live by: Don't talk. Don't trust. Don't feel. Talking, especially about the substance abuse, might cause even more problems. Trusting usually leads to disappointment when parents do not come through with their promises. Feeling is too painful, and expression of feelings is not allowed because it might cause more trouble. These rules are the basis for dyadic and triadic relationships and interactions in the family subsystems that are formed by generation, sex, mutual interest, or duties.

Family Subsystems

The first subsystem in the family is the marital subsystem that has a closed membership in which duties are performed by the husband and wife. The second subsystem, the parental subsystem, emerges with the birth of the first child. These duties are usually carried out by the husband and wife, but in an alcoholic or addict family, the parents may abdicate their roles to a grandparent or sibling who fills the parental gap. This may blur the generational boundaries or turn the child into a parent. This child who takes on early parenting responsibilities is at risk of losing his or her childhood when strapped with the adult responsibilities of raising their siblings.

The third main category is the sibling subsystem. There may be one or many subsystems depending on the number of children, gender of the children, age differences, and common interests. In healthy families the subsystems are fluid, and members can flow between them as the overall system changes and balances. Children can act like adults when they learn to do chores or babysit for their younger siblings for short times. Parents can act like children and play and be silly for short times. Flexibility is important in defining subsystems; however, these shifts to other subsystems need to be temporary. In an alcoholic family these systems may become rigid and uncertain of their tasks. Children get stuck in the parent subsystem; addicts and alcoholics become rigidly childlike and irresponsible. Parenting may be ignored; children may take on adult roles; and children may be allowed into the marital subsystem if incestuous relationships occur between a parent and one or several children.

Boundaries

This concept has been misused in the popular literature and in the chemical dependency field. Boundaries are not rules for the behavior of children, nor are they processes of limit setting. Boundaries exist between each member of the family and between subsystems. They describe levels of comfort with closeness and connectedness within the family and with the family and the larger society. Minuchin (1974) defines three types of boundaries: enmeshed, clear, and disengaged. In reality most boundaries fall somewhere on a continuum from the very rigid (disengaged) to the very diffuse (enmeshed), with the clearly defined boundaries falling in the center.

Clear boundaries are found in most healthy relationships that are based on mutual respect. Clear boundaries allow separateness for each member, yet maintain closeness and connectedness. Freedom and flexibility in these relationships promote clear and direct communication patterns.

Enmeshed or diffuse boundaries leave no room for flexibility and no room for differences. Sameness and unity are stressed in these relationships, and a sense of belonging does occur. However, adolescents, whose job it is to individuate and pull away from their parents in order to find individual identities, become smothered and may turn to alcohol or drugs to set up a distancing mechanism. The fused marital relationship is an example of the loss of self-identity that occurs when the individual personality of one or both partners is sacrificed for the sake of the marriage. Ethnic and cultural factors have an effect on the amount of connectedness a family should have and can tolerate. Many families with a cultural heritage of close relationship with extended families can tolerate a great degree of diffuse boundaries without causing problems for the family members.

Disengaged or rigid boundaries are often seen in alcoholic families and are identified as the isolation of the members or isolation of the family from society. The rules in these families are: (1) do not talk about the alcoholism or drug addiction; (2) do not confront drinking or drug behavior; and (3) protect and shelter the alcoholic or addict so that things do not become worse. These rules perpetuate the drinking or using, which maintains the need for isolation. Often, marital relationships in these families have arrived at a fixed distance where neither partner is getting his or her needs met from the other. Similarly, siblings in this situation lack a sense of belonging, and very little love is transmitted to build self-worth. These children may use alcohol and other drugs to numb the pain of rejection, or they may act out inappropriately to try to get the recognition they want. This pattern of rigid boundaries can be found in families who have children in their twenties who have not left home. They often have chronic drug problems that keep them from gaining steady employment and, thus, moving out. Research has indicated that these young adults and adolescents with drug problems have never felt connected to their families and hang on to try and get those needs met (Friedman, Tomko, & Utada, 1991; Olson & Killorin, 1987). Olson and Killorin (1987) compared chemically dependent families and nondependent families using the circumplex model of measuring family cohesion. One-third of the chemically dependent families perceived their families as disengaged compared to seven percent of the nondependent families. On the outside looking in, these families might look enmeshed and stuck together. It would be tempting for a counselor to tell the parents to kick these drug-abusing kids out, and although this may be an end goal, it can be disastrous if the children do not first feel connected to the family. Too often drug-abusing young adults only feel connected to their families when the families give them money or bail them out of trouble.

Family Values

As family roles, rules, and boundaries begin to develop, so do family values. These values are a blend of those values transmitted from the spouses' families of origin. These values may be shared by the couple or be more strongly supported by one spouse or the other. Things that are valued in families are: athletics, music, money, work, education, power, control, winning, social status, military service, conservatism, or radicalism, to name just a few. Conflict can occur when the mother embraces music and education as her strong values and wants her son to become a musical virtuoso, while the father longs for an athlete who is competitive and values winning. In some cases, children make adaptations and combine values to please both parents, but when the values are in direct opposition, the child must choose one or none of the conflicting values. This is a no-win situation for the child because one of the parents will withhold approval. The children in the family have the option of accepting or rejecting any or all of the family values and are not bound by pure imitation of their parents. However, it is often true that the parent who sees his or her values mirrored in the child will come forth with more approval. Depending on the boundaries and rules of the family, children who choose different values may be allowed this differentiation, or they may defy a family rule that says family members must not be different.

Other conflicts arise when a female child is born into a family that values boys and needs an heir for the family business or when a male child is born to a family that needs a girl for balance or to satisfy a parent's psychological need.

As the family develops, it takes on an overall atmosphere, depending on the amount of conflict involved in balancing of roles, family values, and interaction rules. The interactions produce atmospheres that are friendly, competitive, or cooperative or environments that are hostile, autocratic, or permissive.

While it is important for counselors to understand the values of families and of the family members, it is also important for counselors to understand their own values. In the early years of family therapy the effort to understand each family member's perspective, treat each fairly, and not blame any one person for the family's problems ignored societal realities of power and gender differences in families. Recent criticisms of this pure systems thinking have caused family therapists to be more aware of the values and belief systems that they bring with them to the therapy session. Therapists do not check them at the door. For instance, in working with a married couple, the gender of the therapist is a fact that is easy for the couple to see and may make the same gender person of the couple feel more understood. Counselors who try to hide their belief that women are not treated equally in society are not actually being fair to the woman by assuming everyone is equal in the therapy. Counselors should be aware of their values and biases and address the inequality of men and women in the society with their clients in order to be most effective.

Alliances and Coalitions

Alliances are connections between two people in a family about an issue or a position. Mom and Dad, for instance, can be in alliance about their children's bedtimes. Two sisters can form an alliance as a power base to defend themselves against their brothers. Families, however, most often work in triangles that can operate in many ways: two against one, two for one, one pulled between two others, one bridging a gap between two others, and so forth. It is very difficult for two family members to talk for very long without "triangulating" a third member into the discussion. For instance, if two sisters are debating an issue, it is common to hear, "But Mom said . . ."

Coalitions form in a family when two people are allied against a third. When a wife is afraid to confront her husband directly because he hits her, she may entice her son to fight her battles with her husband for her. A daughter who feels that her father treats her mother badly may pick fights with him to even the score. Many coalitions are problematic because they cross generational boundaries and shift people into inappropriate subsystems.

In healthy families, alliances form in a horizontal pattern within generations. That is, grandparents have an alliance between themselves; parents have a marital and parental alliance; and the children have special alliances among themselves. These alliances can become vertical in nature if, for instance, there is a cross-generational alliance between one spouse and his or her parent or an alliance between a parent and a child that takes the place of marital closeness. "Whenever generational boundaries are consistently violated and members of one generation supply what should be received in another generation, pathology can be expected" (Haley, 1976, p. 39).

These crossgenerational alliances disturb the balance of the family by changing role definitions and pulling members of the family of origin into the dynamics and workings of the nuclear family. Marital issues cannot get resolved if they are only discussed between the wife and her mother. If the maternal grandmother was overprotective of her daughter and is reluctant to allow her to break away and become an independent person, this attachment may continue through their adult lives. If the daughter married and had children because the expectations of society were stronger than the overprotective tie with her mother, she may be very angry with her husband for taking her away from her mother and angry with her children for keeping her in a difficult position. This anger often is not shown directly but is manifested in the same overprotective parenting style with which the mother was raised. The mother's underlying wish to be rid of her husband and children must be repressed and covered with overconcern. Her anxiety and overprotection often produce symptoms in one of the children and may cause an overinvolvement between the parent and child, thus passing on a crossgenerational alliance and maladaptive behavior. Overprotective parenting has been identified as one of the parenting styles that increase the risk of children becoming alcoholic and drug addicted (Lawson, Peterson, & Lawson, 1983).

As the family of procreation develops as a social system, the spouses define themselves in terms of their relationships with their families of origin. Framo (1976) identified four categories of relationships with families of origin. The first category is the overinvolved relationship, which may resemble the enmeshed subsystems in the nuclear family. These families may live close together—maybe even down the street. The people in these families will often talk daily on the telephone. In some families that are forced to move apart, this daily phone contact may continue long distance. These families usually have very little social life outside their own confines and are closed off from the rest of society. The (other) spouse in these relationships may resent the spouse's overinvolvement or may welcome the relationship with a parent substitute. Difficulty occurs in these situations if grandparents give advice on home management, parenting, marital relationships, and areas that are typically roles of the marital and parental subsystems. Self-identity and self-worth as a spouse and parent are sabotaged with messages from the family of origin to the effect that "you are inadequate, and you need our help." What the family of origin may really mean is "we need you to need help so we can busy ourselves with your problems and not look at our own marital difficulties."

The second category is the superficial relationship. It involves infrequent, nonpersonal contact, usually revolving around ceremonies or family rituals. Framo believes that people in these relationships see themselves as having resolved their difficulties with their families in a mature way. They have used space, distance, and time to reduce conflict.

The third category occurs when people completely cut themselves off from their families. They proclaim that the absence of contact is the only way to maintain their own sanity and virtually deny the existence of other family members, treating them as if they were already dead. Framo believes that these people have the greatest chance of repeating the irrational patterns of their parents.

The last category is a positive one in which a person establishes an identity within the family of origin before leaving. This differentiation or individuation occurs when families have clear boundaries and parents can solve their own problems without projecting them onto their children or involving their children in the resolution process. These children consequently have no need to stay in the family or to escape its clutches. There is neither an overattachment nor an angry rebellion. These families do have a sense of belonging, but it is balanced with respect for independence. The parents in this type of family of origin love their children enough to let them leave. In transactional-analysis terms, these adult children relate more in adult-to-adult transactions with their parents than in adult-to-child transactions.

"In general, the more a nuclear family is emotionally cut off from parental families, the higher the incidence of problems and symptoms in the nuclear family" (Bowen, 1978, p. 264). Children from families with alcoholism and drug addiction may leave their families in many ways, but usually they feel like they never really belonged to the family, though they can never really leave. This task of leaving the family is crucial and has an effect on all subsequent relationships. Carter and McGoldrick (1980) stated,

> . . . we see a new family life cycle beginning at the stage of the 'unattached young adult,' whose adequate or inadequate completion of the primary task of coming to terms with his or her family of origin will most profoundly influence whom, when and how he or she marries and all succeeding stages of the new family life cycle. Adequate completion of this task would require that the young adult separate from the family of origin without cutting off or fleeing reactively to a substitute emotional refuge (p. 13).

Symptoms

The family roles, rules, boundaries, values, atmosphere, birth-order roles, alliances, and coalitions all combine to constitute the family homeostasis. Meeks and Kelly (1970) stated:

> Any attempt to shift the family equilibrium either from within (i.e., change in a member) or from without (i.e., input from a therapist) may evoke resistance from the family system which seeks to maintain the status quo (equilibrium). No matter how sick it may appear to the outside observer, the established equilibrium represents that family's attempt to minimize the threats of disruption and pain (p. 400).

In the alcoholic family, a balance is maintained with the presence of alcohol, and the family may resist any attempts to remove this part of the balance, though they may ask for the drinking to cease. They believe that change may be worse than the pain they are already suffering. At least they know how to cope with the problem, and the pattern of coping is familiar. Steinglass (1976) said, "the presence or absence of alcohol becomes the single most important variable determining the interactional behavior not only between the identified drinker and other members of the family but among non-drinking members of the family as well" (p. 106).

When families present themselves to a therapist, it is usually due to a symptom in one member resulting from a disturbance in family homeostasis, or it is a result of the suggestion of someone outside the family. Bowen (1978) defined three areas within the nuclear family in which symptoms are expressed: (1) marital conflict; (2) dysfunction in a spouse; and (3) projection to one or more children. Bowen labels this third area as the family-projection process, which he believes exists to some extent in all families. In this process, families project their problems onto their children, who become symptom bearers for the family. The symptom bearer often unconsciously volunteers for this position and may be instrumental in bringing a family into therapy where alcohol abuse or dysfunctional family patterns can be corrected; thus relieving the symptoms in the child. These children have a stake in saving their families and themselves in the symptom-bearer role. "Children, and adults as well, will forgo their own nature in order to save a parent from going crazy or in order to become the kind of person a parent (or parent representative) can love" (Framo, 1976, p. 207). Children may mirror the behavior of the parent to gain acceptance, but instead they receive rejection. The child's symptoms may be labeled as inappropriate; thus causing conflict and anxiety in the child.

Family therapy has evolved around the notion of the identified patient or the symptom bearer as the person who expresses a particular dysfunction for the whole family. Therefore, the context of the alcoholic or addict person is reframed as the alcoholic or addict family, with the alcoholic or addict as the identified patient. Steinglass (1976) pointed out that, uniquely, symptoms occur in the parental subsystem in the alcoholic or addict family. This is in contrast to the majority of dysfunctional families in which children are the symptom bearers. The adult alcoholic or addict, however, may have developed the seeds of his or her addiction as an adolescent in response to disruption in the family of origin and has just brought it into his or her current family as part of an intergenerational family process. This does not mean that the children are not symptomatic. Children of alcoholics or addicts suffer from a variety of problems.

The alcoholic or addict family may also be unique in the process of triangulation, in which the tension between two people is displaced onto an issue or a substance (e.g., alcohol or other drugs) instead of being projected onto the child. Unfortunately, the removal of the substance may result in a worsening of tension or another displacement. Posttreatment divorces are common.

Because of the intergenerational nature of addictions, however, there is usually more than one person in a family with substance abuse problems. It is not unusual for a family to have a drug-abusing son, an alcoholic father, an obese, compulsive overeater mother, two or three addicted grandparents, and a daughter with anorexia. Chemical dependency is a unique symptom in that it can take on a life of its own. Changing the family system may not stop the addictive behavior. Often the addiction needs to be treated in conjunction with changing the family patterns that maintain the addiction. It can be just as counterproductive to treat the family and ignore the addictive behavior as it is to treat the addiction and ignore the family dynamics and problems of other family members.

THEORIES OF FAMILY THERAPY

This section will provide a brief description of four schools of family therapy. As the field of family therapy developed, family therapists created their own models of doing family therapy. These models were influenced by the therapists' personalities; cultural backgrounds; previous training in psychology, psychiatry, or social work; social trends; and the Zeitgeist of the times. Historical events that led the way for these theorists included the child guidance movement, where usually children were seen with their mothers; the failure of psychoanalysis to treat juvenile delinquency and schizophrenia; and the ending of World War II with an emphasis on families reuniting. The pioneering schools of family therapy that are discussed in this section are Structural Family Therapy, Strategic Family Therapy, Intergenerational Family Therapy, and Experiential Family Therapy.

Structural Family Therapy

The founder of structural family therapy was Salvador Minuchin, a psychiatrist from Argentina. His theory grew out of his work with juvenile delinquent boys at the Wyltwyck School where he worked with poor, multiproblem families. These families required techniques that were concrete and action oriented. Minuchin would have these families enact their problems in the therapy sessions so he could see, firsthand, what was happening in the family in order to determine the organization and structure of the family. Structural family therapists are interested in the structure (rules, roles, and sequences of behaviors), subsystems, and boundaries of families. Minuchin was also concerned with environmental factors and found the family to be the interpreter of societal values, rules, and behaviors. Children, he felt, learn either functional or dysfunctional behaviors in the family through observing and interpreting the family structure.

The family structure is defined as transactions that are unique to a family— levels of authority, power structure, and mutual expectations. The structure is created with the marriage and the agreement of the spouses to satisfy each other's needs. The evolution of spousal functions creates the core of the nuclear family. The structure changes when the first child is born and parental functions are negotiated. With this child rides the potential for family growth or possible destruction. If the family cannot clearly differentiate the spousal and parental functions, dysfunction in the family may occur. This theory is similar to Bowen's concepts of the family projection process and crossgenerational alliances.

Within the family structure, Minuchin defines *subsystems* as one or more family members who share something in common: generation, sex, interests, or family duties. He defines *boundaries* as the rules of the subsystems that are either rigid, diffuse, or clear. Dysfunction occurs with rigid boundaries that create isolation and discourage family communication, or with diffuse boundaries that do not clearly define areas of authority or responsibility, as when children are running the family. These diffuse boundaries discourage individual responsibility and promote random and confused problem solving.

Minuchin's Structural Therapy categorizes the family's method of experiencing stress in four ways:

1. Stress can be caused in one family member by someone outside the family, such as the father's boss, which is then transmitted to other family members.
2. Stress may be caused in the entire family by an outside force, such as economic conditions or a move to a new location.
3. Stress can be caused by life crisis transitions, such as the birth of a child, a child attending school for the first time, adolescence, a child leaving home (particularly the last one), or midlife crises of the parents, which may coincide with adolescence of the children.
4. Stress may result from the presence of a chronically ill person in the family, including an alcoholic or addict.

Minuchin feels that dysfunction in the family occurs when there are unclear levels of authority and power, when expectations are misunderstood, when there is confusion as to the functions of subgroups, or when rigid or diffuse boundaries exist in the family.

The goal of Structural Family Therapy is to alter the family structure so that the family can solve its problems. The therapist alters boundaries and realigns subsystems to change the behavior and experiences of each of the family members (Nichols & Schwartz, 1995). A common goal is to help parents function as a single parental unit without division or conflict. Parents, also, need to be in charge of the children and not act as their buddies or peers.

There are three main overlapping processes in Structural Family Therapy (Minuchin, 1974). First, the therapist joins the family as a director of the therapy process. Minuchin has referred to this as joining the family like a wise uncle. The second process is mapping the underlying structure of the family. Minuchin has devised a system of symbols to graphically map out the family structure, boundaries, and interactions. The third process is the intervention to change the family structure. There are seven steps that the structural therapist follows in doing family therapy.

1. **Joining and Accommodating**—This is the process of the therapist's connecting with the family and establishing rapport. The therapist greets each member and uses his or her position to respect the authority of the parents by first asking them to describe the problem. Children are also respected and given a chance to tell their perspectives. Therapists try to match the families tone and way of speaking, using their language—even their coping mannerisms and postures. This is an important part of the therapy. The therapist must be accepted by the family before they will allow him or her to change them.

2. **Working with Interaction**—This is the process of getting family members to talk with one another so the therapist can observe the interactions. This process is called *enactment*. The therapist may give a directive, for instance, for the parents to have a conversation about their concerns for their son, or may have a parent try to get a child to behave. This gives the therapist a chance to see how they behave at home; to observe boundaries and rules for behavior.

3. **Diagnosing**—This is a process that begins with the first contact with the family. Hypotheses about family structure and interaction are formulated with the first phone call. The therapist carefully watches what the family does, where they sit, who they talk to, how they talk, and what they say. The goal of the diagnosis is to move the family from seeing only one person as having a problem to spreading the problem to all family members and then to finding a solution that will benefit all family members. The diagnosis is established in the first session but is refined and revised as more data are gathered and interventions are tried.

4. **Highlighting and Modifying Interactions**—Once unhealthy patterns have been diagnosed, the therapist must point them out and begin to change them. This can be done by using the therapist's directive position to intensify the problematic interaction and react strongly to it. The other method of modifying interactions is to highlight the times when the family is working in a positive way and get them to do more.

5. **Boundary Making**—Structural family therapists are concerned with altering boundaries so that they are clear. If boundaries are diffuse and relationships enmeshed, therapists find ways of marking boundaries. This can be done in the sessions by changing where people are sitting or between sessions by assigning tasks. If the daughter, for instance, always sits between the parents and seems overinvolved in their relationship, the therapist might ask her to change seats with one of her parents, putting the parents together, with the daughter outside the subsystem. Therapists also

block family members who interrupt others; thus marking a clear boundary. Homework assignments might include assigning the couple to go on a date by themselves. Rigid boundaries can be opened up by connecting family members. During a session, the therapist might ask family members who are distant from the family to become more involved in the process of the session as well as challenge conflict avoidance by family members. A homework assignment might include having a noninvolved father spend time with his daughter. The goal of this process is not only to create clear boundaries, but it can also move a family from thinking about their problems in a linear way to helping them understand circular causality and how all of the family members influence each other.

6. **Unbalancing**—Families become stuck in patterned behaviors that keep them from solving their problems. Unbalancing is an attempt to arbitrarily add importance or weight to one person's perspective in order to make a shift in the process and shake the homeostatic balance. Although this may seem like the therapist is making a value judgment about who is right, it is done simply to shake things up. The therapist takes turns showing preference with other family members at other times to even things up.

7. **Challenging the Family's Assumptions**—As part of changing the family structure, structural therapists may use a cognitive or educational approach to normalize behaviors that the family may see as terrible or to reframe behavior or problems with a positive twist. A child, whom the parents describe as "into everything," may be described by the therapist as "bright and inquisitive." It is the same behavior with different labels. Sometimes the therapist will teach the family about their structure and what needs to be changed to help them see themselves in a different light.

Structural Family Therapy is the most common family approach used in the treatment of chemical dependency. Research in treatment outcome has indicated that this method of treatment is very successful with drug addicts, adolescents with drug abusing problems, and anorexic children. Stanton and Todd (1992) compared a structural-strategic model of family therapy with a placebo condition and individual therapy in treating drug addicts. The level of positive change and symptom reduction in the family therapy condition was double that achieved in the other conditions, and the changes were maintained at six and twelve month follow-up evaluations.

Treatment outcome studies have also been conducted using family therapy based on a structural approach in treating adolescent drug abuse. The Purdue Brief Therapy Model (Lewis, Piercy, Sprenkle, & Trepper, 1991; Piercy & Frankel, 1989) was one of the projects that integrated family therapies that had previously demonstrated their effectiveness and applied this model to adolescent substance abuse. The models included theory from Stanton and Todd (1982), who demonstrated the effectiveness of structural-strategic family therapy with adult heroin addicts; Szapocznik and his colleagues (Szapocznik, et al., 1983, 1986), at the University of Miami School of Medicine, who found strategic therapy effective in decreasing adolescent drug abuse; Minuchin and his colleagues (1978), who found that structural family therapy decreased symptoms of psychosomatic illnesses such as asthma and anorexia nervosa; Alexander (1974) and his colleagues, who used functional family therapy to work with juvenile delinquents; and Patterson (1982) and his colleagues, who repeatedly demonstrated the effectiveness of behavioral contracting with delinquent adolescents. This brief twelve-session model was geared to help change the entire family into a healthier supportive environment. Its goal was to stem the current drug abuse of an adolescent and prevent the development of drug abuse by a younger sibling.

This model was compared to a family drug-education program, with training in Parenting Skills (TIPS) Program and individual-based drug counseling of adolescents. The results indicated that the two brief, family-based drug interventions together appeared to reduce the drug use of nearly one-half (46%) of the adolescents who received them. In commenting on this success Lewis (1991) stated:

> We suspect that this success was due partly to the fact that both of these outpatient interventions focused on the systemic treatment of *entire* family groups. In contrast, however, the family therapy intervention seems to have been more effective in significantly reducing adolescent drug use for a greater percentage of the adolescents (54.6%) than the family education intervention (37.5%). An even more dramatic result of the study was this: Although more than twice as many adolescents in the family therapy condition (40%) were hard drug users at their pretest, *twice as many of these hard users (44.4%) moved to no use at all* by the posttest time, compared to only the 25% of the hard users in the family education condition who moved to no drug use (pp. 2–3).

A similar adolescent treatment outcome study was conducted by Joanning and his associates (Joanning, Quinn, Thomas, & Mullen, 1992). They compared Family Systems Therapy to Adolescent Group Therapy and Family Drug Education. The Family Systems Therapy was based on the structural-strategic model that Stanton and Todd (1982) used with adult drug addicts. The Family Systems Therapy produced twice as many apparently drug-free clients (54%) as the Family Drug Education model (28%) and three times as many as the Adolescent Group Therapy approach (16%).

Strategic Family Therapy

Strategic Family Therapy grew out of the Communications Model that was developed by the Mental Research Institute (MRI) in Palo Alto, California.

Gregory Bateson began working with interpersonal communications in schizo-phrenic families and applying cybernetics to family therapy. Bateson was joined in this project by Jay Haley, John Weakland, and Don Jackson who developed a belief that communication between members was the most important factor of family life (Bateson, Jackson, Haley, & Weakland, 1956). These theorists believed that blocked forms of communication in the individual were symptoms of overall dysfunctional communication in the family. They proposed that dysfunctional communication patterns produced family tension that was projected onto one or more family members.

The MRI group developed the theory of the "double bind" and later related it to clinical work. The double bind is a communication pattern involving a victim or scapegoat and a message sender. The sender gives two messages at the same time. Often one is verbal, while the other is nonverbal. In order for these messages to be defined as a double bind, they must be conflicting and be repeatedly sent over a long period of time. One message must carry a negative connotation or punishment message (which may seem life threatening), while the other is more abstract and contradictory. The victims are trapped in this pattern by their need for love and approval.

Haley (1976) developed a philosophy involving personal alliances in the family. In the healthy family, he noticed mutually satisfying and need-fulfilling relationships. In the dysfunctional family, he found confused communication patterns and shifting alliances. Haley hypothesized that confused, out-of-order communication patterns can lead to misinterpretation, assumption, guessing, and misunderstanding among family members. If children cannot interpret what their parents' needs and wishes are, they certainly cannot fulfill them. Haley also found that crossgenerational alliances produced confused communication and misunderstanding in the power hierarchy of the family. He believed that change in communication patterns and alliances in the family would change the overall functioning of the family and reduce symptoms in the symptom bearer.

Haley was highly influenced by the work of Milton Erickson and Salvador Minuchin as well as that of Gregory Bateson. It is the combination of these influences of communication theory, cybernetics, Ericksonian hypnosis, and structural theory that became Haley's strategic approach. Strategic therapists are more concerned with changing a family's behavior than in changing their understanding; consequently, they are very interested in technique (Nichols & Schwartz, 1995). The goal of therapy is to resolve the presenting problem. They are not interested in insight or understanding. The strategic therapist takes on most of the responsibility for change in the family, and devises novel strategies for bringing about change. Strategic therapists have been criticized for being manipulative and for deceiving the family, but they have responded to these criticisms with treatment outcome data indicating the power of their techniques in producing change.

Strategic therapists borrow concepts from cybernetics and are interested in positive feedback loops, family rules, creating second-order change, and reframing behavior to expose the "function of the symptom." This means the adaptive function that the problem serves in the family and why it is so hard to give up. This is another way of trying to understand why people do things that are apparently opposite the goal they are trying to achieve. Strategic therapists use paradoxical techniques to bypass a family or a family member's resistance to change. A simple paradox is prescribing the symptom. If, for instance, a daughter is doing poorly in school, the therapist might suggest that she continue to fail at her school work. If she continues to fail, she has followed the therapist's directive. If she begins to succeed, that intervention has also worked. If there is strong resistance to change, sometimes going with the resistance will produce more change that confronting it directly. If the therapist believes that the daughter is failing because it gets her mother involved with her around homework and studies and takes her mother's focus away from a failing marriage or her alcoholic husband, the therapist may say, "You really need to continue to fail at school, because your mother feels needed when you do," or the therapist might compliment the daughter for being so sensitive to her mother's need and being willing to sacrifice her school work for her mother. Haley also believes that the symptoms that are presented by the symptom bearer are metaphors for what is really wrong with the family or the marriage, and without changing the family structure, the symptom will either return or change to another one. Another type of paradoxical message is the restraint of change. Since families are used to their homeostatic balance, even if it is unhealthy, change may be very frightening for them. The therapist can acknowledge this ambivalence to change by instructing the family to go slow with change, because it can be dangerous. There is an art to devising paradoxical interventions, and they should not be used if a straightforward directive will be followed or if the therapist has not had sufficient training and supervision in these techniques.

Haley has developed a four-stage process for a first session of Strategic Family Therapy, which he calls Problem Solving Therapy. The stages are (1) social; (2) problem; (3) interaction; and (4) goal setting. This method would be useful for families of recovering alcoholics and addicts, families where alcoholism or other drug addiction is not the presenting problem and is not the central issue of therapy, or with families where the adolescent child is abusing alcohol or other drugs. If the family's presenting problem is not addiction and the therapist redefines the problem as alcohol or other drug abuse, the family may become anxious or may feel unheard and pull out of therapy. It is important to initially begin with what the family has identified as their problem but without forgetting about the addiction. If the therapist can remain flexible and spontaneous, an initial solvable problem can be a good starting point, and then the therapy can shift to the addictive behavior or recovery issues. Usually, the presenting problem can be easily linked to active abuse or unresolved problems from previous addictive behavior.

The beginning period allows the family to experience the "familiness" of their problems. The entire family should attend the early sessions, and the network of support people who are involved with the family are useful for the initial interview. Sometimes it is useful to include the alcoholic's or addict's sponsor. Strategic therapists, however, will work with whomever comes to the sessions.

The first stage is the social stage, and it establishes a comfort level and provides a naturalizing of the social environment. Family members are allowed to sit where they wish. The therapist has a greeting exchange with family members to get their names, ages, and additional innocuous information. The idea is to demonstrate that each person is important and can contribute to the session. At this point, it can be determined who is missing from the family and if any members of the extended family would be important contributors.

The issue of blame may arise at this time with the alcoholic family. Either the family is uncomfortable with the unstated alcohol problem and blames a child for their presence in therapy, or the family continues to scapegoat the alcoholic or addict and remains uninterested in his or her contributions to the family problems. The therapist should focus on the here and now and initially avoid discussions of specific problems. The family will present a dominant mood that the therapist should attempt to match.

With parents and children all in one room, parent-child interactions, discipline modalities, and sibling relationships may also be noted. This, however, only represents how family members act in front of others and may be different from behavior at home. Also, at this time parents may be openly in disagreement, in agreement, or overly agreeable about the child's problems. One of the spouses may be reluctant to participate in the session.

Additionally, the therapist can observe the seating arrangement to see if the identified patient is isolated or sitting between the parents or if the parents have an allied child near them.

It is best at this time to keep all conclusions about the family interaction tentative, and therapists should not share their observations with the family. At some level, the family is aware of these dynamics and would see this as an invasion. Haley (1976) said, "To point out something like a seating arrangement is asking the family to concede something they might prefer not to concede, and thus that action could arouse defensiveness and cause unnecessary difficulties in the therapy" (p. 19).

The second stage is the problem stage, and it begins with an inquiry about the family's view of the problem that has brought them in for therapy. It signals the end of the social atmosphere stage and indicates that it is time to get down to business. It may be very confusing to the alcoholic or addict family to be in family therapy when it is obvious to them who has the problem. The therapist must clarify why the entire family has been asked to participate. The problem orientation can remain, but the therapist may state that it is important to get everyone's opinion of the problem. Usually the therapist has some prior knowledge of the family from a referral source or from the family member who called for the appointment. If the family seems secretive, it is beneficial for the therapist to share this prior information with the family.

During questioning about the problem area, the therapist needs to decide whom to ask and in what way. If the family is simply asked what the problem is, the therapist may receive a long history of all of the negative behavior of the identified patient. The therapist can offer hope for change and ask questions like, "What do you want to change in your family?" To assess what caused the family to ask for help, the therapist may ask, "How did the decision get made to call for this appointment?" or "What has happened recently that motivated you to call for this appointment?" Haley (1976) suggested, "As a rule, the more general and ambiguous the inquiry of the therapist is, the more room there is for the family members to display their point of view" (p. 21).

It is difficult to present these questions to the family as a whole, and usually there is a therapist bias in selecting who is addressed. If the therapists are chemical dependency counselors, their sympathies may be with the alcoholic or addict, who seems victimized by a nagging spouse. If the therapists are child oriented, they may be angry at the parents, who have neglected and hurt the children. A decision about who to address can best be made by first examining the family hierarchy of power and influence. Usually one parent is more motivated to work than the other, and one parent has more power to get the family to return for further sessions. Haley (1976) believes that the person who can get the family back to therapy should be treated with respect, but the underinvolved parent should be engaged first.

Sometimes the most detached family member is a child. In this instance, it is best to start talking with the person who is least involved and sits furthest away and then work through the family to the most involved member. It is inadvisable to begin with the identified patient, as it may look like the therapist is blaming him or her. Identified patients are used to getting attention when the family is anxious, and this pattern must be broken by the therapist. Haley (1976) said, "Every therapist must watch out for a tendency to turn to, or on, the problem person in a benevolent way when he or she (the therapist) is anxious and under stress" (p. 25).

In addition, the problem that brought the family to therapy must be clearly stated and not minimized. If there is a tendency to extend the social stage and not deal with issues, the family will be confused. If alcohol and/or other drug abuse is the presenting problem and a direct discussion of this issue is skirted, the problem will grow in magnitude and take on the aura of being unmentionable. Even if the therapist does not agree that the presenting problem is the main issue, it can be used as a lever to create change. For instance, if the presenting problem is child oriented but the therapist is certain of marital conflict, the marital relationship can be approached by addressing disagreement on parenting issues. Haley (1976) stated, "Usually family members say that one person is the problem. The therapist's job is to think of the problem in terms of more than one person. By thinking that way he [or she] is most able to bring about change" (p. 33).

As the problem is being presented, the therapist should simply listen to the family and observe behaviors. The therapist should avoid making interpretations, giving advice, or encouraging emotional reactions with inquiries about feelings rather than facts. One member of the family must not be allowed to monopolize the discussion. The therapist must have enough control of the session to allow everyone to speak. If the therapist is not in control, things will go as they have in the past, and change will not occur.

If the family requested therapy because of a problem with a child, the chances are good that the parents may be talking metaphorically about marital problems. If the mother says her daughter is unaffectionate, it is possible that the mother is also saying her husband is unaffectionate. These hypotheses should not be shared with the family. There is a reason that things are not talked about directly, and the child's behavior should not be outwardly connected with the marital situation. If the problem statement is left open and ambiguous, it will allow for these dynamics to be expressed to the therapist indirectly through safe subjects.

Alcoholic and addict families have many areas that have become forbidden to discuss, and the children may be protecting the parents by withholding information or by taking the blame for family troubles. The alcoholic or addict couple may be unable to talk about certain subjects in a sober state but can let the therapist know they exist in indirect ways. The therapist can observe all the levels of communication and interaction and can begin to think about the family's problems in a systems context. The therapist does not have to convince the family of this approach; the family will experience it in the process of treatment.

The third stage that Haley described is the interaction stage. Here, the therapist begins to direct people to speak to one another, rather than having all comments directed to the therapist. At this stage, family members may be able to act out some of their problems. A role-play situation of family interactions around a problem can be set up, allowing the therapist to observe the structure of the family and the interaction patterns.

The fourth stage is the goal-setting stage, which requires a more detailed definition of the problem. The desired changes are defined, and a clear therapeutic contract is negotiated. In order for the family to begin change, it is necessary to put the problem into terms that are solvable, observable, and measurable. This is important for observing therapy outcomes and for giving the family a clear direction for working. At this stage, the therapist can ask specific questions about the symptoms, such as when they occur, if they are constant or periodic, if they come on quickly or gradually, or how intense they are. It is useful to find out what everyone does in reaction to a problem. If the problem is drinking, questions can be asked about shifts in everyone's behavior and how it is different from their behavior when the alcoholic or addict is sober. In families who present a problem in an area other than substance abuse, the goal of the family may not be to stop the drinking or the using of one member. If the therapist insists on abstinence instead of the family's goal, they may leave treatment. The therapist should instead see this as an opportunity to carefully tie the presenting problems to times of active use or to times that are complicated by the substance abuse. This is similar to an intervention of several sessions. But if abstinence is the goal, it is easily observable and can be defined in terms of family behavior. The alcoholic or addict may also be in the victim or scapegoat role in the family, and it would be dangerous to try to convince the family otherwise at this stage. If the therapist has been involved with the individual treatment of the alcoholic or addict, the temptation may arise to defend the alcoholic or addict and fight the rest of the family. If the therapist works too hard to free the alcoholic or addict from this negative position, the family may have to make the alcoholic or addict out to be worse, to show the therapist that they were correct. The therapist needs to listen to the pain of all of the family members concerning the effects of living with an alcoholic or addict and not be too quick to explain all of his or her behavior away with the disease model, which leaves family members with anger about behaviors of the alcoholic or addict, such as affairs or abuse, with no outlet except their feeling guilty about justified anger. A situation like this may lead to attempts to sabotage early recovery or retaliate in a more covert way. The same thing is true of a family who has a scapegoat child or adolescent that the therapist wants to save.

In this first session, the therapist is working to join the family by making everyone feel at ease, allowing everyone to contribute, involving everyone with one another, and including everyone in the decision-making process. If done in a genuine manner, this joining allows the therapist to enter the family and to begin to bring about change from within.

If the family seems hesitant about committing to a course of therapy, it may relieve their anxiety to set a certain number of sessions after which an assessment of progress will occur and a decision to continue can be made.

Intergenerational Family Therapy

Although structural and strategic approaches to family therapy are useful in working with chemically dependent families, the process of addiction in families is most clearly understood from an intergenerational perspective. The only definite statement that the chemical dependency field can make is that chemical dependency and other addictions run in families, generation after generation; more in some than in others. Whether this is caused by nature (genetics) or nurture (environment) is really not as important as how to intervene in a family problem that has a tremendous history.

Intergenerational family therapists share an interest in family dynamics across generations and come from a background in psychodynamic theory. Their interest in history is fueled by the belief that people's pasts influence their current behavior and relationships. Three pioneers in the school developed their theories at approximately the same time and were influenced by each other. They are Murray Bowen, Ivan Boszormenyi-Nagy, and James Framo. Bowen was also influenced by biological science, as mentioned earlier. He developed a theoretical model called Bowen Therapy with six interlocking concepts: (1) differentiation of self; (2) triangles; (3) nuclear family emotional process; (4) family projection process; (5) multigenerational transmission process; and (6) sibling position. He added two concepts in the 1970s: emotional cutoff and societal emotional process.

Nagy and Framo worked together at Eastern Pennsylvania Psychiatric Institute developing a process of working with schizophrenic families. Nagy developed a contextual family therapy, which was based on loyalty, trust, and ethics in family relationships (Boszormenyi-Nagy & Spark, 1973). He emphasized the loyalty commitments people have to their families of origin, which is particularly useful in understanding what appears as undeserved loyalty in substance abusing families. Framo was influenced by Bowen, but he drew the foundations for his theory from object-relations theory. Framo brings adult children together with their parents and siblings for intensive family-of-origin therapy sessions (Framo, 1991). The goal of these sessions is to heal old wounds, correct family mythology, and to help the adult children relate on an adult-to-adult level with their parents, instead of regressing to a child in their presence. This is similar to Bowen's concept of differentiation from the family of origin; however, Bowen coaches clients to return to their families and practice a nonreactive response to the presence of their family of origin. Framo brings them all together in the therapy sessions.

Because Bowen directly addressed the intergenerational transmission of alcoholism, this section will cover his theory more in depth. This model can be used with individuals in treatment and is particularly effective with adults who were raised in alcoholic or addict families. Bowen (1974) saw the transmission process that occurs in alcoholic families as involved with levels of differentiation of self in the family. This is a function of the relationship that the child has with his or her parents, and the way the child's unresolved emotional attachment to his or her parents is handled in young adulthood. This model of family theory and therapy, that emerged during the birth of the family movement, defines symptoms in one member as a function of the family system of more than one generation (Bowen, 1974).

This theory can be used to understand the etiology of alcoholism in the family (Bowen, 1974). Bowen's theory was developed during his work with schizophrenic families. He began seeing distinctions in affective states and cognitive processes that led to his *scale of differentiation* or the degree that individuals can differentiate themselves from their family of origin. This early work defined the family as a system that is operated by the same principles as other systems, such as societies, corporations, or institutions. Thus, the family is a system in that a change in one family member would be followed automatically by a change in another. Bowen was willing to work with the most motivated individual in the family to bring about change. He further believed that a person's current behavior is caused by a transference process that inappropriately applied past history and behaviors to present situations. Bowen's initial focus was on the mother-daughter relationship, which fostered his theory of the *family projection process*—the projecting of the problems of the parents onto the child. When he began to add grandparents to his sessions, he developed his theories on *multigenerational transmission*—how symptoms or family patterns were handed down through the generations.

Bowen observed families that exhibited feelings of oneness or lack of individual identities among the members. He further found varying degrees of this oneness in families who seemed overly dependent on one another and labeled it "stuck togetherness." This stuck togetherness was the families' defense against crises or tensions; under threat, the family members pulled together to restore balance. A delicate balance was created, with changes in one member affecting all others. If self-destructive behaviors, such as substance abuse, helped maintain balance, the families would tolerate them.

In this system, the smallest unit is a *triangle*. When two people feel stress they bring in a third person to stabilize the unit. In alcoholic families the third member of the triangle can be the alcohol itself. In states of calm, there are two comfortable sides of the triangle and one conflictual side. Over a period of time, these roles become fixed. When conflict occurs between the two comfortable members, they project conflict onto the third, who develops symptoms in a family projection process. A familiar example is the mother, father, and child triangle. When conflict occurs in the marriage, tension rises in the mother and is projected onto the child who will accept it to maintain the family oneness. In this case, the father may be the adaptive spouse who gives up his identity for the sake of the marriage and supports the other spouse's need as well as her projection to the child. This father may also withdraw from the conflict by working long hours or drinking with his friends in the local tavern. There are several other patterns of response to stress or conflict that might occur among the three members as well.

The child selected for this projection is often the one closest to the mother. He or she may be the oldest, the only child, a child born during crisis, or one born with a defect. When this child leaves the family, another will take his or her place. When all the children have left, the marital problems may come to the fore, or the projection is passed on to others outside the family.

The adolescent who leaves this family will create a pseudoindependence based on anxiety that will be transmitted to that person's marital relationship in a multigenerational transmission process. Therefore, the patterns of the family of origin will be repeated in the nuclear family.

Families with high degrees of stuck togetherness produce children who distance themselves from the family in an attempt to gain self-identity. They may: (1) become rebellious adolescents or withdraw destructively; (2) gain physical distance by moving away from home; or (3) emotionally distance themselves, which may also create physical distance. These children never differentiate themselves from their parents and are consequently unable to become problem solvers in crisis situations. Some of these children may become substance abusers who say, "I can't take pressure or I can't cope; I'm an alcoholic."

Bowen devised a scale for determining self-differentiation in family members. This scale ranges from 0 to 100. The range from 0 to 25 encompasses those who are dominated by their emotions. Essentially, they lack a self; their only feeling of self-worth comes from others. The two rules of behavior for these people are: (1) Does it make me feel good? or (2) Will others approve of me? Moving up the scale, differentiation is added to this profile to create people who begin to use intellectual processes in decision making and who gain personal opinions. The upper half of the scale reflects goal-orientation and encompasses those who can respond with rational principles and have less need to be defensive. They have achieved a self with a high degree of differentiation from their families. These people are able to achieve intimate relationships and are problem solvers.

In Bowen's words, self-differentiation "is the degree to which the person has a 'solid self' or solidly held principles by which he lives his life. This is in contrast to a 'pseudoself' made up of inconsistent life principles that can be corrupted by coercion for the gain of the moment. The 'differentiation of self' is roughly equivalent to the concept of emotional maturity" (Bowen, 1974, p. 263). This rating is based on the amount of a person's differentiation from his or her parents, the type of relationship that exists with the parents, and the quality of emotional separation from the parents in young adulthood.

Bowen states that people with similar scores tend to be attracted to one another, and they pass on similar degrees of differentiation to their children. The child with the lowest degree of differentiation is at highest risk for the family projection process and later problems. It is common for people to flee their families, blaming their parents for their problems and seeking happiness in their marriages. These two pseudoselves fuse together and create impairments in one of the spouses. The most common way that couples handle this marital fusion is by one spouse's becoming dominant and the other adaptive. The adaptive one becomes a "no-self." "If this pattern is continued long enough, the adaptive one is vulnerable to some kind of chronic dysfunction, which can be physical illness, emotional illness, or a social dysfunction such as drinking, the use of drugs, or irresponsible behavior" (Bowen, 1978, p. 263). Families can use marital conflict or the projection of their immaturity onto the children as ways to adapt. This selection of adaptive patterns is not a conscious process. These patterns were programmed into the spouses by their families of origin.

Bowen believed that there is a continuum of behaviors that lead to alcoholism. On one end are the persons who deny the emotional attachment to their families of origin and maintain a superindependent posture. The actual level of emotional attachment, however, is intense. As these persons become increasingly emotionally isolated they find relief in alcohol. On the other end of the continuum are the persons who are so attached to their parents that they are never able to manage a productive life. These people become "de-selfed" in the emotional fusion with the family of origin. They deny their intense need for their parents and begin drinking heavily early in life. Bowen states that most people with drinking problems fall somewhere in between these two extremes. "A high percentage of adult alcoholism is in people who are married, and who have the same kind of emotional attachment in marriage that they had in their parental families" (Bowen, 1978, p. 265).

Treatment would involve helping the patient differentiate from their family of origin and reduce the emotional reactivity to this system. The goal would be to help these patients create their own nuclear families with a minimum of the multigenerational transition process. This is a lengthy process, usually transpiring between the therapist and the family member wishing to differentiate from the family of origin. The therapist coaches the patient in this work with their family of origin.

Framo (1972) described a similar process of symptom development. He stated, "symptoms are concomitants of the universal conflict between individuation, autonomous strivings, and loyalty to the family relationship system" (Framo, 1972, p. 127). In alcoholic families it is difficult to truly belong and nearly impossible to individuate in a healthy way. The effects of living in a disruptive, alcoholic family system may transmit alcoholism into a second or third generation.

Bowen therapists, in contrast to strategic approaches, are less interested in technique than in theory. Bowen therapy does, however, have some overall therapeutic interventions that are used to achieve the goal of differentiation. Therapists construct a multigenerational family map of symbols called a genogram, that includes ages, marriages, divorces, deaths, and other important events in family life. These symbols have been expanded to indicate close, conflicted, or cut-off relationships; addictions; and other intergenerational problems and patterns (McGoldrick & Gerson, 1985). The purpose of this genogram is to help clients see what patterns they are acting out from previous generations. When clients have an awareness of their heritage, they are then free to chose to repeat those patterns or change them (Figure 6–1). Bowen also advocated the therapist's taking a nonreactive position in therapy to lower the reactivity of the client or family. He also taught his clients to be nonreactive to their families by helping them distinguish between thinking and feeling and by using "I" statements. This helps clients take responsibility for their reactions and thoughts and reduces

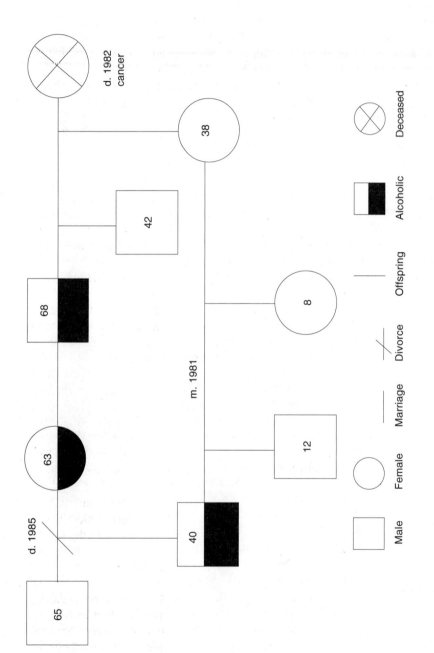

Figure 6–1   Sample of a Genogram

blaming. An example of an I statement could be, "When you call me a drunk, I get angry and defensive. I wish you would stop it."

David Treadway (1989) adapted Bowen's model for working with couples with active alcoholism. He chose this model because of the extreme emotional reactivity in these couples and their inability to take personal responsibility for their behavior. He has outlined a six-stage model for working with these couples.

Stage 1 is *disengagement.* The goal of this stage is to shift the responsibility back to the drinker and to help the spouse change standard responses to the substance abuse, which has helped maintain it. He believes that the chemical abuse is inextricably intertwined with the couple's behavior pattern. This reflects the strategic notion that families develop a circular pattern of behavior around a problem that often becomes part of the problem. He also believes that the spouse may be the most motivated person to change and that a change in his or her behavior will force a shift in the alcoholic's behavior. Another goal of this stage is to get the drinker to stop by changing the spouse's behavior, referring him or her to Al-Anon, or creating an intervention. In a way, he is firing the spouse from trying to get the drinker to quit, and he takes on this role, freeing the spouse to take responsibility for his or her own recovery.

Stage 2 is *differentiation.* The goal of this stage is to help the family tolerate the discomfort and confusion surrounding sobriety and to reduce their unrealistic expectations about early recovery (Treadway, 1989). Treadway acknowledges that couples who have been organized around the substance will be destabilized by the removal of the substance from the balance. Spouses also become more aware of the pain and hurt associated with the struggle with the substance abuse. Treadway uses a Bowen model at this stage to lower the reactivity in sessions by becoming the third point of the triangle and running all of the conversation through him. He does not allow the spouses to attack one another and works to break the fusion of the couple. This is similar to doing individual therapy with the spouse watching. He hopes to develop empathy in each spouse for the other.

Stage 3 is *negotiation.* Usually, couples in early recovery have difficulty negotiating and problem solving because one spouse has been overfunctioning in most areas and the other has been subordinated and treated like a child. Since the overfunctioning spouse has developed some sense of worth, if not martyrdom, from the overfunctioning, he or she may be reluctant to give up this hierarchical position. However, the other spouse has to find something to do in the family besides drink. Treadway teaches the couple how to put their feelings aside and work effectively together. He acts as an arbitrator in this process.

Stage 4 is *conflict management.* One of the most common dynamics of alcoholic or addict families is the ever-present conflict. Conflict can occur during dry stages or wet stages. Substance abuse either dampens conflict or fuels it. Couples in early recovery try to avoid open conflict at all costs because they fear it will lead to drinking or using (Treadway, 1989). Couples need to learn how to tolerate conflict without letting it escalate out of control. Treadway helps couples learn to tolerate unresolved conflict and to fight fairly.

Stage 5 is the *resolution of the past*. Couples who have been struggling with substance abuse for years have a large storage vault full of hurt, anger, and resentment. As they begin to acknowledge the wasted years of dealing with addiction, unresolved pain from childhood may also emerge in this grief process. Treadway's goals for this stage are to unite the spouses around the shared pain and loss, instead of allowing the typical adversarial blaming of each other, as well as to help the couple come to a position of acceptance. Acceptance is not necessarily forgiveness because some things may not be forgivable, especially physical abuse, sexual abuse, affairs, or refusal to participate in sex (Treadway, 1989).

Stage 6 is *intimacy*. Intimacy and sexual behaviors are just as intertwined with substance abuse as is conflict. Sexual dysfunction and sexual abuse are common coexisting problems with chemical dependency. Intoxication may be connected with intimate behavior or avoidance of intimacy, and fear of intimacy can be a problem for adults who were raised in chemically dependent families. It is possible that neither spouse has ever seen a positive model of intimacy in a couple relationship. Treadway (1989) helps couples "separate reasonable expectations for intimacy from attempts to make up for unresolved family-of-origin needs. Coming to terms with their old grief in relationship to their original families is often a prerequisite to setting realistic expectations for their couple relationships" (p. 96). During this last stage of the treatment model, Treadway removes himself from the third point of the triangle and empowers the couple to take more leadership in the therapy and to become more self-reliant.

Couples may not go through all of the stages of the model or may come and go in therapy over a several-year period. This is, however, a good example of how Bowen theory and a focus on intergenerational issues can be used in treating chemical dependency.

Experiential Family Therapy

"Experiential family therapists focus on the subjective needs of the individual in the family and work to facilitate a family process that will address the individuality of each member" (Hanna & Brown, 1995, p. 13). They have elements of the intergenerational theorist, but they put more emphasis on emotional expression and growth. They also resemble the structural and strategic therapist in their focus on the present interactions in the therapy session. Experiential family therapy drew from individual humanistic theories that emphasized here-and-now experiences in therapy, Gestalt therapy, and encounter groups, as well. The arts and psychodrama impacted on techniques of family sculpting and family drawing.

The two most influential therapists in this school were Virginia Satir and Carl Whitaker. Satir began seeing families in her private practice in Chicago, and later joined Bateson, Haley, Jackson, and Weakland in Palo Alto, California at the Mental Research Institute, where she added her perspectives to the Communications Model. She saw communications as a key factor in functional and dysfunctional relationships and believed that homeostasis was more valuable to a family than was an individual member's well-being. Satir also stated that parents bring their faulty patterns of communication to the marriage from their families of origin and that children learn these patterns in a multigenerational process. Satir's version of the Communications Model, however, grew to be a more holistic health model dedicated to self-esteem building, personal growth, and spirituality. Satir was a dynamic, nurturing therapist who genuinely cared for her fellow human beings. She was a master at creating peak experiences in therapy, with her gift of a healing touch that created family dramas in the therapy sessions. Her technique of *family sculpting* has been adapted by the chemical dependency field to help families experience their connections, boundaries, and hierarchies.

Satir developed four basic role types that family members typically adopt when dealing with crises, such as substance abuse, in the family.

1. The placater is a person who reduces tension by smoothing things over. The person may be a martyr, a role often played by the alcoholic or addict's spouse. The placater would avoid confrontation of abusive drinking behavior and deny personal emotions.
2. The blamer role is often played by people with low self-esteem who attack to keep the focus off themselves. The alcoholic plays this role by blaming others and by insisting that his or her drinking behavior was caused by the spouse's nagging or the children's misbehavior. The spouse can also shift to this role when conflict is high.
3. The irrelevant role is played by people in the family who avoid conflict by changing the subject, responding inappropriately, distracting others, or having temper tantrums.
4. The superresponsible role is characterized by ultareasonable communications. These people act calm, cool, and collected, but internally they feel vulnerable.

Satir would use these roles to create family sculptures so that families could experience from a symbolic and dramatic perspective the roles that they played in the family and how this was all part of a family dance in response to family stress or problems. She believed that these roles covered real feelings that people were afraid to share because of their low self-esteem. In her work, Satir clarified communications, helped families find solutions, supported each family member's self-esteem, and taught families how to touch and be affectionate.

Carl Whitaker was raised on an isolated dairy farm in New York. He attributed this experience of isolation to his shyness and his ability to connect with schizophrenic patients. He was originally trained as a doctor of obstetrics and gynecology, but during World War II was pressed into working as a psychiatrist and became fascinated by psychotic patients. Since he had no formal training in psychiatry, he was unencumbered by traditional ideas. Whitaker went on to establish a training program at Emory University, but left with several of his colleagues to establish the Atlantic Psychiatric Clinic, where his version of experiential family therapy, Symbolic-Experiential Family Therapy, was further developed. Whitaker's theory evolved from his work with schizophrenic families and collaboration with other family therapists. The goal of his therapy was individual growth as well as strengthening the family as a whole. He believed that personal growth requires family integration, and family integration depends on the personal growth of its members (Nichols & Schwartz, 1995). Toward this goal of growth, Whitaker created an experience in the therapy process that allowed for the growth. He valued experience for its own sake. He further believed that a therapist should approach a therapy session with the expectation that he or she would also experience growth from these existential encounters.

Whitaker often referred to his therapy as "therapy of the absurd," and he relied on his intuitions and the flashes of thoughts that were created by the encounter with the families. He talked of falling asleep in the sessions and dreaming about the family. Upon waking, he would tell the family what he had dreamed in a symbolic way. He was known to blurt out statements about the undercurrent of process in the family such as, "Someone is having murderous thoughts!" "Whitaker advocates craziness, non-rational, creative experiencing and functioning, as a proper goal of therapy. If they let themselves become a little crazy, he believes, families will reap the rewards of zest, emotionality, and spontaneity" (Nichols & Schwartz, 1995, p. 299).

As opposed to Bowen, Whitaker liked to raise the anxiety of the family and create emotional exchanges. He believed that sometimes family members had to get angry with each other in order to clear the air and allow for closeness and loving feelings.

Although these experiential therapists are difficult to emulate because their personalities were part of their therapies, their beliefs, goals, and processes can be adapted by others. Focusing on feelings, self-esteem, and the experiences of the therapy process can be useful in working with substance abusing families, who usually have low levels of self-esteem and a strong taboo about expressing feelings. They often need to learn to be spontaneous, loving, and growing individuals and families. Couples who have been struggling with addiction for long periods are full of anger, resentment, disappointment, and fear. Experiential therapy can be useful to help couples get beyond these stockpiles of negative emotions that keep them from growing in their recovery process.

DESCRIPTIONS OF THE ALCOHOLIC AND ADDICT
FAMILY SYSTEM

It was important to identify common characteristics of alcoholic families so that assessments and treatment strategies could focus on the recovery of the entire system. Many investigators have looked at the alcoholic family environment (Bowen, 1974; Davis, Stern, & Vandeusen, 1978; Killorin & Olson, 1984; McLachlan, et al., 1973; Pringle, 1976). McLachlan, et al. (1973) studied teenagers with alcoholic parents and found that a sense of secure family cohesiveness clearly differentiated the controls from the alcoholic families. The teenagers from alcoholic families had a much lower sense of family cohesiveness. Pringle (1976) reported that the alcoholic families of origin in his study were controlling, closed systems with little room for self-expression and strongly encouraged competition and achievement, whereas the nonalcoholic families of origin were more cohesive and supportive, and had more open expression and autonomy.

Kaufman has written extensively about the alcoholic family system (Kaufman, 1980, 1984, 1986). He described four types of family reactivity patterns: (1) the functional family system where family members have the ability to wall off and isolate alcoholic behavior; (2) the neurotic, enmeshed family system where drinking behavior interrupts normal family tasks, causes conflict, shifts roles, and demands new adaptation; (3) the disintegrated family system where the alcoholic is separated from the family, but they are still available for family therapy; and (4) the absent family system that is marked by total loss of family of origin (Kaufman, 1984). He further stated, "There is now substantial evidence to conclude that family systems play a significant role in the genesis of alcoholism, as for example in the transmission of marital and family roles of alcoholism from one generation to the next" (Kaufman, 1984, p. 7). In his article, "Myth and Reality in the Family Patterns and Treatment of Substance Abusers," Kaufman (1980) rejected myths about substance abusers' family patterns. He pointed out that families of drug abusers are very similar to families of alcohol abusers; however, the drug abuser may be a child, while the alcohol abuser may be the adult. In over half of the families with an identified patient with a drug problem there is also a parent who is alcoholic. He felt that the family plays an important part in the onset and perpetuation of substance abuse, yet it may not be the cause of all substance abuse. He also cautioned about overgeneralizing about alcoholic families and added that they vary according to ethnic background, sex of the alcoholic, and stage of life cycle of the family. He concluded that there is a need for more research in the area of the substance abusing family environments and implications for directions in family therapy.

In a more recent interview, Kaufman (1991) reviewed his 1980 article on myth and reality in the field and concluded that counselors are learning more and more about the importance of the family in the root and maintenance of substance abuse. The field is acknowledging that there is more to the family system than the mother-son relationship, that the fathers are not all distant, that the mothers are not all enmeshed, and that there are unique dynamics in the family systems of various ethnic groups. Siblings are also incredibly important in family therapy. Kaufman further stated that, though there is still controversy about whether one can treat a family with ongoing substance abuse, the majority of therapists working in the field agree that the substance abuse needs to be stopped before doing family therapy. This follows his previous statement that no study has demonstrated the need for abstinence for effective therapy, though many family therapists state that this is necessary (Pattison & Kaufman, 1981). Although in some cases family therapy may be needed as an interventive process to accomplish the sobriety, Kaufman believes this is part of the debate within the field on whether alcoholism or drug abuse is a symptom or a disease.

Kaufman also updated his subgroups of alcoholic and addict families. He thinks that there are far fewer of the "functional families systems" than he first believed. These families were able to wall off and isolate alcoholic behavior. Berenson (1976) also proposed a category one and a category two of family systems with alcohol problems. Category one was similar to the functional family. These families agreed that alcohol was not a problem or was a minor problem; the problem was acute as opposed to chronic; there was only occasionally a family history of alcoholism and the behavior change when drinking was slight and infrequent. The category two family had high conflict about drinking; saw it as a chronic problem; usually had a family history of alcoholism and often had intense behavior change when drinking. It is interesting to note that he describes the amount and pattern of drinking in both of these families as variable. This differentiation of categories was important because different treatment models were proposed for each category.

A differentiation was also made among various states of operating within a single family in an attempt to understand the alcoholic family dynamics. Steinglass, Davis, and Berensen (1977) observed that families tend to maintain alcoholic behaviors. They studied the *adaptive consequences* of alcoholism by observing videotapes of families when the alcoholic was in a dry state and when drinking, the wet state. They found the family to be more relaxed and talkative when the alcoholic was intoxicated and more rigid and closed during dry states. Steinglass, Davis, and Berenson (1977) further developed a model to demonstrate how drinking behavior is maintained. It is based on three concepts: "interactional behavior cycling between the sober state and the intoxicated state; patterning of behavior that has reached steady state; and the hypothesis that alcohol use in the alcoholic family has become incorporated into family problem solving behavior" (Steinglass, 1979, p. 167). Steinglass (1980) pointed out that chronic alcoholism produces distortions in the normative family lifecycle. Davis, et al. (1974) "postulate[d] that alcohol abuse has adaptive consequences that are reinforcing enough to maintain the drinking behavior, regardless of its causative factors. These adaptive consequences may operate on different levels including intrapsychic, intracouple, or to maintain family homeostasis" (p. 210).

Killorin and Olson (1984) believed that, as a result of these adaptive consequences, the function of the symptom of alcoholism varies and so does the family style. Even though the families may have a common symptom, the way the system interacts can take many forms. Using Olson's Circumplex Model for evaluating family environment, alcoholic families fell into all 16 types of family systems (Olson & Killorin, 1987). They included disengaged as well as enmeshed systems and chaotic as well as rigid systems. Olson and Killorin (1987) compared chemically dependent families and nondependent families. On the scale of cohesion (how connected families feel), about one-third of the chemically dependent families perceived their families as disengaged compared to seven percent of the nondependent. In terms of family adaptability, over 40 percent of the chemically dependent families saw themselves as chaotic, while only 8 percent of the nondependent families rated themselves as chaotic.

There have been several studies that evaluated the alcoholic family environment (Moos & Moos, 1984; Moos, Finney, & Gamble, 1982; Moos, et al., 1979; Moos & Moos, 1976). Moos, et al. (1979) investigated alcoholics with poor follow-ups six to eight months after inpatient treatment for alcoholism. Their family environments revealed more conflict and control problems, and less cohesion, expressiveness, active-recreational orientation, intellectual-cultural orientation, and moral-religious emphasis than those patients who had follow-up treatment. Additionally, Moos and Moos (1984) compared families of recovered alcoholics and families of relapsed alcoholics two years after residential treatment. The recovered alcoholic families did not differ from the control families (families without alcoholism). The relapsed families showed less cohesion (the amount of support family members give and receive), expressiveness (expression of feelings), and recreational orientation (playing together as a family).

Filstead, McElfresh, & Anderson (1981) took a look at the overall family environment of the alcoholic family and compared it to the nonalcoholic family environment. Data were collected on 42 white families of which 59 percent were families in which the male members were alcoholic. Each family member completed the Moos Family Environment Scale covering ten dimensions of family life conceptually organized around: relationships, personal growth, and system maintenance dimensions. These scores were compared to the normal nonclinic group of families previously used by Moos. The alcoholic families perceived their family environments to be much less cohesive and expressive; perceived less emphasis on the independence of individuals, intellectual-cultural activities (like reading and valuing the arts), active-recreational concerns, and organizational tasks than did the so-called normal families. The alcoholic families also reported a much higher level of conflict than the normal families (Filstead,

McElfresh, & Anderson, 1981). This same pattern was found in the families of origin of adult children of alcoholics who themselves became alcoholic and adult children of alcoholics who did not develop alcoholism, and these ACOAs created similar patterns in their nuclear families (Lawson, 1988).

There appears to be a set of family dynamics that are common to many families struggling with addiction. These include a lack of support for family members and a low sense of belonging; a high degree of conflict and fighting; an absence of expression of feelings; difficulties in accepting individual differences and opinions; an expectation of achievement from family members but a lack of modeling intellectual and cultural pursuits; and a lack of family recreational experiences and playing. Although not all families battling addictions have these dynamics, these are good areas of assessment for counselors. When these problems are found in families, goals can be set to modify these dynamics.

This chapter has attempted to help counselors view the entire family as a client in need of treatment. Counselors who are interested in developing their family therapy skills and working with families should continue to read books on family therapy, attend workshops or take classes in family therapy, and find a good supervisor. There is a list of suggested reading for counselors who want to learn more about becoming a family therapist at the end of this chapter. These books can be ordered from any bookstore.

DISCUSSION QUESTIONS

1. Why is it important to examine family history of substance abuse and current family dynamics when treating substance abuse?
2. How is systems thinking different from linear thinking?
3. What are some family dynamics that promote the intergenerational transmission of substance abuse in families?
4. Which theory of family therapy do you believe would be most useful in working with a substance abusing family? Why?
5. What family factors would be important to assess before beginning treatment with a substance abuser?
6. How would you develop skills as a family therapist? What skills would be important?
7. Why is the concept of "adaptive consequences" of alcoholism important?

REFERENCES

Alexander, J. F. (1974). Behavior modification and delinquent youth. In J. C. Cull & R. E. Hardy (Eds.). *Behavior modification in rehabilitation settings* (pp. 79–92). Springfield, IL: Charles C Thomas Publisher.

Bandler, R., Grender, J., & Satir, V. (1976). *Changing with families.* Palo Alto, CA: Science & Behavior Books Inc.

Barnard, C. P. (1981). *Families, alcoholism and therapy.* Springfield, IL: Charles C Thomas Publisher.

Barry H., & Blane, H. T. (1977). Birth positions of alcoholics. *Journal of Individual Psychology, 33,* 62–69.

Bateson, G., Jackson, D., Haley, J., & Weakland, J. (1956). Toward a theory of schizophrenia. *Behavioral Science, 1,* 251–64.

Bennett, L. A., Wolin, S. J., Reiss, D., & Teitelbaum, M. A. (1987). Couples at risk for transmission of alcoholism: Protective influences. *Family Process, 26,* 111–29.

Berenson, D. (1976). Alcohol and the family system. In P. Guerin (Ed.), *Family therapy: Theory and practice* (pp. 284–97). New York: Gardner Press.

Black, C. (1979, Fall). Children of alcoholics. *Alcohol Health and Research World,* 23–27.

Black, C. (1981a). Innocent bystanders at risk: The children of alcoholics. *Alcoholism,* 22–25.

Black, C. (1981b). *It will never happen to me.* Denver: M. A. C. Publishers.

Booz-Allen & Hamilton, Inc. (1974). *An assessment of the needs of and resources for children of alcoholic parents.* Rockville, MD: National Institute on Alcohol Abuse and Alcoholism.

Boszormenyi-Nagy, I., & Spark, G. (1973). *Invisible loyalties.* New York: Harper & Row.

Bowen, M. (1974). Alcoholism as viewed through family systems theory and family psychotherapy. *Annals of the New York Academy of Science, 233,* 115–22.

Bowen, M. (1978). Alcoholism and the family. In *Family therapy in clinical practice.* Northvale, NJ: Jason Aronson, Inc..

Boye-Beaman, J., Leonard, K. E., & Senchak, M. (1991). Assortative mating, relationship development, and intimacy among offspring of alcoholics. *Family Dynamics of Addiction Quarterly, 1* (2), 20–33.

Carter, E., & McGoldrick, M. (1980). *The family life cycle: A framework for family therapy.* New York: Gardner Press.

Davidson, M. (1983). *Uncommon sense: The life and thought of Ludwig von Bertalanffy.* Los Angeles: J. P. Tarcher.

Davis, D. J., Berenson, D., Steinglass, Peter, & Davis, S. (1974). The adaptive consequences of drinking. *Psychiatry, 37,* 209–15.

Davis, P., Stern, D. R., & Vandusen, J. M. (1978). Enmeshment-disengagement in the alcoholic family. In F. A. Seixas (Ed.), *Currents in Alcoholism: Vol. 4. Psychological, Social and Epidemiological Studies.* San Diego: Grune & Stratton.

Ewing, I. A., & Fox, R. E. (1968). Family therapy of alcoholism. In A. Messerman (Ed.), *Current psychotherapies.* San Diego: Grune & Stratton.

Filstead, W. J., McElfresh, O., & Anderson, C. (1981). Comparing the family environments of alcoholics and "normal" families. *Journal of Alcohol and Drug Education, 26,* 24–31.

Framo, J. L. (1972). Symptoms from a family transactional viewpoint. In C. Sager and H. S. Kaplan (Eds.), *Progress in Group and Family Therapy* (pp. 125–171). New York: Brunner/Mazel Publishers.

Framo, J. L. (1976). Famly of origin as a therapeutic resource for adults in marital and family therapy: You can and should go home again. *Family Process, 15,* 193–209.

Framo, J. L. (1991). *Family of origin therapy: An intergenerational approach.* New York: Brunner/ Mazel Publishers.

Friedman, A. S., Tomko, L. A., & Utada, A. (1991). Client and family characteristics that predict better family therapy outcome for adolescent drug abusers. *Family Dynamics of Addiction Quarterly, 1* (1), 77–93.

Haley, J. (1976). *Problem solving therapy.* New York: Harper & Row.

Hanna, S. B., & Brown, J. H. (1995). *The practice of family therapy: Key elements across models.* Pacific Grove, CA: Brooks/Cole Publishing Co.

Jackson, D. D. (1957). The question of family homeostasis. *Psychiatric Quarterly Supplement, 31,* 79–90.

Joanning, H., Quinn, W., Thomas, F., & Mullen, R. (1992). Treating adolescent drug abuse: A comparison of family systems therapy, group therapy, and family drug education. *Journal of Marital and Family Therapy, 18* (4), 345–56.

Kaufman, E. (1980). Myths and realities in the family patterns and treatment of substance abusers. *American Journal of Drug and Alcohol Abuse, 7* (3 & 4), 257–79.

Kaufman, E. (1984). Family system variables in alcoholism. *Alcoholism: Clinical and Experimental Research, 8* (1), 4–8.

Kaufman, E. (1986). The family of the alcoholic patient. *Psychosomatics, 27* (5), 347–58.

Kaufman, E. (1991). An interview with Edward Kaufman, M.D. *Family Dynamics of Addiction Quarterly, 1* (3).

Killorin, E., & Olson, D. (1984). The chaotic flippers in treatment. In E. Kaufman (Ed.). *Power to Change: Alcoholism.* New York: Gardner Press.

Lawson, A. (1988). The relationship of past and present family environments of adult children of alcoholics. (Doctoral dissertation, United States International University, San Diego) *Dissertation Abstracts International, 49* (07), 1979.

Lawson, G., Peterson, J., & Lawson, A. (1983). *Alcoholism and the family: A guide to treatment and prevention.* Gaithersburg, MD: Aspen Publishers, Inc.

Lewis, R. A., Piercy, F. P., Sprenkle, D. H., & Trepper, T. S. (1991). The Purdue brief family therapy model for adolescent substance abusers. In T. Todd & M. Selekman (Eds.), *Family therapy approaches with adolescent substance abusers* (pp. 29–48). Boston: Allyn & Bacon.

Lewis, R. A. (1991). Testimony before the house select committee on children, families, drugs and alcoholism. Hearing on: Adolescent substance abuse: Barriers to treatment, 101st Cong.

McGoldrick, M., & Gerson, R. (1985). *Genograms in family assessment.* New York: W.W. Norton & Co., Inc.

McLachlan, S., et al. (1973). A study of teenagers with alcoholic parents. *Donwood Institute Research Monograph, N3.* Toronto: The Donwood Institute.

Meeks, D., & Kelly, C. (1970). Family therapy with the families of recovering alcoholics. *Quarterly Journal of Studies on Alcoholism, 31* (2), 399–413.

Minuchin, S. (1974). *Families and family therapy.* Cambridge, MA: Harvard University Press.

Minuchin, S., Rosman, B., & Baker, L. (1978). *Psychosomatic families: Anorexia nervosa in context.* Cambridge, MA: Harvard University Press.

Moos, R. H., Bromet, E., Tse, V., & Moos, B. S. (1979). Family characteristics and the outcome of treatment of alcoholism. *Journal of Studies on Alcohol, 40* (1), 78–88.

Moos, R. H., Finney, J. W., & Gamble, W. (1982). The process of recovery from alcoholism. *Journal of Studies on Alcohol, 43* (9), 888–909.

Moos, R. H., & Moos, B. S. (1976). A typology of family social environment. *Family Process, 15* (4), 357–70.

Moos, R. H., & Moos, B. S. (1984). The process of recovery from alcoholism: 3. Comparing functioning in families of alcoholics and matched control families. *Journal of Studies on Alcohol, 45* (2), 111–17.

Nardi, P. (1981). Children of alcoholics: A role-theoretical perspective. *Journal of Social Psychology, 115,* 237–45.

Nichols, M. P., & Schwartz, R. C. (1995). *Family therapy: Concepts and methods.* Boston: Allyn & Bacon.

Olson, D. H., & Killorin, E. A. (1987). *Chemically dependent families and the circumplex model.* Unpublished research report, University of Minnesota, St. Paul, MN.

O'Sullivan, C. (1991). Making a difference: The relationship between childhood mentors and resiliency in adult children of alcoholics. *Family Dynamics of Addiction Quarterly, 1* (3), 46–59.

Patterson, G. R. (1982). *A social learning approach to family intervention: Coercive family process.* Eugene, OR: Castalia.

Pattison, E. M., & Kaufman, E. (1981). Family therapy and the treatment of alcoholism. In M. R. Lansky (Ed.), *Family therapy and major psychopathology* (pp. 117–129). New York: Grune and Stratton.

Piercy, F. F., & Frankel, B. R. (1989). The evolution of an integrative family therapy for substance-abusing adolescents: Toward the mutual enhancement of research and practice. *Journal of Family Psychology, 3* (1), 5–25.

Pringle, W. J. (1976). The alcoholic family environment: The influence of the alcoholic and nonalcoholic family of origin on present coping syles. (Doctoral dissertation, California School of Professional Psychology, Fresno). *Dissertation Abstracts International, 37* (11), 5812 (University Microfilms No. AAC7710809).

Simmons, G. M. (1991). Interpersonal trust and perceived locus of control in the adjustment of adult children of alcoholics. (Doctoral dissertation, United States International University). *Dissertation Abstracts International, 52* (3), 1703. (University Microfilms No. AAC9122858).

Stanton, M. D., & Todd, T. C. (1992). Structural family therapy with drug addicts. In E. Kaufman & P. Kaufman (Eds.). *The family therapy of drug and alcohol abuse* (2nd ed.) (pp. 46–62). New York: Gardner Press.

Stanton, M. D. & Todd, T. C. (1982). *The family therapy of drug abuse and addiction.* New York: Guilford Press.

Steinglass, P. (1976). Experimenting with family treatment approaches to alcoholism, 1950–1975, a review. *Family Process, 15* (4), 97–123.

Steinglass, P. (1979). Family therapy with alcoholics: A review. In E. Kaufman and P. Kaufman (Eds.). *Family Therapy of Drug and Alcohol Abuse* (pp. 147–85). New York: Gardner Press.

Steinglass, P. (1980). Life history model of the alcoholic family. *Family Process, 19* (3), 211–26.

Steinglass, P., Davis, D., & Berenson, D. (1977). Observations of conjointly hospitalized "alcohol couples" during sobriety and intoxication for theory and therapy. *Family Process, 16,* 1–16.

Szapocznik, J., Kurtines, W. M., Foot, F., Perez-Vidal, A., & Hervis, O. (1986). Conjoint versus one-person family therapy: Further evidence for the effectiveness of conducting family through one person with drug-abusing adolescents. *Journal of Consulting and Clinical Psychology, 54* (3), 395–97.

Szapocznik, J., Kurtines, W. M., Foot, F., Perez-Vidal, A., & Hervis, O. (1983). Conjoint versus one-person family therapy: Some evidence for the effectiveness of conducting family therapy through one person. *Journal of Consulting and Clinical Psychology, 51,* 889–99.

Thornton, R., & Nardi, P. M. (1975). The dynamics of role acquisition. *American Journal of Sociology, 80* (4), 870–85.

220   ESSENTIALS OF CHEMICAL DEPENDENCY COUNSELING

Treadway, D. (1989). *Before it's too late*. New York: W.W. Norton & Co., Inc.

Wegscheider, S. (1981a). *Another chance: Hope and help for the alcoholic family.* Palo Alto, CA: Science & Behavior Books, Inc.

Wegscheider, S. (1981b, January/February). From the family trap to family freedom. *Alcoholism,* 36–39.

Wilson, C., & Orford, J. (1978). Children of alcoholics. *Journal of Studies on Alcohol, 39,* 121–42.

Wolin, S. J., Bennett, L. A., & Noonan, D. L. (1980). Disrupted family rituals: A factor in the intergenerational transmission of alcoholism. *Journal of Studies on Alcohol, 41,* 199–214.

Wolin, S. J., & Bennett, L. A. (1984). Family rituals. *Family Process, 23,* 401–20.

SUGGESTED READING

Much more can be learned about family counseling. The following is a list of reading material that is especially pertinent. The titles are listed in the suggested order in which they should be read by someone seeking further training in the area of family counseling.

Alcoholism and the family: A guide to treatment and prevention; Gary Lawson, James Peterson, & Ann Lawson, Gaithersburg, MD.: Aspen Publishers, Inc., 1983.

Conjoint family therapy; Virginia Satir, Palo Alto, CA: Science and Behavior Books, Inc., 1964.

Peoplemaking; Virginia Satir, Science and Behavior Books, Inc., 1972 or *The new peoplemaking,* 1988.

The family crucible; Carl Whitaker & August Napier, New York: Harper & Row, 1978.

Problem solving therapy; Jay Haley, San Francisco: Jossey-Bass, Inc. Publishers, 1973.

Families and family therapy; Salvador Minuchin, Cambridge, MA: Harvard University Press, 1974.

Family therapy techniques; Salvador Minuchin & H. C. Fishman, Cambridge, MA: Harvard University Press, 1981.

Satir step by step: A guide to creating change in families; Virginia Satir & M. Baldwin, Palo Alto, CA: Science and Behavior Books, Inc., 1983.

Dancing with the family: A symbolic experiential family therapy; Carl Whitaker & William Bumberry, New York: Brunner/Mazel Publishers, 1988.

Family therapy: Full length case studies; edited by Peggy Papp, New York: Gardner Press.

Family therapy in clinical practice; Murray Bowen, Northvale, NJ: Jason Aronson, Inc., 1978.

Strategic family therapy; Cloe Madanes, San Francisco: Jossey-Bass, Inc. Publishers, 1981.

Change: Principles of problem formation and problem resolution; Paul Watzlawick, John Weakland, & Richard Fisch, New York: W.W. Norton & Co., Inc, 1974.

The handbook of family therapy; edited by A. S. Gurman & D. P. Kniskern, New York: Brunner/Mazel Publishers, 1981.

The handbook of family therapy. Vol. 2; edited by A. S. Gurman & D. P. Kniskern, New York: Brunner/Mazel Publishers, 1991.

Family therapy: Concepts and methods; edited by Michael Nichols & Richard Schwartz, Boston: Allyn & Bacon, 1995.

Before it's too late; David Treadway, New York: W.W. Norton & Co., Inc, 1989.

Genograms in family assessment; Monica McGoldrick & Randy Gerson, New York: W.W. Norton & Co., Inc., 1985.

Chapter 7

Dealing with Diversity

CHAPTER OBJECTIVES

- Examine the major types of diversity
- Examine how each type of diversity might impact chemically dependent patients
- Identify areas of diversity that may lead to high risk in individuals with chemical dependency problems
- Examine how knowledge of individual diversity issues can be useful to the counselor in treatment planning

Ten years ago when the first edition of this text was written, diversity was not a consideration in the chemical dependency counseling field. Most treatment programs were inpatient and offered a standard treatment that included education on the disease of alcoholism and the 12 steps as well as individual and group counseling. Women, men, Native Americans, adolescents, the elderly—everyone went through the same program. The belief was: One program fits all. All addicts were seen as basically the same. They were believed to suffer from the same disease and the treatment was simple: Break the denial in group and individual counseling, introduce the patient to the 12 steps, give them a Big Book, a thirty-day medallion, and send them off to be sober "one day at a time" and to attend "30 meetings in 30 days." The cost for this "MacTreatment" was usually around $10,000. Insurance companies willingly paid for it. As single-minded as these programs were, some people began a successful recovery in them. But many did not, and the heyday of inpatient treatment programs was short lived. Today, insurance companies are no longer willing to pay for what addicts can have for free in a self-help group.

Today, fortunately, things are changing in chemical dependency treatment. Individual differences, or what is termed here *individual diversities,* are becoming important issues in most treatment programs. Issues such as race, sex, age, and cultural background are considered when treatment programs are designed, and the dynamics of addiction are considered when individual treatment plans are developed. There are more and more publications addressing issues in special populations (Lawson & Lawson, 1989; Sue & Sue, 1990) and there are also books and articles devoted to certain groups with substance abuse problems such as adolescents (Lawson & Lawson, 1992), codependents (Babcock & McKay, 1995), and AIDS patients (Clark & Washburn, 1988). Newer books on addiction usually include a chapter or two on issues of diversity (Lewis, 1994). The authors of books and articles discuss diversity among individuals and how these diversities make a difference when treatment for addiction is planned and implemented.

This chapter will cover more than just cultural diversity. Many forms of diversity that affect chemical dependency will be discussed specifically in relation to the etiology and treatment of chemical dependency. Some case histories will be given to illustrate the important issues. The following areas of diversity will be included in this chapter:

- age and developmental level
- family history and genetics
- gender and sexual history
- mental health and personality
- employment and related issues
- racial and cultural affiliations
- religion
- medical problems
- criminal and deviant behavior
- emotional stress or a history of personal trauma
- drugs of choice

By understanding diversity among clients and viewing the individual as part of a system as discussed in the previous chapter, it will be possible for counselors to interpret addictive behavior in a context that will help determine *all* of the issues that need to be addressed in treatment. This will also help the counselor understand how this diversity can be addressed in issues of recovery. This is not done so the counselor can determine where the patient is wrong; it is done from the perspective of using a knowledge of diversity to help the client recover. It is not really feasible for a counselor to know everything about the culture or race or religion of a client or patient. However, if the counselor is aware of the issues and asks the right questions, the client or patient can help the counselor with what they need to know.

It is important here to acknowledge something. It is possible for an addict to attend a self-help group, or a treatment program, where only the substance use is addressed, and yet they are able to stop using and turn their lives around. This has happened thousands of times and will continue to happen. Many people have stopped destructive behaviors like smoking, drinking, and using drugs without any help at all. If the substance abuse is the only or the major problem that the individual has, they may be quite successful doing this: However, the majority of people with addiction problems have many other related problems and issues to deal with. In addition, there are degrees or stages of recovery, and the ability to stop using drugs without also having a meaningful, happy, and fulfilling life does not offer much. This "unfullfilling recovery" often leads to relapse or even suicide. It is the counselor's job not only to help the client achieve sobriety and maintain it but also to assist them in the search for happiness and meaning in life. This is best done with an understanding of the issues of diversity as described in this chapter.

Each approach to counseling has a theory about how and why people change. There are basically three things that people can change. They can change their behavior, as in changing from a drug user to a nonuser. They can change their cognitions or thoughts, as in thinking of drug abuse as a disease rather than as a moral weakness. Finally, they can change their feelings or emotional response to something or someone, as in feeling they cannot control their use of alcohol when earlier they felt they could. Most people who make significant changes in their lives do so in all three areas. An addict who just changes drug-using behavior by quitting drugs, without changing thinking and feeling about drugs has little chance of maintaining that behavior change. A counselor with an understanding of the issues of diversity will be much better equipped to assist in this change. The next section of this chapter will examine some specific areas of diversity. There is a great deal of overlap. For example, family background and religious affiliation overlap. Most people do not choose a religion; they are born into a family where they are expected to follow the religion of the family. If they choose not to, this may or may not be a major family issue. Because there is overlap, some of the sections on specific diversities will be much longer than others. This has nothing to do with their importance. They are all important to consider in relation to etiology and treatment.

AGE AND DEVELOPMENTAL STAGE

How are age and developmental stage related to substance abuse? They are related in many ways; for example, certain stages in life are high risk for substance abuse. Adolescents are going through a stage in life where experimentation is the norm. This often includes experimentation with drugs. The risk increases if the adolescent is developmentally ahead or behind peers, which means the development of pubic hair, breasts for girls, and deeper voices for boys. Both girls and boys who are early or late developers find drugs, particularly alcohol, to be useful in the transition from childhood to adulthood. Early developers tend to "hang out" with older peers who are more likely to be using. To fit in with the older kids, early developers use as well.

Teenagers who develop late often use alcohol and other drugs to make their peers think they are older and to feel older themselves. Almost all teenagers want to look or be older. They believe drug use will help them. Tobacco companies know this and advertise to take advantage of it.

At the opposite end, the elderly are prime candidates for iatrogenic (induced inadvertently by a physician) and prescription drug abuse. They overuse and underuse. They mix drugs that should not be used together. They use each others' prescription drugs without the doctors' permission. Strangely enough, these two groups, adolescents and the elderly, have a great deal in common. They are both going through major changes in their lives and they are both at risk for substance abuse as a result. The aging process is not easy for many people and using chemicals to soften the blow is very common. Counselors who understand this can help their clients find other ways than using drugs to get through stages that are only natural in life, so an understanding of the stages of life and the aging process will make this task easier for the counselor.

Many alcoholism and drug treatment programs pay little, if any, attention to the past development of their clients. It is felt, by some, that "what is past is past, and there is nothing we can do to change it, so why bring it up?" If the past is brought up during treatment, it is usually only in the context of the recent past. Alcoholics Anonymous (A.A.) deals with the past in the eighth and ninth steps by suggesting that its members make a list of all the persons whom they have harmed, become willing to make amends to all of them, and then make direct amends to such people wherever possible, unless to do so would injure them or others. Although these steps deal with the past and offer the A.A. member an opportunity to rid himself of possible guilt about previous actions, they focus mainly on past behavior with regard to drinking—and that is not taking human development into full consideration; the drunk-a-log is similarly deficient.

The drunk-a-log is often part of an A.A. meeting. Members tell how drinking led them down the path to dependency and how they have turned their lives around through A.A. Then they explain how they have learned to stay sober just one day at a time. This is fine as an attempt to remind the speaker and those listening of history, lest it repeat itself. Too often, though, this dialogue leads the listeners and the speaker to the conclusion that all of these problems began when alcohol or drugs entered the picture. Often they assume that before alcohol and drugs, the speaker lived a normal, happy life, and if alcohol were removed, life would again be the proverbial bowl of cherries, but the very high rate of suicide for those recovering from chemical dependency suggests that this is not true. The number of chemically dependent persons whose family histories include psychological, physical, and sexual abuse suggests that before alcohol or drugs, things were not that rosy either. In short, though each of us starts out much the same, some time between the womb and the beginning of alcohol or drug use, we experience life events that have a direct effect on how we relate to our world. The more information the chemical dependency counselor has about these life events, the better the treatment plan can be—and the greater the chances are that the client will be successful in treatment.

Developmental Stages

Each major theory of counseling or psychotherapy embraces some form of developmental theory. Usually this theory involves a rationale of how a person develops. This rationale is, in turn, related to some type of developmental dysfunction that the particular theory of psychotherapy is designed to treat. The first to theorize in this manner was Freud. Freud's theory involved different stages of development, and posited that for those individuals who could not successfully complete these stages, the outcome was mental illness or exhibited deviant behavior.

Freud believed that every child goes through a sequence of developmental stages, each associated with a specific erogenous zone. He claimed that individuals passed through these stages on the path to a personality that is divided into three major parts: the id, the ego, and the superego. His stages of development were the oral stage, the anal stage, the phallic stage, the latency stage, and finally, the genital stage. Freud felt that each of these stages fulfilled a task in the development of a healthy personality. Freud's theories have had a great impact on how we view the development of personality today. One of the popular theories of psychotherapy, transactional analysis, uses personality divisions called the child, parent, and adult that closely parallel the id, ego, and superego of Freud.

This chapter will not present developmental theories. For a review of these, we would suggest that the reader refer to a basic text on developmental psychology. Our aim is to suggest to the chemical dependency counselor that, in order to provide the best treatment for chemical dependency, one should have an idea about how the chemically dependent person develops.

Chemical Dependency Development

Drinking alcohol or taking drugs is a behavior. The way one acts or behaves under the influence of drugs or alcohol is also a behavior. For each behavior there is an antecedent or a reason. Although an individual's behavior may seem to be self-destructive, there is a reason, a "payoff," for this behavior. At the least, the behavior is leading that person in a direction that, for them, appears to be logical or the only direction available. Removing the alcohol or drugs is just a beginning; something therapeutic must happen to an individual before they will give up drugs or alcohol. Something must also assist individuals in making the choice to change negative or self-destructive behaviors.

Thus, to focus only on alcohol- or drug-taking behavior is a mistake therapeutically. Self-help groups including A.A. appear to have accepted this view. Of the 12 steps toward recovery from alcoholism, only one even mentions alcohol. The others deal with behaviors, emotions, attitudes, and changes regarding control of one's life. These are positive steps toward recovery that can be enhanced by using information regarding early personality development. Information that provides a key to the question: Why does this person behave the way he does? will provide a direction for treatment. This includes what needs to change before the individual can behave in a more rational, self-fulfilling way. For many chemically dependent people, a change in behavior is brought about by a change in attitude. This change in attitude (sometimes known as therapeutic movement) is often brought about by one or more significant events in the person's life. (See the section Emotional Stress or a History of Personal Trauma, p. 245.) When these events are manipulated or caused by the counselor, that is therapy. For example, if a person in a group experience becomes moved by the caring that the other group members show toward him and changes his behavior as a result of this experience, that is therapy. It is only common sense to believe that the more the counselor knows about what motivates the chemically dependent person, the more accurately the counselor can set up these significant emotional events in order to bring about therapeutic change in thinking, feelings, and behavior.

Other Developmental Levels

Although early developmental theories include only the period from birth to early adulthood, it has become clear that we continue to develop in many areas for most of our lives. Erikson's theory of psycho-social development runs from birth through old age, with eight stages altogether. Each of these stages is meaningful to the understanding of individuals as they progress through life. We can best illustrate our point by reviewing a developmental stage and reflecting on how this information might be helpful to the chemical dependency counselor. Let us look at adolescence as a developmental stage and consider the important physical, emotional, and social characteristics of an adolescent. For the sake of simplicity, we will look here only at the male adolescent.

Physically, the adolescent male is in a state of rapid maturation. Some boys mature at an early age and some later. Those who mature later are often not as self-confident and assured as those who mature earlier; however, late maturers often become more sensitive and insightful than their early maturing counterparts. There is likely to be a great deal of concern about appearance at this age, especially with regard to the opposite sex. The male sex drive is at a peak at the ages of 16 to 17. A strong sex drive and severely limited opportunities to satisfy it are sources of much concern to many young males.

Socially, the adolescent male comes increasingly under the influence of his peer group. Often there are conflicts between peer group and family values, which is another source of anxiety for the adolescent. Emotionally, the adolescent may be moody and unpredictable, partly because of biological changes associated with sexual maturation and partly because of confusion about identity. Adolescents also tend to be intolerant and opinionated, partly because of a lack of confidence and partly because of a lack of experience as formal thinkers. In a search for a sense of identity, and in their efforts to become independent, many adolescents experience moments of confusion, anxiety, and anger. They may express their frustration by turning to alcohol or drugs or by otherwise rejecting established values. Adolescents also live for the here and now; they think very little about the future or the consequences of present behavior. They tend to look for immediate gratification rather than work toward some future goal. As a group, they look much the same, but on further examination each is very different.

Adolescents have a completely different set of problems than adults. The goals for treatment may be the same, but the direction they take to reach the goals is dictated by the problems that they encounter on the way. For example, building self-image might be an appropriate goal. For the adult, this might be done through improved relationships with family members and improved performance on the job. For the adolescent, it might only be done through a peer group.

For a forty-five-year-old adult, the reality that alcohol intake is damaging his liver and that he might someday die as a result of this could be a motivating factor to give up drinking. This same news presented to the adolescent might have no effect whatsoever on his alcohol intake. Again, the more you know about the developmental factors of the individual you are working with, the more effective you can be in treatment planning and, thus, in treatment.

FAMILY HISTORY AND GENETICS

In the earlier section of this chapter, we discussed the importance of development and how this relates to problems that clients experience later in life. No period of development is more critical to the development of the adult personality than early childhood. Almost without exception, the personality theorists link major adult personality characteristics to certain categories of childhood experience. (There are exceptions to this contention.) It seems reasonable to conclude, however, that if childhood experiences are so important in molding various personality attributes, the way one interacts with drugs and alcohol would be greatly influencing as well. There is nothing that has a greater impact on these early experiences than the family and the family has a role in the treatment and prevention of chemical dependency problems.

Much of what goes on in families, particularly early on, determines the subsequent risk for substance abuse. The family is where a child develops a self-image. Children begin to feel either good, bad, or indifferent about themselves. The family is where a child learns to make decisions, they learn what sex should be like, and they learn to deal with anxiety and have relationships with others. All of these are important in the development of low or high risk for substance abuse. The family is also where children receive their genetic predisposition for substance abuse and where they develop values related to the use of mind-altering substances. The use or lack of use by parents and other relatives provide children with a model that they either follow or reject. For more information about the family see *Alcoholism and the Family* (Lawson, Peterson, & Lawson, 1983).

In our examination of the family, we will be looking at two types of families that influence the chemically dependent person. First, and perhaps more critical to the development of the individual, is the family of origin. This family includes parents, relatives, or significant others who played a major role in a child's rearing. The major importance of this system is that attitudes and values about self and the world, as well as the use of alcohol and drugs, are mostly formed here, and thus play an important role in present behavior.

The second family we shall examine is the nuclear family. The nuclear family consists of those individuals with whom the person is living at the present time. This system is important because it may serve to create, maintain, or worsen problems that the chemically dependent person is having at the time. The nuclear family is also important because it is a potential mechanism for positive change in the life of the chemically dependent person.

Identifying Family Factors in the Development of Chemical Dependency

There are three major areas where theories of the etiology of chemical dependency have arisen. There are those theories that are biologically or genetically based, those theories that are psychological in nature (these include theories that chemically dependent persons have a distinct personality flaw that leads to chemical dependency), and those theories that are sociocultural in nature (these propose that the largest determiner of drinking and drug use is the culture that the chemically dependent person lives in).

Theories in each of these major areas are based to some degree on research findings and other empirical data. There has been evidence linking drug dependency or alcoholism with genetic factors, psychological factors, and sociocultural factors, but none of the research has demonstrated that any one of these factors is the major contributor to the etiology of chemical dependency. So most theorists believe that a combination of these factors causes one person to become chemically dependent and another person not to become so. One thing that is clear, and is becoming clearer as research in the area continues, is that the family has a major impact, perhaps *the* major impact on the individual in each of these areas. The family influences all of the physiological and a great deal of the psychological and sociological development of the individual. It is the developmental foundation established early by the family that is reflected in how a person relates to his environment, including his relationship with drugs and alcohol.

We cannot conclude from this that the family is the cause of chemical dependency. But it seems clear that the family cannot be ignored in regard to the etiology, treatment, or prevention of chemical dependency. To establish a clearer picture of the role that the family plays in physiological, psychological, and sociological factors, let us look at each factor from the perspective of the development of a risk level for chemical dependency. Remember that each of us has a potential risk for problems with chemical dependency; however, some of us are at greater risk than others.

Meeting Interpersonal Needs through Alcoholics Anonymous and Other Self-Help Groups

If the family is not available, the second best approach to treating chemical dependency is to provide a surrogate family to meet these needs: A.A. and other self-help groups serve this purpose for many. A problem may arise, however, if A.A. meets these needs at the expense of the real family (if it is intact). We have known many an alcoholic who took refuge at an A.A. meeting rather than working out unresolved family matters at home. When used properly, these groups are often very successful at reducing both the psychological and sociological risk levels enough to allow individuals to seek family therapy to resolve family problems.

Sociologically, they provide a new social group with a new set of values with regard to drinking or using. Often this means a change from a group where using or drinking to excess is not only acceptable but encouraged to a group where drinking or using in any fashion is not acceptable. This group, if it becomes a major influence on the individual, lowers the person's sociological risk level; if the individual maintains contact with the group and group members, he or she will continue to have a reduced sociological risk level.

Psychologically, people reduce their risk level if they respect and identify with the other members of the groups whom they meet. They reduce their own feelings of hopelessness by seeing people, who have had problems similar to theirs, who became better because they were able to stop using. There is some psychological relief in the knowledge that others in the world share similar problems; there is a feeling of acceptance that helps people feel better about themselves. Perhaps most importantly there is a feeling that by sharing experiences with other members, there is a chance that one could be helping other members stay sober. This is carried even further when the member is asked to do 12-step work, which includes their making house calls and home visits to individuals who are suffering from drug addiction or alcoholism and volunteering to share how they have been successful in maintaining sobriety. The 12-step call is a great esteem builder, and it serves to further reduce the psychological risk level by making the caller feel needed and useful.

Yet risk reduction is best done through the family for several reasons. (Even if A.A. or other self-help groups are used in the beginning, the counselor should help clients work toward meeting their goals through the family.) The first reason is that the family is the logical place for these needs to be met. Second, the family needs help just as much, or perhaps more, than the chemically dependent person. By conducting family therapy, the counselor helps family members meet their own personal needs through the family system. This pays off not only for the chemically dependent person but for the children in the family as well by teaching them to meet their interpersonal needs through the family; thus reducing their risk of future problems.

Genetic Predispositions

It has long been established that alcoholism runs in families (Cotton, 1979; Schuckit, 1995). The evidence is not as conclusive for other forms of drug abuse or addiction, but more and more research has indicated a link between the generations of those who experience chemical dependency problems, just as research has indicated a link between the generations of those who experience depression and other mental disorders. A number of studies have shown higher rates of alcoholism among relatives of alcoholics than in the population in general. While their findings suggest that genetic factors are involved, they provide no details on how a predisposition to alcoholism is transmitted. We can assume that just as eye color or metabolism rates are passed on genetically, so is the *capacity* for drug or alcohol abuse. The chemical dependency counselor can determine the physiological risk level for a client by asking if parents or grandparents have had chemical dependency problems. If the answer is yes, it can be assumed that the person is physiologically at a high risk to develop chemical dependency problems. However, it cannot be assumed that they *will* have problems. Too many factors are involved to make that assumption.

The chemical dependency counselor can use the information about parental problems with chemicals to let clients know that they are at high risk and to establish the importance of reducing the risk levels in other areas, both psychological and social. Although physiological susceptibility can be established, environmental factors will still play a major role in the development of chemical dependency. The client can simply be told: "We don't know for sure what causes chemical dependency, but we do know that each of us reacts differently to drugs or alcohol based on our size, chemical makeup, and other genetically predisposed factors. Because your parents or grandparents had a problem, you are physically at risk to have such problems, as your children will be, too. If you have a problem now or if you think you will at some time choose to use drugs or alcohol, you must pay particular attention to any signs of impending problems, you must work to keep your risk levels low in the other two areas." Table 7–1 is useful for conceptualizing the primary goals in the treatment or prevention of chemical dependency, that is, identifying and lowering one's risk levels.

Sociological and Psychological Family-Based Risk Factors

The person who is sociologically at high risk is the one whose primary support system, most often the family, either condones excessive chemical use (as a parent who is alcoholic might do) or does not tolerate the use of one or more chemicals (for example, a religious group with strong sanctions against the use of chemicals, commonly alcohol). In the first instance, the person is at risk because the abuse of chemicals is an option as a coping mechanism, or it is an expected behavior. Groups such as American Indians, Irish Catholics, and others have been identified as having high rates of alcoholism and other chemical dependency problems. The degree to which these social and cultural groups have influenced the individual is relevant to the sociological risk factor.

The others at high risk sociologically are those whose values about the use of drugs or alcohol were established while they were young. The message from the family, and usually the church, was clear: Those who use are wicked. At the very least: They (users) have not chosen God's way. If these values are followed throughout life and there is no use of drugs or alcohol, there can be no chemical dependency problem. But if, after becoming older, a person chooses to use alcohol or drugs, he will have a very difficult time not feeling guilty because of the messages received as a child. Problems are compounded by the fact that most drugs provide a temporary respite from guilt. The cycle becomes: use, feel guilty, use more to relieve guilt, feel even more guilty, use even more. It is a difficult cycle to break. To complicate matters even more, the family of origin sometimes rejects the person because of the drug use, thus confirming the user's belief that he is truly bad and deserves to be punished. (For more on this see the section Religion, p. 242.)

Table 7–1   Risk Levels for Various Etiological Factors and Treatment Goals

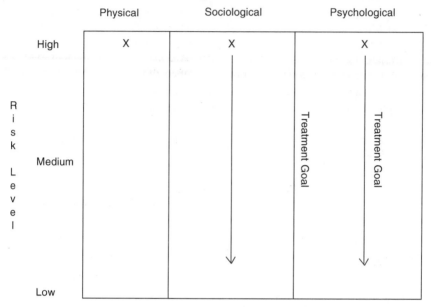

In the above instance, there is not a clear distinction between a sociological risk and a psychological risk; in fact, these are often interrelated. It is not necessary, however, to be totally precise to understand that the family has had a dramatic role in the development of the individual's risk level for chemical dependency problems. The psychological dynamics are there. One clear motivational factor for chemical use and abuse is to feel better. For reasons that are closely linked to the family, the person who becomes dependent on chemicals very often has a poor self-image, seeing himself in relation to others ("I am not as good as my parents") or in relation to how one perceives one should be ("I haven't come close to living up to my potential and I should"). Either way, the family of origin plays a vital role in these feelings. These factors have been explained in detail elsewhere, and for the counselor who is serious about providing a complete treatment program for clients, a highly recommended text is Lawson, et al., *Alcoholism and the Family: A Guide to Treatment and Prevention,* Aspen Publishers, Inc. For our purposes here, it will suffice to say that these factors determine how individuals feel about themselves—whether they feel in control of the world around them. If these feelings are essentially, "I am not OK" and "I do not have a great deal of control over things that happen around me or to me," these persons are psychologically at high risk to develop some form of chemical dependency problem if they use chemicals.

The one variable that remains constant is, of course, use. It is impossible to become chemically dependent if one does not use chemicals. This is not to say that it is impossible to have chemical dependency problems after one gives up the use of chemicals. On the contrary, very often the problems only begin when the person stops using. This is where the nuclear family becomes important: We believe that the family is a system, and if one or more members of that system are chemically dependent then the whole system suffers, not just the person who is chemically dependent. The system must be treated, and is best treated as a unit. That does not translate to placing the chemically dependent person in treatment while educating the family about the disease of chemical dependency and teaching them to live with, yet psychologically apart from, the chemically dependent person. The family system, when functioning as a unit, is the place where family members should meet many of their needs (the need to be loved, and the need for security, among others). If the family does not meet these needs, the system needs repair or redirection. When the family is intact, we highly recommend that family therapy be used to restructure the family system so that all members are meeting appropriate needs through the family. (See Chapter 6.)

GENDER AND SEXUAL HISTORY

Just like human development, gender issues and human sexuality are often neglected in training programs for chemical dependency counselors. Consequently, many chemical dependency counselors feel ill-equipped to deal with their clients' sexual problems, and often these problems are neglected in the treatment plan. However, sexual problems rarely resolve themselves, and, if nothing else, it is the responsibility of the counselor to make an appropriate referral to a therapist trained to deal with problems of a sexual nature. This section of the chapter will view sexuality as it affects the chemically dependent person and will suggest some prospects for treatment and referral. Human sexuality is heavily intertwined in the development of each individual. The role that sex plays in establishing a positive self-image cannot be overstated. In turn, this variable also becomes critical to the treatment and rehabilitation of the chemically dependent person. Very often, the chemically dependent person has used drugs or alcohol to ease the anxiety or conflicts surrounding the issue of sexuality. These conflicts can easily complicate the rehabilitation effort if they are not considered and dealt with as a primary part of treatment.

It has been suggested that the most appropriate way to deal with problems of a sexual nature is to consider the distinctive needs of chemically dependent women and men and to place them in gender specific (same sex) therapy groups where these issues can be best addressed (Kaufman, Morrison, & Nelson-Zlupko, 1995). Studies of addicted populations have found that certain characteristics peculiar to chemically dependent women should be addressed in treatment (Beckman & Bardsley, 1986; Nelson-Zlupko, Kauffman, & Dore, 1995; Wallen, 1994). For example, women are far more likely to have a history of sexual abuse. Much of it involves the family and happened in early childhood. Women who abuse drugs are more likely to be socially isolated than men. They are more likely to be in an interpersonal relationship with an addicted partner. They are more concerned with interpersonal relationships than men and they express many more issues about parenting and child-care. Given these differences, it is not suprising that the treatment needs of women have been better met in women-only treatment groups (Kauffman, et al., 1995). Men also have issues both of a sexual and a nonsexual nature that women may not understand or relate to. These should also be dealt with in men-only groups. There may, however, be many things that men and women can teach each other about one another in a group setting. The choice of group membership criteria should be considered in relationship to the goals of the group. (See Chapter 5.) But the impact of diversity should definitely be factored into the decision.

Sex as a Source of Guilt

For the chemically dependent person, sex has often been instrumental in the establishment of a negative, rather than a positive, self-image. Guilt about sexual behavior is sometimes a primary motivation for drug- or alcohol-taking behavior. This guilt need not be connected to sexual behavior that occurred while the person was drinking or using; it might be sexual behavior that took place during a predrinking or drug-taking period. For example, victims of childhood incest have many issues surrounding their sexuality that cause them guilt, great pain, conflict, and self-doubt. If incest is ignored as a factor by the chemical dependency counselor, the treatment for these individuals will be incomplete or altogether unsuccessful.

In other instances, sexual behavior that occurred during drinking or using may be a great source of guilt. The values regarding sex that a person has when sober are often violated when under the influence. Promiscuous sex, homosexuality, and incest are all potential guilt producers. It is the responsibility of the chemical dependency counselor to determine the client's primary sexual issues and to establish how these factors are involved with the drinking or drug-taking behavior. The counselor can then intervene therapeutically to help the client resolve these matters. If this is done successfully, sexual problems will no longer be a source of negative feelings for the client.

Obtaining the Sexual History

As is suggested in Chapter 4, assessment, or diagnosis, is the cornerstone of a successful treatment program, and a successful diagnosis is only complete with an accurate sexual history. In order to gain access to information that is of a very personal nature, it is critical to ensure that rapport has been established between the counselor and the client. This rapport should be a natural part of a therapeutic counseling relationship. However, this may take time to establish, and the counselor should not rush to deal with sensitive subjects. Other, less threatening aspects of the client's history can be reviewed until the client is more comfortable with the counselor. With a subject such as sex, where values and feelings differ, it is only natural that some clients will be reluctant to bring up the subject regardless of the quality of the client-counselor relationship. This does not mean that the counselor should not bring up the matter. If the client is reluctant to talk about sexual subjects, the counselor should discuss the importance of such issues with the client and model openness toward sex. This might be done with a certain amount of self-disclosure by the counselor about his or her own experiences, which may be more comfortable for the client if the counselor is the same sex.

With regard to the sexual history of the individual, the counselor needs to pay particular attention to issues surrounding patterns of dominance and control; dependency; intimacy; and childhood experiences, including parental attitudes toward sex. Dominance issues should be examined with regard to the client's present and past interpersonal relationships. Questions concerning who has control, the level of control (Is there overcontrol? When? How?), and what this does to the self-esteem of the parties involved should be considered.

Dependency issues should be examined with regard to who is dependent upon whom, when, and under what circumstances. Levels of intimacy should be determined, and the influence of childhood experiences on sexuality should be considered with regard to parents and siblings. How did they relate to one another? Were they given opportunities for self-expression? What were, and are, the patterns of self-restraint that they developed? For chemically dependent persons, it is important to assess self-image and the role sex has played in the development of that self-image. It is also of interest to note how they see their spouses. What kind of image do they have of their spouses? What is their image of their relationships? After clients' relationships have been evaluated from the point of view of both parties, a more profound sexual history can be developed.

The sexual history should include an attempt to ascertain any specific dysfunction and a history of that dysfunction. It should also include the client's feelings with regard to the dysfunction. To complete the picture of the client's sexual background and how this background might be influencing current destructive behavior, a sexual history of the childhood, adolescent, and teen-age years should be taken. Feelings regarding family, cultural, religious, and social influences should be explored. Premarital sexual experiences and feelings (first sexual experiences, first knowledge of sex, masturbation, and homosexuality) and courtship and marital history are also important.

Some additional areas to explore in a sexual history would be the details (onset, duration, circumstances) of a specific problem and how the client views the problem. It is also important to consider the possibility of an HIV infection or AIDS. The client's physical and emotional condition plus forewarnings of the dysfunction and associated symptoms should also be considered.

Sexual problems have a variety of causes, both physiological and psychological. And, as noted earlier, these sexual problems are manifested in other psychological problems. It is not always clear which problem precedes the other; either way, the important issue is the current affect and how it can be dealt with therapeutically.

Physiological and Psychological Sexual Dysfunction

Some possible psychological causes of sexual dysfunction include anxiety, religious orthodoxy, hypertension, lack of arousal in one's partner, inability to communicate sexual desires, lack of knowledge, relationship problems, and, of course, alcoholism and drug abuse. Additional possible physiological causes of sexual dysfunction include diabetes, arthritis, central nervous system damage, vaginal infection, endometriosis, irritation from vaginal foam or jellies, menopausal atrophy, mumps, cancer, dietary insufficiencies, and drug and alcohol use.

Some specific female dysfunctions that women report are:

- not yet having had an orgasm
- pain during intercourse (dyspareunia)
- an involuntary vaginal spasm preventing penile penetration (vaginismus)
- absence of sexual feelings during intercourse
- little or no sexual desire

Some specific male dysfunctions that men report are:

- premature ejaculation (ejaculatio precox)
- erection with delayed or no ejaculation (ejaculatio retardata)
- inability to produce an erection (this may be called impotence and can occur as a primary or secondary dysfunction)
- absence or diminution of sexual feelings during intercourse
- little or no sexual desire

It is not essential for a client to report any one of these problems for sex to be a major issue in chemical dependency. In fact, more often than not the client will not report a specific problem. Sexual problems in the chemically dependent person are more likely to revolve around issues of guilt and self-image regarding prior sexual behavior and beliefs than around specific dysfunctions. The counselor should be aware, however, that specific dysfunctions do sometimes occur and that they are treatable when they do.

Should You Refer the Client to a Sex Therapist?

Whether the chemical dependency counselor wants to do sex therapy herself or himself or refer clients with sexual dysfunctions to a competent sex therapist is an individual choice. This choice should be made with several things in mind. The first factor to take into consideration is the counselor's personal comfort level when it comes to dealing with sexual problems. Do the counselor's own values and personal experiences make it difficult to work on issues involving sex? If so, we would recommend that the counselor refer clients with sexual problems. Counselors who are not comfortable with their own sexuality can hardly expect to be good sex therapists. Counselors should also consider their training; sex therapy is not something one does without proper training and instruction. There are many good books on the subject and there are excellent workshops offered across the country on sex therapy. These workshops are most useful to the beginning sex therapist.

The second factor to take into consideration is the availability of sex therapists in your community. If they are widely available and of good quality, the counselor may choose not to seek additional training in this area. However, if the counselor lives in a community where there are no competent sex therapists, the extra effort expended on training in sex therapy will be well worth the effort. Clients will benefit from the counselor's additional skills, and the counselor's understanding of the role sexuality plays in chemical dependency will be increased. Even with additional training, however, there may be times when it is more beneficial to send the client to an intensive inpatient sexuality treatment program such as the one established in St. Louis by Masters and Johnson. (See the reference list for their book.)

The third factor to take into consideration is whether the chemical dependency counselor is willing to use marriage counseling to deal with the client's sexual problems. Sex is only part of a marital relationship, and often sex between marital partners is hampered by other issues in the relationship. For a relationship to thrive, it must have mutual understanding, trust, and acceptance. These qualities have sometimes eroded in a relationship where one member of the couple is chemically dependent. The counselor who can assist in establishing a positive marital relationship will not only resolve many sexual issues but will be working toward the resolution of the chemical dependency problem as well.

This book is not designed to train chemical dependency counselors as sex therapists or marriage counselors. Its purpose is to alert the counselor to potential problems that chemically dependent clients may exhibit and to direct the counselor to resources wherewith they can confront these problems as they become apparent. Marital and sexual problems are two of the complicating issues that a chemical dependency counselor must confront. They must be included as necessary parts of most treatment to provide a complete treatment plan for each client.

To summarize the counselor's goals with regard to sexual problems: The counselor should uncover the client's sexual problems, freely examine the issues, and clarify problem areas. The counselor should also provide insights and interpretations as to how these problems are affecting the client's chemical dependency; provide emotional support and reduce anxiety and hostility; and educate and give permission, when necessary, in an effort to reduce guilt and increase positive feelings of self-worth in the client.

MENTAL HEALTH AND PERSONALITY

Those who suffer from substance use or abuse are a diverse group with regard to mental health. Some of them are mentally healthy except for the inappropriate use of drugs. Others suffer deeply from all manner of mental disorders from clinical depression to anxiety or even schizophrenia. Counselors who work with the chemically dependent make three major mistakes regarding mental health issues and chemical dependency. First, they do not diagnose the mental illness and only focus on the drug abuse. This is usually because they believe that the symptoms of the mental health problem are only a result of the drug abuse. Second, they misdiagnose the mental illness because some of the symptoms of drug withdrawal are the same as the symptoms of mental illness. And, finally, they diagnose the mental illness and ignore the substance use. It is usually counselors who work primarily in the mental health area who make this third mistake.

So-called dually diagnosed patients are a complex group. It is difficult for even the most experienced and highly trained person to sort out the symptoms caused by drug use or drug withdrawal from those of mental illness. The only accurate way is to make sure the patient is free of drugs and has been for some time.

Another issue that is raised regarding the mentally ill drug abuser is that of treatment by psychotropic drugs. Some see giving a mentally ill drug abuser any drug, even a prescription drug, as counterproductive. They feel that it reinforces the idea that one cannot live happily without drugs. It is highly advisable for the chemical dependency (CD) counselor to have a solid background in pharmacology. This also includes a knowledge of drugs that are used to treat mental illness and a solid knowledge of mental illness such as that usually found in an abnormal psychology course.

Although it is beyond the scope of this text to detail mental health issues, it is important to stress that the CD counselor who does not have a basic knowledge of mental illness will most assuredly make some tragic errors. For a review of this issue see the chapter on dual diagnosis in Lawson and Lawson, *Alcoholism and Substance Abuse in Special Populations,* Aspen Publishers, Inc., 1989.

Closely related to mental health issues are issues of personality. The idea of an "addictive personality" has never really achieved favor among most chemical dependency counselors, but it is still accepted by many in the mental health field. Although each counseling approach has its own theory regarding personality constructs, all agree that much behavior is learned, and developmental events influence the image of humankind that each individual has. The degree of emphasis placed on prior learning varies from theory to theory. Whether this should be a central focus of CD counseling is a decision each individual counselor will need to make.

Personality can be defined as the way in which each person interacts with the world. This involves an awareness of who we are in relation to others. What makes this difficult to understand and to track in each individual is that we all have different roles that we play in different situations. There are some personality characteristics that seem to be common to many chemically dependent people. These include being manipulative, dependent, blaming, irresponsible, sensation seeking, and many others. There are those who believe that the pathological effects of mood-altering chemicals have an impact on personality functioning, particularly in the area of regression. Regression is a return to an earlier developmental stage of psychological functioning, or a shift to a less mature level of psychological defenses. Regression includes acting out, passive-aggressive behavior, and somatization (conversion of anxiety into physical symptoms), as opposed to the more mature mechanisms of suppression, humor, or anticipation (Vaillant, 1971).

EMPLOYMENT AND RELATED ISSUES

Dr. William Glasser, founder of reality therapy, once said in a presentation on mental health, "The two things a person needs to be in a state of good mental health are someone to love who loves them and something to do that makes them feel worthwhile." The importance of feeling good about what one is doing has been almost absent as a treatment issue in most programs and individual treatment plans. Yet, if some thought is given to the issue, it is easy to see many cases where what the individual does on a daily basis relates directly to self-image and therefore to substance abuse. Some examples might include:

- A man or woman retires from a job that they derive great satisfaction and self-worth from. With too much extra time on their hands and lowered self-esteem because they are not contributing like they used to, they begin to drink too much or used too many prescription drugs. The fact that they may suffer from aches and pains that go with aging makes intoxication even more attractive.

- A woman who derives a great deal of pleasure from being a mother, suddenly has an empty nest. She feels empty and useless, and she turns to drugs to dull this feeling.
- A young man who has never drunk or used drugs in his life because of his family's values against doing so, goes to college or joins the military. The majority of his peers drink or use drugs because it is the "cool thing to do." He begins to emulate their behavior so he can fit in. He feels guilty going against his family's values, so he uses even more to subdue the feelings of guilt.

In other situations certain vocations are high risk for encouraging substance use. This may even be specific to a certain substances. Baseball players use snuff. Cowboys chew tobacco. Construction workers drink beer. Lawyers hang out with their peers in bars after work. Doctors and dentists have easy access to prescription drugs and are at risk of abusing them. Painters have nothing to do between jobs or when the weather is bad, so they drink. Sailors have long periods of work, and then they are off for long periods with little to do, so they drink. The unemployed spend their unemployment checks on drugs that will help them forget about their dilemma.

At the other end of the continuum are the individuals who have very high-paying jobs such as actors or professional athletes. One might wonder why people with so much talent and money would ruin their lives by using drugs. It does not seem to make sense. However, in many cases, especially when these individuals, seemingly overnight, go from being relatively poor to having literally millions of dollars, there is a burden that goes with the wealth. It allows these people to have access to an unending supply of drugs. There are always those who will sell drugs, especially to those with a great deal of money. So if the person used drugs even a little before, it is tempting for them to use all they want, especially when it relieves them of the guilt they could easily feel about having so much when most of their friends and relatives have so little. They often ruminate on the questions, "Why was I born with this talent?" and "Why should I have all of this when most others do not?"

These conditions sound stereotypical and can all be viewed as just excuses to use, but they surely play a part in an individual's substance abuse problems, and they should be addressed in treatment. The prime issue here is helping patients have something that they are interested in either as a vocation or an avocation that gives them a sense of achievement or adds meaning to their lives. If they do not have this, permanent recovery from addiction is unlikely.

RACIAL AND CULTURAL AFFILIATIONS

One's racial and cultural identity and affiliation have everything to do with self-image and, thus, chemical dependency. Race and culture affect our behavior. They determine how well we fit into the world we live in. They make us minorities or majorities. They make us politically strong or weak. They provide us with a feeling that we fit in or that we do not. They give us our values. They teach us what is normal. They influence our views on gender and family. They are vitally important as an aspect of the treatment process.

However, these issues first need to be understood by the counselor and client and then acknowledged and accepted. They may not be the focus of substance abuse treatment but they often offer a background from which the individual addiction can be understood. What counselors need to address first and foremost is their own assumptions, beliefs, and biases regarding other races and cultures. It is not the job of the counselor to change the culture of a patient, though some counselors try. Rather, counselors should do all that they can to understand the relationship between the patient's race and culture and the accompanying chemical dependency problems.

Each race and culture has its own set of issues, depending on the setting and surroundings that the individual is in. Gender, as well, often plays a role in each culture (Comas-Diaz & Greene, 1994). A black man in Kenya, Africa has a different set of problems than a black man in Alabama. A Native American on a reservation has a different set of problems than one living in an urban setting.

It is beyond the scope of this chapter to address the specific issues of Native Americans, Asians, African Americans, Hispanics, and other cultures and races. Native Americans alone represent over four hundred different cultures. Each tribe is a culture unto itself. Asians and Hispanics come from many different cultures. It is imperative that we stress the importance of these issues in the overall etiology and treatment of addiction.

Crosscultural counseling cannot be separated from the broader sociopolitical environment. How therapy is rooted in and reflects the dominant values, beliefs, and biases of the larger society, how the minority experience in the United States has influenced the worldview of the minority patient, and how counseling might represent cultural oppression are all issues to be addressed (Sue & Sue, 1990).

Is it possible for a counselor of one race or cultural background to truly understand what it is like for someone from an entirely different racial and ethnic background? And if the differences are vast, can the counselor accept the differences? Even if the counselor can do these things, will the patient ever be able to trust someone who is different than they? These issues are not unlike other issues in addictions counseling. Issues of whether a nonalcoholic can really help an alcoholic, or whether an alcoholic can help a cocaine addict are issues that can be and should be discussed in treatment. Patients who can tell their counselors that they do not trust them and why, have made progress. A patient who holds racial hostility or cultural issues inside will be more likely to relapse or not respond to treatment at all.

Important issues such as race and culture are covered in detail in Lawson and Lawson, *Alcoholism and Substance Abuse in Special Populations.* (See the reference list at the end of this chapter.) They believe that a CD counselor should take at least one entire course on race and culture, since a small bit of information on a race or culture often leads to stereotypes and further generalizations that may be harmful during the counseling process. A CD counselor with a few simple ideas about a specific race or culture may generalize them and falsely attribute these to individual patients. Race and culture is a subject to which there is no end when it comes to information that can be acquired and be useful. The most important issue, though, is the attitude of the counselor. Being open and accepting and willing to learn from your clients will go a long way to make up for a lack of knowledge about a culture or race.

RELIGION

Organized religion affects personal values, provides direction, defines meaning, and meets spiritual needs for many people. Religious beliefs can also affect an individual's risk for substance use or abuse. Some religions condone alcohol use and others do not. As mentioned in the subsection, Sociological and Psychological Family-Based Risk Factors, of this chapter, those who grow up in a religion that disapproves of alcohol use are at risk for problems if they choose to use alcohol. At the other end of the spectrum are some religions (the Native American church) that use mind-altering drugs in a ceremonial fashion. Alcohol is often used in religious rituals, for instance to represent the blood of Christ. Why should a CD counselor get involved in something as personal as religion?

If religious beliefs affect patients' self-image, their views on drug or alcohol use, or their beliefs in the spiritual meaning of life, they are important and should be addressed in treatment. Also, as has been often pointed out by Father Leo Booth, there have been abuses of religion as well as appropriate uses. Addictive behaviors are often related in some way (e.g., guilt) to religious beliefs. The CD counselor is not expected to be an expert in any one religion, and if counselors feel uncomfortable or inadequate dealing with such issues they should make a referral to someone who does not feel that way—perhaps a minister or a priest or a rabbi. Religion is an important issue for many people and it should not be overlooked in the overall treatment of chemical dependency or addiction.

MEDICAL PROBLEMS

Those with life-threatening medical problems or those who have medical conditions that involve a great deal of pain are at risk to abuse drugs. In today's world a client's AIDS or HIV infection must be an important consideration for the chemical dependency counselor. As everyone knows, having unprotected sex while under the influence of a mind-altering substance or while using IV drugs are two of the major ways in which substance abusers contract AIDS, which becomes a medical problem to be dealt with. Then, the fear and anxiety that go with such conditions are eased by mind-altering drugs, whether they are prescription or illegal. In addition, alcohol is often used alone or in combination with drugs to deaden the pain or reduce the anxiety. While there may be some short-term relief, the client's physical problems are often worsened by this behavior. The CD counselor can assist patients who are in physical pain by recommending biofeed-back, hypnosis, or pain clinics in order to help reduce the use of mind-numbing drugs to relieve pain. There is a point, however, when the values of the CD counselor may be challenged when clients choose to use drugs to reduce suffering. For example, it may be hard for a counselor to condone any use of marijuana, yet a patient may choose to use it to reduce the symptoms of chemotherapy. For some counselors, this would be a dilemma. There are no black-and-white answers to these kinds of questions.

Unfortunately there is a reverse problem here also. In some cases, doctors have being accused of inducing drug addiction in patients, and because of the fear that many people have of addictive drugs, many people in the United States are undermedicated for their pain and as a result are suffering. Contrast this to the fact that in most other countries in the world heroin and marijuana are medically available as pain relievers. In the United States both substances remain illegal even to cancer and AIDS patients who might respond to these drugs better than to any other prescription drug now available. The CD counselor can help resolve this social issue by educating themselves and the public not to overreact to heavy drug use or even addiction in those who are in pain or dying.

Other physical problems such as blindness, deafness, or muscular-skeletal disorders increase the risk of substance abuse. Each of these conditions has its own special set of problems. If a client has one or more of these conditions along with a chemical dependency problem, the counselor needs to understand what that person's specific issues are. For an excellent review of some of the major problems encountered by the disabled, see Glow (1989).

CRIMINAL AND DEVIANT BEHAVIOR

Recently in the United States the number of individuals in jails and prisons reached the one-million mark. Over half of these individuals are incarcerated as a result of some type of substance abuse. Statistics on the relationship between drugs, including alcohol, and criminal behavior are astounding. It is also not suprising that many of those who are in jail for drugs are also cultural or racial minorities from impoverished backgrounds. For the counselor who works in corrections, racial, cultural, and other issues of diversity are important but far less important than the issues that all of these individuals have in common, which is criminal behavior. Regardless of their cultural, racial, economic, religious, family, or any other diversity factor, they have used, sold, or bought drugs, and as a result they suffered the legal consequences—probation or jail.

In all criminal substance abuse cases, regardless of developmental or family history, personality, race, sex, or other conditions, those who are involved made the choice to use or sell drugs, which led to their being in jail or on probation. Therefore, the first and foremost issue in therapy should be helping these individuals take responsibility for their choices and decisions and helping them learn from their mistakes and make better choices in the future.

In order to do this, counselors in the federal prison system are taught to teach the inmates the three "Cs"—conditions, choice, and cognitions (Walters, 1990). To teach conditions, the counselor asks inmates in a group situation, "Why are you here in prison?" The counselor then lists on a blackboard the conditions that the inmates provide. Usually these include: poor family background including verbal and physical abuse from parents, poverty, poor school teachers, lack of love, poor religious background, among many others. The counselor then talks about how these are important variables and asks if the inmates know anyone who lived in such conditions but who is not in prison and did not use drugs. The answer is always yes. In fact, most inmates can recall someone who came from the same conditions they did and who has, by anyone's criteria, had a very successful life living within the law. The counselor then asks the inmates what the difference is between them and those who did not end up in trouble with the law. If, after discussion, the inmates do not come up with the fact that the difference between the two is the choices they made, the counselor brings up the issue of choices. The counselor then points out how conditions often limit the choices for a person, but there is always a choice that does not involve using drugs and risking jail time. The next hour or two is used to teach about choices with the inmates being asked to talk about the choices they made that led to their being in jail.

Then the counselor brings up another difference between the two groups, which is what they told themselves about the choices they had. These are called cognitions; thus making up the three Cs. Cognitions are discussed and each inmate is asked what they told themselves about the behavior that led them to jail. Sometimes they have told themselves that they had no choice, but the counselor can always provide another choice. For example, the inmate might say, "I had to sell drugs, it was the only way I had to make money." The counselor would then point out that other choices might have been made, such as a job, welfare, or borrowing money. If the inmate starts with, "Yes, but," the group usually confronts their behavior, otherwise the counselor confronts it.

There has been a great deal of research and a number of theories about criminal behavior (Walters, 1990; Blackburn, 1993). It is difficult to determine if the substance abuse led to the criminal behavior or the criminal behavior led to the substance abuse. Neither is an excuse for the other, however. They both involve choices and cognitions and they both have conditions that affect these cognitions and choices; consequently the three Cs is a good place wherewith to begin treatment.

Walters (1990) has suggested that criminals have developed a lifestyle that is characterized by a global sense of irresponsibility; self-indulgent interests; an intrusive approach to interpersonal relationships; and chronic violation of societal rules, laws, and mores. All of these need to be explained and dealt with both in group and in individual therapy. Each inmate should be asked to give examples of these lifestyle characteristics in their own life and to tell what the effect was on those around them.

Treatment programs in corrections settings can be programmed into the daily routines of inmates. Lessons of therapy can be reinforced and strengthened each day in the prison community by counselors, staff, and other inmates. Examples of inappropriate behavior are abundantly there for inmates to recall and learn from.

Counseling this population can be rewarding for the counselor, and substance abuse treatment as part of jail time makes a great deal of sense since it is very cost-effective in the long run for society. It costs only slightly more than no treatment at all, and it pays off in reduced recidivism rates, lower overall crime rates, and fewer behavior problems from inmates. Society has only begun to see the benefits of such treatment.

EMOTIONAL STRESS OR A HISTORY OF PERSONAL TRAUMA

It is not too difficult for the counselor to identify major negative emotions in chemically dependent persons. Sadness, grief, anger, fear, and rage often erupt in various ways when patients are in group or individual counseling. Positive emotions (joy, happiness, love, and caring) are usually less visible and then only as a sign that the patient is starting recovery. It is usually a goal of treatment to get clients to let go of, or change, highly charged negative emotions and replace them with positive emotions.

Anger is one of the most common emotions seen in addicts or alcoholics. Anger may or may not appear to be directed toward a specific person or event. In some cases, the alcoholic or drug addict may deny that this anger even exists. They may mask this emotion with another, such as sadness. Yet, they display repeated destructive, aggressive behavior toward others, usually while under the influence. A look into the chemically dependent person's developmental history might reveal a family background where anger and violence were not tolerated; thus the only time it becomes alright to get angry or aggressive is while intoxicated. Then they have an excuse. Further examination might find that a great deal of unexpressed anger toward a parent or a sibling exists and that the issues involved therein have never been resolved. If this is the case, the therapist can help resolve the issue by bringing in the family or providing some type of substitute treatment such as the "empty chair technique" (where the empty chair represents a person unable to attend therapy) for dealing with unresolved past issues. The therapist will also want to provide the client with alternative, positive ways of expressing anger. For some persons, just the knowledge of how they have been affected by past events is motivation enough to assist them in changing their feelings, their thinking, and their behavior.

Persons who come from alcoholic families often have the type of difficulties described above. As we know, about 50 percent of all alcoholics come from alcoholic families. What we do not know for sure is why only some of the children of alcoholics become alcoholic themselves and why others drink only moderately or choose not to drink at all. Of the ones who do become alcoholic, it is clear that their lives as children in alcoholic families had a great deal to do with their existing alcoholism. We know that modeling played a part in the development of their problem drinking. We also know that they may be at higher risk biologically or genetically. But most of all, we know that they were affected psychologically and emotionally. It is important to remember that not all children who grow up in alcoholic families are emotional cripples or suffer from negative psychological conditions. Two of our last three presidents grew up in alcoholic homes. As Wolin and Wolin (1993) point out in their book, *The Resilient Self,* many children who grow up in a destructive family environment gain strengths from the experience.

Stress and Psychological Factors

It has been the authors' clinical experience that psychological factors are very important in determining why some people develop chemical dependency. Children from alcoholic homes who themselves have drinking problems generally do not like themselves, and they do not feel in control of what they see as their hostile environment. Furthermore, most, if not all, of their basically negative attitudes can be traced directly to their experiences as a child in an alcoholic family. What is unfortunate is that many of their ideas and attitudes are erroneous and based on the sometimes-distorted view of the world that they had as children. For example, because of their parents' behavior they believed, and still believe, that their parents did not love them. Therefore, they see themselves as unlovable. After all, if one's own parents do not love them, who will? This is seemingly logical reasoning, but a child has no understanding of the complexities of alcoholism and other addiction and the behavior connected with it. To the child, the behavior is clear and the message is clear. Because my parents treat me as they do, I must be unloved and unwanted. At the very least, the message is confusing, "Daddy loves me but Daddy has a disease?" For a child, and even for many adults, a disease does not excuse past or future behavior. A parent's missing a birthday or missing

Christmas is a disappointment to a child, disease or no disease. And if the child resents the drinking parent for his neglectful behavior, telling the child not to drink because the parent has a disease only makes the child feel guilty about natural feelings. For the child, the only real option is to have the parent demonstrate his love through consistent, loving behavior.

For adults who grew up in an alcoholic family, an understanding of their parents' behavior—and the connection to why they are now behaving the way they do could change some of their own destructive behavior. Most alcoholics do not make a connection between their own behavior and that of their parents. They have also given little, if any, thought as to why their parents behaved the way they did and to the impact their grandparents had on their parents. It is a common belief that we all have a set of choices and are free to make whatever choice we want. The reality is that long before we make many choices, we are programmed to make one choice over another and our choices are not always in our own best interest. However, if we know how we have been programmed, we can override our programming and make choices that are truly in our best interest. Hence, adults who grew up as children of alcoholics should reexamine the issue of their self-worth. Given additional information and evidence—i.e., people who care about them, past successes, parents who perhaps are now sober and can express love to them—they can decide that they need to reassess their feelings of worthlessness and examine how they could make new decisions regarding their future behavior. For them, this might mean remaining sober and allowing themselves to enjoy life.

In most instances, it is possible to trace the antecedent of a behavior and to develop patterns of past behavior. It is also possible to predict, with some degree of accuracy, which future behavior will be based on past behavior. It is almost impossible, however, to do this without a knowledge of each person's developmental history. This should also include a history of past trauma. As mentioned, the family is often a source of this trauma, though not always. Veterans of Viet Nam for example often live with the trauma of not only the war but of an unpopular war, unlike any other where returning soldiers were spat on and called baby killers. This, after their risking their lives and seeing many of their friends killed. It is no wonder that this group is a high-risk group for substance problems. However, substance abuse is not the only issue that should be addressed in therapy. The trauma must be dealt with perhaps even before the substance abuse. Patients will be unlikely to give up drugs unless they have resolved the issues of the war.

A trauma may also be caused by a random event that changes lives forever. A patient of the authors, who was a cocaine abuser and a heavy alcohol user when he could not get cocaine, had been to inpatient treatment four different times. During the initial interview it was revealed that at age eighteen while he was in high school, this now twenty-eight-year-old young man had been driving with a friend when an accident occurred. The friend was not only killed, he was decapitated in full view of the patient. Further inquiry revealed that although this patient was still feeling a great deal of guilt over this incident, not one of the treatment programs had even asked him about it. It was very unlikely that this individual would be able to give up drugs unless this issue was resolved or at least addressed.

Because of the many similarities among persons who are chemically dependent, it is easy for a chemical dependency counselor to come to believe that each client is basically like the others. There are, however, far more differences among chemically dependent persons than there are similarities. The knowledge of these differences often separates a counselor who is mostly effective from one who is mostly ineffective.

DRUGS OF CHOICE

The drug, or drugs, that an individual chooses to use or the type of addiction is another consideration that the counselor will use in designing an appropriate treatment plan. There has been concern that some drugs, stimulants like crack and cocaine in particular, are more treatment resistant than more familiar drugs such as alcohol or heroin. However, treatment for problems with the major stimulant drugs, such as methamphetamine and cocaine and its altered forms, which were all in widespread use, was found to be just as effective as was treatment for alcohol problems, and somewhat more effective than treatment for heroin problems (CALDATA, 1994).

There are some differences that need to be considered. For example, a cocaine or stimulant user may present very differently than an alcohol or depressant user. The effects of heavy stimulant use include symptoms of paranoia and agitation that may not be seen in depressant use. Of course, the facts that a cocaine user has had to break the law to use and an alcohol user may not have will play a part in this. And, other addictions like gambling or food addictions have their own special issues that the CD counselor needs to be aware of. For example, the concept of abstinence is not really useful in the treatment of eating disorders. It is beyond the scope of this text to detail each addiction or each drug and what the similarities and differences are, however some excellent books on pharmacology are available to cover this material. Chapter 4 also provides additional information on this. We also suggest that all chemical dependency counselors take a course in pharmacology and be aware of all the different effects and side effects of drugs of abuse as well as psychotropic medications.

SUMMARY

The chemical dependency counselor who has a knowledge of the diversity issues, skills in identifying these issues and treating resulting problems, the ability to treat the family as a system, and the willingness to look at society's role in all of this will find the field of chemical dependency treatment rewarding and a continual challenge. Counselors who do not possess this knowledge or these skills will be constantly perplexed by the chemically dependent client. They will have to rely on the old standby: This client was not ready for treatment, when one person after another is unsuccessful in treatment. They will be unable or unwilling to see that it was not the client who was not ready for treatment; it was the counselor who lacked the skills to identify appropriate treatment plans. Meanwhile, the counselor with an understanding based on knowledge in these and other areas that make each client diverse will be able and willing to take the appropriate responsibility for what happens in treatment and to make adjustments as necessary to provide a successful treatment plan.

DISCUSSION QUESTIONS

1. What makes me diverse?
2. How comfortable am I with diversity in others?
3. What was my family of origin like and how has it affected me?
4. How can I use diversity to improve my counseling outcomes?
5. Are there important areas of diversity that were left out of this chapter? If so what are they?
6. What are the diversity issues a counselor might need to deal with in an alcoholic Native American woman with six children all under the age of 15?
7. What diversity issues would likely exist in an African American male, adolescent crack addict whose mother is also a heroin addict and whose father is unknown?
8. What could be the diverse issues of a forty-six-year-old male, Viet Nam veteran, who is unemployed, confined to a wheelchair, who smokes marijuana all day, and uses cocaine when he can get it?
9. What are the diverse issues of an alcoholic, retired Air Force general, who is sexually impotent, separated from his wife, and never sees his three grown children or his 12 grandchildren?
10. Make up your own case and list the issues that need to be addressed in treatment. Make it diverse.

REFERENCES

Babcock, M., & McKay, C. (1995). (Eds.). *Challenging Codependency: Feminist Critiques.* Toronto: University of Toronto Press.

Beckman, L. J., & Bardsley, P. E. (1986). Individual characteristics, gender differences, and drop-out from alcoholism treatment. *Alcohol and Alcoholism, 21,* 216–24.

Blackburn, R. (1993). *Psychology of criminal conduct: Theory, research & practice.* New York: Wiley & Sons.

CALDATA (1994). Evaluating recovery services: The California drug and alcohol treatment assessment, general report. Sacramento CA: Health and Welfare Agency: Department of Alcohol and Drug Programs.

Clark, W., & Washburn, P. (1988). Testing for human immunodeficiency virus in substance abuse treatment. *Journal of Psychoactive Drugs, 20* (2), 110–17.

Comas-Diaz, L., & Greene, B. (1994). (Eds.). *Women of color: Integrating ethnic and gender identities in psychotherapy.* New York: Gilford Press.

Cotton, N. S. (1979). The familial incidence of alcoholism: A review. *Journal of Studies on Alcohol, 46* (1), 89–115.

Glow, B. A. (1989). Alcoholism, drugs, and the disabled. In Lawson, G., & Lawson, A. (Eds.), *Alcoholism and substance abuse in special populations.* (pp. 65–91) Gaithersburg, MD: Aspen Publishers, Inc.

Kauffmen, E., Morrison, D., & Nelson-Zlupko, L. (1995). The role of women's therapy groups in the treatment of chemical dependence. *American Journal of Orthopsychiatry, 65* (3), 355–63.

Lawson, G., & Lawson, A. (1989). (Eds.). *Alcoholism and substance abuse in special populations.* Gaithersburg, MD: Aspen Publishers, Inc.

Lawson, G., & Lawson, A. (1992). *Adolescent substance abuse: Etiology, treatment and prevention.* Gaithersburg, MD: Aspen Publishers, Inc.

Lawson, G., Peterson, J., & Lawson, A. (1983). *Alcoholism and the family: A guide to treatment and prevention.* Gaithersburg, MD: Aspen Publishers, Inc.

Lewis, J. A. (1994). Issues of gender and culture in substance abuse treatment. In J. A. Lewis (Ed.), *Addictions: Concepts and strategies for treatment* (pp. 37–43). Gaithersburg, MD: Aspen Publishers, Inc.

Masters, W., & Johnson, V. (1966). *Human Sexual Response.* Boston: Little, Brown & Co.

Nelson-Zlupko, L., Kauffman, E., & Dore, M. M. (1995). Gender differences in drug abuse and treatment: Implications for social work interventions with substance abusing women. *Social Work, 40,* 45–54.

Schuckit, M. A. (1995). *Drug and alcohol abuse: A clinical guide to diagnosis and treatment.* (4th ed.). New York: Plenium Publishing Corp.

Sue, D. W., & Sue, D. (1990). *Counseling the culturally different: Theory and practice* (2nd ed.). New York: John Wiley & Sons, Inc.

Vaillant, G. E. (1971). Theoretical hierarchy of adaptive ego mechanisms. *Archives of General Psychiatry, 24,* 107–18.

Wallen, J. (1994). A comparison of male and female clients in substance abuse treatment. *Journal of Substance Abuse Treatment, 9,* 243–48.

Wolin, S., & Wolin, S. (1993). *The resilient self: How survivors of troubled families rise above adversity.* New York: Villard Books.

Chapter 8

Aftercare and Relapse Prevention

CHAPTER OBJECTIVES

- Define aftercare and relapse prevention
- Examine how several different treatment programs provide aftercare and relapse prevention
- Examine what the research on aftercare indicates about its effectiveness
- Examine the relapse prevention models of both Marlatt and Gordon, and Gorski
- Identify Marlatt and Gordon's specific and global relapse prevention strategies
- Examine the outline of Gorski's Developmental Model of Recovery
- Outline the basic principles and procedures of relapse prevention employing the Gorski model
- Examine the research on relapse prevention and the factors that have an impact on relapse
- Identify characteristics of relapsing and nonrelapsing alcoholics
- Examine the role of self-efficacy in relapse prevention

INTRODUCTION

This chapter, unlike the others in this book, focuses on what happens to substance abusers after they have completed primary treatment. While usually thought of as following treatment, both aftercare and relapse prevention actually begin with primary treatment when the person decides to stop using a mood-altering substance. For example, one can see the typical 12-step program as being designed to provide aftercare and to prevent relapse, and both of these goals are built upon the first step of Alcoholics Anonymous (A.A.). However, aftercare and relapse prevention have specific aims that are somewhat different from the aims of primary care. For this reason, it is important to define what is meant by *primary care, aftercare,* and *relapse prevention.*

Primary care has been defined in different ways by different people. The Institute of Medicine's (1990) special report on alcohol problems provides some of the more widely accepted definitions in the substance abuse field. The authors of this report define *primary care* as

> the application of therapeutic activities to help the individual reduce alcohol consumption [could read drug use also] and attain a higher level of physical, psychological, and social functioning while in either independent living or in a sheltered living environment. (Primary care includes both brief intervention and intensive intervention.) (p. 65)

The Institute of Medicine's (1990) report defines several other subphases of treatment that will not be included here. However, it is necessary to include one additional subphase outside our discussion because some people may define this type of treatment as aftercare. What this report calls *extended care-stabilization* is defined as, "the consolidation of gains achieved in primary care through continued participation in treatment and supportive activities while in either independent living or in a transitional supportive, sheltered living environment" (p. 65).

Aftercare is defined by this same report as, "the continued provision of some therapeutic input to maintain the gain in functioning achieved through intensive intervention and stabilization while in either independent living or in transitional or long-term supportive, sheltered living environment" (p. 66). (It is important to note that there seems to be some overlap between this definition and the one given for earlier extended care and the one that follows for relapse prevention.)

Relapse prevention, according to the Institute of Medicine's (1990) report, is

> the continued provision of therapeutic activities to avoid the return to prior patterns of drinking [or drug use] and to maintain the gains in functioning achieved through brief intervention or intensive intervention and stabilization while in either independent living or in a transitional or long-term supportive, sheltered living environment (p. 66).

What these definitions illustrate is that treatment phases overlap. For example, it is often difficult to know where aftercare ends and relapse prevention begins. The Institute of Medicine's report attempts to break down treatment into three major phases. The first is acute intervention and includes emergency treatment and detoxification. The second phase is rehabilitation, which subsumes the attempts to get patients to change their drinking behavior. Individuals may have to learn new ways of living and thinking during this phase and develop some new coping skills. The third stage is called maintenance and extended care (which is seen as an extension of primary care) and aftercare. However, aftercare is used by the Institute to describe patients' long-term efforts to maintain the changes they have made in formal treatment.

These various ways of dividing up the phases of treatment may be quite artificial because patients may actually get the first so-called formal treatment in a particular area of their lives only when they are in aftercare or the first day of formal treatment may play a critical role in aftercare. Thus, as noted earlier, treatment may not always occur in precisely arranged stages or phases. However, for the purposes of this chapter, each of the treatment phases will be discussed as if they were clearly separate.

This chapter focuses on aftercare and relapse prevention. First to be described and evaluated will be aftercare. Then relapse prevention, which is one of the major issues confronted in aftercare, will be discussed. This chapter will include some examples of aftercare and relapse prevention programs, descriptions of procedures and instruments used in these programs, and any research available that supports and/or argues against the effectiveness of aftercare and relapse prevention.

AFTERCARE

Getting a stable definition of aftercare has been difficult. They way it has been defined has changed over time and is partially dependent on who is proposing the definition. For example, aftercare, as originally defined by the Joint Commission on the Accreditation of Health Care Organizations (1983), included all the services provided for the patient following their discharge from the treatment agency. One must remember that, in the early 1980s the Minnesota model, a twenty-eight-day intensive inpatient treatment program based on Alcoholics Anonymous' 12 steps, was in vogue. Aftercare was seen as any services that helped recovering persons deal with the abrupt transition from an intense treatment program to life in the everyday world.

We will compare and contrast three current programs that provide treatment that extends beyond what one might call primary care. Two of these programs are built on what is called the Minnesota Model (see above), but they differ in the degree to which they use psychosocial treatment. A major portion of the difference is the use of clinical psychologists and/or a psychological approach. The third program is based on a developmental model. In the developmental model the 12-step program of Alcoholics Anonymous (A.A.) is not employed as a central component of treatment philosophy or as a main focus of treatment. Because of these differences and because of the differing populations that they serve, the three programs have different programs following primary care. Economic factors, such as what type of aftercare third-party payers will fund, are also important.

Aftercare: Three Examples

Valley Hope is a chemical dependency program located in several midwestern and southwestern states. Treatment facilities managed by the Valley Hope Association, Norton, Kansas, can be found in Kansas, Nebraska, Missouri, Oklahoma, Colorado, and Arizona. This is a nonprofit organization that has been very successful, as demonstrated by its growth from one agency in Norton, Kansas, to locations in six states. All of Valley Hope's treatment centers share a common philosophy. Much of the philosophy is based on the Minnesota Model and the use of A.A.'s 12 steps. Each of Valley Hope's programs is currently responding to the economic realities of managed care in the alcohol and drug field at different speeds. The Parker, Colorado, Valley Hope residential program has been one of the first to publish new materials on the program, as it has made the changes necessitated by managed care economic realities (Dr. Kenneth Gregoire, Valley Hope Association, Personal Communication, August 1993). Therefore, the Parker Valley Hope descriptions will be used here.

Parker Valley Hope has an "intensive residential chemical dependency" program. (This quote and others to follow are based on Parker Valley Hope literature, August 1993.) This program is individualized so that each person has a separate treatment program. An assessment is conducted on each person who enters Valley Hope to establish the individualistic treatment program. "In-depth biopsychosocial assessments . . . [are] . . . conducted on all admissions . . . [and] . . . include a medical history and physical, substance abuse and psychosocial history, psychological assessments as well as pastoral and recreational service assessments. Assessments are usually completed within the first three to five days."

A sense of the type of treatment programs that Parker Valley Hope provides can be gained from their description.

> Behavioral and affective stabilization occurs within an intensive recovery-oriented treatment millieu stressing 12 step involvement and reinforcement of sobriety based attitudes and behaviors. Rehabilitative [treatments] include individual, group, pastoral, family and marital counseling provided by certified addiction counselors and pastoral counselors. Over 45 hours of active treatment are provided weekly and 12 step meeting attendance is strongly encouraged. A patient's involvement in these specific services is dictated by their identified clinical needs and individualized treatment planned. Each patient is assigned a primary counselor when admitted to coordinate treatment planning, assessments of patient programs, and case management. Psychiatric consultation and other ancillary medical services are utilized as needed. Continuing care is provided in a weekly aftercare counseling group [see below]. Parker Valley Hope also offers a weekend outpatient program

and makes referrals for continuing care for patients who live in geographic areas that are less convenient to our facility (Parker Valley Hope program information materials, August 1993).

This same facility offers a partial care program that runs from 8:00 A.M. to 6:00 P.M., Monday through Friday. The same type of programming is followed with programming that is individually based on the biopsychosocial assessment procedure noted above. The partial care program is part of what this agency calls the "continuum of care" and it is seen as perhaps less restrictive than the residential program. As noted in the Parker Valley Hope information materials (1993), "partial care is provided by a caring, multidisciplinary team comprised of certified counselors, chaplains, nursing staff, physicians and psychologists."

As might be expected from a program that is concerned with the continuum of care, Parker Valley Hope also offers an aftercare program. The aftercare program may be obtained as part of the primary care treatment or may be purchased separately. Aftercare takes place within six months (13 counseling sessions) or one year (27 counseling sessions). Parker Valley Hope views these sessions as furthering gains made in primary treatment and as assisting both the patient and the spouse or significant other in adjusting to the new, nonalcoholic and/or nondrug lifestyle. Most of these services are delivered in group settings.

Participants in the aftercare groups are encouraged to attend Al-Anon, Al-Ateen, or other self-help programs. The Valley Hope material also indicates that individual sessions are available within the framework of the aftercare program.

Another view of the issues that drive aftercare in the Valley Hope system is given in the association's newsletter, *Coffee Cup*. This view was written by Harry Gard of the Wichita Valley Hope Outpatient Center (in some locations Valley Hope does not have a residential treatment program). Gard suggests that aftercare involvement be stressed as "a tool of ongoing recovery." He cites sources that suggest that the field should move away from two discrete types of treatment (primary treatment and aftercare) and see treatment needs as being on a continuum. He notes that one can (and perhaps should) anticipate that treatment outcome for both alcoholics and drug addicts is more dependent on what happens following primary treatment than on what happens in intensive treatment. He uses a lengthy quote from Shulman (1993) to bolster his point.

It is noteworthy that a significant number of people relapse during the first 3 months after discharge, almost as if the treatment they were provided "wore off." Another very significant factor is the shorter lengths of treatment, which is an impact of managed care. More and more issues that are identified during inpatient treatment must now be treated in an outpatient setting (Shulman, 1993 [as cited in Valley Hope Association, 1993]).

Gard cites changes in treatment due to managed care as the reason that a variety of aftercare services are provided at Wichita Valley Hope. These services include group therapy, marital groups, individual sessions, and marital and family sessions. An intake is conducted to plan aftercare services. The results of psychological testing completed at the beginning and end of preliminary treatment are frequently used for aftercare planning. (It should be noted that a pretreatment and posttreatment battery of tests is routinely given to Valley Hope patients. This battery includes, among others, the Minnesota Multiphasic Personality Inventory (MMPI), the Rotter Incomplete Sentence Blank, and the Marlowe Crowne.) To complete planning for aftercare, patients' current stressors and potential for relapse are assessed.

The **Independence Center,** located in Lincoln, Nebraska, has been in place since the beginning of the 1970s. It is truly a Minnesota Model program since it was established by trainers from the Johnson Institute in Minnesota. Early in its history the program was well known for a heavy controntational approach to treatment. As time passed, the program gained a reputation in some parts of the community for being perhaps too confrontational. This was particularly true when used with women who had low self-esteem and fewer of the sociopathic personality characteristics with which a heavy confrontational approach works better. Over the years, this approach has been modified by a more informed set of counselors, and the treatment rationale for the facility has gradually changed. In the majority of cases, a less confrontational, more caring approach is now used. Historically, the Independence Center has depended heavily on third-party payments. A recent change in payment by insurance companies hit all freestanding treatment programs very hard, but this billing change was particularly trying for the Independence Center. Reduced inpatient bed occupancy was difficult for an agency that had previously depended on this part of the program to fund some of its outpatient and aftercare services. In a recent publication, the shift in emphasis and programming was noted.

> In response to a rapidly changing health care environment, the Independence Center has developed creative ways of treating patients and their families for addiction and co-dependency. With goals of (a) reducing the overall cost (b) improving the quality of care, Mr. Engel [*the Director of the agency*–italics added] and his staff have devised multiple interventions designed to be flexible and individualized (Eiel, 1993, p. 32).

Today, treatment is seen as a continuum of care that includes inpatient and partial care for both adults and adolescents. Added to these treatment programs is a residential program that Engel describes as a "step-down" level of care for those patients needing long-term primary treatment. The patient's status is documented by a nonmedical charting of progress. This program is designed for patients who are physically stable and who do not have serious psychiatric problems. It costs 40 percent less than inpatient treatment.

Cost containment is one of the factors that has heavily influenced the changes in the program at the Independence Center (as it has for most alcohol treatment programs in the U.S.). The Independence Center has dealt with the need to provide good care while still providing less expensive treatment. Mr. Engel describes movement through treatment as integrated with variable lengths of stay. According to Independence Center program literature, treatment is enhanced because patients stay with the same counselor as they progress through the different intensities of care. This new integration of services helps patients move to less expensive methods of care as soon as they are deemed ready. Upon admission, patients are informed about different levels of care and how these levels will affect treatment progress. Hopefully, this process helps them feel more secure in therapy.

The Independence Center's response to less funding for inpatient treatment was to find other ways to provide services for their clients. At present, they do not have a traditional aftercare program. Instead, the goal in aftercare is to make personal contact with patients. Treatment is seen as being something that may occur over 18 months. The agency uses aftercare to meet needs in clients as they arise following intensive care.

The Independence Center sees alcohol abuse as a chronic, potentially relapsing condition. There is an attempt to deal with relapses before the recovering person drinks. As the director of the agency suggests, what they now do should not be called aftercare but rather continuing care, since that is closer to what the agency provides. A great deal of this care is carried out through the use of several groups. These include, "fighting right," Relapse Prevention, Adult Children of Alcoholics, Co-dependency Group, and Youth Specialty Group.

The length of treatment varies for each person. All patients are no longer put through the same program. Instead, treatment starts where the person is at the time that they are first seen and progresses from there. The program is based within the local community and planned so that patients can return to the community as soon as they are ready. For example, a patient might go from detox to daycare (a nonresidential program that keeps the patient involved in a program of treatment for the full day). From the daycare program the patient might go to outpatient, which is a less intense level of treatment usually meeting several nights of the week. Following outpatient programming, patients may be assigned to one or more of the specialty groups listed above.

The new program is still in the process of being finalized. It is likely that more frequent and continuous assessment over the span of treatment will be necessary so that the patient's needs can be more carefully met. That is not always easy to do, as the following excerpt from Eiel (1993) suggests.

Since many patients move through the treatment system quite rapidly, some treatment consistency has been lost. This loss of consistency has resulted in less bonding between patients and their counselors. This problem is exacerbated, according to Mr. Engel, by increasing amounts of clinical documentation and lack of computerization. The director readily admits that, at times, his treatment center needs a "traffic cop" to keep track of the location, clinical disposition, and status of the patients as they move through the many levels and intensities of care. (p. 33)

(*Note:* The people in treatment are called patients here because the Independence Center is administratively and physically tied to a general hospital in Lincoln, Nebraska.)

The Independence Center's program is trying to find a way to meet patients' treatment needs by providing a program that is flexible, is customer oriented, and is sensitive to the current managed care reimbursement system. They also face (as do all of the examples here) the uncertainty of what changes nationalized health care will demand from freestanding alcohol treatment programs. Being attached to a medical facility (but relatively administratively independent) may or may not help this facility.

The **Lincoln Lancaster Drug Projects** (LLDP, formerly Full Circle) is not an A.A. or 12-step based program. Instead, it is based on a "biopsychosocial model: A holistic approach which attempts to combine all other models (except of course, the moral model); views other models as reductionistic" (Lincoln Lancaster Drug Projects, 1992). The individual and the application of the holistic approach are the focus of this treatment center. The holistic approach assumes that biological events affect psychological functioning, that psychological functioning affects social functioning, and vice versa. "An event in one realm (biological, psychological, or social)—an event such as substance abuse—not only impacts and is impacted by the other two, it **IS** an event in all three realms" (Lincoln Lancaster Drug Projects, 1992, capitals and bold in the original).

This holistic approach requires an understanding of the whole person. Without looking at the whole person, all the problems or all the possible resources that could be used to assist recovery cannot be recognized. The treatment of the whole person means treating several presenting problems at the same time. "This approach to treatment, coupled with the agency's mission to serve the disadvantaged, has attracted referrals of many individuals with long histories of multiple problems." (Lincoln Lancaster Drug Projects, 1991) This approach has led to the agency's treating dual-diagnosis clients, i.e., clients with coexisting substance abuse and mental health problems, with neither disorder being primary. Because of the nature of the clients' histories (many are homeless, most are people with limited resources, and up to 10 percent have dually been diagnosed), the treatment is often longer than in most substance abuse centers. Treatment runs as long as three to six months for a large percentage of clients. A description of a typical client is given in Exhibit 8–1.

Exhibit 8–1 A Description of a Typical Lincoln Lancaster Drug Projects Client

---

Client: Adult Female, approximately 30 years of age.
HISTORY: Sexual abuse beginning age 3, continuing at least 5 years; severe physical abuse as a child, resulting in permanent injury; history of alcoholism in the family; foster home and group home placements beginning approximately age 9 (perhaps sooner, records unclear); several abusive relationships as an adult, one failed marriage; lengthy history of alcohol abuse including consumption of up to one quart of vodka daily, numerous blackouts, delirium tremens, potentially fatal blood concentrations; extensive drug history, including IV, cocaine, and methamphetamine usage; 3–5 DWI arrests (records unclear), several other misdemeanor arrests, several brief incarcerations, probation; several failed efforts at employment; at least two prior inpatient treatments for substance abuse, unknown number of detoxifications, seven years of "psychotherapy," unknown number of hospitalizations and other medical treatments for substance abuse, unknown number of hospitalizations and other medical treatments for injuries (some self inflicted) and disease (including liver disease); at least two serious suicide attempts; dependent on friends or public assistance throughout most of adult life; evidence of several mental disorders in client's history, including post-traumatic stress disorder, major depression (recurrent), and documented concerns about a possible thought disorder and personality disorder.
ECONOMIC COSTS: At least 18 years in and out of the "system," including several years in group homes or foster care; criminal justice system costs (including several brief incarcerations, court costs, probation); unknown number of hospitalizations and other medical treatment for physical injuries (accidents, physical abuse, suicide attempts), liver disease, delirium tremens, one partial-care substance abuse treatment, several detoxifications, 7 years of outpatient therapy, direct public assistance payments; per-client administrative costs of public assistance programs, virtually none of these costs borne by client, conservatively estimated costs of $15,000 per year in the system for a total of $270,000 in public monies.
COURSE OF TREATMENT: Admitted to residential program in late 1988, withdrew early 1989, reentered in fall of 1989, completed in February of 1990; approximately 9 months in treatment.
OUTCOME OF TREATMENT: Client drank shortly after discharge, required one more detoxification; has since maintained longest period of drug free status since early adolescence, and has remained employed and self-sufficient for the past 9 months (also a record); receives no public assistance; regularly utilizes YWCA, involved in other appropriate leisure pursuits; involved in long-term relationship with no abuse; remains in contact with us.
Update 2/20/92: Returned for outpatient counseling after becoming involved in another abusive relationship and subsequent drinking again. Also reported mood swings; maintains sporadic contact; utilizes psychiatric consultations and case management services. Stabilized but prognosis uncertain.

Case study from materials from Lincoln Lancaster Drug Projects, Inc. and is used with permission.

The agency has outlined its basic characteristics in a fact sheet. These characteristics include:

- **HISTORY**—Lincoln Lancaster Drug Projects was founded in 1973 to fill unmet needs in the community for (1) a treatment program for persons using drugs other than alcohol; (2) a program that would serve clients regardless of their abilities to pay or other life circumstances that were barriers to their getting help; and (3) a program that offered an alternative to the traditional A.A.-based treatment. Only adult programs were offered in the early years. In 1979 those same community needs gave rise to the development of the agency's youth programs. In 1983 the agency assumed responsibility for the Drug Crisis Center. In 1991 programming was enhanced and expanded to include specialized services for persons with mental health and substance abuse problems.

- **MISSION STATEMENT**—Through the years, the agency has grown to meet an increasing demand for services. Over 40 staff now provide service to approximately 400 clients and 800 crisis line callers per year. Lincoln Lancaster Drug Projects recognizes the individual's right to treatment regardless of socioeconomic status or any other life circumstances that might serve as a barrier to access.

- **TREATMENT GOALS/OBJECTIVES**—The goals of treatment at LLDP are to: (1) reduce drug and alcohol misuse; (2) assist individuals in coping with the fundamental problems that led to the drug or alcohol use in the first place; and (3) provide individuals with skills for becoming more effective students, workers, and family members. These are achieved through educational and counseling groups, individual and family counseling groups, individual and family counseling, life-skills training, and activity therapy.

- **UNIQUE APPROACH**—Our model of treatment is unique in several respects. It offers an alternative to more traditional, A.A.-based treatment programs. The length of treatment is longer, averaging three–six months. Each client's treatment plan is individually designed. Success is measured by several criteria, including educational involvement, legal involvement, work history, use of drugs or alcohol, and interpersonal relations. Finally, treatment costs are less than other comparable programs and a sliding-fee scale is used. No one is denied services due to an inability to pay.

- **TARGET POPULATION**—LLDP is committed to serving anyone in need of assistance, regardless of socioeconomic status or other barriers to accessing service. Ninety percent of residential clients and 50 percent of outpatient clients should be low income. Ten percent of all clients served should be from ethnic minority populations. Homeless persons and dual-diagnosis clients, i.e., clients with concurrent mental illness and substance abuse problems, are priority populations for the agency. Special outpatient programming is offered for gay/lesbian/bisexual clients (Lincoln Lancaster Drug Projects, Inc., 1993 and used with permission.)

Perhaps because of its individualized approach, this agency does not have an aftercare program in its structure. One could speculate that this is in reaction to the changing reimbursement policy of insurance companies. It is unlikely that this is a major issue with this agency, though. Because of its commitment to treat *all* clients, almost none of the people treated by this agency are on third-party payments from insurance companies.

The above three program descriptions point out that the way in which aftercare is incorporated into treatment varies in important ways across different alcohol treatment programs. These differing aftercare programs make it difficult to compare the effectiveness of aftercare in general and its specific effects in particular in the overall recovery rate of persons who have been treated for alcohol and drug problems. One way to resolve whether these varying aftercare programs are effective is to utilize research findings on aftercare. Such research should help clarify the effectiveness of aftercare in alcohol and drug treatment.

Research on Aftercare

There is a great deal of research that has been done on aftercare. However, there is what can be called a natural confound between participation in aftercare and the degree of investment in what Littrell (1991) calls the "packaged treatment program" that precedes aftercare (p. 191). A confound is where two factors that could conceivably account for the outcome of a research study cooccur and make it difficult to establish causality. In the case of aftercare, it is the motivation that the client initially brings to treatment that may (with or without the treatment offered in aftercare) affect outcome. The higher the motivation, the more likely clients are to do well in treatment and the more likely they are to attend aftercare. Thus, clients' choices to attend and to complete aftercare treatment may be heavily influenced by the level of motivation and desire for change with which they leave the prepackaged program. Despite this possible confound, several studies have looked at the rate of participation in aftercare treatment in terms of the percentage of people who participated and how much they participated.

It should be first noted that participation rates in aftercare are low. In one study, only 66 percent of 122 patients attended aftercare following an intense treatment program and only 28 percent attended more than three sessions (Pokorny, Miller, Kanas, & Valles, 1973 [as cited in Littrell, 1991]). Other programs' attendance rates at aftercare have been even lower. Of 90 Veterans Administration patients who completed an eight-week inpatient treatment program, only about one-third attended one aftercare session. Only 9 percent attended more than four sessions (Pratt, Linn, Carmichael, & Webb, 1977. The alcoholic's perception of the ward as a predictor of aftercare attendance [as cited in Littrell, 1991]). Littrell reports that the mean number of aftercare sessions attended in most studies is about three.

Studies that allow a causal statement to be made usually involve random assignment to an aftercare treatment, no follow-up treatment, and/or a differing treatment like a telephone aftercare service where patients call in. The findings from these studies are that aftercare has no effect. That is, these more carefully controlled studies fail to support the prediction that aftercare will produce a more positive outcome than no aftercare and/or a lower level of aftercare. This might mean that *when allowed to choose aftercare,* those patients who are most invested in staying sober attend, and those less interested in remaining sober do not. An alternative hypothesis is that those patients who are most likely to comply with program recommendations are the ones who attend aftercare. Littrell (1991) suggests, from her review of the literature, that compliance is a personality factor that is positively associated with outcome in alcoholics.

In another important study by Connors, Tarbox, and Faillace (1992), male and female problem drinkers participated in an eight week drinking-reduction program. Following this program they were randomly assigned to either a six-month group aftercare program, a telephone aftercare program, or no aftercare. Regardless of aftercare program, the majority of patients (64 percent) reduced their drinking following treatment. As the authors of this study note: "Aftercare, at least as operationalized in this study, did not moderate treatment outcome" (p. 471).

In an earlier study, McClatchie and Lomp (1988) divided a group of 155 subjects into three aftercare groups. One group was placed in a mandatory aftercare group, another in a voluntary aftercare group, and a third were asked to not participate in aftercare for three months following treatment. The findings from this study illustrate some of the difficulties in understanding the results of aftercare studies. The researchers found no differences in outcome in those attending aftercare. They did find, though, that 66 percent of the voluntary aftercare group requested aftercare services. The authors concluded that:

> the results of this study are consistent with the body of literature which contends that there is no advantage to extended therapy in the treatment of alcoholism. Furthermore, the possibility is raised that previous research efforts that have found a positive relationship between aftercare and outcome may have been confounded by the issue of 'patient compliance' with the terms of treatment. That is, subjects who comply with the terms of treatment tend towards better treatment outcome irrespective of whether the terms of treatment call for aftercare or not (p. 1045).

Most of the current research seems to support the contention that aftercare has little differential impact on treatment outcome when proper experimental controls are included. This does not necessarily mean that individuals who attend aftercare voluntarily do not receive many benefits from aftercare programs. It does mean that whatever clients obtain from this extended-care experience cannot be demonstrated to have an impact under appropriate experimental conditions, or at least not enough impact to influence treatment outcome. It may be that when more precise diagnostic instruments are developed, the matching of alcoholic patients to the appropriate postcare conditions may demonstrate a significant role for aftercare. It is important that the patients who are most likely to gain from this type of extended care be assigned to this longer-term treatment.

RELAPSE PREVENTION

Because alcohol and drug abuse are seen as "relapsing conditions," one of the key factors in keeping a person drug free is whether or not the danger of relapse can be minimized. Two approaches to relapse prevention will be discussed in this section. The first one (by Marlatt & Gordon, 1985) is a biopsychosocial model based on learning principles and some limited research by various investigators. Marlatt and Gordon take a social learning approach to relapse prevention, but their writings do not seem to be widely known and used by chemical dependency counselors. This may be due, in part, to their use of learning concepts. Marlatt and his associates have been a major influence in the substance abuse field through their research on relapse prevention. (A discussion of research findings will follow the presentation of the two relapse models.)

The second approach (Gorski & Miller, 1986) is much better known by chemical dependency counselors. This is primarily because Terry Gorski has outlined his model in workshops that he has conducted throughout the country. While Gorski and Miller's model is also a biopsychosocial one, the principles have been simplified and described with less learning based, psychological jargon than has Marlatt and Gordon's approach. Also Gorski's model is based on the 12 steps used by most of the Minnesota Model treatment centers.

Relapse Prevention: Marlatt and Gordon

Relapse and relapse prevention can be viewed from several perspectives. Marlatt and Gordon (1985) review some of those perspectives in order to clarify the reasons why approaches to relapse prevention can vary depending on the philosophy on which they are based. For example, the paradox of control in the disease model (which is the base for the Minnesota Model and most other models of treatment in this country) is that alcoholics are told that alcohol problems originate from physiological factors that lead them to lose control of their drinking. They are told they must abstain, but the paradox is that abstaining is a *form of control*. Marlatt and Gordon say, in fact, that the individual can only maintain control if they abstain. To relapse is to lose control.

One of the problems of this disease-model approach is that, while it absolves the alcoholic from blame for their abusive drinking, it can potentially make them see themselves as helpless to change it. Some research suggests that if people are told that their drinking is genetic (and by implication that they can do little about it), they feel that they can do less about the problem than people who are given a social learning explanation.

Of course, in both of these models, the disease model and the social learning model, clients benefit from knowing that they are predisposed to a drinking problem, and, thus, they remain vigilant (Marlatt & Gordon, 1985). The disease model is successful if it can teach the alcohol abuser what Wallace (1982) calls an esoteric belief, i.e., abusive drinkers are convinced that they are sick, that they are suffering from a medically recognized illness, and that they are no longer capable of drinking without losing control. According to Marlatt and Gordon, teaching this esoteric belief does not seem to be very effective in preventing relapse. Some research suggests that only 10 percent of alcoholics in various treatment programs manage to abstain for as long as two years. Relapse may be the turning point where disease theory may fail (Marlatt & Gordon, 1985). Acceptance of the A.A. position that you are always just one drink away from being a drunk means even a one-drink lapse can precipitate a total, uncontrollable relapse. Thus, in the disease model, just one lapse is tied to the expectancy that you have total failure.

Another way of seeing drinking problems is as an addiction; as nothing more than an acquired habit pattern. From the social learning perspective, addictive behaviors are viewed as overlearned habits that can be analyzed and modified in the same manner as other habits (Marlatt & Gordon, 1985). Using this conceptual perspective, Marlatt (1985a) has outlined the relapse process.

Marlatt's overview of relapse factors that contribute to slips will be followed by a more extensive discussion of these factors. First, Marlatt is careful to specify that his description of relapse applies to those people who have chosen voluntarily to abstain from the addictive behavior. Coerced change has not been tested in the Marlatt model. A representation of the Marlatt model of relapse is given in Figure 8–1.

In this model, individuals are assumed to experience perceived self-control while they are maintaining abstinence. The longer persons can maintain abstinence or control over the addictive behavior, the greater their perception of self-efficacy. (Self-efficacy is defined as, "the individual's expectation concerning the capacity to cope with an impending situation or task. A feeling of confidence in one's abilities to cope with high risk situations is associated with an increased perception of self-efficacy—a kind of 'I know I can handle it' feeling" [Marlatt, 1985a, p. 40]).

Perceived control continues until the individual is exposed to a high-risk situation. (Any situation that is a risk to the person's sense of self-control is defined as high risk.) By looking at a number of relapse episodes from a variety of addiction problems (problem drinking, heroin addiction, compulsive gam-

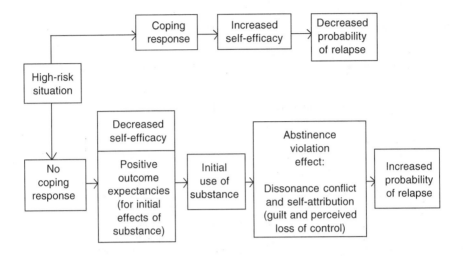

Figure 8–1 A cognitive-behavioral model of the relapse process. *Source:* Reprinted from *Relapse Prevention* by G. A. Marlatt and J. R. Gordon, p. 38, with permission of Guilford Press, © 1985.

bling, and overeating), researchers have arrived at three categories of high-risk behaviors that are closely related to relapse.

The first of these three categories is *negative emotional states* (35 percent of all relapses occur during this type of state). The person in this state is seen as experiencing negative (and unpleasant) affects. These emotions can include frustration, anger, anxiety, depression, or boredom, which occur at or before the relapse event occurs. The source of these emotional upsets are intrapersonal.

When another person or a group of people are the source of relapse, another category of high-risk behaviors, *interpersonal conflict* (accounting for 16 percent of relapses), is involved. Interpersonal conflict percipitators of relapse include negative, conflictual interaction such as with the marital partner, with friendship relations, or with family members or employers. Arguments with other people and confrontations at work or in social situations would be other interpersonal conflicts that could potentially contribute to relapse in the "sober" addicted person.

When the individual is placed under *social pressure,* it means that pressure is being placed on the addict to engage in the addictive behavior by another person or group of people. This third relapse precipitating factor accounts for 20 percent of all relapses.

Marlatt presents a more detailed and more finely honed analysis of the three factors and their influence on relapse. This elaboration is detailed in Exhibit 8–2.

Exhibit 8–2 Categories for Classification of Relapse Episodes

Intrapersonal-Environmental Determinants. Includes all determinants that are primarily associated with interpersonal factors (within the individual), and/or reactions to nonpersonal environmental events. Includes reactions to interpersonal events in the relatively distant past (i.e., in which the interaction no longer has a significant impact).

Coping with Negative Emotional States. Determinant involves coping with a negative (unpleasant) emotional state, mood, or feeling.

- **Coping with frustration and/or anger**—Determinant involves an experience of frustration (reaction to a blocked goal-directed activity), and/or anger (hostility, aggression) in terms of the self or some nonpersonal environmental event. Includes all references to guilt and responses to demands ("hassles") from environmental sources or from within the self that are likely to produce feelings or anger.
- **Coping with other negative emotional states**—Determinant involves coping with emotional states other than frustration/anger that are unpleasant or aversive, including feelings of fear, anxiety, tension, depression, loneliness, sadness, boredom, worry, apprehension, grief, loss, and other similar dysphoric states. Includes reactions to evaluation stress (examinations, promotions, public speaking, etc.), employment and financial difficulties, and personal misfortune or accident.

Coping with Negative Physical-Physiological States. Determinant involves coping with unpleasant or painful physical or physiological reactions.

- **Coping with physical states associated with prior substance use**—Coping with physical states that are specifically associated with prior use of drug or substance, such as the "withdrawal agony" or "physical craving" associated with withdrawal. (Note: References to "craving" in the absence of withdrawal are classified under Giving into Temptations or Urges below.)
- **Coping with other negative physical states**—Coping with pain, illness, injury, fatigue, and specific disorders (e.g., headache, menstrual cramps, etc.) that are *not* associated with prior substance use.

Enhancement of Positive Emotional States. Use of substance to increase feelings of pleasure, joy, freedom, celebration, and so on (e.g., when traveling or on vacation). Includes use of substance for primarily positive effects—to "get high" or to experience the enhancing effects of a drug.

Testing Personal Control. Use of substance to "test" one's ability to engage in controlled or moderate use; to "just try it once" to see what happens; or in cases in which the individual is testing the effects of treatment or a commitment to abstinence (including tests of "willpower").

Giving in to Temptations or Urges. Substance use in response to "internal" urges, temptations, or other promptings. Includes references to craving or intense subjective desire, in the absence of interpersonal factors. (Note: References to craving associated with prior drug use or withdrawal are classified under Coping with Physical States . . . above.)

- **In the presence of substance cues**—Use occurs in the presence of cues associated with substance abuse (e.g., running across a hidden bottle or pack of cigarettes, passing by a bar, seeing an ad for cigarettes). (Note: Where other individuals are using the substance, refer to Social Pressure below.)

continues

Exhibit 8–2 continued

- **In the absence of substance cues**—Here, the urge or temptation comes "out of the blue" and is *followed* by the individual's attempt to procure the substance.

Interpersonal Determinants. Includes determinants that are primarily associated with interpersonal factors: Reference is made to the presence of the influence of other individuals as part of the precipitating event. Implies the influence of present or recent *interaction* with another person or persons who exert some influence on the user (reactions to events that occurred in the relatively distant past are classified in Intrapersonal-Environmental Determinants, above). Just being in the presence of others at the time of the relapse does not justify an interpersonal classification, unless some mention is made or implied that these people had some influence or were somehow involved in the event.

Coping with interpersonal conflict—Coping with a current or relatively recent conflict associated with any interpersonal relationship such as marriage, friendship, family patterns, employer-employee relations.
- **Coping with frustration and/or anger**—Determinants involve frustration (reaction to blocked goal-directed activity), and/or anger (hostility, aggression) stemming from an interpersonal source. Emphasis is on any situation in which the person feels frustrated or angry with someone and includes involvement in arguments, disagreements, fights, jealousy, discord, hassles, guilt, and so on.
- **Coping with other interpersonal conflict**—Determinant involves coping with conflicts other than frustration and anger stemming from an interpersonal source. Feelings such as anxiety, fear, tension, worry, concern, apprehension, etc., which are associated with interpersonal conflict, are examples. Evaluation of stress in which another person or group is specifically mentioned would be included.

Social Pressure. Determinant involves responding to the influence of another individual or group of individuals who exert pressure (either direct or indirect) on the individual to use the substance.
- **Direct social pressure**—There is direct contact (usually with verbal interaction) with another person or group who puts pressure on the user or who supplies the substance to the user (e.g., being offered a drug by someone, or being urged to use a drug by someone else). Distinguish from situations in which the substance is obtained from someone else at the request of the user (who has already decided to use).
- **Indirect social pressure**—Responding to the observation of another person or group that is using the substance or serves as a model of substance use for the user. If the model puts any direct pressure on the individual to use the substance, then the lapse should be categorized under Direct Social Behavior above.

Enhancement of Positive Emotional States. Use of substance in a primarily interpersonal situation to increase feelings of pleasure, celebration, sexual excitement, freedom, and the like. Distinguish from situations in which the other person(s) is using the substance *prior to* the individual's first use (classify these under Social Pressure above).

Scoring Rules. For each relapse episode, only one category can be used for scoring. When multiple categories seem to apply, choose the most significant precipitating event for scoring (the event *immediately* preceding the relapse). When it is impossible to decide between two equally likely categories, assign the score on a priority basis. Category 1 takes precedence over Category 2; within each major category, the ordering of categories indicates the priorities.

From their analysis of relapse episodes, Marlatt and Gordon concluded that there were more similarities than differences across various types of addictions. In other words, the three high-risk situations are involved in similar ways among relapses from cigarette smoking, gambling, overeating, heroin, and alcohol.

The level of self-efficacy determines how effectively individuals can cope with these high-risk situations. Positive coping responses in the high risk situations outlined above increase self-efficacy as well as increase future self-coping responses in high-risk situations. However, positive expectations about the use of alcohol (or other addictions) compete with these positive coping responses. Therefore, addicts are at risk for violating their abstinence from the substance they have previously abused. If substance abusers do consume a drug while in a high-risk situation, then another cognitive process, the abstinence violation effect (AVE) occurs. The AVE has both a cognitive and an affective component in reaction to substance consumption, e.g., alcohol. These components are aroused by the knowledge that substance abusers have violated their commitment to abstinence from ethyl alcohol. The AVE includes: (1) a sense of guilt or failure; and, (2) persons recategorizing themselves as "drinking" rather than as abstinent persons (McCrady, 1989).

The following is a summary of Marlatt and Gordon's model of relapse prevention.

- Telling persons how to deal with a relapse is viewed by some professionals as indicating to alcoholics that they will relapse, and this leads to a self-fulfilling prophecy. Marlatt (1985b) points out that fire drills and lifeboat drills are conducted for ship passengers to prevent disasters should the worst happen. The same could be argued for alcohol relapse prevention. How to deal with a relapse should be seen as part of an ongoing treatment program.

- Involving clients in working out their relapse-prevention program is emphasized. The overall goal is to increase their awareness of the choices that they have in dealing with their problem. There is also a focus on developing individualized coping skills and self-control abilities. All of these factors contribute to a sense of mastery and self-efficacy. The teaching of these skills is done gradually, at a pace that allows mastery without clients' being overwhelmed by too much too soon. Thus, the sense of mastery also helps build self-efficacy.

- Marlatt utilizes two types of intervention strategies to prevent relapses: specific intervention strategies and global self-control strategies. Specific intervention strategies are procedures directed at immediate precipitants of relapse. Global self-control strategies are designed to help modify clients' lifestyles and to deal wtih covert threats to relapse. The procedures used in both strategies can be subsumed under the categories of skill training, cognitive reframing, and lifestyle intervention.

- Skill training involves learning both cognitive and behavioral responses to deal with high-risk situations. Cognitive reframing techniques have several uses. They help the client see the habit-change process as a learning experience, they help in introducing coping imagery to deal with urges and cravings, and they help in restructuring how clients see the initial relapse. This latter use involves coping with what Marlatt calls the abstinence violation effect (AVE). This effect is a sense of failure and guilt, or the feeling that everything gained in recovery is lost as a result of a drinking slip.

- An examination of the specific intervention and global self-control strategies suggested by Marlatt gives a clearer picture of how relapse prevention techniques are operationalized. Specific intervention strategies involve teaching clients to recognize the high-risk situations that may trigger a relapse. These must be individualized because the risks are different for each person. It is important for clients to recognize as early as possible in a chain of behaviors that the behaviors are leading them closer to high-risk situations that may trigger a relapse. The earlier that individuals are aware of the risks, the sooner they can intervene by using coping skills and by using these cues as both warning signals and as reminders to engage in alternative or remedial actions. Clients should be taught to monitor their reactions, check their sense of competency, and use relapses and descriptions of previous relapses to alert themselves to modify their behavior. They should be taught relaxation, stress management, and efficacy-enhancing imagery as coping responses. In the face of decreased self-efficacy and the perception of a positive outcome from drinking (alcohol will make them feel better), efficacy-enhancing imagery again helps. Education about the immediate positive and the long-term negative delayed effects of alcohol use may also be beneficial. Two other procedures that help clients limit the impact of relapse are (1) contracting with them that should they drink, they will limit alcohol's use; and (2) using a reminder card that tells them what procedures to follow if they slip.

- Another training device sometimes used to anticipate relapse is "programmed relapse." That is, letting clients drink in the presence of the counselor so they discover that they can go back on the wagon after this programmed slip. To deal with AVE, cognitive restructuring is involved. Clients are taught to see the slip as a mistake and not as a total failure. They learn to attribute blame to the situation and not to themselves. These examples are not exhaustive, but give some of the major preparations for preventing and limiting relapse with these risk sources.

- Global self-control strategies help clients establish a broader framework for resisting relapse. To deal with lifestyle imbalances, clients are trained to develop a balanced daily lifestyle and to utilize positive addictions such as jogging or meditation. To deal with the client's desires for indulgences, substitute indulgences such as recreational activities or massage. Global self-control strategies that are used to deal with urges and craving for alcohol include coping imagery, stimulus control techniques, labeling, and detaching oneself from the feeling state (that is, recognizing that the urge to drink will occur and that it will eventually pass). Indivdiuals must deal with rationalization and denial by becoming aware of these defenses and by treating them as aids to alert themselves about drinking risks. To deal with high-risk situations, alcoholics should make up relapse "road maps" that show where risks are likely to occur and how to avoid those situations. Avoidance strategies can then be used (Rivers, 1994, pp. 152–53).

The above quote suggests some ways of using relapse prevention strategies that are primarily based on clinical work in the area of relapse prevention. Unlike many areas in the alcohol field, at least a modest amount of research has been conducted on Marlatt's and his colleagues' paradigm of prevention. This research will be reviewed following the summary of Gorski's relapse prevention model.

Gorski's Model of Relapse Prevention

While Marlatt and his colleagues developed their model of relapse prevention around laboratory and clinically based research, Gorski's work seems to have been generated from clinical work and observations. His own description on how his model was developed is given in several places, but one of the best summaries is in a book by Gorski and Miller (1986) entitled *Staying Sober: A Guide for Relapse Prevention*. Gorski's work on developing procedures to prevent relapse of substance abusers began when he was exclusively assigned to a group of relapse-prone patients. He found that while they knew the A.A. principles well, they somehow could not put the principles to work in their lives. Following the Minnesota Model, he developed a model of relapse prevention that is tied very closely to the A.A. 12 steps and to treatment approaches that are typical for most U.S. alcohol and drug treatment programs.

Gorski has also described the operationalization of his relapse prevention program far more completely than has Marlatt and his colleagues. An important aspect of Gorski's model of relapse prevention is that he perceives recovery as a developmentally based disorder and uses that model to help monitor where the client-patient is at any given time in terms of the relapse process. He sees his model as being based in a biopsychosocial model despite the fact that he has tied it closely to the strongest advocates of the disease model, Alcoholics Anonymous. As one might suspect, since his model has sprung from clinical work, there is not a great deal of research using this model. Gorski and his followers seem to depend on others' research, especially that of Marlatt and his colleagues, to help validate this model. In addition, Gorski's energetic proselytizing of his relapse prevention model through numerous workshops designed for treatment centers has helped spread the use of his model and the discussion of relapse prevention in general.

Gorski has outlined what he calls the Cenaps Model of relapse prevention in a 1990 journal article. He suggests that for some patients there may be a need for a special form of treatment that builds "on current strengths while effectively managing the problem of relapse" (p. 126). He sees a disruption in biological, social, and psychological function to be present in all alcoholics. Therefore, to prevent relapse, treatment must be designed to deal with problems in all three areas specified in the biopsychosocial model. Total abstinence as well as personality and lifestyle changes are seen as essential for full recovery.

In what he calls the developmental model of recovery (DMR), he suggests that there are six stages that persons who are addicted to alcohol usually go through on their way to recovering from a substance abuse disorder. As these are described, paraphrasing Gorski's description given in 1989, it is interesting to note how traditional 12-step programming is built into the developmental process. In stage one, transition, patients discover that they have a problem with alcohol. However, they initially believe that they can deal with this problem by simply learning to control the use of the substance. This stage ends when they learn they are unable to control their use and are powerless over the substance being used. While individuals do not know why they are out of control or how to be sober, they now know that they must stop using the substance if they want to turn their life around.

In stage two, stabilization, addicts are aware that they have a problem with alcohol and drugs but are unable to stop their abuse of the substance. At this point, they have to deal with postacute withdrawal syndrome, including being shaky and confused. In this stage, alcoholics must learn "to stay away from one drink (or one dose of drugs) one day at a time" (Gorski, 1989, p. 6).

In stage three, early recovery, addicted persons must make internal changes. As the physical craving for the drug is relieved, they learn to be comfortable with abstinence. It is a time of both expanding their knowledge about the addiction and learning how to cope with daily problems without the addictive substance(s).

In stage four, middle recovery, addicts learn how to put balance back in their lives. Relationships with people must be mended and significant relationships must be reevaluated. The role of a career in their lives must be assessed. If there are areas of discontent and unhappiness, they must personally acknowledge these, and actions must be taken to change things. If someone close to them has been harmed by their actions, they must take responsibility and attempt to repair the damage.

This stage is followed by the fifth stage, late recovery, where the focus is on ineffective patterns of living that have been learned in childhood. Since so many addicts report coming from dysfunctional families, they may not have learned how to be happy and how to deal with concerns like intimacy and affection when relating to others. Late recovery ends when recovering persons have accomplished the following three things.

1. We recognize the problems we have as adults that were caused by growing up in a dysfunctional family.
2. We learn how to recover from the unresolved pain that was caused by growing up in a dysfunctional family.
3. We learn how to solve current problems in spite of the obstacles caused by how we were raised. (Gorski, 1989, p. 7.)

In stage six, maintenance, alcoholics or addicts learn that their addiction is for life. They realize that they can never again use alcohol and drugs. There is also a recognition that for the rest of their lives they must practice a daily recovery program to avoid addictive thinking. They also realize that they must continue to grow as people.

These developmental stages are important because the factors emphasized in developing a relapse prevention program for a person in stage one would differ dramatically from the planning of a relapse prevention program for someone who is in stage six. Therefore, the developmental model of relapse, postulated by Gorski, is important for planning relapse prevention techniques. The intervention needed is thought to be tied to where the person is in terms of the six-stage model outlined above.

The Cenaps Model of relapse prevention views abstinence from alcohol and other mood-altering drugs as the most effective goal for all chemical dependency treatment. However, this is not the exclusive goal. Improvement in biopsychosocial functioning is also an important aspect of the approach.

The Cenaps Model integrates recent advances from the medical, psychological, and social sciences. It consists of a theoretical model, educational materials, therapy procedures, and self-help methods. The treatment and self-help approaches are directed toward three areas: assessment, recovery planning, and relapse prevention planning (Gorski, 1990, p. 125).

As a result of the multidimensional nature of the relapse prevention program, the Cenaps Model programs organize themselves around three basic components—a stabilization and assessment program, a primary recovery program, and a relapse prevention program.

The stabilization and assessment program is early in treatment and relapse prevention and provides detoxification and psychosocial stabilization. Here the patients are evaluated for placement in primary care or in a relapse prevention program. Self-assessment, professional diagnosis of disease stage and type of disease, stage of recovery, and the kind of relapse warning signs that are present are included in the evaluation.

In the primary recovery program, Gorski indicates that the patient (and therapist) should recognize that addiction is a biopsychosocial disease. They should also understand that the addictive disease will require lifelong abstinence from mind-altering drugs, and the development (and use) of an active recovery program to maintain abstinence. During primary care, other problems (e.g., personality, vocational, family, social, marital) that can interfere with sobriety should be treated. It is here that recovering addicts begin working through the DMR by beginning at the transition stage; patients have decided that they have a problem and need a life change, i.e., that they must deal with their substance abuse problem. During the stabilization stage patients deal with acute and postacute withdrawal and with threatening life issues that may be immediate threats to sobriety. Early stage is a stage where a deeper understanding of the recovery process is gained and more profound understanding of drug dependence is developed. Management of problems and feelings without the use of alcohol or drugs is also begun during this stage. It is in the middle recovery stage that lifestyle changes are made and/or lifestyles are repaired. The need to develop a balanced lifestyle, one of the chronic problems of recovering people (see Chapter 9), is emphasized during this stage.

During late recovery, the next-to-last stage, patients move to work on broader psychological issues that may cause either discomfort or pain during the recovery process. The final stage, the maintenance stage, is the lifelong process of growing and developing, making transitions in life, and confronting the *possibility of relapse*. It is the latter issue that adds extra work to the recovering addict's life. Everyone moves through life and deals with the issues as outlined for this stage by Gorski. However, for recovering persons, maintaining sobriety through these transitions is something they must have as a lifelong constant. They must always work on *relapse prevention*. The reader should keep in mind that Gorski sees his relapse model as tied to a developmental model of recovery (DMR); therefore, dealing with each stage in a successful way ultimately affects relapse prevention.

Basic Principles and Procedures of Relapse Prevention

An elaborate discussion of Gorski's model is beyond the scope of this chapter. The reader is referred to original sources (Gorski, 1988a, 1988b, 1989, 1990; Gorski & Miller, 1986) for a more complete presentation of the procedures used at each stage. However, a presentation of the principles of this model and brief examples of procedures related to them will be outlined below. It should be noted here that this summary is based almost entirely on Gorski's 1990 article outlining the model, and it is a succinct description of his position.

Principle 1: Self-regulation

"The risk of relapse will decrease as the patient's capacity to self-regulate their thinking, feeling, memory, judgement and behavior increases" (Gorski, 1990, pp. 128–29).

Relapse Prevention Procedure 1: Stabilization. One of the basic measures of whether patients have mastered this stage is whether or not they can carry out the basic tasks of everyday living. One must provide seclusion from drug use, i.e., provide a drug-free environment. Treatment personnel must also help patients deal with the way that they justify the use of alcohol or drugs, e.g., "I am not ever going to get well anyway so why shouldn't I drink?" Patients must be reminded over and over again about the past disasters that have accompanied substance use and abuse. At the same time they must be provided with ways of coping with immediate threats to sobriety and decisions about what can be done if they should use chemicals. Having a plan to work with is very important during this early stage of recovery. Not noted by Gorski, but important just the same, is the need to return some type of structure to the addict's often chaotic life.

Principle 2: Integration

"The risk of relapse will decrease as the level of conscious understanding and acceptance of situations and events that led to past relapses increases" (Gorski, 1990, p. 129).

Relapse Prevention Procedure 2: Integration. Relapse prevention is built on the patients' self-assessment. Here, careful exploration of presenting problems helps to establish where there are relapse risks. The therapist can identify immediate problems that could lead to relapse and provide interventions that will reduce the risk. Once the immediate relapse-threatening issues are ascertained and appropriate interventions are provided, the second type of self-assessment is undertaken. This is a careful exploration of their life history. What were things like in grade school, high school, and college? What are patient's lifelong friendships and romantic relationships like? One of the goals of reconstructing a life history is to find self-defeating behaviors that are threats to relapse. Other goals include building rapport and relationships between therapist and patient as well as between patient and therapy group. The third goal is to resolve pain associated with painful memories. The final step in the procedure is to carefully reconstruct a relapse history for patients.

This history includes a so-called recovery-relapse calendar that shows the date of recovery and relapse. This calendar helps reinforce the past number and severity of relapse and the dangers that addicted persons face during recovery.

Principle 3: Understanding

"The risk of relapse will decrease as the understanding of the general factors that cause relapse increases" (Gorski, 1990, p. 130).

Relapse Prevention Procedure 3: Understanding. The task here is to provide accurate information to the addict about what contributes to relapse. Gorski is very precise about what he believes is the best procedure to follow in providing this education. The education process should incorporate a minimum number of lectures, since he sees this as the poorest way to communicate effectively with recovering substance abusers.

> The recommended format for a relapse education session is the following: (1) introduction and pretest (15 minutes); (2) educational presentation—lecture, film, or videotape (30 minutes); (3) educational exercise conducted in dyads or small groups (15 minutes); (4) large group discussion (15 minutes); and (5) session posttest and review of correct answers (15 minutes) (Gorski, 1990, p. 130).

Principle 4: Self Knowledge

"The risk of relapse will decrease as the patient's ability to recognize personal relapse warning signs increases" (Gorski, 1990, p. 130).

Relapse Procedure 4: Warning Sign Identification. In group, a warning sign list for relapse is reviewed by all group members. The initial step for all group members (each member develops their own warning list) is to select five warning signs that they feel are representative of them from a composite list. The group members then take their lists and during warning-sign-analysis time individually present examples of how each of the warning signs preceded relapse in the past. Both therapist and group members listen to these warning signs, and try to detect hidden warning signs that the patient is not aware of. Through this process, each patient, the therapist, and the entire group move toward a final warning list for the patient. The final warning-signs list has two types of warning signs; those stemming from core addiction issues and those arising from core psychological issues. Core psychological issues cause pain and discomfort but do not, says Gorski, lead the patient directly to relapse. It is the addictive thinking that does that, i.e., the core addictive warning signs.

Principle 5: Coping Skills

"The risk of relapse will decrease as the ability to manage relapse warning signs increases" (Gorski, 1990, p. 131).

Relapse Prevention Procedure 5: Warning Sign Prevention. Gorski feels that the better addicts are able to manage warning signs, the better they will be at managing threats to relapse. He advocates the use of mental rehearsal, role playing, and therapeutic assignments. Management training takes place at three levels. At the first level, patients deal with situational-behavioral issues. They are taught to avoid situations that arouse warning signs and to change behavior patterns should these situations appear. The second level is cognitive-affective. Patients must be trained to challenge irrational thoughts and instructed on how to deal with overwhelming and/or unmanageable feelings. The "self-talk" that one uses must be modified. Patients learn how to use imagery and to deal with such imagery. The third level, the core-issue level, is where patients are taught to recognize core addictive and psychological concerns that produce warning signs that they have recognized mean that they are at risk for relapse. For example, Gorski sees patients' core beliefs that they must be better than everyone else as being driven at the core level by low self-esteem. It is the low self-esteem that is behind irrational thinking that they must be best at everything. Low self-esteem underlies the unmanageable feelings that they must always prove themselves and the associated self-defeating behavior. They really do not deserve success, so why not make a fool of themselves while drinking? (These concrete examples are ours, not Gorski's.)

Principle 6: Change

"The risk of relapse will decrease as the use of daily inventory techniques designed to identify relapse warning signs increase" (Gorski, 1990, p. 132).

Relapse Prevention Procedure 6: Inventory Training. Patients are taught to monitor how well they are keeping to a relapse prevention program. This daily inventory is an ongoing check on the emergence of relapse warning signs. There is a morning planning inventory to plan the day (e.g., identifying three recovery goals for the day), and in the evening, individuals complete an inventory to review their progress and to detect any problems (e.g., patients review their warning-signs list and check to see if they have completed assigned duties).

Principle 7: Awareness

"The risk of relapse will decrease as the use of daily inventory techniques designed to identify relapse warning signs increases" (Gorski, 1990, p. 132).

Relapse Prevention Procedure 7: Inventory Training. Here Gorski suggests that patients susceptible to relapse keep two daily inventories to help monitor compliance with individual recovery programs. The morning inventory helps persons check for possible relapse warning signs that might arise on any given day. In the morning a patient might be asked to identify three primary recovery goals and to create a "to-do" list. An evening inventory is employed to review progress and to assess possible problems. The evening inventory is used to review how well the recovering person has completed their required recovery activities.

Principle 8: Significant Others

"The risk of relapse will decrease as the responsible involvement of significant others in recovery from co-dependency and in [the] relapse planning process increases" (Gorski, 1990, p. 132).

Relapse Prevention Procedure 8: Involvement of Others. Gorski is adamant about the involvement of significant others with the patient. This support helps increase the effectiveness of the relapse program. The more psychologically and socially well-adjusted the people are around the addicted person, the more effective they can be in relapse prevention. Gorski and others have developed a protocol to be used by significant others who work with the patient on relapse prevention.

Principle 9: Maintenance

"The risk of relapse decreases if the relapse prevention plan is regularly updated during the first three years of sobriety" (Gorski, 1990, p. 132).

Relapse Prevention Procedure 9: Relapse Prevention Plan Updating. Gorski calls for a monthly updating of the patient's relapse plan for the first three months, quarterly updates for the rest of the year, and semiannual updates for the next two years. Thereafter, the relapse plan should be done annually. He warns that while the largest number of relapses occur during the first six months following primary treatment, relapse warning signs constantly change as the person's life changes. He also notes that less than one quarter of the variables that cause relapse can be detected in initial treatment.

This brief outline of the two different views of relapse prevention suggests that both are incomplete. In the case of Marlatt and Gordon, there is less clear-cut operationalization of just what is needed and how this learning-based relapse prevention program can be tied to existing programs. In the majority of cases, existing U.S. alcohol and drug treatment programs have a disease orientation. On the other hand, Gorski has his relapse prevention model tied closely to the Minnesota Model and the 12 steps of Alcoholics Anonymous. His model is definitely close to the majority of existing programs and thus is readily usable by them. Unfortunately, to date, Gorski's model has not been supported by research studies to evaluate its effectiveness with patients. For this reason, relapse prevention programs are still being conducted for the most part on the basis of clinical observations and are being evaluated by the same means. There are few clinical trials using Gorski's more elaborated disease model and too-few programs that have utilized the Marlatt and Gordon model of relapse prevention. In the next section we review what research says about relapse prevention. Almost all of this research is based on Marlatt and Gordon's approach. There is litle research currently available on the Gorski and Miller model.

Research on Relapse Prevention

One of the factors that plays a role in relapse prevention is the amount of time since the last drink. The longer the time interval since sobriety began, the more likely there is to be a relapse in the recovering person. Marlatt (1985) has suggested two relapse models. Where there is a passive patient and a powerful treatment program (like aversion treatment), over time there is a decay of the treatment, and thus the possibility of relapse increases. This means that a larger number of relapses will occur as a function of time since discharge from treatment. Marlatt (1985a) proposes a second model where patients are in an active role. Following treatment, patients acquire social skills that help them deal with situations that might precipitate relapse. In this model, treatment is directed toward development of those social skills that will help patients navigate those situations that formerly elicited drinking or will help them avoid those situations entirely. As Littrell (1991) puts it: "Social skills are developed as coping strategies which defuse the eliciting capability of relapse precipitants" (p. 91).

Research also suggests (Littrell, 1991) that most people (and sometimes all) will relapse in the first few months following treatment. However, many of these relapsers reinstate abstinence following a loss of sobriety.

In terms of establishing factors that precipitate relapse, Marlatt has suggested that negative emotions and social pressure are the conditions accounting for the largest number of relapses. Positive emotions and tests of personal control also play a role in relapses by alcohol-involved people and other addicts. Littrell (1991) has summarized the research reported on these factors as precipitants of relapse.

Negative emotions, which Marlatt (1985a) found to be a precipitant in 59 percent of relapses by alcoholics, can be either intrapersonal or interpersonal. Intrapersonal negative emotions include feelings like frustration, free floating anger, fear, sadness, loneliness, and so forth. These feelings accounted for 38 percent of the precipitants of relapses in Marlatt's research. Negative emotions resulting from interpersonal conflict were responsible for 18 percent of the relapses. Included here were feelings associated with a lack of appreciation from others, guilt feelings, and perceptions of being accused unjustly. Feeling bad physically (negative physical state) accounted for 3 percent of relapse precipitants. Marlatt's research of relapse precipitants has been complemented by others. Some (e.g., Chaney, Roszel, & Commings, 1982) have found with heroin addicts that emotions aroused by interpersonal conflict were more likely to result in relapse in later (more long-term recovery) abstinence.

Negative emotions can also be seen as being aroused by external stressors. Rosenberg's research (1983) on a sample of recovering alcoholics found those addicts who experienced more negative life changes and fewer positive life changes had a higher probability of relapse. An earlier study by Hore (1971) found that the overall sample of subjects studied demonstrated no relationship between negative life events and relapse. However, he did find a subset of alcoholics for whom the experiences of negative life events led to relapse and suggested that this subset may be more sensitive to life events.

Others have also suggested an interaction between alcoholic history and stress in the environment. For example, if the alcoholics' drinking has disrupted their relationships with family, and then some negative event occurs involving the family, there is likely to be relapse. Littrell (1991) in her summary statement regarding negative emotions indicates that "stress can be a factor in precipitating or increasing drinking, but there are individual personality differences, and the sources of stress may make a difference" (p. 93).

Littrell also reviews the research on social pressure, the second leading cause of relapse in Marlatt's (1985a) research. She notes that social pressure can be direct, as when a friend encourages you to take a drink, or indirect as when the people around you model drinking as the appropriate behavior in which to engage. She reiterates that the Chaney, et al. (1982) findings with heroin addicts indicate that social pressure is most likely to cause relapse in early abstinence. Intuitively, this finding makes sense because early abstinence alternative sources of social support (e.g., nonusers and fellow recoverers) that could buffer against substance-using friends are not yet strongly developed.

The test of personal control as a cause of relapse accounted for 11 percent of relapses in Marlatt's (1985a) study. Relapsers seemed to be testing whether they could control their drinking or avoid the negative consequences of alcohol use of this specific drinking occasion. One of Marlatt's surprising findings was that only 3 percent of relapsers reported their lapses as due to interpersonal positive emotions (none reported intrapersonal positive emotions as a cause of relapse). Other writers (e.g., Baker, Morse, & Sherman, 1987) have suggested that positive emotions may play an important role in precipitating relapse. Intuitively, a major role for positive emotions in precipitating relapse would make sense, because so much occurs around individuals' having a good time with people they have not seen for some time or around holiday celebrations. Good feelings toward others are often present and drugs like alcohol are associated with having a good time. Littrell (1991) cites some research that does offer tentative support to the importance of positive emotions in precipitating relapse. She notes that some people stay sober because of the fear arousal of the long-term consequences of drinking. Having a pleasurable and good time tends to undermine this fear type of motivation for staying sober. If a person does not have some other type of motivation, like pride in being sober, then when a pleasurable event occurs in their life they may turn to drinking, because drinking is one of the few activities that has been previously associated with positive events in the person's life. Strack, Carver, and Blaney (1987 [as cited in Littrell, 1991]) in research predicting successful completion of an aftercare program following treatment of alcoholism suggest that the role of disproportional optimism established a relationship between the number of positive events in the person's life and dropping out of aftercare (which they equated with high risk for returning to drinking).

Cravings and urges were present in 11 percent of alcoholic relapses in the Marlatt (1985a) study. However, there is some concern that there may be internal and external cues for cravings and developing a "drug urge" (Baker, et al., 1987).

Apparently irrelevant decisions also play a role in relapse. Akin to what A.A. calls "stinking thinking," this terminology refers to thinking that moves the sober individual closer to taking a drink. This includes things like buying alcohol so a guest will have it available and dropping the use of Antabuse because its continued use is inconvenient. As Littrell (1991) notes, these decisions are made with the potential relapser partially aware that the motivation to change behavior is to move them closer to drinking again (or using some other addictive substance). "Unfortunately, Marlatt did not report the frequency with which apparently irrelevant decisions precede relapse. Pomerlau, Adkins and Pertschuk's 1978 work, 'Predictors of Outcome and Recidivism in Smoking Cessation Treatment,' found that those ex-smokers who seek situations in which they are exposed to risk are more likely to relapse" (as cited in Littrell, 1991, pp. 94–95).

The above discussion of the research on precipitants of relapse should be understood in the light of what Littrell calls "unanswered questions." For example, does the drinker's pattern of drinking prior to starting the recovery process suggest future precipitants of relapse? Do people who drink in a bad mood also have high potential for drinking when alone or under stress? Those whose drinking occurred most often in convivial situations might be more likely to relapse in a pleasurable party atmosphere or after having some type of personal success. At present, these guesses are still at the hypotheses stage and need additional research before they can be established as principles for relapse management.

The finding that problem drinkers and alcoholics differ from other drinkers in terms of the expectations that they hold about what alcohol will do for them is another issue of importance. For example, a positive relationship has been found between the expectation that alcohol will enhance self-esteem and relapse (Carle, 1993). Expectancy has become a major concept in the alcohol field. The operationalization of the expectancy concept by Brown, Christiansen, and Goldman, (1987) is perhaps the most widely researched. In their review, they define expectancy as follows:

> Expectancy refers to an intervening variable of a cognitive nature . . . the term expectancy, rather than attitude or belief is usually involved when the author refers to the anticipation of a systematic relationship between events/objects in some upcoming situation. The relationship is understood to be of an if-then variety; if a certain object is registered then a certain event is expected to follow. (Goldman, et al., 1987, p. 18, [as cited in Carle, 1993, p. 1]).

To measure this concept, Goldman, et al. have developed the alcohol expectancy questionnaire (AEQ). The AEQ is designed to measure what people expect from the use of alcohol. These expectancies seem to have a bearing on relapse risk. For example, Brown (1985) found that alcohol expectancies enhanced the prediction of drinking outcome at one year following treatment (Carle, 1993).

Another unanswered question is whether planned relapses differ from impulsive ones. Some individuals may feel that they cannot continue their sobriety and that they are pressured daily to drink. When these individuals do drink they may fully expect disastrous, long range consequences, yet they simply feel that they can no longer maintain their "white knuckle" sobriety. Still others plan their relapses, believing that they are alcoholics but also believing that they will drink for a short time and then return to sobriety or to normal drinking and escape the difficulties of long-term destructive drinking. These two diverse thoughts may lead to differing outcomes when relapse occurs. It is probable that cognitions about relapse differ in more subtle ways and that these subtle differences may have an effect on the accuracy of predicting a relapse in a particular person's case.

A final unanswered question is whether the core motivation for ceasing to use an addictive substance is related to relapse. If a person quits substance abuse for health reasons, will they be more likely to relapse when they feel good? Persons who quit drinking to please their family may be more vulnerable to relapse when they feel that family members have treated them unfairly. One way to understand the importance of these factors is to look at the characteristics of relapsing and nonrelapsing alcoholics.

Characteristics of Relapsing and Nonrelapsing Alcoholics

Littrell has outlined some of the major factors that determine addicts' resistance to and risk for relapse. One of the factors determining relapses is the degree of self-efficacy about staying sober that the person has. Littrell (1991) sees self-efficacy as a corollary of self-perception theory. "Self-efficacy is a specific corollary of the more central tenant of self-perception theory. The theory predicts that given valuing of some goal (say sobriety), people who *believe* they can achieve the goal (that is stay sober), will more often do so" (p. 96).

The difficulty is: How do you measure self-efficacy? What factors in these measurements predict relapsing and nonrelapsing individuals? Littrell's review of the literature suggests that individuals in treatment are themselves good predictors of whether they are going to relapse or not. They also can predict the situations in which they are likely to relapse (Chapman & Huygens, 1988; Condiotte & Lichtenstein, 1981; DiClemente, 1981; McIntyre, Lichtenstein, & Mermelstein, 1983). How individuals see themsleves in relation to dealing with substance abuse use and dealing with temptation also appears to be important to Littrell (1991). In summarizing those factors that describe people who successfully deal with relapse, she stated:

> Feelings of self-efficacy, a propensity to use positive self-reinforcement
> and positive images (offering themselves thoughts of the benefits of

sobriety, and experiencing pride in accomplishment when maintaining sobriety), and the permission of strong coping skills were recognized as important . . . (p. 105).

When one looks more closely at the characteristics of relapsing and nonrelapsing alcoholics, it is clear that Littrell and others have found multiple differences between the two groups. For example, people who believe that they can achieve the goal of sobriety tend to be more likely to achieve the goal. Littrell (1991) cites Donovan and O'Leary's 1983 study that divided alcoholics on their subjective estimate of whether they would succumb to pressure to drink. Those alcoholics who reported that they would be highly likely to give in to pressure to drink reported drinking in a more chronic and obsessive fashion, said they used more external resources to cease drinking, reported higher rates of loss of control when they did drink and had more physical, psychosocial, and psychological damage as a result of drinking. In addition, those who saw their sobriety as being the result of chance or the result of fate were more likely to relapse.

Another factor is the degree of complacency that persons have toward their own ability to manage their recovery. The more complacent the person is about achieving sobriety, the more likely the person is to stay in treatment for a shorter period of time and to be discharged prematurely for violation of treatment-program rules. One of the danger signals for persons who may not do well in treatment is for them to say, particularly early in treatment, that they now believe that they will be able to easily handle their treatment in the future. It does seem to be necessary for persons in treatment to have some doubts, some sense of a real struggle before them, in order to maximize the impact of their treatment.

How does this match up with feelings of self-efficacy? In general, those people with high self-efficacy avoid relapse. However, persons who develop skills for dealing with threats to relapse are the ones who seem to do better. Those people who simply have faith that they will not relapse do more poorly. In addition, coping skills of nonrelapsers, both behavioral and cognitive, are employed in greater number and diversity than by those individuals who relapse. The effective use of these skills may build self-esteem and may lead to greater use of the tools to stay sober. People who do better in terms of relapse do not shower themselves with self-recriminations; instead, they are able to see themselves as doing something positive, as coping and as acting as good role models for others. In fact, having a positive attitude toward life in general is associated with positive outcome, i.e., a reduction in relapse.

What recovering persons must always deal with is their cognitive appreciation of what the addictive substance does for them. One of the important cognitive factors is expectancies about what the drug will do. "Youthful drinking [and, by implication adult drinking] is influenced by the modeling of alcohol consumption; the creation of specific expectations of the benefits of drinking via media portrayals of sexual prowess, power, and success and by social reinforcement from peer groups" (Monti, Abrams, Kadden, & Cooney, 1989, p. 6).

All of these factors add up to the fact that nonrelapsers must make, over time, considerable lifestyle changes. They need to develop a life interest that takes the place of the time formerly spent drinking. Whether it is just having the activity alone or perhaps a more global change (now perceiving oneself as a runner not a drinker) is still unknown (Littrell, 1991). In addition, social support from one's family is associated with a reduced relapse rate. Of course, there is always a possible confound with the severity of the drinking history of the recovering person and the amount of social support a family may be willing to give.

While there are clear indications in the literature about what may determine a relapse, what is still unknown is how best to intervene with those people who are potential relapsers. Just exactly how do we intervene with someone who is not motivated to recover? How does one teach relapse prevention skills to someone who still has positive feelings toward using the abused substance? These things await more research. We need better measurement tools, better intervention strategies, and more outcome research to evaluate the effectiveness of treatment and relapse prevention. It is also probable that ongoing assessment of drinking potential will be needed to fully exploit both aftercare and relapse prevention strategies. These two areas of alcohol rehabilitation, aftercare and relapse prevention, seem to loom prominently in the future intervention and treatment of substance abuse problems.

DISCUSSION QUESTIONS

1. Why is it so difficult to precisely divide primary care, aftercare, and relapse prevention? Describe at least two conditions where at least two of the above overlap.
2. What is the importance of offering both A.A.-based treatment programs and programs not based on A.A.? Make a list of reasons why both approaches together might be potentially helpful to substance abusers seeking treatment.
3. Why does client motivation affect the positive and negative outcomes of aftercare? Describe in as much detail as possible the type of person who is likely to be most successful in aftercare and contrast this person with the individual least likely to be successful.
4. Visit three alcohol and drug treatment agencies and ask them to describe their treatment, aftercare, and relapse prevention programs. What are the similarities? What are the differences? Is there a clean break between each of the program treatment components? How do the three programs measure the effectiveness of treatment, aftercare, and relapse prevention?

What do you think are the strengths and weaknesses of their measurement procedures?

5. Look at the other chapters in this book that deal with treatment (e.g., the chapters on individual, family, and group therapy). Do each of these chapters mention aftercare and relapse prevention? If so, do they show specific aftercare and relapse prevention strategies that fit the treatment modality being discussed? Or, do all of them have a similar program? If aftercare and relapse prevention are not specifically discussed, what type of aftercare and relapse prevention programs would you design for the treatment modality in question? Why?

6. Using your own personal experience (or an interview with a close friend) outline a time when you, while dieting or trying to change another habit (including alcohol and tobacco use, etc.), suffered from the *abstinence violation effect* (AVE). Be sure to outline in detail what happened and how you felt. Describe what you did immediately after your slip and the AVE was experienced by you.

7. Using Gorski's six stages (Developmental Model of Recovery [DMR]) and your reading of his relapse model, plan a relapse program for persons in stages one, three, and six of recovery. Are the programs you planned similar? Do they differ in any important way? Why or why not?

REFERENCES

Baker, T. B., Morse, E., & Sherman, J. E. (1987). The motivation to use drugs: A psychological analysis of drug urges. In P. C. Rivers (Ed.), *Alcohol and addictive behavior: Volume 34 Nebraska symposium on motivation* (pp. 257–323). Lincoln, NE: University of Nebraska Press.

Bem, D. J. (1972). Self perception theory. In L. Berkowitz (Ed.), *Advances in experimental social psychology* (Vol. 6, pp. 2–61). New York: Academic Press, Inc.

Brown, S. A. (1985). Reinforcement expectancies and alcoholism treatment outcome after a one year follow-up. *Journal of Studies on Alcohol, 46*, 304–8.

Brown, S. A., Christiansen, B. A., & Goldman, M. A. (1987). The alcohol expectancy questionnaire: An instrument for the assessment of adolescent and adult alcohol expectancies. *Journal of Studies on Alcohol, 48,* 483–91.

Carle, D. (1993). *Predicting drinking patterns of college students: The AEQ vs. the AEQ-A.* Unpublished doctoral dissertation, Department of Psychology, University of Nebraska, Lincoln.

Chaney, E. F., Roszell, D. K., & Cummings, C. (1982). Relapse in opiate addicts: A behavioral analysis. *Addictive Behaviors, 7,* 291–97.

Chapman, P. L. H., & Huygens, I. (1988). An evaluation of three treatment programmes for alcoholism: An experimental study with 6- and 18-month follow-ups. *British Journal of Addictions, 83*, 67–81.

Condiotte, M. M., & Lichtenstein, E. (1981). Self-efficacy and relapse in smoking cessation programs. *Journal of Consulting and Clinical Psychology, 49,* 648–58.

Connors, G. J., Tarbox, A. R., & Faillance, L. A. (1992). Achieving and maintaining gains among problems drinkers: Process and outcome results. *Behavior Therapy, 23*, 449–74.

DiClemente, C. C. (1981). Self-efficacy and smoking cessation maintenance: A preliminary report. *Cognitive Therapy and Research, 5,* 175–87.

Donavan, D. M., & O'Leary, M. R. (1983). Control orientation, drinking behavior and alcoholism. In H. M. Lefcourt (Ed.), *Research with the locus of control construct: Development and social problems* (Vol. 2, pp. 107–53). New York: Academic Press, Inc.

Eiel, C. (1993). A hospital based program evolved to survive. *Applications, 4*(5), 32–33.

Gorski, T. T. (1988a). *Do family of origin problems cause chemical dependence?: Exploring the relationship between chemical dependence and codependence.* Independence, MO: Independence Press.

Gorski, T. T. (1988b). *The staying sober workbook: Instruction manual.* Independence, MO: Independence Press.

Gorski, T. T. (1989). *Passages through recovery: An action plan for preventing relapse.* Minneapolis: Hazelden Foundation.

Gorski, T. T. (1990). The Cenaps Model of relapse prevention. *Journal of Psychoactive Drugs, 22,* 125–33.

Gorski, T. T., & Miller, M. (1986). *Staying sober: A guide for relapse prevention.* Independence, MO: Independence Press.

Hore, B. D. (1971). Life events and alcoholic relapse. *British Journal of Addictions, 66,* 83–88.

Institute of Medicine (1990). *Broadening the treatment for alcohol problems.* Washington, DC: National Academy Press.

Joint Commission on the Accreditation of Health Care Organizations (1983). *Consolidated standards manual for child, adolescent and adult psychiatric, alcoholism and drug abuse facilities.* Chicago: JCAHCO.

Lincoln Lancaster Drug Projects (1992). *Annual report.* Lincoln, NE: Lincoln Lancaster Drug Projects.

Lincoln Lancaster Drug Projects (1993). *Fact sheet.* Lincoln, NE: Lincoln Lancaster Drug Projects.

Littrell, J. (1991). *Understanding and treating alcoholism: Volume 1.* Hillsdale, NJ: Lawrence Erlbaum Associates, Inc.

McCrady, B. S. (1989). Extending relapse models to couples. *Addictive Behaviors, 14,* 69–74.

McIntyre, K. O., Lichtenstein, E., & Mermelstein, R. J. (1983). Self-efficacy and relapse in smoking cessation: A replication and extension. *Journal of Consulting and Clinical Psychology, 51,* 632–33.

Marlatt, G. A. (1985a). Relapse prevention: Theoretical rationale and overview of the model. In G. A. Marlatt, & J. R. Gordon (Eds.), *Relapse prevention* (pp. 3–70). New York: Guilford Press.

Marlatt, G. A. (1985b). Situational determinants of relapse and skill training. In Marlatt, G. A., & Gordon, J. R. (Eds.), *Relapse prevention* (pp. 71–127). New York: Guilford Press.

Marlatt, G. A., & Gordon, J. R. (Eds.) (1985). *Relapse prevention.* New York: Guilford Press.

MClatchie, B. H., & Lomp, K. G. E. (1988). An experimental investigation of the influence of aftercare on alcoholic relapse. *British Journal of Addiction, 83,* 1045–54.

Monti, P. M., Abrams, D. B., Kadden, R. M., & Cooney, N. L. (1989). *Treating alcohol dependence.* New York: Guilford Press.

Parker Valley Hope (1993). Informational literature. Parker, CO: Parker Valley Hope.

Rivers, P. C. (1994). *Alcohol and human behavior: Theory, research and practice.* Englewood Cliffs, NJ: Prentice Hall.

Rosenberg, H. (1983). Relapsed versus non-relapsed alcohol abusers: Coping skills, life events and social support. *Addictive Behaviors, 8,* 183–86.

Strack, S., Carver, C. S., & Blaney, P. H. (1987). Predicting successful completion of an aftercare program following treatment for alcoholism: The role of dispositional optimism. *Journal of Personality and Social Psychology, 53,* 579–84.

Valley Hope Association (August–September, 1993). *Coffee Cup.* Norton, KS: Valley Hope Association.

Wallace, J. (1978). Working with the preferred defense structure of the recovering alcoholic. In S. Zimberg, J. Wallace, & S. B. Blume (Eds.), *Practical approaches to alcoholism psychotherapy* (pp. 19–29). New York: Plenum Publishing.

Chapter 9

How To Survive in a Chemical
Dependency Agency

CHAPTER OBJECTIVES

- Examine general problems that occur in social service agencies
- Examine the roles inter- and intra-agency conflict play in agency effectiveness
- Identify the demands of early job adjustment in chemical dependency agencies
- Examine the importance of maintaining communication with outside agencies
- Explore ways to live with the demands of long range counselor adjustment
- Explore ways to avoid burnout
- Examine the importance job choice plays in counselor survival in chemical dependency agencies
- Examine the need to adjust to changing job demands and roles as the field adjusts to managed care and other professional changes

Each year, new counselors enter the alcoholism treatment field. Each counselor has survived some selection process, some type of training experience, and other stress-related activity. However, many will discover that the field of alcoholism counseling is filled with experiences that they did not anticipate and for which they were poorly trained. Most alcohol counselor training programs give little attention to the types of system-level problems that exist in all agencies, and they spend a minimal amount of time dealing with the system issues peculiar to alcoholism treatment agencies.

As a result of the failure to deal with these issues and to help prepare the counselor for the adjustment needed to work effectively within a given job setting, many counselors experience anxiety, frustration, and anger as they attempt to adjust to their jobs. While most of these counselors survive the process of adjustment from the idealism of training to the reality of the job place, many are unaware that the frustrations, anxieties, and self-doubts that they experience are also occurring in their colleagues, and thus, they lose a valuable opportunity to share their feelings with others. As for those who do not survive the intensity and work demands of the alcohol workplace, some leave without doubting that the job change was the correct vocational decision for them. Some leave because they cannot deal with the ambiguity or the mixed messages so frequently given in caregiving systems. Others leave with anger and, due to their frustration, display hostility toward the system. Still others leave with the feeling that they have failed in some basic and personal way, both as a human being and as a professional.

Survival is defined here as the ability to adjust to job demands without being overwhelmed by stress, i.e., avoiding burnout. It is of course possible to survive in an agency by simply becoming less involved with clients and disengaging from the agency, i.e., by suffering burnout. This latter condition is defined as existence.

This chapter addresses some of the problems and raises issues that the author has observed in his work as a staff member, an outside consultant, and a trainer of personnel in the alcoholism treatment field. The chapter will focus on issues common to most social service agencies, e.g., dealing with internal staff relations and roles, as well as those specific to alcohol agencies, e.g., dealing with the potential problems that can develop between staff members who are themselves recovering from chemical dependency (referred to here as recovering counselors) and staff members who are not (referred to here as nonrecovering counselors). Counselors should be aware that many of the specific issues that they will confront may be ignored or treated too briefly in this chapter. A complete coverage of all the possible issues that substance abuse counselors will confront in the job place is clearly beyond the scope of this chapter. However, it is hoped that some of the issues raised here will be helpful to counselors by making more public and explicit issues that were previously experienced but not articulated. Making these issues a labeled part of the experience of counselors makes it possible for much of the frustration, anxiety, and anger generated by these experiences to be shared with colleagues and dealt with as real staff-maintenance issues. This awareness will improve counselors' morale and help them focus on the job of providing better services to their clients.

SOME INITIAL CONSIDERATIONS

This chapter deals with issues applicable to most social service agencies and some that are specifically relevant to the alcohol service system. We shall first turn to a consideration of problem issues that are applicable to most service agencies, including those in the substance abuse field.

One of the things that you, as a counselor, may not be initially aware of is that like your clients, the agency you work in has its own ability to adjust and meet its problems or to behave in irrational and destructive ways. There are several reasons why social service agencies may have more problems than agencies not dealing with the personal problems of people. These considerations are discussed below.

Daily Demands of Clients

Frequently, clients attempt to set one staff member up against another either to get something they want or to vent unresolved hostility. Because clients may have dealt with many agencies in the past, they frequently have developed a highly manipulative style of dealing with such. For example, they may have found that being demanding or extremely dependent is an effective tactic for dealing with bureaucracies. They may have also learned that setting one counselor against another can keep the pressure off them when they enter treatment. It is possible for counselors to react negatively to these behaviors rather than to see them as a part of the clients' problems. In an agency where there is not adequate communication among staff members these problems can escalate and lead to deterioration in staff relations.

Communication Breakdowns

Client demands can cause problems when there is poor communication in an agency. In fact, like a marriage relationship, an agency rapidly begins to show serious difficulties when there is a breakdown in communication. While breakdowns in communication frequently occur, they are usually corrected if the basic structure and process of communication are in place. However, we are talking here about chronic problems in communication. These may occur as vertical communication problems (e.g., a supervisor with a counselor) or as a horizontal problem (e.g., between two counselors doing the same type job). Left unchecked, these problems can develop into distrust, with the result that communication exists only in smaller cliques, and a type of war can break out between these cliques. Regardless of the pattern, the efficiency of the agency is seriously affected, and the functioning of the agency can be distorted in drastic ways. Like a family, agencies will adjust to communication breakdowns and may well continue to function for considerable periods of time. However, both work efficiency and the morale of many of the agency's workers are lowered when these negative adjustments are made.

Emotional Involvement with Clients

One of the factors that is involved in most social service agencies is the need for counselors to become emotionally involved with clients. Emotional investment in individuals is a characteristic usually found in the effective caregiver. However, when a caregiver invests himself in a client, there is a potential that the client will disappoint or frustrate the caregiver. This frustration can lead to a drop in the self-esteem and general morale of the staff member, which is particularly true in the substance abuse field where chemical dependency counselors work with clients who show a pattern of frequent relapse. Therefore, working with these clients can be particularly frustrating to new counselors who are already concerned about their ability to become competent counselors. In this situation, new counselors are constantly seeing clients relapse and asking themselves if they are doing all they can for their clients. In many cases, novice counselors blame the failure on themselves and, consequently, suffer self-doubt and a loss of self-esteem. An interesting consequence of emotional investment and caring is that, generally speaking, the counselor who is able to empathize with the client, and project warmth and concern, is usually the most effective counselor. In other words, being concerned and caring leads to more effective treatment in most caregiving situations. However, it is frequently the most committed and caring counselors who suffer counselor burnout. Conversely, many of the people who are not emotionally invested in their clients may well be survivors in the agency but at the cost of the clients. (Many counselors may be people who had originally been very caring but, due to disillusionment, have become cynical and less caring about their clients.) Another danger for substance abuse workers is that they may vent all of their job frustrations on the client, who is the most visible source of their frustrations. Therefore, a balance between the ability to emotionally invest in a client and to maintain some emotional distance is basic to survival in caregiving agencies.

Ambiguity of Tasks

Another issue faced by staff in social service agencies is the general ambiguity of the tasks that they are asked to perform. Few therapists, for example, can ever say that their counseling was the major factor (or sometimes, even a minor factor) in a given client's recovery. In fact, a counselor who does carry out a specific intervention will only know if the intervention led to a positive outcome by waiting to see how the client changes. Frequently these delays between intervention and outcome are quite lengthy and even very effective therapists can feel they have done little to help the client.

Conflict between Recovering and Nonrecovering Staff

One of the most important differences between substance abuse agencies and other caregiving agencies is that in many, perhaps most, chemical dependency agencies, both recovering and nonrecovering personnel are employed. There are very few caregiving systems, outside the substance abuse field, where people who are recovering from the problem become therapists. While many agencies manage the relationships among people with differing entrance credentials quite well, some agencies do not spend enough time or energy dealing with the potential problems that may ensue, some of which are discussed below.

Staff Motivation

Recovering staff in chemical dependency agencies are frequently suspicious of the motivation of the nonrecovering staff, particularly in alcoholism agencies. For example, recovering alcoholics may wonder why a person who has not suffered through an alcohol problem would care anything about the welfare of alcoholics. (Many alcoholics, despite their own recovery, still view the active alcoholic in a moralistic way. They assume that other people also have this viewpoint.) And while they seldom voice their concerns to the nonrecovering counselors, the recovering counselors frequently wonder if the nonrecovering counselors are working in the agency simply because the jobs were available, or if they plan to "rip off the agency by drawing their pay and doing little to earn it." In some cases, they may see the nonrecovering counselor as a con artist who is trying to gain control of the agency, i.e., become the head of the agency. In general, recovering staff may see nonrecovering staff as less dedicated than they are and may resent their equal or superior status in the agency.

Education Differential

Recovering staff can sometimes be threatened by the fact that the nonrecovering staff have more training. Because many recovering counselors enter the alcoholism treatment field through on-the-job-training or workshop experiences, they do not receive the academic credentials that go with formal education. Many of these counselors are extremely sensitive about their lack of formal education and seem to fear that, someday, the better educated, nonrecovering counselors will reveal the recovering counselors' ignorance to the world in one fell swoop of intellectual ambush. Obviously, this fear makes the counselor who is a recovering alcoholic very cautious and circumspect in his dealings with the better educated, nonrecovering counselor. While this attitude may seem quite irrational to the casual observer, it is better understood when one remembers the problems with self-esteem and lowered self-worth that many alcoholics must struggle with for an extended period of their life following the achievement of sobriety.

A regrettable consequence of these first two points of friction is that although the recovering alcoholic counselor has much to offer the nonaddicted counselor, because of the suspiciousness and hostility generated between the two groups, a beneficial exchange between them may not be possible. It is also true that the degreed counselor may have skills and points of view that might benefit the recovering counselor. Unfortunately, the frequent antagonism between the two camps may not allow for constructive dialogue—a dialogue that might eventually lead to better care for both types of counselors' clients.

Formation of Cliques

The nonrecovering counselor may resent the in-group cliquishness of the recovering counselors. The fact that the recovering counselors have a built-in bond of Alcoholics Anonymous (A.A.) association and some experiences that they perceive as shared can make the nonrecovering counselor feel excluded. Another aspect of this same issue is that the nonrecovering staff member may see recovering staff members as exercising a reverse sort of snobbery. That is, the recovering counselor may insist that the only way one can really understand an alcoholic is by being one and that, as a result, the nonrecovering counselor can never really be effective.

Differing Attitudes toward Alcoholism

There may be differences in the way the recovering and nonrecovering alcoholic view alcoholism. In many cases, the counselor who is a recovering alcoholic will see alcohol problems in less differentiated ways than the academically trained counselor who, through education, has been exposed to widely differing models of alcoholism. For example, on the one hand, the recovering counselor may see alcoholism as an either/or issue, i.e., either you are alcoholic or you are not. The notion of alcoholism as a disease may have been fundamental in the recovering counselor's training history, and close ties with the philosophy of A.A. may be seen as the sole basis for treatment.

On the other hand, the academically trained counselors may have been exposed, through university training, to a multicausal model of alcohol abuse and may see differing types of interventions as appropriate where there are differing developmental histories for the alcohol abuse. It goes without saying that these differing approaches can frequently become the basis for a communication breakdown and neither group really appreciates that a major part of the problem is in the model that they are using to treat alcoholism and alcohol abuse.

Academic versus Craft Training

Another difference exists in the source and philosophy of training for the degreed professional and the recovering alcoholic counselor. Kalb and Propper (1976) have characterized the differences between these two types of substance abuse professionals as science versus craft training, respectively. On the one hand, the scientist-professional background of the degreed counselors usually means that they have learned their caregiving skills not only experientially, as an apprentice to a skilled counselor, but that also through didactic training, they have been exposed to the teachings of many others regarding alcohol problems. In this type of training, counselors will normally be exposed to a wide range of differing viewpoints and are encouraged to exercise independence in establishing their concepts of the issues. The ability to engage in original, independent thinking and to critically evaluate the work of one's teachers and peers is the highest calling of the scientist-professional model.

On the other hand, craftsmen obtain their qualifying skill or knowledge primarily through observing and experiencing the actual tasks required under the tutelage of a master craftsman. The knowledge that they acquire is a product of the experiences of their teacher, and the acquisition of the craftsman's skills is demonstrated by the ability to consistently replicate the performance of the master craftsman. In mastering these skills, only limited elaborations of style are allowed, and critical examination of the traditions of the craft are actively discouraged. In fact, shared agreement on the traditions of the craft is the criterion for loyalty in a craft-like organization.

In the past, paraprofessional preparation in the alcoholism treatment field has primarily followed the craft model. Trainees are usually indoctrinated in the philosophy and principles (the 12 steps) of A.A. by trainers who are themselves recovering alcoholics and who have used this approach in their own recovery. These students are expected to emulate their teachers' thinking and actions. Their goal is to one day be like their teachers and teach others what they have learned. As a result, most paraprofessionals in the alcoholism treatment field are committed to traditional concepts and are resistant to alternative views of alcoholism. The steadfast refusal to question their own premises, despite conflicting evidence, helps to create and maintain an intense loyalty and unity among these recovering counselors. While this problem between the recovering and nonrecovering counselors has been an ongoing one, it could become more severe in the next few years as more alcohol counselors complete training in more formal settings and are exposed to competing models of alcohol use and abuse.

Appropriate Modeling Behavior versus Emotional Catharsis

The nonrecovering counselor may sometimes view the recovering counselor as having as many psychotherapy needs as the clients he is trying to help. Of course, lay counselors may very well tie their recovery to helping other people, particularly since twelfth stepping is a tenet of A.A. Frequently there is a close tie between the treatment philosophy of an alcohol treatment program and the philosophy of A.A. Therefore, recovering counselors may use their own histories with alcohol abuse extensively to teach other patients how they managed their personal recoveries. There is, of course, a fine line between illustrating appropriate recovery behavior and experiencing some emotional catharsis that may be useful to the mental health of the recovering counselor. It is also probable (and possibly necessary in order to appropriately model the desired behavior) that the recovering alcoholic will use a group or individual session to deal with his own personal problems. It is imperative, however, that counselors, whether recovering or nonrecovering, remember that they are there to help the people in treatment, not themselves. Whenever a counselor's problems become the predominant, ongoing focus of treatment, then the concern of fellow counselors is justified, and it may be necessary to intervene, in some way, to find outside therapy for the counselor having difficulty.*

Alcohol Counselors and Other Mental Health Professionals

Problems for new alcohol counselors may be especially pronounced when it becomes necessary for them to work with people from other disciplines. It may be particularly difficult, for example, for those substance abuse counselors working in mental health agencies. There one must relate to disciplines such as psychology, psychiatry, and social work, which have different ideological and philosophical training histories. Bridging the gap to form a collegial relationship may be very difficult for the substance abuse counselor, for a number of reasons. First, the philosophical and ideological differences among the above training disciplines are great, and these differences are even more pronounced between the substance abuse counselors and these professions. For example, the center of client motivation for most mental health professionals is in the client, i.e., the client must want to change before therapy can be effectively instituted. In working with the alcoholic and drug abuser, considerable external coercion may be used to get persons to enter treatment and to get them involved in the initial stages of treatment. Second, many mental health personnel view individuals who are working with alcoholics as paraprofessionals. As Kalb and Propper (1976) have noted, the paraprofessional has operated as an adjunct to, and under the supervision of, the professional in mental health settings. The paraprofessional in the alcohol field, however, has been a teacher or colleague rather than a student. These differences in expectations about roles add to communication difficulties. Finally, a considerable amount of hostility toward, and avoidance of treatment of, alcoholics has historically been present in all of these disciplines. Many of them see

*The reader is referred to Knauert and Davidson (1979) and to Wegscheider (1981). The latter author has generated a checklist so that people working with substance abusers can evaluate their own levels of adjustment at a given point in time. Wegscheider (1981, pp. 248–53) has introduced what she has labeled "the whole person inventory." This inventory covers both personal and job-related issues and may be helpful to counselors who are experiencing difficulty.

alcoholics as a lower level of client, and may see the alcohol counselor, regardless of level of training, as a person who is competent only to deal with these hopeless clients. Many mental health agencies insist on both physical and administrative separation of the two caregiving systems. Frequently, very little communication is maintained between these two groups, and considerable resentment and hostility can develop.

As noted above, this is not an exhaustive list of the potential problems that may exist between recovering and nonrecovering counselors. It is hoped, however, that it will alert alcohol counselors to some of these issues and lead to the issues being discussed among staff members.

Inter-Agency Conflict

Because the alcohol field began as a grassroots movement, primarily through A.A. and the National Council on Alcohol,* it has developed as a highly personalized, very politicized system. In particular, there has been a major concern with protecting one's turf against competing agencies, both in and out of the alcohol field. Part of this paranoia is historically justified, since alcohol treatment has traditionally been underfunded. Individuals in the field have had to fight for scarce resources with other caregiving systems (e.g., mental health agencies) and even with competing alcohol agencies. As a result, the system has not only become paranoid toward agencies outside the alcohol field, but also within the field one agency may become suspicious of other agencies that might be competing with it for patients. With this view of internal and external agencies as threats to their survival, alcohol agencies are frequently susceptible to rumor, internal fantasy generation, and the distortion of facts. While all of these problems can be present in human service agencies generally, the degree of severity seems to be greater in the alcohol field. Of course, this means that some forum for open discussion of the issues and some mechanism for resolution of differences must be rigorously maintained. When clear channels of communication are not maintained, then alcohol agencies can engage in very destructive behaviors.

Inter-Agency Conflict and Client Care

None of the above issues would be of much importance if they had little bearing on the care of clients. However, relationships within and between agencies can

---

*A fact frequently overlooked by the alcohol field is that the field actually had considerable professional-scientific input at its inception and that the founder of the National Council, Marty Mann, actually received considerable support from Jellinek and his group at Yale (see Jellinek, 1960).

directly and indirectly affect the quality of care provided to the clients of these agencies. We will consider only a few of the more important consequences of disrupted internal and external agency relationships. The main point to remember here is that agency functioning is not an abstract event, unrelated to day-to-day client care. As we shall see, there are rather direct tie-ins between some of the above issues and the quality of client care provided by an agency.

One example of the direct impact of problems among agencies is that the appropriate referral of clients can be disrupted. For example, if you do not have good relations with a long-term care agency and a client discharged from your treatment center needs this care, the probability of adequate referral is lowered. The reader could doubtless supply many other illustrations of how poor relationships with other agencies can potentially affect client care, ranging from referral to aftercare.

Indirect effects of internal and external agency conflict are more difficult to observe (and frequently more difficult to correct). However, if you concentrate on a given agency, you can readily see how many of the indirect effects discussed here are operating in that agency. Whenever there is internal or external strife surrounding an agency, the amount of emotional energy left to caregivers to do their daily counseling is reduced (and thus their effectiveness is reduced). In addition, the frustration, anger, and anxiety felt by the counselors are communicated to the clients under their care. Therefore, in agencies where staff are spending considerable time and energy dealing with internal or external conflict, clients receive less effective treatment. The clients frequently begin to show acting-out behavior in response to the caregiver's emotional reactions being transmitted to them. This trickle-down effect usually occurs about two weeks following the initiation of the caregiver's conflict and for the same amount of time following the resolution of the conflict.

These problems indicate that the frequently held notion that inter- and intra-agency planning meetings are a waste of valuable treatment time is not necessarily accurate. The provision of structure (e.g., regularly scheduled meetings) to discuss issues, and the existence of an ongoing process (an openness and honesty between staff members in communication) are important for substance abuse agencies. Ensuring open communication can lead to more effective treatment of clients and a reduction of acting-out behavior on the part of the people in treatment.

EARLY JOB ADJUSTMENT IN AN AGENCY

Most counselors would agree that alcohol agencies are not unchanging, static organizations. However, one of the things that caregivers frequently overlook is the fact that they themselves also change in a number of ways in the course of their careers. The ability to manage psychological and philosophical adjustments is crucial to survival in caregiving agencies. In this section we shall examine some of the adjustments that caregivers entering an agency may need to make over a period of time. We will also suggest some strategies that can be helpful in dealing with these issues. A cautionary note: The sequence of adjustments described here is typical, but may not occur for all counselors in all settings. The timing of each of the following phases is also highly variable, both across settings and for caregivers in the same setting. Therefore, the phases described should not be perceived as automatic procedures that will be experienced by all alcohol counselors or all caregivers.

The Honeymoon Period

Part of the problem new counselors face is that they simply do not know the agency very well. Another problem is that the new counselor may approach the job in an idealized way. If we were to have an organizational chart of the agency drawn from the new counselor's perspective, we would expect that much of the agency would be left out, and the counselor's role in the agency would be much larger than it would be from the perspective of an objective observer. The new counselors' egocentric behavior is initially reinforced, since in the early days and weeks people in the agency usually welcome them in and attempt to be very supportive. Additionally, the counselors are, ideally, not yet swamped with a heavy caseload and have time to interact with their new colleagues. None of this is necessarily maladaptive since we would hope that a new counselor would enter the job with enthusiasm and excitement. However, this period, sometimes called the "honeymoon" period, is not generally characteristic of the experiences that counselors will encounter once they become fully involved with their job in the agency.

One reason for highlighting the honeymoon period is that some counselors suffer early severe doubts about whether they have chosen the right job, right career, because of the contrast between this period and the emotional letdown that they experience following it. After the honeymoon period, some counselors may feel that they have chosen the wrong job, the wrong career. While these feelings may be correct, leaving the agency at this point may be a serious mistake simply because the counselor may not have enough information on which to base a rational decision. The point for counselors to remember if they suffer some early disillusionment within the first three to six months is that other very competent, committed, and dedicated counselors in the same agency may have had the same feelings and stayed with the job until the initial adjustments were made.

Mastering Routine Tasks

Several other adjustment phases in caregiving agencies have been described (Sarata, 1979). These phases are usually filled with ambivalence and uncertainty for the caregiver. We will call the first of these phases "mastering standard operating procedures." This stage usually overlaps the honeymoon period described above. In mastering procedures, the counselor is preoccupied with learning things such as the clerical demands of the agency, e.g., how to fill out the necessary forms correctly, how to get progress notes typed up, and procedures for setting up an interview with the family. Many counselors may experience this period as a time when there are an overwhelming number of things to learn. Many fear that they will never learn it all. Generally, counselors at this point in this phase are so busy with the nitty-gritty functions of the agency that they have relatively little concern about their comparative job performance. To their disappointment, new counselors discover that a portion of the work they will be doing is routine, monotonous, and uninteresting. The boring routine of learning the right forms to use, the appropriate channels through which to get things done, and so forth, may be tasks that the new counselors did not anticipate. In addition, they learn that their general training in counseling did not provide many of the technical details needed in their new job. Close relationships with a more experienced counselor or their supervisors are needed for them to handle the adjustments in this phase. However, novice counselors must be mature enough (and assertive enough) to seek out this technical advice and support in order to reduce the stress of this period.

Comparing Work Attitudes and Philosophies

In the third phase, counselors may begin to compare their work attitudes and philosophies with those of coworkers and superiors. Each interaction seems to provide an opportunity for the new workers to compare their ideas to those of relevant others in the job place. While some counselors may be concerned with what supervisors think, more often counselors are interested in what their fellow counselors are thinking and doing. The sharing of experiences with fellow counselors is important because new chemical dependency counselors face what has been called the "crisis of competence" (Cherniss, 1980). The comparison of their performance with those of their peers allows feedback about the relative quality of their performance. Being able to share experiences and receive support from their peers provides several benefits for the neophyte counselors. First, colleagues can offer the neophyte counselors a sympathetic ear when they want to talk about work problems, resulting in an emotional release of tension and anxiety. Second, a better perspective and understanding of the problem is frequently possible after sharing job problems with colleagues. Third, supportive colleagues are particularly important when the novice counselors find themselves in conflict with administrators or agency policy. Fourth, colleagues also offer a readily available resource for the large amount of technical information that must be acquired. Fifth, colleagues offer feedback on one's performance, feedback that is important for the feeling of professional competence. Finally, colleagues can help the new counselor confirm or disconfirm his perception of his performance on the job.

Self-Doubts about the Caregiver Role

Eventually, the fourth phase of early job adjustment is reached. This phase involves a preoccupation by the caregivers with their fitness for, or commitment to, the caregiver role. Counselors may begin to examine how far their clients have progressed and to question whether or not they are doing an effective job. Counselors may also begin to reflect on the stresses and satisfactions experienced in the job. The paramount question that seems to be asked during this phase is: Are the job and I suited for each other? Moving to another agency is one way to resolve the uncertainties of this issue. However, the counselor should be aware that working through the above phases and learning to pace oneself seem to be necessary adjustment procedures for assuming the caregiving role.

The above adjustments are frequently experienced by the counselor in a lonely, internal struggle. It is frequently lonely because caregivers find it difficult to request assistance for themselves and often relegate their own cares and concerns to another time. It is important, then, for counselors to seek out peer and supervisor support as they progress through these phases. The question: Should I share my concerns with others in the agency? is one that must be answered by counselors based on their perception that other staff will be supportive and on their own ability to be open. If the counselor does decide to risk asking for support, a potential long-range advantage is that, even if specific questions are not answered, the counselor has built a network of support that can be utilized in the future.

An awareness of the above phases should be helpful in two ways to new counselors entering an alcohol agency.

1. Like their clients, it is better if counselors have some preliminary understanding of some of the things they may experience. Daily adjustment requires the ability to label and understand experiences. If neophyte counselors are aware that the above experiences are relatively common, they are less likely to be hesitant in sharing their experiences with coworkers. In particular, if other counselors at the same level are present, it may encourage the counselors to form a minisupport and discussion group. Support from peers may be readily available in the agency.
2. If a particular job situation is not going well, an awareness of the existence of ongoing workplace adjustments may allow the counselor to more readily put things in perspective. For example, when the above phases are being

worked through, the occurrence of a frustrating event can have a heavier impact on the counselor's morale. An awareness that experiences may have a greater impact on people when they are already feeling perplexed and confused (something counselors tell their clients all the time) can be helpful in maintaining a more objective and long-range perspective. Both of these points can be useful in surviving the initial adjustments necessary in the work place.

COMMUNICATION ISSUES WITHIN AN AGENCY

One of the factors frequently overlooked in assessing the quality of care provided to clients in an alcohol agency (or any caregiving agency) is the degree to which an agency communicates internally and externally. This section focuses on internal agency communication; external communication (communication with other agencies) will be considered in the following section.

Open Communication

One of the most obvious advantages of open communication within an agency is that if counselors talk to each other, then clients are likely to get better and more appropriate care. This function is frequently (but certainly not always) appreciated by alcohol caregivers and can be seen in daily staffing meetings, where lively discussions of client progress and what types of interventions may be needed occur. What is often ignored is that adequate communication regarding clients requires clear communication among staff in that agency.

This staff communication network frequently involves a highly personalized series of interactions. When these personalized interactions are characterized by openness, sensitivity to other colleagues, candor, and trust, then the agency is more likely to perform well such tasks as evaluating client progress and planning treatment. However, when the communication network is characterized by defensiveness, insensitivity, dishonesty, and mistrust, even basic client evaluation and treatment planning sessions become distorted by the overall breakdown in communication within the agency. The breakdowns can occur for a number of reasons. Some examples include the following: competition for what may be considered a more ideal job assignment; distance that may be created because co-workers have little in common in terms of outside interests; or a situation where one person may be perceived as the favorite of the supervisor and the rest of the counselors scapegoat that person. Whatever the reason, jealousy, envy, or simple lack of interest can create communication gulfs in an agency (Cherniss, 1980).

As implied above, the lack of sensitivity on the part of counselors toward colleagues can lead to defensive behavior and to closing down communication between counselors and their colleagues. Much of what has previously been discussed would apply in the area of defensive behavior; however, one additional point should be made. All people have vulnerable points. If they are attacked at these points, they will overreact and behave in irrational ways. Counselors should become aware of these vulnerabilities in their colleagues and avoid arousing defensiveness whenever possible. If they do, however, make a fellow counselor defensive, counselors should remember that their colleague is likely to behave in an irrational manner. Frequently, it is better to apologize for making the person angry and then to try another tack in communicating with the individual about the issue.

Personal Insensitivity and Communication

Personal insensitivity within an agency can have a powerful impact on communication. There will be times when counselors do not get the support and concern they need from their fellow counselors, simply because the other counselors are so preoccupied with their own job responsibilities. Also, it is frequently forgotten (or overlooked) that it is the small, sensitive things that count in day-to-day interaction. Being human and humane with colleagues can reduce emotional and psychological distance and make communication both easier and more open. Since counselors are human, they tend to talk more to the people who are sensitive to their needs and to become more defensive (and so, less communicative) toward those people who are not sensitive to their needs. A common error for counselors is to attend so much to the needs of their clients that they ignore entirely the needs of their peers. Counselors frequently show sensitivity, warmth, care, and concern with their clients, then leave the counseling session and greet their colleagues as if they had been trained in the Attila the Hun School of Therapy. Again, the empathy and warmth shown to patients is not transferred to counselors' interactions with colleagues.

Areas of Potential Insensitivity

One area of potential insensitivity comes out of the differing training histories of the personnel typically employed in an alcohol agency. The degreed, professional counselor may be insensitive to factors such as the role that A.A. plays in the lay counselor's life. Professional counselors may, in the beginning, be insensitive to the fact that for people using A.A. as a support group, an attack on A.A.'s principles is similar to an attack on a person's religion (i.e., they are touching on an area that is a central value for these people). New counselors will quickly be made aware that for the counselor who is a recovering alcoholic, the strengths and weaknesses of using A.A. as a support group is not a topic for academic discussion. Obviously, an early encounter of this type can lead to anger, defensiveness, and less effective communication between the two groups.

Recovering counselors, on the other hand, sometimes are insensitive toward the nonrecovering counselors. For example, the recovering counselor may make caustic remarks about the degreed counselors' lack of a true understanding of the problem they are trying to treat. Attempts to belittle the utility of education also reflect insensitivity and defensiveness on the part of the recovering counselor when such comments are directed at their academically trained peers. These patterns of interaction affect the degree and level of communication and lead to the formation of cliques within an agency.

Communication Structures

In order to better understand communication breakdown, counselors need to understand or make explicit some factors that are so much taken for granted that they are never really looked at closely. To begin with, there are format and form issues involved in communication within any agency. For example, setting up daily meetings implies that some format has been provided within which communication can occur.

New counselors must learn the format of communication in their agency. This structure can vary from highly formal meetings, with someone acting as chairperson, to a casual hallway meeting system where things are decided in a very informal way. In some cases, a highly formal system may be set up, but this system is not really involved in how things get communicated (e.g., things may be communicated and decisions consensually agreed upon prior to the formal meeting). The issue is not which one of the above formats is most effective (both can be effective or ineffective) but rather which one or which combination is used in the agency. When counselors first enter an agency, part of the honeymoon period described earlier should be spent studying how things are communicated and how tasks are accomplished in the agency. If counselors are initially aware that two systems of communication and decision making can coexist, they may be less frustrated when they discover that issues that they bring to the more formal session are not extensively debated or considered before a decision is made.

The Communication Process

In addition to understanding the structure of communication, it is also important to recognize and monitor the process of communication. As noted earlier, if people in the agency are basically honest, open, sensitive, and supportive toward their colleagues, then there is likely to be a relatively free and easy exchange of information. If the members of an agency cannot talk to one another, then the best series of structured meetings will not lead to effective communication. While the structure of communication patterns may provide the vehicle for communication to occur, open, trusting communication with colleagues will determine whether the communication patterns will be clear and effective.

In some agencies, disagreements are avoided or played down in order to maintain a surface harmony. Inevitably, this results in distorting the process of communicating, and dealing with some issues among counselors is avoided at all cost. For example, feelings toward one staff member may be so intense that some or all of the counselors avoid confronting that staff member about issues where there is disagreement. Again, not only communication processes, but also decision-making procedures, can be distorted.

Communication Breakdown and Mistrust

Mistrust in an agency is frequently a byproduct of a breakdown in communication, but, obviously, it also can contribute to communication problems once it is present. Sometimes mistrust occurs because an individual has dealt with personal confidences in a destructive manner. At other times an individual (or the agency hierarchy) has not followed through on promises or supported staff members in the agency when a difficult issue is being dealt with. Mistrust is a threat to the fabric of intra-agency communication and, once established, can seriously erode the quality of staff interaction. The question that is sometimes asked is: Can anyone be trusted or is everyone out for number one?

Mistrust, like communication, can either be vertical or horizontal, or it can be present at all levels when the entire agency has problems with trust. When there are problems throughout the agency, an easy way out is to make some outside threat a greater problem than the problems that need to be dealt with internally. While such a strategy may be effective for a short period of time, it does not provide a long-term solution. Like the marriage relationship, relationships within agencies can only be assured by continually dealing with issues as they arise. As with other communication issues, a common mistake is believing that only a single intervention is required to deal with mistrust. An agency maintenance issue can be dealt with routinely where communication and trust levels are high, but becomes difficult to deal with when they are not. Some strategies that seem to be helpful here include the following:

- Keep messages between counselors and their peers clear and deal with interpersonal problems as they occur, rather than putting them off. Reducing ambiguity in communication with peers is an important goal in this respect.
- Remember that personal fantasy and rumor are like gas on a burning fire when trust is an issue. Counselors should attempt to confirm or disconfirm rumors as soon as they hear them. They should also check out their fantasies

of what is going on in the agency; it is remarkable how easily messages can become distorted. If counselors would like to confirm this, they should try passing a verbal message through 10 or more people (at a party, for instance). Usually even a simple message will show some dramatic change. Another way to confirm that multiple modes of communication work better is to write the message down and pass it both in written and verbal form, which should result in a significant reduction in the distortion of the message. A similar issue occurs in counselors' anticipation of what is going to happen when they fantasize about what is occurring in an agency: These fantasies are usually partially, or entirely, wrong.

- If counselors are not physically located in the same facility, they should remember that they may have difficulty managing communication with their colleagues. Here you may have to create some method of maintaining contact with your coworkers. Some possible solutions might include (1) having coffee once a day in the central agency; or (2) having lunch with fellow counselors once a week or more if counselors are located in the field rather than in a central office. The practical side of regular contact is that it allows counselors to deal with ongoing problems in the agency. Of more central importance is the fact that physical and psychological distance is reduced between counselors and their peers through regular contact. If people see and talk to one another on a daily basis, there is less likelihood that mistrust will become a problem. It should again be noted that colleagues provide a powerful support system for new counselors. Without the moral support of colleagues, many new counselors would not make an active effort to resolve their job-related difficulties and could withdraw into mindless conformity.

- Remember, there is a need to provide internal support for communication. Counselors should be aware that they have the most control over their own behavior. They should make every attempt to deal openly and honestly with their peers. Also, they should remember that overcoming mistrust can take time and, in an agency where there are problems, they may not receive much reinforcement for their attempts to deal with issues in a clear and straightforward manner. That will be particularly true when issues of peer insensitivity and defensiveness coexist in an agency; this is not an uncommon occurrence where mistrust is an issue.

A common failure in dealing with communication process issues is to assume that a one-time intervention that results in better communication is all that needs to be done. However, the same breakdowns in communication are likely to recur in an agency. Counselors should be aware that ongoing sessions devoted to specific breakdowns in communication may be necessary. They should not conclude, simply because there is decay in the communication process over a period of time following an intervention, that what they tried was ineffective or that repairing the communication pattern is hopeless. Rather, the problem should be viewed as a maintenance issue in which previously successful interventions can be utilized again.

Communicating with Supervisors

No matter what his position is as a newcomer to an agency, a counselor will need to manage effective communication with people superior, and subordinate, to him in rank or status. One factor that may directly affect counselors' survival is how they deal with people in authority over them, i.e., their supervisors. It is interesting that counselors can sometimes deal so effectively with clients and yet be very ineffective in using identical principles when they interact with their supervisors.

One thing that is very helpful is for counselors to become aware of their own personal feelings and reactions to authority. Frequently, counselors react to supervisors on the basis of long-held emotional reactions to authority figures. When they have a disagreement with a superior, the first question they should ask themselves is how much of this is their own emotional response to an authority figure. A good rule of thumb is that counselors should never confront a superior when angry and out of control (even if they are right), because they may not present their ideas as clearly and precisely as they would like. If counselors are angry but are under control and can verbally express their anger (and their reason for it), their ideas are more likely to be well received. One thing that might be helpful to counselors when communicating something they feel strongly about is to ask themselves how they would feel if someone attacked them personally when complaining about some of their actions. One should not forget that people in positions of power are also feeling human beings. Counselors might also ask themselves if their motive is simply to let off steam, or if they really want to communicate with the person.

A common error in communication is for counselors to avoid interaction with their supervisor. It is almost as if counselors feel that the best way to manage their situation is to blend into the woodwork. If counselors get to know the supervisor as a person, the tendency and need to maintain distance are usually lessened and communication is improved.

Supervisors As a Factor in New Counselor Survival

Supervisors are critical to the initial development and continuing survival of chemical dependency counselors. Some specific ways that supervisors can aid in the development of competence in novice caregivers are outlined below. These include the following:

- Supervisors can provide technical suggestions and advice that can increase the counselors' effectiveness.
- Supervisors provide feedback to the new counselors; positive feedback can help alleviate anxiety, while negative feedback delivered constructively can help the counselor correct weaknesses.
- When the supervisor is readily available to the new counselor for consultation, the counselor feels less alone and isolated, and the fear of harming a client through ineptitude is decreased.
- Supervisors provide a reference point for the new counselor (e.g., if the new counselor sees the case in the same way as the supervisor, then the counselor is reassured that his own competence in understanding a case is adequate).

In general, for the new professional, a supportive, but discreet, supervisor has been found to be associated with positive career development, i.e., positive survival (Chemiss, 1980).

Interacting with Support Personnel

Regardless of their status in the agency, counselors will probably find someone with lower status than themselves with whom they must interact. For example, how will they, as entering counselors, deal with clerical personnel? Obviously, they will want to be sensitive to secretarial needs and will want to promote as much productivity as possible. One rule of thumb is to adopt a style of interaction with subordinates with which they can be comfortable. If counselors are easygoing individuals, it is likely that a brusque, business-like style with secretaries will be difficult to maintain. If counselors try to assume roles that are not consistent with their usual style of interaction, then typically they will under- or overplay them. Remember, a wide variety of approaches work in communicating with people. This can be confirmed by observing the different styles that fellow counselors use in interacting with people.

Cutting Through the Bureaucracy

One area that frequently seems to be overlooked is the general insensitivity of bureaucracies toward people. One result is that the professional role that the counselor has been trained for may be difficult to carry out in the face of bureaucratic demands. For example, bureaucrats may see what is needed and demanded from a different point of view than the counselors do; this is particularly true in the area of professional autonomy. The irrational and sometimes destructive rules and policies of chemical dependency agencies may be a major source of frustration and stress for novice counselors. The new counselors find that one of their tasks is to mediate between bureaucratic demands and client demands. Frequently, alcohol counselors personalize some of the bureaucratic indifference that can occur in care agencies. This can lead counselors to assume that what is occurring is a personal vendetta directed toward them. In point of fact, what is occurring may be totally unknown to the person (or persons) who could correct it, and it will remain that way unless counselors initiate action to open communication and resolve the problem. Frequently, counselors find that the person responsible is just as eager to have the problem corrected as they are. In other words, counselors should check out perceived injustices to see if they are simply oversights.

The solution to another problem in communicating with the bureaucracy is also in the hands of the counselor. As noted above, many counselors find that keeping charts up to date, writing treatment plans, and so forth, is unexciting and boring. Counselors may do these tasks but gripe incessantly about doing them; or resist doing them at all. It may well be that this lack of response to the bureaucracy by counselors can lead to poorer care for their clients and more work for their colleagues. What can be overlooked is that these bureaucratic tasks, as onerous as they are, do help maintain communication within an agency and can ensure better care for the client.

In fairness, it should be noted that general griping about the bureaucracy is characteristic of care agencies. In fact, if not taken to extremes, this griping can allow anger and frustration to be expressed toward a nonreactive source. However, when the griping includes passive resistance or active sabotage of the system, then a vital communication link is threatened.

The importance of establishing open, positive communication with colleagues cannot be overemphasized for new counselors. The role of a novice counselor is psychologically stressful and can be emotionally demanding even when the new counselors have open access to their more experienced peers and can depend on their advice and support. Without this support, the adjustment is infinitely more difficult.

If counselors could always rely on working out problems with colleagues, the world of work would be a happier place. However, the reality of life is that despite their strong efforts to communicate with peers, there will be some colleagues with whom counselors simply cannot communicate. At this point, they have to attempt to find ways to go around these colleagues and to do their job in spite of them. That is, they may have to live with these so-called problem colleagues if they choose to stay in the agency. One question the counselor may have to answer is: Can I work out a way to live with this person or must I leave the agency for my own peace of mind? Another way of phrasing the question would be: Do I like what I'm doing well enough to put up with working with this person? In other cases, they will encounter colleagues who are already burned out and who have very negative attitudes toward the job. For the new counselors, these negative attitudes can be extremely contagious, and they can quickly lose their enthusiasm and drive for the job. Therefore, avoiding contact with such colleagues is essential for the new counselors, particularly during the first months on the job.

MAINTAINING COMMUNICATION WITH OUTSIDE AGENCIES

The practical importance of maintaining open and effective liaisons with other agencies, in terms of meeting the needs of clients, has already been demonstrated. The lack of adequate communication with other agencies also affects the overall morale and functioning of the entire agency and its personnel. Many of the same factors that apply to intra-agency communication also apply here. For example, openness, sensitivity to colleagues, candor, and trust are as necessary for inter-agency communication as they are for intra-agency communication. When the communication network is characterized by negative factors such as mistrust and insensitivity, poor communication will exist among the agencies in a community.

The establishment of positive inter-agency communication requires effort at several levels. For example, Rivers, Sarata, and Book (1974) have pointed out the potential role that chemical dependency agency secretaries can play in maintaining inter-agency communication. It is important for counselors to understand that adequate communication involves many levels. (They may sometimes assume that communicating with outside agencies is the responsibility of their superiors.) The actions of counselors can add to or detract from, in significant ways, how well agencies may communicate. Another issue is that since interactions among some agencies may be very infrequent, the perception that one agency has of another may be based on the quality of interaction an agency had with a specific counselor.

As in intra-agency communication, it is critical that what is to be communicated is specified as clearly as possible. To reduce inter-agency ambiguity, it is necessary that the agency's intra-agency communication be firmly established and operating properly—a necessary but not sufficient condition for effectively communicating with outside agencies.

Some of the same factors that make intra-agency communication difficult are also problematic in inter-agency communication. The only difference is that inter-agency problems may occur more often and require more effort to deal with than the communication problems within a single agency. There is one built-in problem in inter-agency communication: that is distance, both physical and psychological. If the physical locations of agencies are close, some natural communication might occur through various staff members who bump into each other in the parking lot, and so forth. However, these casual interactions are not as likely when agencies and their staffs are physically located in various parts of town. This physical distance can retard the development of close personal relationships among the various staffs. When these close personal relationships are not present, then it is possible for rumor and fantasy to increase drastically and for many imagined slights to occur. These negative fantasies can interfere with inter-agency functioning.

Distance As a Factor in Inter-Agency Communication

When groups of people are separated from each other, they attempt to maintain order in their perception of an outside group by filling in any missing blanks. Frequently, when they do not know the people in the outside group, they fill in these missing blanks in a negative fashion (i.e., they imagine the worst thing that these people could do to them and their agency and proceed to make it fact). An illustration of how rapidly suspicion, paranoia, and negative fantasy in fellow professionals can be provoked is given in an exercise that was conducted with a group of professionals who were midway through a year-long training program.

The group was initially broken into two subgroups. The exercise required one subgroup to learn an anagram task and then to teach it to the second subgroup. The subgroup that was to teach the task remained on the first floor and, like many community agencies, became totally focused on mastering the task. The members of the second subgroup were sent out of the room, with no explanation of their role or what was to be expected of them, except that the first group would teach them a task and that they were to remain in an upstairs room for about two hours. Shortly after reaching the second floor, the subgroup to be trained began to wonder what was going to happen to them. Then they began to wonder if, perhaps, the first subgroup would not try to present the material in such a way as to confuse them and to make them appear silly. As time passed (the first subgroup continued to be totally involved in learning the anagram task), the second subgroup's fantasies about being humiliated became more real. To deal with the anticipated humiliation, they established a password that, when called out, would signal the entire group to leave the building and abandon the training exercise. After two hours, the second group was brought back to the first floor for training by the first group. The waiting group's initial reaction was so defensive that someone in the first group eventually thought to ask what was going on. Once the fantasies of the second subgroup were shared with the first group, an attempt was made to deal with their fears. Considerable time and energy were needed to dissipate the suspiciousness and anxiety of the second group by members of the first group.

What is amazing about this situation is that the people in the two subgroups were well acquainted with one another and had formed close working relationships over the previous six months of training. They also had regular group meetings, where problems could be worked out. Despite the apparent closeness, separation for a short time—in a situation where one group had been given ambiguous information about the intentions of the other group—produced immediate paranoid fantasies. Following the completion of the exercise, it was pointed out that the first group could have kept the second group in the room while the first group learned the task, and that this not only would have reduced the destructive fantasies of the second group but also would have facilitated the teaching and learning of the task.

Two things are apparent from this exercise. First, if well-acquainted colleagues can become suspicious of one another's motives within a two-hour period, separated by only a single floor in the same building, imagine the possible difficulties that can arise among agencies separated by several miles and without close working relationships. Second, if the first group had involved the second group in the task from the beginning, all of the problems could have been avoided. When one agency is planning policies that may affect another agency, bringing the second agency into the planning process from the beginning may significantly reduce the fantasies held by personnel in the second agency.

Dealing With Inter-Agency Fantasy and Rumor

Another problem created by distance and inadequate communication patterns is rumor. While the need to check out intra-agency rumors is important, the need to deal constructively with rumors concerning outside agencies is imperative. This is particularly so when these rumors consist of possible negative actions by the outside agency. (Unfortunately, these types of rumors are most frequently negative in nature.) As is the case with intra-agency communication, there is a strong need to confront these inter-agency fantasies and rumors and to build channels of communication that assure that they can be dealt with quickly. Some principles that are potentially helpful in dealing with these problems are outlined below.

Maintaining an Avenue of Communication

In every community, it is necessary to maintain some vehicle of communication among agencies. A coordinating committee (with representatives from all local chemical dependency agencies) that meets regularly is essential. Not only do the meetings allow for people to deal with ongoing practical issues, but they also offer the opportunity to establish a network of people who can check out rumors and fantasies between meetings, quickly and definitively. Delay in dealing with these problems only allows them wider circulation and therefore makes them more "real." Not being as definitive as possible when debunking these erroneous communications gives credence to such rumors and fantasies.

Unambiguous Communication

An agency has the same responsibility to communicate clearly and with minimum ambiguity with other agencies as do individuals. Whenever agencies are dealing with issues and announcements that could draw strong reactions from another agency (e.g., because it is potentially threatening to that agency), it is wise to use multilevel channels of communication. Do not just send a memo! One possible approach might be to first go and talk with an agency representative, discuss the proposed issue at some length, and ask for feedback. Whenever possible, incorporate any suggestions and ask the agency or agencies affected if they would like a representative to come and discuss the issue at a staff meeting. While this may not be necessary with minor issues, the time spent may be less than that needed to resolve poorly communicated messages later. Also, it leaves a given agency with better, not worse, communication links with other agencies.

LONG-RANGE COUNSELOR JOB ADJUSTMENT: DEALING WITH ETHICAL ISSUES

While new counselors may be overwhelmed with the adjustments necessary to manage a new job in a seemingly brief period of time, they may also be making adjustments to long-term problems of the profession. For example, the new counselor may enter the agency with considerable eagerness to change its policies and procedures and effect rapid and drastic change. The young counselor may see his enemy as the entrenched bureaucracy. One of the adjustments that young counselors must make over time is the transition from neophyte to member of the establishment. While this transition may not seem important to new counselors initially, most counselors will eventually face adjustment to the increased job demands and responsibilities of the experienced counselor (i.e., they will be faced with the responsibility for setting and maintaining the policies of the agency). In brief, every counselor will eventually become part of the establishment.

In the process of surviving in the agency to reach the point of being a part of the establishment, counselors must learn to pace themselves, to cope with the ethical dilemmas confronted in the job place, and to avoid job burnout. A consideration of some of the ethical issues that counselors may face will be presented first. Finally, a discussion of job burnout will be presented and steps that may reduce burnout will be outlined.

Dealing With Unethical Behavior in an Agency

As an alcohol counselor, you will be entering a caregiving area where problems with appropriate ethical behavior abound. It is not true that alcohol counselors are more, or less, ethical than other caregivers; however, they will face as many ethical issues as counselors in the mental health field and the guidelines provided for them are frequently less well-defined than those of mental health professionals.

In order for new counselors to manage their own ethical behavior, it is frequently necessary for them to consult counselors more experienced than themselves. Neophyte counselors should never hesitate to ask about an ethical issue, and most professional counselors will continue to seek advice about ethical dilemmas throughout their careers. While concern for following proper ethics should be a central value for counselors, it also has practical survival implications. Every year, one of the major reasons that a significant number of counselors are dismissed from alcohol and drug agencies is that they are judged to have behaved unethically.

It would be impossible to specify all the possible ethical dilemmas that counselors could encounter in their work. To do so would require a listing lengthy enough to fill the entire New York City phone book. This section will cover only some of the more obvious potential ethical problems.

Propriety in the Client-Counselor Relationship

A key factor for counselors to consider, when dealing with clients, is that, in the treatment situation, the counselor has considerable power over a person who may be very vulnerable emotionally. Whenever counselors are in a power relationship in a professional setting, they should provide safeguards for themselves and their clients so that this power is not deliberately, or inadvertently, misused. One of the best safeguards is to be alert to the power relationship. Counselors should ask themselves if their actions are likely to be interpreted as taking advantage of the client. Of course, counselors are frequently attempting to get their clients to try new behaviors—to do something that the clients do not choose to do, i.e., to change. Counselors often use the relationship they have with clients to get things accomplished. Most of these interventions are both appropriate and necessary. However, there will be times when counselors' actions toward clients could be seen as questionable. A brief discussion of some of the ethical issues that are most problematic for chemical dependency counselors follows.

Dating a Current or Ex-Client. While this situation is one most chemical dependency counselors would be acutely aware of, it is surprising how many violate this taboo. Most fail to remember that the relationship begins in an unequal power relationship and that this differential power can place the client at a strong disadvantage. Dating an ex-client seems to be less of an ethical issue until it is remembered that the relationship began with this same power differential while the client was in a vulnerable and impressionable position. Therefore, posttreatment dating has some of the same problems that exist in dating a client in active treatment.

Sexual Intercourse with Current or Former Clients. This represents the epitome of taking advantage of the unequal power relationship and the client's vulnerability and is by far most frequent with a male counselor and a female client. Many alcohol counselors see this action as grounds for dismissal from the agency.

Failing To Maintain the Confidentiality of a Client. This is a very shady area and one that is sometimes more difficult for chemical dependency counselors than it is for some other caregivers. In many settings, considerable treatment is done by volunteer counselors, and personal data are shared in a casual and open manner. While this atmosphere may be helpful in treatment, it opens up the possibility that information that is shared by a counselor about a client may be revealed unthinkingly by one of these volunteer counselors. Also, there are frequent visitors to chemical dependency settings, and counselors must be careful about whom is within hearing distance when discussing a client. A related problem occurs when information about the client has to be shared with outside agencies. Frequently, law-enforcement authorities or the client's employer may request a report on the client's progress and possible prognosis; making the judgment of just what should be included in these reports must be done very carefully. Here, the seeking of advice from more experienced counselors and finding out how the reports will be used are important steps.

Sharing Information with Family and Friends. While the client may frequently give blanket permission to share information, the counselor may still have to make judgments as to how much information is shared and how it is presented.

There are several other less dramatic examples of unethical behavior: not assuming professional responsibility for clients and not maintaining adequate supervision for oneself is one example; another is misrepresenting one's credentials to an agency in order to gain employment.

The preceding ethical dilemmas are based on the individual actions of a counselor. Frequently, however, the agency in which a counselor is employed may have a supervisor who is engaging in actions that are unethical or not in the best interests of clients or staff. For example, supervisors in an agency may attempt to use their positions to seek sexual favors from subordinates. Or, an agency may not systematically obtain its clients' permission before releasing information. In many states, the latter action would be a violation of state law (in addition to violating federal regulations).

Of course, there will be other situations that are not so clear-cut. In many cases the counselor will have to make more subtle decisions. When agency policy or actions do not agree with one's perception of correct procedure, it would seem wise to think of these problems as lying on a continuum. For example, counselors might want to see problems of agency procedure improved but allow their supervisors to deal with such problems. A second point on the continuum might be, "I hold the agency responsible, and I intend to document what is happening."

A final point on the continuum might be, "These are actions I can't be a party to, and if I cannot get them changed, I must resign. These actions violate my professional (or personal) ethics and values." In other words, some actions by an agency involve minor borderline violations; others are more serious and may need to be monitored carefully by counselors; still others are so clearly beyond the pale that counselors can only opt for leaving the agency if things are not changed.

Resolving Ethical Problems

In terms of proceeding to deal with these issues, counselors might discuss their concerns on the first level with colleagues, soliciting their opinion, and perhaps even talk to their supervisors about the changes that they perceive are needed. This approach might lead to the elimination of agency policies that the counselors find annoying; of course, it is possible that the counselors will simply have to live with the issue. On the second level, the problems are more acute, and the documenting of the issues should occur after the counselors have approached their supervisors and pointed out the problem. If no solution is provided, the counselors verbally (or in writing) should inform superiors that they will be documenting events because they view the issue as an ethical problem for the agency and as one that causes the counselors considerable concern. On the final level, it is assumed that the counselor has gone through the steps described above and, in addition, has met with trusted colleagues inside and outside the agency prior to deciding to leave. Leaving an agency because of unethical practices is sometimes the only thing that can be done; however, the counselor should remember that leaving the agency usually means losing powerful leverage in getting unethical actions and policies changed.

LONG-RANGE COUNSELOR SURVIVAL: JOB ADJUSTMENT AND AVOIDING BURNOUT

Modifying Work Goals

Over the span of their careers, social service workers change in the way they approach their jobs. A study of professional workers in several social service agencies found the following changes in new professionals:

- Professionals modified the work goals they had set out to accomplish. The modification was frequently in the direction of accepting more modest goals in terms of job accomplishment.

- There was a strong tendency for professionals to reduce their level of personal involvement in the job. Physical and emotional withdrawal from clients was a common occurrence. This reduced investment in clients was accomplished by reducing the role of work in their lives and increasing fulfillment in their lives outside the workplace.
- There was a tendency for new professionals to shift responsibility for failure from themselves to things outside themselves (e.g., they blamed the clients or the system for failures on the job).
- Over time, young professionals became less idealistic, less trusting, and more conservative in their attitudes toward clients and people in general.
- There was increased concern about self-protection and enhancing their own lives (e.g., gratification of their own needs at work became more important). Also, there was increased concern about salaries and maintaining freedom of action in the job place (Cherniss, 1980).

Reality Shock

These changes were described as occurring because of reality shock. Most of the professionals discussed had little experiential or internship training and thus entered their jobs with idealistic expectations that were not based on the realistic demands of the job. Most chemical dependency counselors do have considerable experiential training before taking their first job; however, while the proportion of the training occurring in real-life settings is high, most chemical dependency counselors spend much less absolute time in training than did the professionals in the above study. In other words, while the experiential training certainly helps to insulate chemical dependency counselors against some of the stresses suffered by these professionals, it is probably still insufficient to prevent many of these same changes from occurring in the lives of substance abuse counselors. In fact, some degree of change in job perception and attitudes toward work in the direction of the changes noted above is probably normal and to be expected. These changes may be necessary for counselors to survive in the workplace. However, when pressures in the job place are extreme, there is the danger that chemical dependency counselors may experience job burnout.

Counselor Vulnerability to Burnout

Burnout has been described as a frequently occurring event in the lives of those counselors working with chemically dependent people. It has been noted, for example, that one in the role of alcohol counselor is extremely vulnerable to burnout (Knauert & Davidson, 1979). One writer has suggested that social service workers are affected in the following ways:

- Social service work is psychologically fatiguing or stressful.
- Service providers experience and exhibit an identifiable pattern of burnout reactions.
- Behaviors associated with burnout reduce the individual's effectiveness with clients; indeed, burnout can cause the service provider to act in ways that are harmful to clients. (Sarata, 1982)

The effects of burnout are not only potentially harmful to clients but also to the counselor's job performance, job satisfaction, and morale. Thus, burnout can play a crucial role in determining whether the counselor survives in the chemical dependency agency. It is important to first examine the characteristics of burnout that have been experienced and reported by alcohol counselors. The ways these same counselors describe the recognition of burnout in their colleagues is secondarily important. As the following findings indicate, both perspectives are important, because one's perception of burnout changes drastically depending upon whether it is being experienced personally or is being viewed in another person.

Personal Responses to Burnout

Sarata presents a list of the personal responses to burnout given by participants in a burnout workshop for alcohol counselors (see Table 9–1). As Table 9–1 shows, the response reported by the largest percentage of counselors was that of being drained, exhausted, and tired of listening and thinking so hard. The fact that burnout can affect self-esteem is reflected in the counselors' responses of feeling helpless, incompetent, and overwhelmed.

A chemical dependency counselor would be wise to become well acquainted with the types of experiences reported by Sarata's alcohol counselors. These warning signs can be used to alert counselors that they either need to spend some time away from their jobs or increase their involvement in the maintenance strategies and behaviors that are outlined below. Sarata found that 65 percent of the counselors involved in his workshop were at a point where they should examine their lives for some possible change; 7 percent of the counselors were clearly experiencing burnout. These findings suggest that chemical dependency counselors need to spend more time monitoring their job reactions and taking corrective action where needed.

Burnout as Viewed by Others

Table 9–2 presents the ways in which burnout was observed in others. As Table 9–2 shows, counselors suffering burnout are perceived as reacting in ways that are

Table 9–1 Phrases Used by Alcoholism Counselors To Describe Their Burnout Experiences

Respondents (N = 93)	Responses (N = 348)	Type of Phrase
71%	19%	Drained, exhausted (e.g., "tired of thinking so hard and listening so intently")
45%	12%	Helpless, incompetent, overwhelmed (e.g., "the faster I worked, the behinder I got")
34%	9%	Angry (e.g., "wanting to lash out")
30%	8%	Depressed
30%	8%	Anxious, fearful (e.g., "scared for self and clients")
26%	7%	Emotionally troubled, volatile (e.g., "losing control of self, uptight")
26%	7%	Irritable
17%	4%	Frustrated (e.g., "about what I failed to accomplish")
16%	4%	Alone (e.g., "dumped upon and unsupported")
16%	4%	Wanting to escape (e.g., "hoping clients don't show, dreaming about my vacation")
12%	3%	Resentful (e.g., "everyone is making demands")
10%	3%	Misunderstood and/or sorry for self
10%	3%	Uncaring
7%	2%	Caring too much (e.g., "taking cases home")
	6%	Other (e.g., "rigid, controlling, critical of others, having tunnel vision")

Source: Sarata, P. B. V. *Burnout workshops for alcoholism counselors.* Unpublished paper. Lincoln, Neb.: University of Nebraska, 1982.

destructive to inter-agency communication; they behave in ways that can affect the morale of the people around them; and their style of dealing with their clients becomes drastically countertherapeutic. If these descriptions are accurate (they do agree with the author's observations), they stand as evidence that people who have been outstanding counselors and colleagues can show extreme deterioration as a result of not maintaining themselves on the job. Of course, one should remember that things occurring at home and in the counselor's personal life can be the cause of many of the behaviors linked to burnout; in other cases, the strain of the job is reflected in the person's home life. Not infrequently, there is an interaction between what is going on at work and the reaction of people at home. However, in some cases, the person will report feeling better and more relaxed away from work and then report headaches, anger, and frustration shortly after arriving at the workplace. Such dramatic changes may reflect burnout or extreme dissatisfaction with the job, or both.

Table 9–2 Phrases Used by Alcoholism Counselors To Describe Indicators of Burnout Among Coworkers

Respondents (N = 93)	Responses (N = 298)	Type of Indicator
45%	16%	Withdrawn, isolated, silent, shuts office door, won't discuss work with others.
35%	11%	Complaining, bitches about everything.
32%	10%	Spaced-out, can't follow conversation, only half listening, forgetful.
20%	7%	Avoids work, absent, clock watching, does personal errands, tardy.
19%	7%	Critical of others, blames coworkers, scolds clients, terminates problem cases.
16%	6%	Depressed, loss of confidence, perseverates about mistakes, turns every conversation to pessimistic side.
16%	5%	Procrastination, does only enough to get through each day.
13%	5%	Loss of objectivity, gets overinvolved with clients, misreads clients.
12%	4%	Emotionally flat, flat affect, lacks enthusiasm, loss of concern.
12%	4%	Emotionally volatile, paranoid, screams, throws things.
10%	4%	Physical problems.
10%	4%	Very busy, hassled, too busy for anything.
	15%	Other, e.g., inflexible, tunnel vision, poor hygiene, smokes too much.

Source: Sarata, P. B. V. *Burnout workshops for alcholism counselors.* Unpublished paper. Lincoln, Neb.: University of Nebraska, 1982.

Maintaining Peak Counselor Efficiency: Avoiding Burnout

At this point, it is important to outline some ways in which chemical dependency counselors may maintain themselves at peak work performance as well as point out some of the traps that many chemical dependency counselors fall into in the workplace.

Maintaining a Life outside the Agency

Many counselors feel that a measure of devotion to their job is the fact that they are totally committed to it. Counselors should be acutely aware that they need to discriminate between values directed toward work and values directed toward

other things in life. Both are important in maintaining long-range peak performance on the job. For example, maintaining relationships with family and friends
can give counselors a time-out from the job place, allowing them to get needed
emotional support and psychological repair following a bad day at the office. A
counselor's failure to maintain an outside life may not have drastic effects on
counselor performance in the short run, but grave risks are run if the counselor
remains totally involved over a long period of time (e.g., several years). For one
thing, the necessary network to emotionally support the counselor once he
experiences burnout simply will not be there when it is needed (i.e., family and
friends will be more distant and less readily available when the counselor needs
their support). With individuals who have not practiced personal maintenance, it
may be necessary to leave the alcohol or drug field for several years in order to
recharge their batteries—a practice common to chemical dependency counselors
who simply do not, or cannot, work without making the job their total life
commitment.

Making a more qualified commitment to the alcohol field is particularly
difficult for those counselors who are themselves recovering alcoholics. For
example, it is frequently difficult for recovering counselors to discriminate among
the job, the work needed for A.A. maintenance, and maintaining close relationships with friends (many of whom are recovering abusers themselves). In this
situation, there is generally considerable mutual support. However, there is also
the tendency to get into a pattern where one talks shop constantly, and the arena
of one's life is drastically narrowed. Thus, the very necessary distractions of doing
other things and not obsessively dwelling on job-related issues are lost.

Modeling a Balanced Life

While the above adjustments are important for preventing burnout, there are
some other issues that are just as crucial. Alcohol counselors, like all caregivers,
are modelers of appropriate behavior for their clients. In fact, modeling is
emphasized by recovering counselors, and they will frequently point out similarities between their history and personality and those of clients. In some cases,
counselors give specific advice about methods and procedures that clients can use
to deal with their alcohol or drug problems from the perspective of: "This is the
way I managed it and so can you." However, when recovering counselors also
model a life that is filled with little but work, they are modeling behavior that the
large majority of people would see as inappropriate. In other words, the counselor
who maintains a balanced life presents a healthier model for the client to emulate.
This notion of a healthy, balanced life as a useful tool in caregiving has frequently
been underestimated by substance abuse counselors. Many recovering counselors
seem to turn their obsession with alcohol into an obsession with work; they
become workaholics.

Dealing With Excessive Agency Work Demands

Recovering counselors (and many nonrecovering counselors) are extremely dedicated and committed to the alcohol field and to the clients they serve. Frequently, chemical dependency agencies take advantage of these dedicated counselors. They are the ones who are persuaded to spend extra hours at the facility and who can be counted on to volunteer for the many extra services needed by the agency. Often the supervisor will involve the dedicated counselor in additional tasks simply because the supervisor is not alert to the possible consequences of his actions. Yet other supervisors are unscrupulous in their use of people or are eager to find a quick and simple solution. Whatever the reason, the counselor should be alert to the possibility of being used, since it increases the risk of early job burnout.

Maintaining a Reasonable Caseload

The heavier the workload, the greater the tendency for counselors to suffer burnout. It has been pointed out that it is not simply the long hours that create burnout; rather, it seems to be the increased direct contact with clients (Cherniss, 1980). Since intense involvement with clients is characteristic of the substance abuse field, counselors should be particularly wary here. A heavier client workload is manageable if there are frequent time-outs from client contact; another way of saying this is that the quality of workload as well as the amount of time spent with clients affects the burnout rate.

Another quality-of-workload factor is the scope of client contact, i.e., the range of problems addressed by a professional working with a particular client and the extent to which the counselor sees the client in different kinds of situations. For example, counselors may never have the opportunity to follow up their successful cases; thus, they only see those clients who are readmitted for treatment. Therefore, counselors only receive negative feedback from populations who typically experience high relapse rates (e.g., a detox unit) and receive almost no feedback about the people they have helped, because all their time is spent meeting the needs of their so-called failures. For this reason, establishing some sort of follow-up system for successful cases may be a useful strategy, not only to better evaluate effectiveness but also to help prevent burnout. In brief, counselors will deal more effectively with job stress when they are exposed to the full range of clients' lives—from detoxification to long-range recovery.

Ambiguous Agency Goals and Objectives

A factor that seems to affect a new professional's burnout rate (and one that is present in some substance abuse agencies) is a lack of clarity about agency goals and expectations (Cherniss, 1980). When the guidelines that counselors are expected to follow are changed from week to week, counselors, who are still uncertain about their competence, face an additional stress in the job place. When counselors survive the initial stress created by a lack of structure, they may, with more experience and confidence, exploit this ambiguity. For example, in an unstructured situation, it may be possible to secure more advantageous working conditions for counselors and better services for their clients. However, in the initial stages, the ambiguity or conflict in goals only increases the new counselors' sense of helplessness.

Maintaining a Reasonable Job Perspective

Frequently, counselors fail to maintain a reasonable perspective regarding their own job and the agency in which they work. The ability to maintain an awareness of one's own limitations, the limitations of the agency where one works, and the limitations of the substance abuse field in general is crucial to chemical dependency counselors. In order to obtain a realistic perspective on these factors, the chemical dependency counselor may need to do several things. For example, counselors should attend outside conferences and communicate with other agencies in and out of the substance abuse field as often as possible. If counselors do not maintain contact with other agencies, they begin to see the way their agency does things as the only way to approach the treatment of substance abuse, which causes an egocentric approach to treatment—a particular problem in the substance abuse field.

Maintaining Contact with Other Professionals

The author has been at several conventions where different groups described approximately the same type of program as new and innovative. None of the groups were aware that the other groups had similar programs (and similar problems), so an opportunity to compare how specific problems could be dealt with was lost. This tendency to become self-centered and self-satisfied can lead to a selective gathering of information and a failure to appreciate other ways of doing the job.

Being open to new information and seeking it out are important in preventing burnout. One of the things that seems to work to prevent burnout is to explore new and different ways of thinking about the job. Maintaining in-service training programs and attending outside workshops and various other outside training experiences is one way of insulating against burnout and the consequent drop in the quality of care for clients. A penny-wise-and-pound-foolish stance by an agency is to fail to subsidize attendance at these training experiences and to insist that all of the counselor's time be spent with clients. The result of this lack of professional stimulation is that counselors become less motivated and show many of the signs of burnout noted above. An indirect benefit of having counselors involved in outside training experiences is that they become more open to other points of view (and to other agencies), thus improving communication possibilities with other community agencies. They also keep up with new ideas and innovations in the field much better.

Staff Support Groups

There are some additional strategies that may help to prevent burnout. These methods of dealing with job burnout are somewhat more dependent on the existing structure, policies, and attitudes of an agency than those noted above. One strategy is for newer counselors to develop a staff support group. These groups provide opportunities to regularly discuss and analyze burnout experiences with others who are working in similar situations, which tends to reduce burnout and its effects. In support groups, counselors from the same agency or from different agencies come together, usually on a regular basis, to talk about their work experiences. There is usually no formal leader and as little structure as possible. Typically, counselors share job-related satisfactions, frustrations, and uncertainties. Those with specific problems can present them to the group and receive concrete suggestions. There is also an atmosphere of acceptance and concern by group members. The danger here is that these groups can turn into "bitch" sessions. A genuine effort must be made to go beyond simply sharing emotions to suggesting new attitudes and strategies for dealing with problems. A real danger is that the group can become dominated by members who have already burned out. Since the attitudes that are associated with burnout are highly contagious, especially where a high degree of burnout already exists in an agency, the forming of a support group from existing staff may be counterproductive for the less experienced counselors.

Rotating Workloads

Another strategy that is designed to provide variety for counselors in the workplace is to rotate counselors' workloads. For example, taking a turn at performing the intake sessions in an agency offers an opportunity for relief from ongoing routine. One alcohol intake-and-referral agency asks each counselor to spend one day each month visiting clients who have been referred for inpatient treatment (and their agencies). These visits improve communication with outside agencies and provide some variety for the alcohol counselors. Another possible adjustment is to make sure that counselors see a variety of clients. In some alcohol agencies, new counselors may initially be assigned more revolving-door alcoholics because these clients are seen as less rewarding by the rest of the staff. While many of these alcoholics recover, the success rate is usually low, further placing stress on new counselors who may already be struggling with feelings of self-doubt about their competence.

Performance Feedback

Still another procedure to help reduce the burnout rate is to increase performance feedback for new counselors. Many agencies are casual about feedback, and the new counselor must be assertive enough to ask for it. (This is sometimes difficult for counselors to do when they are already unsure of their ability.) Feedback is particularly important during the first six months of the job and should be given frequently.

One way that an inexperienced counselor can obtain feedback is to work with a more experienced counselor in seeing one or more clients. For example, the new counselor might work with an experienced counselor on a family case or a marital problem or colead a group with another counselor. These experiences are instructive and a chance to gain some estimate of one's performance relative to that of a more experienced counselor in the agency. This procedure also helps reduce the new counselor's social isolation in the agency.

Finally, factors that are not under the counselors' control may reduce or speed up burnout. For example, burnout is less likely for those counselors working in agencies with clear and consistent goals. Defining clear and consistent goals is, unfortunately, a task that is difficult for many substance abuse agencies. New counselors should be aware of this job stress and realize that it may have a severe impact on them. They should also be aware that changing this may be beyond their control; learning to live with the ambiguity or leaving the agency may be the only choices they have. An associated issue is that the agency should have realistic goals. Many agencies have grandiose notions about their missions. Administrators in these agencies may demand that counselors carry 40 clients per week in individual counseling, maintain liaison with local agencies, and keep all records and charts up to date. Unfortunately, these high work demands cannot be met, and it is precisely those dedicated and committed counselors who hate cutting corners and doing shoddy work who suffer the most (i.e., they are the staff most likely to burn out in their attempt to keep up with the unrealistic work demands).

As this discussion shows, burnout is indeed a very serious problem for substance abuse agencies. However, the points outlined above should allow the chemical dependency counselor to avoid many of the problems associated with burnout. In the final analysis, it may be necessary for some people to work at other jobs periodically in order to regain the motivation and drive to work effectively in the alcohol or drug field.

JOB SELECTION: A CRITICAL CHOICE IN COUNSELOR SURVIVAL

Taking a job is a difficult experience under the best of circumstances, especially for a new counselor. Whether the job applicant is a newly trained counselor or very experienced, he or she will be making choices about whether to take a job with incomplete knowledge of how a given agency functions. Knowledge about the agency may be so scarce that the counselor may not even know what questions to ask. In some cases, counselors may feel that they should not ask too many questions since that might make them appear too pushy to the potential employer.

In the author's experience, most agencies are impressed by an applicant who is able to ask informed and appropriate questions about a position. Most interpret such questions as reflecting interest in their agency and as coming from an applicant who will be a thoughtful, knowledgeable, and invested employee. Of course, the major issue here is how questions are asked about the job. On the one hand, applicants who are insensitive to the needs of the interviewer, or are too blunt in posing questions, may do themselves considerable harm. On the other hand, most agency employers will respond positively to well-thought-out questions that reflect some knowledge of the agency and a genuine interest in learning more about the job.

Finding Out About Your Potential Employer

Getting to be an informed job applicant does require some effort, but it will usually pay off in better job selection. Some of the procedures for getting prepared to ask sensible questions about the job are discussed below.

Read As Much About the Agency As Possible

Frequently, agencies will put out pamphlets to describe their mission, types of clients served, and so forth. While these pamphlets are frequently idealized descriptions of the agency and therefore should be accepted with caution, they do give the counselor an idea of how, ideally, the agency sees itself functioning. They can also allow the counselor, in conjunction with information gathered through other sources, to find out how well the agency has met its idealized goals. If there is minimal overlap between how the agency sees itself and how it seems to function, it would be important to ask, in the interview, what the agency does, how it functions, and what its mission is (to see if these inconsistencies can be resolved). An agency that has gross inconsistencies between its mission statement and what it actually does may be an agency in considerable turmoil—and it may be a tough place in which to work.

Find Out As Much As You Can About the Agency from Other Community Agencies

Information from other agencies must be used with caution. The intense politicization of the alcohol field can produce some distortion in one agency's views of another agency (because of vested interests), and this factor must be weighed when very negative impressions of a given agency are being expressed. Coordinating groups made up of local alcohol and drug counselors who deal with several chemical dependency agencies in the community may provide some important feedback. In any case, it would be wise to ask several agencies, in an informal way, how they see the prospective employing agency. As noted below, an agency that maintains clear and open communication with other agencies is likely to be more efficient and create less frustration for its employees. Less conflict with outside agencies means that counselors will have more resources available to do their job and will be less likely to suffer burnout.

How the Agency Fits into the Overall Community System

Another factor that job applicants are likely to overlook is how the agency fits into the overall service delivery system in a community. For example, what need is the agency meeting in the community, and is it likely that the need will continue to be a high priority for the community? The reality of all job situations is that they are more likely to continue if they are perceived as needed by the people who provide the funding. Therefore, establishing whether the agency plays an important role in the continuum of care (in the opinion of coordinating agencies and other agencies in the community) may give the counselor a sense of job security potential for the agency. In this same vein, it might be important to ask outside sources (and try to glean from the written information on the agency) what the future role of the agency is likely to be. Not infrequently, agencies can make drastic changes in role and function, and counselors who thought they were taking a job in an agency with one mission suddenly find that they are in an agency with another mission altogether. Also, even if the counselors have worked in agencies with the same explicit role and function, they cannot take for granted that they know what the new agency does. It is wise to treat each new job situation as one in which the counselor goes through considerable data collection prior to the interview, regardless of how much the counselor thinks he knows about the agency. Both the counselor and his future employer will benefit from this approach.*

---

*The author is indebted to Phillip Tegler, Director of Directions, an employee assistance program, for suggestions about things that counselors should inquire about prior to taking a job at an agency. Mr. Tegler is a former staff member of the survival skills program, Southeast Community College, Lincoln, Nebraska.

Agency Overseeing Authority

A question that may initially escape the counselor (but that may prove to be important once employment is undertaken) is: To whom does the agency answer in terms of ultimate responsibility? Is it the city council, county commissioners, a state agency, a board of directors, or some other group? If possible, you should also try to find out how actively the overseeing body is involved in agency decisions and day-to-day administration. Generally speaking, overseeing authorities are responsible for setting policy, while supervisory personnel in the agency are responsible for day-to-day decisions on how the work is done (i.e., how the policies are to be implemented). A rule of thumb is that overseeing authorities should not be involved in program administration because they are not as aware of how the agency functions as are the on-site administrators. Where the overseeing agency is heavily involved, it frequently means that the agency has serious internal problems. For example, it may mean that the board has lost confidence in the administrative head of the agency. It could also mean that the governing board is composed of people who will not allow the agency to function without their steady input. Or, it could mean there have been serious blowups within the agency or between the agency and the community at large. None of these things bode well for a counselor and will most surely increase the job stress under which the counselor must work.

Basic Personality Types in Caregiving Agencies

In addition to what you find out about the agency, it is important to have an awareness of who you are and what you want from a job, before you proceed with the interview. While there are several ways to answer this type of question, one way may be to look closely at what your primary needs are. Cherniss (1980) has outlined four basic types of people whom he found working in human service agencies. While any general description of caregivers is bound to be an oversimplification, these career orientations may be helpful to counselors in outlining their own primary needs.

Social Activists

These individuals want to do more in their daily work than provide help to a given client. Personal security and status seem to mean very little to these people: Their primary objective is to bring about some type of social and institutional change that would better the lives of the people they seek to help. In brief, these individuals seem to be concerned with social values and wish to work with people who share their ideology and commitment to social change. In the chemical dependency field there are many people seeking to change the way the system delivers services or meets the needs of chemical dependency clients. Many of them are frustrated because they have entered agencies where it is difficult to be involved with or bring about these system changes. The types of agencies in the chemical dependency field that are most apt to accomplish these goals are not likely to be direct-service agencies; instead, they are likely to be state agencies, coordinating and advocacy groups such as the local alcohol and drug councils, or alcohol and drug foundation groups.

Careerists

Cherniss sees the individuals in this group as seeking success as it is conventionally defined. Prestige, respectability, and financial security are what is important to careerists. These individuals want to make a good impression on colleagues, supervisors, and anyone else who might control their career advancement. While the chemical dependency field frequently disparages people who seek career advancement, these individuals usually are sympathetic, caring, and helpful to the clients they serve, and they provide a high level of service—it is just that their primary goal is to secure recognition and advancement. If career and job advancement are important to counselors, then they should find out which opportunities exist in the agency for advancement and whether a job there can be a solid preparation for seeking a better job in another agency. The use of a job to advance one's career may initially seem distasteful to some counselors, but careful career planning may mean that they get to where they want to go in a more efficient and better prepared manner.

Artisans

To these individuals, the issues of career advancement and financial success are less important than the intrinsic quality of their work. Professional service and growth are also important to these service givers. They wish to perform well, according to their own internal standards. Cherniss sees the individuals in this group as the most individualistic. They tend to value autonomy and independence more highly than do social activists or careerists, they tend to be less competitive than individuals in these other groups, and they like working with people who know more than they do because they can learn from them. Cherniss found that artisans will tend to leave a job (even when seen as successful by the agency that employs them) simply because the job is no longer stimulating and challenging. Those who feel that this description fits them should be concerned about things like the ability to work independently with minimal constraints from supervisors. Individuals such as these would probably prefer an agency that stresses the individual professional responsibility and authority of the counselor; they would also like to be in an agency with stimulating personnel from whom they can learn. Frequently, these attributes are found in agencies that are trying a new approach to treatment or are trying to deal with chemical dependency issues in a new way. These individuals would be very unhappy in an agency where there were severe bureaucratic barriers and demands and where there is a rigid authoritarian chain of command in terms of supervision.

Self-investors

Self-investors are more involved in their life outside work than in their careers. These individuals are not motivated by work-related concerns. In general, they seek interesting work that is moderately challenging but that does not demand too much of them. They also desire pleasant, friendly coworkers and supervisors. If your job is not going to be the central part of your life, you may want an agency that is less demanding in terms of workload. You might also seek a place where the people seem to get along well with one another and value their interaction with one another very highly. While some people might view this role as inferior to some of the others mentioned, it may be realistic for many counselors. For example, if a man or woman has a major investment in maintaining the family, such a job may be the most appropriate choice. It should be noted that Cherniss found that people with this career orientation were committed to maintaining an adequate performance level and that they would work extremely hard to bring their work level up to an acceptable standard.

Cherniss has been careful to point out that most people are really a mixture of all four of these types. In fact, he has a fifth category called a "mixed type" that combines qualities of the other four types. At the very least, a consideration of these types of career orientations should allow counselors to come up with their own set of job requirements: requirements that will fit their specific needs. Such a procedure should help clarify exactly what the counselor may want from a job and lead to their asking appropriate questions in the job interview.

The Job Interview

If you are well prepared and have an understanding of the things you want to ask, you can obtain a considerable amount of important information from a job interview. For example, you will want to get as precise a job description as possible from the person who is responsible for hiring you. You may want to know who will supervise you and to whom you will answer in the agency. It may be important to ask about where you will be housed, office availability, and so forth. It goes without saying that you should also ask about salary and the possibility of raises. All of these questions are relevant and important; however, there may be other issues that are even more important.

Orientation Period

Find out if the agency usually has an orientation period where the new counselor can become acquainted with the agency and the job, which will provide the means and the time for new employees to learn the tasks that will allow them to do their job more easily and effectively. Cherniss found that if counselors were dropped into a new job without orientation or a chance to get their feet on the ground, they were less likely to have a positive attitude toward the job and more likely to suffer burnout.

Workload Demands

Try to establish the workload demands that the agency expects. Generally speaking, the greater the workload, the greater the probability for burnout. Even a heavy workload can be managed, though, if there are frequent opportunities for time-outs from face-to-face contact with clients. It is also important to determine the range of client contact available. Being responsible for a variety of different clients and being able to follow the same client through the system can help prevent burnout.

Degree of Job Stimulation

It is important to determine the amount of intellectual stimulation, challenge, and variety in the job. These factors will determine whether a counselor suffers burnout: The more of these characteristics that are present in the job, the less likely it is that the counselor will suffer burnout.

Degree of Job Freedom

Try to find out how much freedom you will have on the job because rigid bureaucratic control of a counselor's actions in the job place can lead to more rapid burnout. (This may be an important thing to find out about an agency during the interview. For example, psychiatric hospitals usually have more rigid bureaucratic control than does an out-patient alcohol treatment center.) If freedom to do the job your way and on your own schedule is important to you, it would be especially wise to ask current employees about the amount of autonomy that they feel they have.

Clearly Defined Agency Goals and Expectations

Try to find out in the interview (or from counselors currently working in the agency) how clearly the goals and expectations of the agency are spelled out to counselors. If guidelines and policies are unclear or if they change from week to week, the danger of job burnout increases.

Compatible Outlook and Beliefs

Try to establish whether the agency and the people working in it have beliefs and an outlook on life that are compatible with your own. Differences in outlook and beliefs are major sources of dissension in social care agencies. An awareness of these issues will give you a chance to ask questions about all of the above areas of concern. Finally, you should establish the job's time demands. You must also ask yourself whether these time demands are consistent with your life roles. If you are married, with heavy family responsibilities, fifteen-hour days may not be appropriate for you. In conjunction with this question, you should try to ascertain whether the agency has realistic expectations and goals. Sometimes chemical dependency agencies expect staff to work extremely long days because the agency is unrealistic about the goals it is attempting to accomplish. One final comment is in order: It is totally unrealistic for applicant counselors to believe that they can come into an agency and bring about dramatic change. That is why it is so important to know the agency as well as possible before becoming a part of it: To not be fully aware of the agency eventually leads to lowered morale, frustration, and fatigue (i.e., burnout), and the counselor is unlikely to survive.

This chapter has outlined some of the problems that are faced by chemical dependency counselors in working with clients and the agencies that employ the counselor. As we have seen, chemical dependency counselors are faced with heavy, sometimes unreasonable demands from the clients that they have in treatment. These demands are exacerbated by the fact that the treatment of the substance abuser requires a counselor's strong caring commitment in order to be effective. This situation places the chemical dependency counselor at risk for burnout. Stress on the counselor increases when emotional energy goes to deal with communication problems within and among agencies. These intra-agency staff struggles (e.g., between lay and professional counselors) rob counselors of emotional energy and negatively affect the clients under their care. It has been pointed out here that there are actions that alcohol counselors can take to ensure their survival as viable helping therapists throughout their employment in the chemical dependency field. Factors to consider when choosing a job (such as matching oneself with the appropriate agency depending on one's own needs and the agency's expectations of counselors) have been noted. It has also been pointed out that chemical dependency counselors should be aware of some of the possible adjustments they may need to make over time in their role in an agency. Finally, an attempt has been made to illuminate some of the issues that counselors will face in the chemical dependency field and how they can often effectively prevent or reduce problems that could affect their emotional and vocational survival.

This chapter has focused on issues of survival for the chemical dependency counselor working in a substance abuse agency. Adjustments that a chemical dependency counselor might have to make in other agencies (e.g., a correctional facility, the general hospital, industry, and the many other settings where the counselor could be employed) have not been dealt with specifically. It is hoped that chemical dependency counselors working in these settings will find many of the things discussed here useful to them. As chemical dependency caregivers become involved in new agencies, there will doubtless be workplace adjustments that differ somewhat across all settings.

At the present time, the growth of personnel in the chemical dependency field has increased markedly. While some of this increase is no doubt tied to increased funding in the substance abuse area, it is also due partly to the discovery, by many people, that working with chemically dependent people is highly rewarding. While this chapter has focused on managing some of the difficulties of working as a chemical dependency counselor, it should be noted that most chemical dependency counselors find the work exciting and gratifying. There are few places in the human caregiving system where a remarkable turnaround in a person's life can be accomplished as dramatically and as rapidly. It is hoped that the issues covered in this chapter will help counselors maintain the enthusiasm and excitement with which they initially entered the field. In our opinion, their excitement is justified.

AN ADDENDUM

When the material in this chapter was first written in the early 1980s, much of the direct work with clients and patients in the field was done by alcohol and drug counselors. While that is still true in most states, there have been some significant changes in the type of personnel used in many agencies. There was

> a reinfusion of psychologists and psychiatrists in the treatment force in the late 1970s after the development of a network of nonmedical programs in the 1960s and early 1970s. . . . Today, given the need to develop programs that could receive third party health insurance funding, program accreditation standards often require that physicians take on supervisory and administrative responsibility for clinical operations and that treatment be carried out only by primary therapists who meet specific educational or licensing standards (Institute of Medicine, 1990, p. 125).

These shifts in who is ultimately responsible for treatment have been accompanied by more reasonable perceptions of the alcoholic by professionals. In a survey of 100 mental health professionals working in a Veterans Administration Hospital the majority were found to be open to diagnosing and referring for treatment people who had alcohol problems. For example, 96 percent of the sample reported that they would refer an alcoholic client to Alcoholics Anonymous even though many of them did not know what the Big Book was. These researchers conclude that there has been "a marked improvement noted in professional attitudes toward alcoholic patients" (Schwartz & Taylor, 1989, p. 322).

These shifts in attitudes may explain part of the reason why there is an increasing involvement of professionals in the substance abuse field. Of course, these changes in attitudes are also related to the fact that there has been an increasing demand by third-party payers that the services they pay for be done by licensed professionals.

These shifts during the 1980s and 1990s in what and who third-party payers will fund have had a tremendous impact on the alcohol and drug field in general and on the alcohol and drug counselor in particular. Many programs have had to find new funding and many counselors have found that they no longer fulfill the requirements such programs must meet in order to be reimbursed for evaluation and treatment.

In addition, many programs have gone out of business because the previous funding from insurance companies no longer will support inpatient treatment programs. This closing of programs means that there are many more alcohol counselors who have had to find new employment with another alcohol or drug agency or else leave the field entirely.

> This shift has led to a transitional period in which many of the personnel working in the field are identified as "alcoholism counselors" regardless of their original discipline and training, and which the non-degreed, recovering person who has become a counselor or administrator is feeling shunted aside by the professionals and the funding agencies (Institute of Medicine, 1990, p. 125).

This change in how the field is manned is still in flux. For the purposes of this addendum, the possible changes that the alcohol counselor must adjust to will be discussed. In addition, some ideas will be explored as to how current counselors who find themselves deficient in credentials might approach retraining. Finally, the possible impact of increased training on the alcohol and drug treatment field will be examined.

There are several possible ways in which alcohol counselors may be asked to change. There may be more emphasis on a multicausal approach to substance abuse. This will mean that alcohol counselors must become aware of how a combination of factors can contribute to a person's becoming a substance abuser. Knowledge of the differential effects of family history, genetic factors, and personality factors on substance abuse must be understood. In addition, social and economic contextual issues will have to be factored in as possible concerns that could have elicited the problem. While these issues are often currently asked about in alcohol agencies, it is rare to see a selective, differential treatment plan that is based on that information.

To be able to establish differential treatment plans, the alcohol counselor of the future must have a background that includes both general information about the precursors and associated problem areas *and* specific technologies that can be used to intervene. This future counselor must be educated in multiple areas including psychology, sociology, social work, and health education in addition to intervention technologies. It seems probable that this type of sophisticated training will require someone who is educated at the masters level or beyond.

Many of today's counselors would probably agree that training to this new level is either beyond them or of little interest to them. They would like to continue the role they have had over the past several decades, a role that has placed an emphasis on a close, understanding, and personal relationship with the person trying to recover from substance abuse. Some will resist any retraining and may be lost to the field as it moves beyond the disease model or the Minnesota Model approach.

Others will be quick to understand that the substance abuse field has always been one that "uses what works" and that the focus of concern should be helping the client. Many of today's alcohol counselors may play important roles at what Rosenberg (1974) calls "paraprofessionals" and that future labelers might call "addiction technicians." That is, they will be individuals who carry out treatment plans established by the "alcohol counselor" or masters-level supervisor.

Of course, the new roles will carry with them not only differing levels of responsibility but also differing levels of pay. While alcohol and drug counselors have never been paid salaries appropriate to their work demands and dedication, these lower level jobs may be reduced in pay scale in order to hire the more advanced trained and more credentialed "alcohol counselor" of the future.

However, no one can fully predict the future. As this is being written, health coverage is being debated in Congress and by the public. It may well be that little will change in the substance abuse field and things will return to their previous form if the national health debate is resolved. It may be that there will be a mandate for thirty-day inpatient treatment as the treatment of choice. However, that seems unlikely. Whatever the choice of care, the issue of accountability and the need to demonstrate positive outcome for treatment that is economically viable will be an important treatment demand. Program evaluation and outside monitoring is likely to be required in any federal- and state-funded programs of the future. Similar and perhaps even more demanding proof of effectiveness may be asked of those agencies who are funded primarily by third-party payers.

One of the reasons that there is so much pressure on the alcohol and drug field at this time is that several studies have demonstrated that there is little difference between relatively longer term inpatient treatment and lower cost outpatient therapy (Jung, 1994). In brief, this finding has forced a reevaluation of alcohol and drug treatment by those who pay, i.e., the insurance companies.

Since the longer term disease-based inpatient programs have not been demonstrated through rigorous research to be more effective than shorter and less expensive outpatient programs for the majority of alcoholics, insurance companies have been given the data to challenge these inpatient programs. At the same time, the concept of managed care has been developed to reduce costs. For example, if a person in treatment, say an alcoholic, is suicidal when first admitted, just as soon as he is detoxed enough and his depression has lifted he will be declared as not needing inpatient treatment because he is no longer depressed and thus is no longer suicidal.

The fact that third-party payers will not now fund inpatient programs is not the only change. At the heart of this change has been the change in the way alcohol and drug problems are perceived. There has been a new emphasis on viewing substance abuse as a multifactorial problem (Rivers, 1994; Jung, 1994). There has also been an increasing emphasis on outcome-related research to demonstrate which types of programs and treatments work best for which types of patients. In the main, much of this outcome research has come out of behavioral and family therapy approaches because these approaches have had more of a research focus than have programs with an A.A. or Minnesota Model orientation. In addition, two recent introductory texts have taken the position that alcohol abuse should be viewed as a multicausal problem. Similar positions have previously been taken by theorists in the illicit drug treatment area. Thus, the field is beginning to see alcohol and drug problems as more complex disorders and as needing more varied approaches to treatment. For example, Witters, Venturelli, and Hanson (1992) have indicated that "drug use and misuse . . . go beyond body and mind reactions. Drug problems involve families, places of employment, neighborhoods, communities, educational and religious institutions, local, regional, national and even international social, political, and economic boundaries . . ." (p. xii).

This increasing complexity has led to the notion that patients should be matched with programs. This has become important because it has been found that patient involvement in treatment is, at least in some studies, dependent on whether their perception of what is needed for them to get better is consistent with the philosophy of the treatment program. Marlatt (1988) puts it this way:

> In our own laboratory, my colleagues and I have found that personal beliefs about the nature of the addiction problem and associated approaches to treatment are important determinants of treatment compliance. [In a study on smoking] . . . it was found that subjects mismatched in treatment assignment (based on their underlying beliefs about the etiology of the problem) were significantly more likely to discontinue treatment than subjects who received a treatment program that was matched with their personal belief system (p. 478).

The idea that patients can be matched with the treatment philosophy that they are most in agreement with is certainly not new. However, while the Minnesota Model has been the one often applied to treatment in the past two decades, the increase in knowledge about new treatment approaches means that more individualized treatment for each client is now possible. Programs that previously emphasized a single approach to treatment (or offered an unmatched "cafeteria plan" where all patients were exposed to several types of treatment programs, e.g., from individual to group therapy to "rapping with the chaplain") must now demonstrate that they are effective with a wide range of patients. They must also show that they can match treatment to patient needs.

There will be a new need for retraining many of the counselors so that they can effectively use the new treatment technologies. While some people might feel that it would be better to start from scratch and train a new cadre of treatment agents for alcohol and drug abusers, the "old" counselors (and especially the recovering ones) bring a commitment of care and concern for their patients that is rarely seen in the caregiving systems of this country.

In order to profit from retraining, these counselors must be open to new ways of getting their job done. For example, they may have to try techniques not usually included in 12-step treatment programs. It a word, this will require some dramatic changes in how counselors approach treatment. Change is never easy. It is even more difficult when one is asked to even slightly deemphasize a method that has been self-validated. This is very likely the case with the 12-step model in so many recovering counselors' lives. If, however, these new technologies, including motivational counseling (Miller & Rollnick, 1991), guided self-change (Sobell & Sobell, 1993), and other more recent specific approaches to treating problem drinking and alcohol use problems can be utilized by these dedicated counselors, then both clients and the alcohol and drug treatment field will profit.

Learning these new skills will not be easy. But there is excitement in change. And the alcohol and drug counselor who has been in the field for as long as a decade or more can look back at the many changes he or she has faced and dealt with already. So the best way to deal with future change is to view it as an opportunity that can reinvigorate the field and the counselor. And, more importantly, it can provide better care for clients, which is the bottom line for all caregivers in the alcohol and drug field. Such change should be faced with some comfort since almost all alcohol and drug counselors have survived major changes in the field in the past and, for the recovering counselors, major changes in their lives!

DISCUSSION QUESTIONS

1. You have just been hired as a counselor in a chemical dependency agency. Briefly outline some of the initial adjustments you may have to make. How

many of these adjustments are characteristic of social service agencies in general and how many are specific to a chemical dependency agency?

2. Visit several alcohol and drug treatment agencies. Interview the directors and find out if they employ both recovering and nonrecovering counselors on their staffs. If they do not, try to find out why. If they do, ask the directors what strengths each kind of counselor brings to the agency. How do the directors' answers compare to this text? What additional things did you learn about the utility of recovering and nonrecovering counselors in chemical dependency agencies?

3. Interview a new counselor (i.e., someone who has worked in the field for less than a year) and a counselor who has been in the field for five years or more. Ask each what is most worrisome about the job and what is most interesting and exciting. What are the differences in the answers of the "new" and "old" counselors?

4. What do you think are your strengths and weaknesses in communicating with people? Ask several people with whom you interact daily what they think are your strengths and weaknesses in communicating and listening to others. Are there differences of opinion depending on the various situations in which you interact with people? Are you stronger or weaker in more intimate (e.g., friends, spouse) or more formal communications (i.e., superiors and colleagues at work)?

5. Try to find out from several substance abuse agencies the agencies with which they have the most communication and the agencies with which they have the least communication. Ask the directors if they can give a reason why one agency is an easy one with which to communicate and why the other is more difficult.

6. Interview counselors who have worked in the field for over five years. Ask them how their interest and excitement about work have changed over the years. If they cite either positive or negative changes (or both) ask them what factors have most powerfully affected their interest and excitement in the field. Try to categorize their comments in terms of total field changes, bureaucratic problems within the agency, and personal/professional relationships within and external to the agency in which they work.

7. In the same interview, ask the counselors what their greatest fear is in their current job and what their greatest fear is for the substance abuse field in general.

8. Suppose you plan to be a substance abuse counselor but due to insurance and government requirements your role is dramatically changed. What factors in your training and in your personal characteristics will facilitate your ability to make a major role change? What factors in your training and personal make-up will inhibit your ability to change?

REFERENCES

Cherniss, C. (1980). *Professional burnout in human service organization.* New York: Praeger Publishers.

Institute of Medicine (1990). *Broadening the treatment for alcohol problems.* Washington, D.C.: National Academy Press.

Jellinek, E. M. (1960). *The disease concept of alcoholism.* New Brunswick, N.J.: Hillhouse Press.

Jung, J. (1994). *Under the influence: Alcohol and human behavior.* Pacific Grove, CA: Brooks/Cole Publishing Co.

Kalb, M., & Propper, M. S. (1976). The future of alcohology: Craft or science? *American Journal of Psychiatry, 133,* 641–45.

Knauert, A., & Davidson, S. (1979). Maintaining the sanity of alcoholism counselors. *Family and Community Health,* 65–70.

Marlatt, G. A. (1988). Matching clients to treatment: Treatment models and stages of change. In D. Donovan, & G. A. Marlatt (Eds.), *Assessment of addictive behaviors* (pp. 474–83). New York: Guilford Press.

Miller, W. R., & Rollnick, S. (1991). *Motivational interviewing: Preparing people to change addictive behavior.* New York: Guilford Press.

Rivers, P. C., Sarata, P. B. V., & Book, T. (1974). The effect of an alcoholism workshop on attitudes, job satisfaction, and job performance of secretaries. *Quarterly Journal of Studies on Alcohol, 35,* 1832–88.

Rivers, P. C. (1994). *Alcohol and human behavior: Theory, research and practice.* Englewood Cliffs, NJ: Prentice Hall.

Rosenberg, C. M. (1974 [Spring]). The responsibility of direct treatment. *Alcohol, Health and Research World,* 3–5.

Sarata, P. B. V. (1979). Beginning employment as a child care worker. An examination of work experiences. *Child Care Quarterly, 8,* 295–302.

Sarata, P. B. V. (1982). *Burnout workshops for alcoholism counselors.* Unpublished paper. Lincoln: University of Nebraska. (A later edition of this paper, with the same title, is currently in press in *The Journal of Alcohol and Drug Education.*)

Schwartz. L. S., & Taylor, J. R. (1989). Attitudes of mental health professionals toward alcoholism recognition and treatment. *American Journal of Drug and Alcohol Abuse, 15,* 321–27.

Sobell, M. B., & Sobell, L. C. (1993). *Problem drinkers: Guided self-change treatment.* New York: Guilford Press.

Wegscheider, S. (1981). *Hope and health for the alcoholic family.* Palo Alto, CA: Science & Behavior Books, Inc.

Witters, W., Venturelli, P., & Hanson, G. (1992). *Drugs and society* (3rd ed.). Boston: Jones & Bartlett.

Chapter 10

Some Questions and Answers

CHAPTER OBJECTIVES

- Explore differences in treating male and female alcoholics
- Examine information on the inheritability of alcoholism
- Examine how recovering and nonrecovering counselors compare in terms of their treatment effectiveness as therapists
- Examine current issues in the debate on whether alcoholism should be considered a disease
- Identify effects of alcohol on sexual performance
- Identify differences between alcohol dependence and alcohol abuse
- Explore ways in which the alcohol counselor can use Alcoholics Anonymous and Narcotics Anonymous
- Explores effectiveness of treatment modes in outpatient and inpatient programs
- Give recommendations from skilled counselors on how to confront a close friend or colleague about his or her alcohol or drug problem

INTRODUCTION

In our experience, alcohol counselors frequently have certain questions about clients and the counseling field that they would like answered. We have gathered together several of these frequently asked questions in this chapter and have attempted to provide answers. These answers are based on the current clinical research literature and our own experiences; however, these questions can only be answered in terms of what is known by the authors at this time. The rapid explosion of information in the alcohol field means that new information may shortly make these answers incomplete or insufficient. However, with these questions as examples, we hope to illustrate to counselors that keeping up with new clinical experimental research in the alcohol field can potentially be very helpful to them. We also hope to encourage counselors to continue to read the research literature and to attend meetings where new research information is disseminated. As these questions and their answers will illustrate, the newfound information in the alcohol field has great potential for program planning and for direct treatment of alcoholics and their families. However, until the new information is utilized by counselors, it will be not be employed to provide better care for the alcoholic—a goal all counselors should share.

ARE THERE DIFFERENCES BETWEEN MALE AND FEMALE ALCOHOLICS, AND HOW SHOULD THEY BE TREATED?

If one examines the literature, the answer is, yes, there are differences between male and female alcoholics. For example, Bourne and Light (1979) outline several psychological and sociological differences between male and female alcoholics that they have gleaned from the research literature. These differences include the following:

- Women usually begin drinking (and problem drinking) at a later age than do their male counterparts.
- Women move more rapidly from the early stages to the later stages of drinking than men do.
- Women, more often than men, will cite a specific stress or traumatic event that precipitated their problem drinking. Frequently the events cited have to do with female physiological functioning.
- Women appear to do more solitary drinking, much of it in the privacy of their homes. This presumed isolation may be due to the female's greater sensitivity to social disapproval of public drinking and general guilt and shame about using alcohol. (Author's note: Bear in mind that alcohol abuse and alcoholism are frequently viewed as a graver social risk by the female alcohol abuser. Therefore, the female drinker may be more strongly motivated to disguise her problem than the male drinker, although both generally attempt to hide their abuse of alcohol.)
- A frequent finding is that female alcoholics are more likely to have affective (emotional) problems and that males are more likely to be sociopathic.
- The consequences of alcohol for men and women show different patterns. Men feel the consequences more frequently in the work situation, whereas

women feel them more often in the family situation. Women alcoholics are more likely to be divorced than are male alcoholics.

- Women are more likely than men to have an alcohol model in their family. The frequency of alcohol problems among alcoholic women's husbands is markedly greater than in the general population or in the wives of alcoholic men.
- There appear to be different medical consequences for alcohol abuse, depending on the sex of the individual. In general, women get sicker earlier and develop health problems associated with alcohol abuse more rapidly (and, thus, earlier in their drinking careers).
- Alcoholic women, as noted above, are more frequently characterized as feeling guilty, depressed, or anxiety ridden than are alcoholic men.
- Another factor, identified by Schuckit and Morrissey (1976), is the correlation between drinking practices and socioeconomic status among women. Lower socioeconomic status women have drinking histories similar to those reported for males; higher socioeconomic status women fit the stereotype of the woman alcoholic described above.

Considering these differences (and there may be others that will become known in the near future), the question can be properly asked: Have these differences led to differentiated treatment strategies for men and women?

Much of what has been written about the treatment of the female alcoholic has appeared in the past two decades. Even today, little is known about what procedures work best with women, and only recently have treatment programs modified their approaches to meet women's needs. Therefore, the reader is cautioned that what follows is the best reading, at the moment, of differential treatment of females, which surely will change in the next few years. Another limitation is the current absence of broad-based empirical research. What is given here has, in the main, been gleaned from clinical reports and the observations of those working with alcohol-addicted women. One of the writers who is cognizant of both research and clinical data is Wilsnack (1982). She sees at least two issues that must be considered in meeting the treatment needs of women.

Subtypes of Alcoholic Women

First, it is important to distinguish among subtypes of alcoholic women. For example, if a woman is suffering from an affective disorder, it may be necessary to seek psychiatric consultation to determine the extent of the depression and the potential usefulness of antidepressant medication. If the depression has preceded the alcoholism and is long-standing, it may be important to consider using antidepressant medication.

Other areas in which it is important to distinguish among female subtypes is when women drink in response to stressful life events and drink in response to sex role-related conflicts and stresses. It is possible that each of these subgroups may account for 25 to 30 percent of female problem drinkers. For those alcoholic women who are reacting to stressful life events, resolving their feelings about precipitating life-transition issues and helping them find alternatives to alcohol and other drugs for coping with the crisis and its associated stress should be the main focus of treatment. Treatment of women in the second group should include attention to the woman's feelings about herself and her roles as a woman. Women's therapy and support groups may help such women identify social pressures to conform to traditional sex-role expectations and may increase their acceptance of themselves as persons, independent of sex-role stereotypes. This means that alcohol counselors must be acutely aware of their own expectations of male and female behavior so that they do not unwittingly reinforce rigid and contrasting sex role stereotypes.

Enhancing Self-Image

Second, it is important to address the alcoholic woman's negative self-image and low self-esteem—areas that Wilsnack sees as crucial in the treatment of alcoholic females. These negative feelings should be actively addressed during treatment. To help the woman feel better about herself, pleasant and attractive surroundings are helpful. Helping the woman restore her physical appearance and at the same time introducing her to other recovering alcoholic women who can serve as role models are also important. Expressive activities under the direction of activity therapists to help restore confidence and self-esteem (e.g., dance, physical fitness, sports, and movement therapy) are also important adjuncts to traditional counseling. The alcoholic woman's vulnerable self-esteem may mean that a somewhat less confrontive but more supportive counseling approach is needed.

Because unexpressed anger is believed to be a major source of low self-esteem in alcoholic women, counseling that explores the source of anger and provides direct training in assertive behavior can help women identify, accept, and express appropriately the anger that they feel. In other cases, where the woman's low self-esteem is linked to destructive interpersonal or living situations, direct environmental intervention may be required in order to provide an environment supportive of both the woman's self-image and the recovery process. What should be emphasized here is that enhancement of self-esteem early in treatment may increase the alcoholic woman's sense of personal worth and may result in increased motivation to change her drinking behavior. Therefore, early self-esteem enhancement may prove more effective than simply waiting for self-esteem to improve as a result of changes in drinking behavior.

Since interpersonal crises and losses are more likely to precipitate alcohol abuse in women, it is possible that the involvement and support of significant others may play an even greater role in the treatment of women. Understanding, concern, and expressed affection from significant others all seem to be very powerful tools in the treatment process. In point of fact, however, some alcoholic women are surprised to learn how much those around them care about them (such relationships not previously shared may be first encountered around the alcoholic crisis). Because the alcoholic female so frequently reports problems associated with her marriage or her children, at least one writer (Tamerin, 1978) feels that the most appropriate therapeutic approach for all alcoholic women is marital or family therapy.

What Are the Counseling Needs of the Alcoholic Woman?

Because sexual problems and concerns seem to be so prevalent in alcoholic women, sexual counseling should be made available to them and their partners. This means that counselors should be comfortable discussing sexual experiences and sexual problems and should know well-qualified professionals to whom they can refer clients with problems that they do not feel competent to treat.

Another special area of concern is the use of psychoactive medication. In particular, women are more at risk for multidrug abuse. This is because physicians are more likely to prescribe a wide variety of psychotherapeutic drugs for women than they are for men. However, the use of major tranquilizers and mood-control agents may not only be appropriate but also necessary for women with major psychiatric difficulties.

In 1992, Burman made a strong clinical case for treating alcoholic females in all-women groups. She pointed out that many factors (e.g., need to care for children, breakdown in support systems, low self-esteem, financial difficulties, lack of health insurance coverage, and the strong stigma associated with alcohol abuse in women) limit females' access to treatment. Current research findings are limited and inconclusive; however, there are suggestions from research that females may do better in single-gender treatment programs than in mixed-gender programs. Whether future studies will confirm these initial findings is unknown at present (Littrell, 1991).

Burman also suggests that the same inequities that exist for women outside treatment agencies also exist within these agencies. Thus, women are often given the message in treatment that they are inferior and subordinate to males. The message is reinforced by the fact that female treatment staff often do not have the same status levels as their male counterparts in alcohol treatment centers. Such stereotyping is even more likely if women are outnumbered by men in a particular setting (which often occurs). One of the reasons that women are outnumbered in alcohol treatment centers is that they are proportionately fewer in the total population than male alcoholics. For example, Littrell (1989) estimated that only 20 percent of the alcoholic population in the United States is female. There are some differences, however, in the ways that females drink in the United States. There are higher rates of abstention in women in the lower socioeconomic class but also a higher percentage of abusive drinkers in this class (Littrell,1989). At the same time, at least one research team (Leavy & Dunlosky, 1989) have concluded that when everything is considered, females are more likely to be labelled as problem drinkers than are their male counterparts.

As noted above, earlier research established that the pattern for developing alcoholism was different for men and women. Not only do women develop their problems with alcohol more rapidly than males (their alcohol problems develop more frequently over a 10–14 year period while males' seem to show problem development over a 20–25 year period), but females are less likely to report morning drinking, blacking out, or withdrawal symptoms. And, of course, women are less likely to be involved with the criminal justice system as a result of their abuse of alcohol. They also score much higher than males on scales measuring psychological distress (e.g., the Minnesota Multiphasic Personality Inventory [MMPI] clinical scale). Perhaps as a result of this psychological distress, women are more likely to endorse escape drinking and more frequently report tension reduction as the reason for their drinking. They are also more likely to identify a triggering event for their alcohol abuse, and this event is, of course, usually related to stress.

What is also frequently overlooked is that a woman with alcoholic problems may lack some very basic survival skills. Retraining in vocational skills, financial management, life and career planning, and parenting skills may make life less overwhelming and give the woman a sense of mastery of her problems.

Another often overlooked issue that affects treatment is that women need to have child care available in order to maintain treatment. Child care may reduce a woman's ambivalence about entering treatment and reduce the guilt about how her drinking has affected her children. (Another possible benefit is that intervention with children with potential problems is possible. If the counselor works with the children while the mother is in treatment, potential readjustment problems for the children can be reduced or eliminated. Without this treatment, it is possible, particularly in adolescent children, that problems will occur after intense treatment for the mother has been completed.)

Finally, there is the need to have specialized care (e.g., Women for Sobriety) available for the recovering alcoholic female following treatment.

IS ALCOHOLISM INHERITED?

This question has been raised because of the fact that alcoholism seems to run in families. For example, Goodwin (1979) has noted that the children of alcoholics are four times as likely to become alcoholics as are the children of nonalcoholics. Therefore, the risk to the children of alcoholics is high; as Goodwin notes, alcoholism does run in families.

However, the fact that alcoholism runs in families is insufficient, by itself, to support a genetic cause of alcohol abuse; we need other supporting data before we can say that alcohol abuse is inherited or genetically linked. To obtain these types of data, researchers have followed several strategies. (See Goodwin [1979] for a complete discussion of all these strategies.) We shall focus here on the two types of studies that have produced, over the past decades, the most dramatic evidence in support of a genetically linked cause of alcoholism—twin studies and adoption studies.

Twin Studies

Twin studies assume that monozygotic twins (born from a single egg and fertilized by the same sperm) and dizygotic twins (born from two separate eggs fertilized by two different sperm) differ in the amount of genetically linked characteristics they share. For example, monozygotic, or identical, twins have almost exactly the same genetic makeup; fraternal twins share only about 50 percent. It is further assumed that the fraternal and identical twins' environments will not differ significantly. Given these assumptions, it is predicted that alcoholism will tend to co-occur more often in identical than in fraternal twins.

This strategy has been applied in at least two major studies. Kaij (1960), in a Swedish study, located 1,974 male twin pairs where at least one was registered at a temperance board because of conviction of drunkenness or some other indication of alcohol abuse. The concordance rate for alcohol abuse in the identical twin group was 54 percent; in the fraternal twins the concordance rate was 28 percent (a statistically significant difference in concordance rates for the two types of twin pairs). Kaij also divided the alcohol abusers into subgroups, based on severity. When this was done, the 14 identical twin pairs classified as having the most severe alcohol problems showed a concordance rate of over 71 percent; there was no significant increase in concordance rates for the fraternal twins when one member of the pair was classified as having severe alcohol problems.

In a Finnish study, Partanen, Bruun, and Markkaners (1966) found less definitive support of a genetic predisposition to alcoholism. Using male twins, these researchers found no differences between monozygotic and dizygotic twins in terms of the consequences that alcohol had on their lives (the primary criterion used for diagnosing alcoholism). However, more or less normal patterns of drinking, i.e., frequency and amount, were more concordant in identical than fraternal twins.

These two studies reflect the mixed findings in twin studies. While they do not provide conclusive evidence that a predisposition to alcoholism is inherited, the results do suggest that heredity is a factor in alcoholism and should be considered when diagnosis and treatment are initiated.

Adoption Studies

Adoption studies have also shown somewhat mixed results. However, the recency of some of this research and the increased sophistication in viewing the issue has made these studies highly visible in the alcohol literature. Goodwin (1979), in a study of 55 Danish male adoptees with an alcoholic biological parent and 78 control adoptees without such a history, found that the adoptees with alcoholic biological parents were nearly four times more likely to be alcoholic themselves than were the control adoptees. Adopted away sons of alcoholics were then compared with their own brothers, who had been raised by the alcoholic biological parent. Alcoholism rates were similar in the two groups, suggesting that regardless of whether one was reared by or away from the biological parent, the alcohol risk would be the same. These findings argue strongly for a genetic predisposition to alcoholism and tend to call into question the importance of family environment.

Bohman (1978) reported on an adoption study of 2,323 illegitimate children born in Stockholm, between 1930 and 1949, who were placed in adoptive homes before three years of age. Male adoptees whose mothers or fathers had been registered as alcohol abusers were themselves more likely to be registered. Following this, Bohman and his colleagues selected 50 male adoptees whose fathers had been repeatedly registered for alcohol abuse (i.e., they were probably alcoholic) and very carefully matched them with adoptees whose parents had no history of alcohol abuse. Bohman found that 20 percent of the sons of frequently registered parents were also registered as alcohol abusers, while only 6 percent of the male children from nonalcohol-abusing parents were registered. Thus, this study also suggests a genetic contribution to alcoholism in men.

As these studies show, the significance of the genetic factor is clear in males, but the findings do not indicate a major genetic transmission factor in females. Cotton (1979) found, in a review of 39 English-language studies, that 27 percent of the fathers of alcoholics were themselves alcoholic but that less than 5 percent of the alcoholics had mothers who were alcoholic, suggesting that genetic predisposition may be sex linked. These findings, taken in concert with those of Goodwin, would certainly suggest such a conclusion. However, the possibility that drinking (and, particularly, abusive drinking) occurred at such low levels in Scandinavian females (and elsewhere) over the time period studied may also account for the different results in terms of sex-related alcoholism.

Familial and Nonfamilial Alcoholism

So what conclusion can we draw from this type of research? Goodwin (1979) has suggested dividing alcoholism into two types: familial and nonfamilial. On the one hand, familial alcoholism would be characterized by early age of onset, rapid development, and an explosive course that requires early treatment at an early age. On the other hand, intervention into nonfamilial alcoholism would require somewhat more diverse approaches and treatment programs.

Nonfamilial alcoholism would occur in a substantial number of alcoholics, according to Goodwin (1979). Another pair of writers (Murray & Stabenau, 1982) conclude:

> the better of the studies of normal drinking have suggested a modest but significant genetic influence. . . . The family, twin, and adoptive studies concur in finding more evidence for male drinking being under genetic influence than female drinking. . . . One of the reasons why researchers have been slow to elucidate the exact nature of genetic predisposition is that they have been looking for simple answers. The present evidence is incompatible with simple Mendelian inheritance through a single dominant or recessive gene. . . . Any successful etiological model must obviously take into account environmental factors such as price and availability of alcohol, plus the effect of occupation and family attitudes to alcohol. . . . (p. 142)

Littrell (1991) after reviewing twin and adoption studies had the following to say:

> A number of twin studies have provided findings consistent with the case for the inheritance of alcoholism. Of course, there is a crucial flaw in the twin methodology. The environment of the monozygote [identical] twins is more similar than the environment of the dyzygote [nonidentical] twins. Hence, findings from twin studies are not definitive. The adoption studies have been consistent in their support of inheritance. There is still a question about what type of alcoholism is inherited, the primary type or the type associated with criminal, socially disruptive behavior. Although the case for male inheritance emerges from the studies, the case for inheritance of female alcoholism is less clear (p. 17).

In brief, the status of the genetic predisposition research suggests that genetic factors can account for some part of alcohol problems. However, even when this factor is most clearly isolated, environmental factors probably mediate its effects.

ARE RECOVERING ALCOHOLICS MORE EFFECTIVE ALCOHOLISM COUNSELORS THAN NONALCOHOLICS?

A large number of observers have debated the advantages and disadvantages of utilizing counselors who themselves are recovering alcoholics (e.g., Blume, 1977; Falkey, 1971; Pattison, 1973; Rosenberg, 1974; Strachen, 1973). In their favor, it has often been noted that recovering alcoholics, because of their personal experience with alcohol abuse, may have a greater understanding of the problem. This understanding gives the counselor the ability to quickly form a close relationship with the alcoholic—an ability that never-alcoholic counselors supposedly do not have. Both through the use of the close relationship and their personal awareness of denial, recovering counselors can challenge denial more forthrightly and forcefully than other counselors. Involved in this ability to confront and to treat the alcoholic in general is the recovering counselor's greater ability to select and use language that is appropriate and understandable to the alcoholic client.

Potential Problem Areas with Recovering Counselors

Some of the same writers who have noted the positive qualities of the recovering counselor have also noted negative characteristics. Specific problems include the defensiveness of the recovering counselor; overidentification with clients; overcommitment to one mode of treatment (usually Alcoholics Anonymous [A.A.] oriented); and hostility toward the use of medication, toward the value of research, and toward mental health professionals in general.

Several writers have suggested that alcoholic counselors' defensiveness is linked to their need to maintain their own sobriety. The argument is that if recovering counselors do not maintain the view of alcoholism that is keeping them sober, then their self-esteem will be threatened. A common example is the individual whose own recovery rests on A.A. principles; this individual may be deeply and personally threatened by information that calls these A.A. principles into question. Conversely, the never-alcoholic counselor may see the challenge to traditional beliefs as an academic matter in need of discussion, debate, and further investigation.

Another area of potential threat to the recovering alcoholic is the frequent disparity in education between recovering and nonrecovering counselors. Because the pattern seems to be for the recovering counselor to be comparatively older and less well educated, the constant fear is that "these young guys" may know more than the recovering counselors. This sense of being one down also contributes to the alcoholic counselor's defensiveness. Resistance to new learning, however, may also be based on economic reality. Personal experience with alcoholism and a personally successful recovery may constitute marketable certification to work in the field. When new treatment concepts are not (or cannot be) incorporated into the recovering counselor's own experience, then that counselor may view new treatment concepts as potentially undermining his expertise and source of livelihood. Whatever the reason, all of the above stances tend to produce a counselor with a narrower view of caregiving; one who may not be able or willing to use knowledge and skills that are potentially helpful to clients.

Possibly as a result of this narrower view, recovering counselors exhibit a tendency to utilize one approach to treatment (usually A.A. oriented) for all clients, regardless of the individual problems they present. Kalb and Propper (1976) as well as Rossi and Filstead (1976) have suggested that recovering counselors tend to avoid serious consideration of alternative views on the nature of alcoholism and refuse to question their own premises in light of new research evidence. Therefore, despite new research findings that suggest new directions for treating alcohol abuse, these counselors cling to empirically invalidated approaches. Kalb and Propper maintain that clinical knowledge is governed by the craftsmanship of A.A.-oriented recovering counselors. Thus, established traditions have become sacred wisdoms, which survive because of the protection of loyal disciples. As Jellinek (1960) noted:

> In spite of the respect and admiration to which Alcoholics Anonymous have a claim on account of their great achievements, there is every reason why the student on alcoholism should emancipate himself from accepting the exclusiveness of the picture of alcoholism as propounded by Alcoholics Anonymous (p. 38).

As Wallace has pointed out (1978), many recovering alcoholics employ assimilative projection, i.e., the tendency to see everyone else as much like themselves. This identification with the client can be used to rapidly establish a client-counselor relationship and to reduce defensiveness in the alcoholic client. However, the individuality of the alcoholic client can be overlooked when this strategy is used and specific treatment needs may not be met. Thus, overidentification with the client can blind the recovering counselor to the real and special needs of a specific client and interfere with recovery.

The recovering counselor is frequently opposed to medication of any type. This means that in those alcoholics who need psychotropic medication for a psychotic disorder, the counselor's insistence on a drug-free approach could contribute to a psychotic breakdown. In other clients suffering from depressive disorders, the elimination of lithium could lead to severe depression and suicide. This attitude toward the use of psychoactive drugs is related to a general tendency of some recovering counselors to discount mental health issues and mental health professionals. In many cases these counselors' own discounting of mental health problems and their not using mental health personnel deprive those alcoholic clients, who need these services, of the best possible care. The best possible care for a client should be the professional goal of every caregiver; therefore, learning to wisely use other professionals in the mental health area would seem to be an important goal for all alcohol counselors.

Just as mental health resources should be used when needed, any new information or approaches that could be used in client treatment should be reviewed by counselors. The constant upgrading and learning of new skills and ideas would seem to be an appropriate goal for all counselors. Discounting all research as useless is a failure on the part of counselors to better prepare themselves to deal with problems. To the degree, then, that an alcohol counselor ignores new information that might be helpful, that counselor is being unprofessional and destructive of client welfare.

We have spent some time discussing these potential problem areas because the positive aspects of recovering alcoholics as therapists are frequently noted, but the potential dangers and blind spots of the recovering alcoholic are seldom discussed. However, these problem areas are usually more than balanced by the empathy and commitment of the recovering counselor.

A few studies comparing recovering alcohol counselors with their nonrecovering counterparts have been completed over the past few decades. This research has been reviewed by Littrell (1989). Rosenberg, Gerrein, Manohar, and Liftik (1976) failed to find any differences in the rate of dropout by clients who had been referred because of driving-while-intoxicated charges. Note that this research focused on the ability of both recovering and nonrecovering counselors to keep their clients in treatment. Earlier, Covner (1969) found no differences in the professional evaluations of recovering and nonrecovering counselors. A third study (Argeriou & Manohar, 1978) also failed to demonstrate any major differences between the two types of counselors. In more recent years, the burden of proof has been placed on the shoulders of the nonrecovering counselor. For example, Kirk, Best, and Irwin (1986) showed a tape of a counseling session to alcoholics who were actively involved in therapy. During some of the presentation they identified the counselor on tape as recovering and provided no such designation in the rest of the presentations. Designation of the counselor as a recovering counselor had no impact on the viewers' ratings of counselor empathy. These studies are few in number but there is converging information that indicates that there have been no demonstrated differences in counselor effectiveness when recovering and nonrecovering counselors are compared.

IS ALCOHOLISM A DISEASE?

Deciding whether alcoholism is a disease is made more difficult by the disagreements about just how one should define disease. Even physicians are often uncertain about what should be called a disease (Vaillant, 1995). However, Jellinek (1960) has labeled gamma alcoholism (characterized by tissue tolerance, progressive symptoms, and loss of control of drinking) a progressive disease. But he also acknowledges that many other types of abusive drinking, which he did not label as a disease, exist. Clark and Cahalan (1976) suggested that "the common conception of alcoholism as a disease fails to cover a large part of the domain of alcohol problems and a more useful model would place greater emphasis on the development and correlates of *particular problems* related to drinking, rather than assuming that alcoholism as an underlying and unitary, progressive disease is the course of most alcohol problems" (p. 251). In another place, Clark (1976) stated, "What is questioned is the usefulness of conceptualizing alcoholism as a progressive entity that is sufficiently different from other drinking problems to receive separate consideration" (p. 1257).

Does the labeling of alcoholism as a disease serve a useful purpose? Vaillant (1995) stated the case for and against the utility of labeling alcoholism a disease in the following way:

> Alcoholism does reflect deviant behavior that can be often better classified by sociologists than by physiologists; alcoholism is often better treated by psychologists skilled in behavior therapy than by physicians with all their medical armamentarium. But unlike giving up gambling or fingernail biting, giving up alcohol abuse often required skilled medical attention during the period of acute withdrawal. Unlike gamblers and fingernail biters, most alcoholics as a result of their disorder develop secondary symptoms that do require medical care. Unlike gamblers and fingernail biters, alcoholics have a mortality rate two to four times as high as that of the average person. In order to receive the treatment they require, alcoholics need a label that will allow them unprejudiced admission to emergency rooms, access to medical insurance coverage, detoxification, and paid sick leave—all of which are denied to (and rarely required by) compulsive gamblers . . . and nail biters (pp. 21–22).

The disease concept of alcoholism has been an important impetus in changing the public's perception of alcohol problems as being based on moral failings to a perception where the alcoholic is seen as medically ill. This shift in perception has led the general public to see alcoholism as a treatable disease. Following this change in perception has been the reduction of the stigma that has so long been associated with the disorder. It has also led to considerable support, from legislators and other policy makers, in the form of financial support for instruction and treatment of the alcoholic. In brief, the positing of alcoholism as a disease has had considerable positive benefit for the alcohol field in general and the alcoholic specifically.

HOW DOES ALCOHOL ABUSE AFFECT THE SEXUALITY OF ALCOHOLICS?

The general impact of alcohol on human behavior has been described in the frequently quoted line from Shakespeare:

> Lechery, sir it [alcohol] provokes and unprovoked; it provokes the desire, but it takes away the performance: therefore much drink may be said to be an equivocator with lechery . . . (from *Macbeth,* Act II, Scene III)

This view of how alcohol affects human sexual behavior is shared by both the public and professionals. More specifically, alcohol is a central nervous system depressant that progressively disrupts sensorimotor performance in a dose-related manner.

Sexual Difficulties of the Alcoholic Male

A general finding from animal research is that ingestion of alcohol leads to a delay in ejaculation and reduced duration of erection (Gantt, 1940, 1952). Some researchers believe that alcohol abuse in men can result in irreversible damage to the neurogenic reflex arc serving the process of erection (Masters & Johnson, 1970). Other, less severe psychophysiological responses may be suffered by the male. For example, several studies have suggested that penile tumescence is severely reduced by moderate to heavy ingestion of alcohol, with significant reduction of tumescence occurring after the ingestion of 75 milligrams or more of alcohol (e.g., Farkas & Rosen, 1976). In addition to these difficulties, reports of more severe consequences abound in the clinical literature. Atrophy of the gonads and enlargement of the breasts are frequently reported in men with chronic, long-term heavy-drinking histories.

In addition to these difficulties, male alcoholics suffer from the sexual difficulties that occur in the population at large. Clinical information would suggest, however, that these difficulties occur much more frequently in the abusive drinker than in the nonabuser. These difficulties include:

- **Erectile insufficiency**—The inability to achieve or maintain an erection sufficient for successful sexual intercourse. (This disorder was previously called impotence.) There are two types of erectile insufficiency: primary and secondary. We will focus on the latter since alcohol can most clearly contribute to this disorder. The male with this problem is unable to maintain the required level of penile rigidity. While prolonged difficulty with erections is rare in the population at large, it occurs more frequently in the heavy-drinking male because alcohol tends, at high dosages, to reduce sexual responsiveness. In addition, failure to achieve erection can set up an expectancy of sexual inadequacy that can become a self-fulfilling prophecy. As Masters and Johnson (1970) have noted, the greatest contributor to sexual inadequacy is fear of sexual inadequacy.

- **Premature ejaculation**—This refers to an unsatisfactorily brief period between the commencement of sexual stimulation and the occurrence of ejaculation. This results in the failure of the female partner to achieve satisfaction. In the drinking male, the needs of the female partner are lost in the general dulling of interpersonal sensitivity that occurs with heavy alcohol intake. Therefore, the male frequently focuses on satisfying his own needs and ignores those of his partner. Upon recovery, it may be necessary for the male to relearn the needs of his sexual partner (or learn them for the first time if sexual intercourse was usually conducted while the male was drinking). Sex counseling with both partners may be necessary in order to deal with this problem.

- **Retarded ejaculation or ejaculatory incompetence**—Here the problem is that the male cannot ejaculate while inside the female or cannot ejaculate at all. While the clinical literature would suggest that some alcoholics have sexual difficulties that lead them to use alcohol in order to perform the sexual act (and hence, alcoholics with the inability to ejaculate while inside the female are likely to be part of this problematic population), the more frequently occurring problem in abusive drinkers is the inability to ejaculate at all. This inability is frequently keyed to the alcoholic's attempting intercourse while severely intoxicated and when the sexual response is so depressed that ejaculation is impossible. Or, the alcoholic attempts intercourse after drinking for several days and while in a physiologically exhausted state. In both cases, several failures will lead to an expectation of ejaculatory incompetence that may result in a continuation of this difficulty when the alcoholic begins recovery. In these cases, intense sexual counseling may be needed to deal with the recovering male's psychological apprehensions.

These characteristics are certainly not exhaustive, and we are still learning how alcohol affects the male sexual response. Generally speaking, alcohol at low levels may be disinhibiting and even increase the pleasure of the sexual act. At moderate to high levels it clearly impairs sexual performance and can make the sexual act impossible. While in some cases, heavy drinking may permanently impair the male sexual response, a more likely outcome is that negative psychological expectations about sexual performance will be established; these expectations will have to be dealt with by the counselor during the recovery process.

Sexual Difficulties of the Alcoholic Female

Sexual difficulties also occur in females who abuse alcohol. While the initial literature regarding alcohol and the female described the alcoholic female as a "loose woman" and as very promiscuous, more recent research *does not* support this generalization.

Many females do report that alcohol has a disinhibiting effect on their sexual performances. Interviews by P. Clayton Rivers (one of the authors of this chapter) with women in treatment for alcoholism indicated that the vast majority of these women reported that sexual intercourse after drinking was much more exciting and enjoyable. However, studies of actual physiological responses suggest that the sexual response is inhibited even when the females are reporting more arousal in response to erotic stimuli. For example, Wilson and Lawson (1976) measured vaginal pulse pressure of women at differential dose levels of alcohol. The more alcohol consumed, the lower the vaginal pulse pressure was (i.e., lower physiological arousal). So, while physiological arousal seemed to be reduced by alcohol in this study, the subjective experience of arousal increased.

Despite the heightened psychological expectation, studies of women with severe alcohol problems suggest that orgasm is severely curtailed by chronic alcohol intake (Levine, 1955) and that the sexual drive is inhibited (Glatt, 1961). Other factors that are closely associated with alcoholism in women are sexually related physiological difficulties. For example, one of the earliest descriptions of alcoholic women reported that problem drinking was associated with dysmenorrhea, abortion, childbirth, and sexually-related physical disease. Menstrual periods have also been shown to be instrumental in precipitating excessive drinking in females (Lindbeck, 1972). Wilsnack (1982) has noted the prevalence of sexually related physical problems among alcoholic women and has suggested that alcohol may be used by many women to compensate for feelings of inadequacy. (This brief overview does not do justice to the complexity of alcohol use by the female: the reader is referred to Schuckit and Morrissey [1976] for more information.)

Although the following problems also occur in nonalcoholic women, they should give substance abuse counselors some awareness of potential sexual problems and will aid the counselor in diagnosing these problems in alcoholic females and in the spouses of alcoholic males.

- Orgasmic dysfunction—This can be primary or secondary in nature. The former refers to the failure by the female to ever achieve orgasm (by any means), whereas secondary orgasmic dysfunction occurs in women who have experienced orgasm but who have since lost that ability.
- Vaginismus—This is a psychophysiological difficulty (a spastic contraction of the muscles of the perineum and outer third of the vagina) that prevents

the woman from completing intercourse. It is an involuntary response brought on by imagined, anticipated, or actual attempts at vaginal entry. Assessment of this problem should include a thorough history and a pelvic examination.

- Female Dyspareunia—Dyspareunia denotes pain that occurs during or following intercourse. Causes can range from physiological difficulties (e.g., infection, cysts, lack of lubrication) to psychological difficulties (including lack of interest in the sex act or fear of intercourse). In some instances, the spouse of an alcoholic male has been subjected to sexual abuse and rape. These factors should be carefully explored and evaluated in the therapy situation. Lack of interest in sex can sometimes be a complex issue in the female and may reflect more widespread problems in a couple's relationship.

Littrell (1991) summarized alcohol's effects on sexual responses this way:

> Alcohol does influence sexual behavior. Both sexes believe that alcohol will enhance their sexual response. Drinking an alcohol placebo has been found to increase sexual responsiveness to erotic, nondeviant material. Actual drinking does increase interest in sexual material, however, the physical response is reduced. The impact of alcohol on deviant sexual material requires an elaborate explanation. Belief that alcohol has been consumed does increase sexual interest and response to deviant material. The effect seems to occur because alcohol provides people with an excuse for their behavior (pp. 251–52).

Outlining specific treatment approaches for these problems is beyond the scope of this chapter. The reader is referred to Miller and Mastria (1977, pp. 103–24) for an excellent overview of alcohol-related sexual problems and their treatment in the alcoholic.

The Counselor's Personal Comfort Level in Discussing Sexual Issues

A topic that Miller and Mastria also cover (and which is frequently overlooked or downplayed by the alcoholic counselor) is the counselor's personal acceptance of his own sexuality and the counselor's personal comfort and openness in discussing sexually-related issues with clients. As Miller and Mastria indicate, discussing, clarifying, and thinking through one's own feelings about sex is a necessary first step for the counselor in preparing to help others with their sexual problems. In fact, this may be more important than knowing about all the technical problems and treatment information available on sex. While treatment manuals, research information, and other literature can be helpful, Miller and Mastria suggest that the use of formal discussion groups with other counselors, where opposing views are presented, is helpful to many counselors in desensitizing themselves to the topic and exposing them to views that are different from their own. They also suggest that blind spots in sexual counseling with couples can be compensated for by pairing male and female counselors. Such an arrangement allows both clients to feel that they have an ally; it also provides the opportunity for the counselors to model how men and women can relate to each other in an adult and constructive manner.

IS THERE A DIFFERENCE BETWEEN ALCOHOLISM AND ALCOHOL ABUSE?

The first problem faced in answering the question is to define alcoholism and alcohol abuse. Unfortunately, these definitions are not well established and agreed upon across the substance abuse field. More accepted are the Diagnostic and Statistical Manual of the American Psychiatric Association (DSM-IV) definitions of alcohol dependence and alcohol abuse. The DSM-IV has grouped all the substance abuse syndromes together, including alcohol, because the professionals working on this manual thought there was considerable overlap of alcohol and other drug abuse. Lets first look at substance abuse. The DSM-IV describes substance abuse as:

> A maladaptive pattern of substance use leading to clinically significant impairment or distress, as manifested by one (or more) of the following occurring within a twelve-month period. (1) a recurrent substance use resulting in a failure to fulfill major role obligations at work, school, or home (e.g., repeated absences or poor work performance related to substance use; substance-related absences, suspensions, or expulsions from school; neglect of children or household); (2) recurrent substance use in situations in which it is physically hazardous (e.g., driving an automobile or operating a machine when impaired by substance use); (3) recurrent substance-related legal problems (e.g., arrests for substance-related disorderly conduct); and/or (4) continued substance use despite having persistent or recurrent social or interpersonal problems caused or exacerbated by the effects of the substance (e.g., arguments with the spouse about consequences of intoxication, physical fights).

The symptoms listed above have never met the criteria for substance dependence for this class of substance. The DSM-IV describes alcohol dependence as:

A maladaptive pattern of substance use, leading to clinically significant impairment or distress, as manifested by three (or more) of the following occurring at any one time in the same twelve-month period. (1) Tolerance as defined by markedly increased amounts of the substance to achieve intoxication to the desired effect; and markedly diminished effect with continued use of the same amount of the substance. (2) Withdrawal, as manifested by either the characteristic withdrawal syndrome for the substance (refer to criteria A and B of the criteria sets for withdrawal from the specific substances); or the same (or closely related substance) is taken to relieve or avoid the withdrawal syndrome. (3) The substance is often taken in larger amounts or over a longer [time period] than was intended. (4) There is a persistent desire or unsuccessful efforts to cut down or control substance use. (5) A great deal of time is spent in activities necessary to obtain the substance (e.g., visiting multiple doctors or driving long distances), use the substance (e.g., chain smoking), or recover from its effects. (6) Important social, occupational, or recreational activities are given up or reduced because of substance use. (7) The substance use is continued despite knowledge of having a persistent or recurrent physical or psychological problem that is likely to have been caused or exacerbated by the substance (e.g., current cocaine use despite the recognition of cocaine-induced depression or continued drinking despite recognition that an ulcer was made worse by alcohol consumption). (DSM-IV, 1995, pp. 182–83.)

The diagnostician should also specify With Physiological Dependence or Without Physiological Dependence with items 1 and 2 above present in the first diagnosis and absent from the second.

To be more specific, yes, there is a difference between an alcoholic and an alcohol abuser. However, neither term is totally satisfactory when used to describe the condition of an individual. Abuse and misuse are unsatisfactory concepts within a scientific approach because they involve value judgments. Terms such as *unsanctioned use, hazardous use, dysfunctional use,* and *harmful use* are less value laden and go further toward describing the situation (just as *uncontrolled drinking* or *uncontrolled behavior* go further toward describing a situation than the term *alcoholic drinking*). As Jellinek (1960) has pointed out, there are many types of alcoholism, each type representing different behaviors and different levels of addiction to alcohol. (For those who are not familiar with it, Jellinek's classic *The Disease Concept of Alcoholism* is highly recommended.) Many people quote Jellinek and speak of alcoholism as a disease. But they hardly ever mention that Jellinek himself only saw two of the several types of alcoholism that he described as a disease; that he presented his work as a "working hypothesis," not fact; and that he took no explicit stand on issues such as irreversibility of the syndrome. It is, then, the person's own behavior in relation to alcohol or drugs that we must examine. What does this behavior mean in the context of the individual's own life? One man's normal drinking could be another man's alcoholism. Or with regard to the original question: One man's alcohol abuse might be another man's alcoholism. The bottom line is: How will you, as a counselor, treat clients differently according to their needs?

HOW SHOULD THE COUNSELOR USE ALCOHOLICS ANONYMOUS OR NARCOTICS ANONYMOUS IN THE OVERALL TREATMENT PLAN?

First, the counselor should have a thorough understanding of the A.A. or Narcotics Anonymous (N.A.) program. For the nonalcoholic counselor this would involve reading the Big Book of A.A. and attending open meetings. For the recovering alcoholic or drug abuser who is a member of either group, this would include a recognition of the limits of A.A. or N.A. It is important for counselors, regardless of whether they are recovering alcoholics or not, to recognize both the assets and limitations of the self-help group.

Again, this realization leads us to an appropriate differential diagnosis that is translated into an appropriate treatment plan. There are some individuals who will respond very favorably to a referral to A.A. or N.A. There are others for whom this type of referral would be inappropriate or at least insufficient as a total treatment plan.

For example, American Indians, who have been taught to keep their problems to themselves, often do not respond to the traditional A.A. meeting where they are expected to share their drinking history with other members. This is especially true when all other members of the meeting are white. Chicanos with a macho self-image might have problems with the idea of admitting one's powerlessness over alcohol (the first of the 12 steps). The nonbeliever might have problems with the concept of a "higher power," even with the addendum "[God] as we understand him." As a patient once explained to this author, "They told me at A.A. that I needed to turn my life over to my higher power as I see him, even if my higher power was a door knob." He then looked up at me and in all seriousness said, "They wanted me to turn my life over to a door knob!"

Perhaps this understanding of A.A. was a bit distorted. But it is hard to convince an antireligious person that A.A. is not a religious program, when 6 of the 12 steps mention God or "your higher power" specifically. Some people are unable or do not want to differentiate between religious and spiritual. This does not mean that these people are untreatable or a poor treatment risk. They may very well respond to an alternative to A.A. Thus, use A.A. and N.A. where appropriate, but do not depend solely on them for the treatment of the chemically dependent person.

WHAT IS THE MOST EFFECTIVE TREATMENT MODEL FOR CHEMICALLY DEPENDENT PEOPLE?

This is a difficult question to answer. Evaluations of various treatment models are either not available or are not generally agreed upon by various theoretical orientations. Outcome results are subject to question because programs are often self-selective with regard to clients. For example, private programs that require payment end up mostly treating people who have money or a job with an insurance policy to pay for treatment. The outcome with these people is likely to be better than with those who have no job and no money. Often the success rate reported by a program does not include the people who started the program but dropped out during treatment.

The most widely accepted approach to treatment is Alcoholics Anonymous. The 12 steps of A.A. are used in more treatment programs than any other approach. These steps have been revised for a variety of programs including overeating, gambling, and others. The success of A.A. is perhaps overrated when viewed in an overall perspective, though. The latest reported number of A.A. members is around one million. Given that there are over ten million alcoholics, that would mean one in ten alcoholics has found A.A. to be an acceptable program for their sobriety, one in ten is not enough.

What is needed in the field of chemical dependency is a variety of treatment approaches that meet the needs of a variety of individuals. This should include the family members, as suggested by Lawson, Peterson, and Lawson (1983). This family approach has the added appeal of preventing intergenerational alcoholism or chemical dependency and working as a prevention program for the children of alcoholics or chemical abusers. The most effective treatment program will look at all aspects of a person's life and will provide treatment for each of these areas as necessary.

One of the model considerations now under debate is the relative effectiveness of inpatient vs. outpatient treatment. In one of the first comparisons of inpatient and outpatient programs, Edwards and Guthrie (1966) randomly assigned middle-class alcoholics to inpatient treatment (eight plus weeks) or to outpatient group therapy of seven plus weeks. They found no differences in treatment effectiveness after assessing outcome at six months and one year. In a more recent study, Chapman and Huygens (1988) used six- and eighteen-month follow-ups to measure outcome in patients who had been in either inpatient or outpatient treatment. They failed to find any differences in treatment outcome for patients who had received inpatient or outpatient therapy. While there are a few exceptions, there has been a general trend of no differences between inpatient and outpatient programs when adequate control conditions are utilized (e.g., random assignment of patients to either inpatient or outpatient therapy).

Of course, one should not forget that most real-world alcohol treatment does not have random assignment and instead involves a crude matching of patients to treatment. That is, patients choose and stay with a program that they feel they can get something from, in the best of real world matching. A few studies have attempted to find out whether particular types of patients would do better in inpatient vs. outpatient therapy. A 1985 study by Meyer, Berman, and Rivers found, surprisingly, that the stable, financially and socially secure patients did better in inpatient therapy while the less socially stable, lower socioeconomic, and more severe alcoholics did better in outpatient therapy. As Littrell (1989) suggests, such a result is counterintuitive and may well be a spurious finding. However, a similar outcome was obtained by McLellan, Luborsky, Woody, O'Brien, and Druely (1983). Whatever the nature of the effects of inpatient vs. outpatient treatment, they are likely to be complex as the above research findings suggest. It is likely that the new emphasis on individualized, variable-stay treatment programs will lead to a discovery of several important ways in which one can combine inpatient, outpatient, and even self-care to the best advantage of the client.

The most effective treatment model for the chemically dependent person is a treatment model that meets the unique treatment needs of the individual. This may seem like a simple answer to a complex question; however, it is as simple as it is true!

HOW WOULD YOU APPROACH AND CONFRONT A CLOSE FRIEND, COLLEAGUE, OR COWORKER ABOUT HIS ALCOHOL PROBLEMS?

To answer this question we obtained the assistance of some special people who have a great deal of experience in the chemical dependency field. We have summarized their interviews and have attempted to capture, as accurately as possible, the flavor of their comments. The interviewees' answers to this question are given below. (Authors' Note: Since the above question was asked in 1983, many things have changed in the substance abuse treatment area. To see just how much the response to this question might change, the first three contributors from the 1984 volume were recontacted and asked to answer the question from their current perspective on confronting someone and getting them to treatment. For comparison purposes, the original statement appears first and the new statement follows.)

Ellen McCrory, Director
St. Monica's Halfway House
Lincoln, Nebraska

I'd start out by shooting the breeze—make them comfortable, get their defenses down a bit. Then come right out and talk to them directly about their problems. I'd share my concerns and feelings about what I've seen and how they've changed. If I know them well, I'll point out what they used to be able to do. I'd also point out that their job is suffering. Most of the time when I confront it is from a feeling level—they know that I care about them. I feel that many times an alcoholic is waiting for someone to say something. I usually go into these sessions with the same plan—I let them know I'm willing [to help]. I've never had someone turn me down. I also place the responsibility [for doing something about their problem] on them, except at work, where it is an either/or proposition.

Women are, in a sense, easier to confront; [there is] almost a sense that they're supposed to do what is expected of them. If you know the individual, you know where they are vulnerable. For example, you can break through a woman's defenses through her children—if the woman is guilty about the children [or it can be assumed they will be better off without her while she's in treatment in terms of long-term effects] then the woman is more likely to be able to accept treatment.

If the family is involved, the better off you are; the more leverage you have. That is why late-stage alcoholics are hard to intervene with, i.e., there's no leverage. Also, when a family member is alone they may be rather ineffectual in confronting the alcoholic; however, when the same family member is part of an intervention team confronting the alcoholic, they have considerably more impact. Generally speaking, when confronting the alcoholic it is better to have more than one person, and it is better to have more than one family member whenever possible.

1995 Statement by Ellen McCrory, who has just retired as Director of St. Monica's.

My recommendation wouldn't change much. A recent confrontation with an employee who had resumed substance abuse comes to mind. I told her that it was either treatment or no job. I also told her I would help her set up what she needed in terms of treatment, and I would see that she got it. I didn't guarantee the job, but I told her that future employment depended upon her ability to resolve her problems.

In point of fact, our referrals have changed over the past ten years or so. Dual diagnoses are now more frequent referrals. We are now dealing with an entirely different client—more emotional problems. These women are more fragile. We have to deal with them in a much softer way. I have found that I like working with the dual-diagnosis client. They are more ready to work [on their problems]. They bond more with staff. They take longer to treat but they are committed to treatment. What is different is that one must take the time to provide the treatment they need and we have that time at St. Monica's.

Dealing with dual-diagnosis clients has meant that we had to become more knowledgeable as a staff to deal with their more complex problems. Our learning is reflected in the way we use our psychology extern, who no longer has to do so much individual therapy and can now act more as a consultant to counselors who are seeing more clients individually themselves.

We must have a more trained staff, because we now get referrals from treatment agencies, which [because of managed care] have been able to provide only a small part of the total treatment the client needs. So, we have become the ones that provide the long-term care that these dual diagnosis women need. [*Author's Note:* Recently St. Monica's level of care was officially upgraded to what the State of Nebraska labels a "therapeutic community."]

Duke Engel, Director and Intervention Specialist
Independence Center
Lincoln, Nebraska

Originally our confrontation [at Independence Center] was based on a heavy confrontational model, i.e., lay out the facts very hard and without qualification. But with co-workers and friends this is not appropriate. We are now moving to a more invitational model. We think this model suggests four things.

1. Get across your personal concern for the person being confronted.
2. Talk about the facts of alcoholism and how these facts relate to the confrontee's problem, if at all possible.
3. Stay away from moral judgments. And stay away from opinions and use facts when discussing the drinker's drinking behavior. For ex-

ample, don't say, "You are drinking too much," but instead indicate that the person had 10 beers, i.e., be specific.

4. Give an open invitation—put forth hope that the drinker can get better, that treatment can help. Leave the door open, but don't nag them. These types of interventions may go on over a period of several months. With a friend or co-worker, it may take months, years, and may involve several people talking to the abusive drinker before they agree to enter treatment.

We do more interventions of this type now, i.e., the open invitation kind. We expect that this type of intervention approach [involving gentle persuasion instead of harsh confrontation] will be the one we will use in the future. If you are successful using this approach, the friend, co-worker, or relative enters treatment with a better attitude. We may still use heavy confrontation if the alcohol problem has placed the person and those around them in crisis (i.e., something bad might happen if we don't take action). However, it is only in this type of situation that we would really put pressure on the drinking individual.

Duke Engle's 1995 statement. Duke is now the Director of the Independence Center, Lincoln, Nebraska.

Today, we work with an intervention model that is slower, more humane, more natural, more flexible, and more easily put to work by all kinds of people. It does not depend on "an intervention posse" to create a crisis.

We do not ask friends or family to ignore problems created by alcohol or other drugs nor do we ask them to take responsibility for it. We ask them to "flash their brights" at it. This technique is similar to what a motorist does when he sees an oncoming vehicle at night without lights. He does not try to turn on their lights for them but he does not ignore the problem either. He flashes his brights at them.

We see six methods involved in flashing your brights.

1. Be factual about the behavioral issues and other problems that you see the alcohol or drug use creating. Report observations about their behavior or its results. Tape recordings are sometimes ideal for this technique. Being factual about observations helps the intervenor avoid diagnosis, judgment, and opinion, e.g., "I think you drink too much."
2. Express your personal concern about those problems and your care for the individual involved. One wife repeatedly had angry morning-after confrontations with her husband. When she calmly told him one

morning how much his abuse of himself with alcohol concerned her, she found a different reaction from him.

3. Offer education about substance abuse and recovery. Not only are many substance abusers ignorant about the nature of abuse, they also often have substantial pieces of misinformation. When asked whether his kids had ever intervened with him, one father said, "Not exactly. I mean, every time there is a drunk driving commercial on television my six year old makes sure that I see it." The child intervened with his father by offering him education about substance abuse.

4. Hold them accountable for their behavior. There are two ways to express this idea—first, enforce logical consequences; second, solve your own problem. As friends and family we cannot solve their problems with drinking or drugging, but we can solve the pain and the problems we are having with it. When we do so, we naturally enforce logical consequences on them. When family members begin attending Al-Anon or Naranon they are solving their own problem. They are also enforcing a logical consequence on the problem drinker (or drug user).

5. Offer hope and choices for help. The knowledge that other people have found ways to recover is a powerful motivator for overcoming the hopeless sensation that change is an impossibility.

6. Network with other concerned persons. In the course of two weeks, six different friends at various times approached a drug addict with their individual facts and concerns. Each one laid down the same counselor's business card to encourage the person to seek help. They were networked together, providing a consistent picture and consistent invitation to him. Their impact was as dramatic as a single major "intervention confrontation."

Our survey of 259 patients at Independence Center revealed that 10 to 11 different people (or agencies) had flashed their brights at them before they sought help for themselves. We now encourage intervenors to go in for the long term and not to worry about putting all their eggs in one big intervention basket. Because friends and family are more comfortable with these methods, they act more often and more consistently than with older intervention-posse techniques.

Dr. William Leipold, one of the originators and former director of the first Valley Hope Alcohol Treatment Center, Norton, Kansas. He is currently president of the Valley Hope Association, Norton, Kansas.

I try to create a crisis in their lives. I try to get the alcoholic to confront his/ her drinking problem. Frequently, their denial system is so well established that they will not accept that they have a problem and will not enter treatment. In these cases, I try to persuade people close to the alcoholic to create a crisis in their life. For example, we recently suggested to the wife of an alcoholic that the next time he went driving while he was intoxicated that she should call the police and have him arrested for DWI. She would not do it because she was afraid it would create difficulty for the family. It is interesting that similar circumstances finally created the crisis that brought the man to treatment. Whether it is a friend, colleague, etc., we have to work with anything that gets past denial—we try to get them to face up to their denial. In another case, the person soiled himself, vomited, and generally was a filthy person following his drunken bouts. We suggested to the wife that she put in a full-length mirror in the basement, where he normally drank himself into unconsciousness. While the alcoholic refused to accept that this dirty and disheveled person was really him, he did enter treatment for his problem. If the individual is an alcoholic, you try to get him to treatment any way you can. If they come to treatment angry and resistant, we will deal with that issue in the treatment setting as a part of treatment. You must remember that frequently when we get calls about someone's drinking problem, it is generally very late in the person's drinking history, and there is some type of emergency for the person who is drinking and/or for those around them.

In recent years we are getting more and more cases where we get someone who is still in the early stages of alcoholism. This is because our education of the public has made the detection of alcoholism possible earlier [in the person's drinking career]. Here we may make a more subtle approach, e.g., leaving brochures about alcoholism and alcoholism treatment in the living room.

We have also found that if we have family members come into treatment [before the alcoholic is willing to come], that not only does the family feel better and happier, but we eventually get the alcoholic into treatment in 95 percent of the cases. In other words, anything that can be utilized should be utilized; what we find most effective for referrals are the employee assistance and industrial programs. We have also found that the education of judges and probation officers and prosecuting attorneys is also helpful in getting people into treatment. To sum up, it depends on the severity of the problem what confrontation methods you use. Helping the families and getting them involved in pressuring the alcoholic seems to be the best approach. In several cases we've had alcoholics come to treatment [following the treatment of their families] saying that all the happiness and relief in the family brought them to treatment. They just could not stand all that happiness around them!

William Leipold's 1995 statement. Dr. Leipold is now President emeritus of the Valley Hope Association and enjoys retirement in Colorado.

Ten years later and the average age of the alcoholic at our Valley Hope Centers runs between 33 to 35 years of age. That is down from the 48 years of age when we opened our first Valley Hope Center in 1967.

It is a different ballgame today, although the basics of alcoholism have not changed. Denial still ranks as the number one problem and the answer to this denial is pretty much the same.

What has changed is length of stay, which today is 19 days or less. Outpatient is the treatment of choice for most HMOs and other insurance companies. If a person fails outpatient, inpatient may be utilized; albeit at a reduced rate. If denial is still the number-one problem, and it is, then with shorter days of stay the treatment centers have to make adjustments.

The family becomes really important, not only as a confrontational mechanism but as a treatment resource for individual recovery. The legal system has a better understanding of what to do to help, but in many ways tougher laws have made it more difficult to get the alcoholic into treatment.

While it is still imperative to use confrontational methods to get the alcoholic into treatment and to work through the denial defense, there is a greater denial that needs to be worked on as well. That denial is focused in the HMOs' and other insurance companies' approach to alcoholism. It is now easier to deny benefits than to give them. The alcoholic denial system keeps them from help and the insurance denial system helps keep them from treatment. What should be done?

Ralph Fox, Executive Director
Houses of Hope, Inc.
Lincoln, Nebraska

I feel pretty strongly about this. I would refer them to someone else who could be objective.

James S. Peterson, PhD
Professor of Rehabilitation Counseling
Southern Illinois University
Carbondale, Illinois

This is a ticklish situation; not only due to its very personal nature, but also because one expects the response to be defensive and hostile.

However, most professionals agree that ignoring the problem is not the answer.

Circumstances and individual differences do dictate [the response] to a certain extent, but there are a few things to keep in mind when approaching the problem drinker.

First, do your homework. It is important to cite specific examples; a general accusation can be easily denied and/or discounted.

Second, use a straightforward but supportive approach. Avoid uses of guilt, blaming, or angry confrontation. This will prevent the problem drinker from reacting to the way it is said, and focus more on the content of what is being said.

Third, have some resources at your fingertips that you can recommend. Be specific, cite a name and a phone number, and offer to help make some arrangements. If possible, do it right then and there—often the problem drinker will agree to seek help, but never follow through on his own.

Finally, be willing to come away with less than a completely successful encounter. Don't press on indefinitely once you have made your point—it is often enough to "plant the seed" and allow some time for reflection. Leave the door open for future contact.

Ann Lawson, Ph.D.
Associate Professor
Psychology and Family Studies
U.S. International University
San Diego, California

Having lived in an alcoholic family as a child, I learned not to confront people about their drinking. This is a strong taboo for those who are close to the person with the drinking problem. It allows the person to drink more comfortably.

If I were concerned about a friend or family member, I would use a family-systems approach to define the drinking as it affects the family system and each of the members. I would work with all of these people together, including the children. With this approach it is necessary to help each person describe specific behaviors of the drinker and how the behaviors have affected them. Often it becomes more difficult for that person to continue drinking with the new knowledge of how this affects those closest to them.

It is advisable to look for adaptive consequences of the drinking in a family—what does the family gain when the person is drinking? This may be closeness, distance, sexual intimacy or avoidance, freedom, martyrdom, or a number of complicated relationship dynamics that may stem from the families of origin.

It is important to remember that one person cannot force someone else to change a drinking pattern, but the family can express themselves and reduce enabling behavior, thus making it more difficult for the drinking to continue. There is also help for those family members who hurt as a result of another's drinking. Children who live with alcoholic parents need counseling to reduce the risk of intergenerational alcoholism.

DISCUSSION QUESTIONS

1. After reading the questions and answers in this chapter make up a list of questions and answers that the chapter did not include. Are there questions for which you believe others would also like to know the answer(s)? Are your questions about issues of concern for the field as a whole or are they peculiar to your interests? Can you find answers to the questions in the clinical and empirical research literature? Do a brief library search on your most important questions.

2. If someone close to you had an alcohol/drug problem, which of the examples given in this chapter would you feel most comfortable following in confronting him or her about the problem? Would you feel more comfortable using your own method of confrontation instead of those suggested in this chapter? Why?

3. After reading the material on the different needs for treatment of women with substance abuse problems, outline an ideal treatment program for women. What parts of the typical substance abuse treatment program would you keep? What major changes would you make in the traditional program of treatment? Why?

4. Look up the findings in the research literature that compare inpatient and outpatient treatment. After reading this literature which is more effective? Why are both modalities necessary? What type of patient does better in an inpatient program and what type of patient does better (or as well) in outpatient treatment?

REFERENCES

American Psychiatric Association (1995). *Diagnostic and statistical manual IV*. Washington, DC: American Psychiatric Association.

Argeriou, M., & Manohar, V. (1978). Relative effectiveness of nonalcoholics and recovered alcoholics as counselors. *Journal of Studies on Alcohol, 39,* 793–99.

Blume, S. (1977). Role of the recovered alcoholic in the treatment of alcoholism. In B. Kissen, & H. Begleiter (Eds.), *The biology of alcoholism: Treatment and rehabilitation of the chronic alcoholic* (Vol. 5). (pp. 545–65). New York: Plenum Publishing Corporation.

Bohman, M. (1978). Some genetic aspects of alcoholism and criminality. *Archives of General Psychiatry, 35,* 269–76.

Bourne, P. G., & Light, E. (1979). Alcohol problems in blacks and women. In J. H. Mendelson, & N. K. Mello (Eds.), *The diagnosis and treatment of alcoholism* (pp. 84–123). New York: McGraw-Hill Publishing Co.

Burman, S. (1992). A model for women's alcohol/drug treatment. *Alcoholism Treatment Quarterly, 9,* 87–98.

Chapman, P. L. H., & Huygens, I. (1988). An evaluation of three treatment programmes for alcoholism: An experimental study with 6- and 18-month followups. *British Journal of Addictions, 83,* 67–81.

Clark, W. B. (1976). Loss of control, heavy drinking and drinking problems in a longitudinal setting. *Journal of Study on Alcohol, 37,* 1256–90.

Cotton, N. S. (1979). The familial incidence of alcoholism. *Journal of Studies on Alcohol, 40,* 89–115.

Covner, B. J. (1969). Screening volunteer alcoholism counselors. *Quarterly Journal of Studies on Alcohol, 30,* 420–25.

Edwards, G., & Guthrie, S. (1966). A comparison of inpatient and outpatient treatment of alcohol dependence. *Lancet, 1,* 467–68.

Falkey, D. B. (1971). Standards, recruitment, training, and use of indigenous personnel in alcohol and drug misuse programs. *Selected papers of 22nd Meeting of Alcohol and Drug Problems Association, 38–41.*

Farkas, G. M., & Rosen, R. C. (1976). The effect of alcohol on elicited male sexual response. *Journal of Studies on Alcohol, 37,* 262–65.

Gantt, W. H. (1940). Effect of alcohol on sexual reflexes in dogs. *American Journal of Physiology, 360.*

Gantt, W. H. (1952). Effects of alcohol on sexual reflexes of normal and neurotic dogs. *Psychosomatic Medicine, 14,* 174–81.

Glatt, M. M. (1961). The drinking habits of English middle class alcoholics. *Acta Psychiatria Scandinavia, 37,* 88.

Goodwin, D. (1979). Genetic determinants of alcoholism. In J. Mendelson, & N. Mello (Eds.), *The diagnosis and treatment of alcoholism* (pp. 59–82). New York: McGraw-Hill Publishing Co.

Jellinek, E. M. (1960). *The disease concept of alcoholism.* New Brunswick, NJ: Hillhouse Press.

Kaij, L. (1960). *Studies on the etiology and sequels of abuse of alcohol.* Department of Psychiatry, University of Lund, Sweden.

Kalb, M., & Propper, M. S. (1976). The future of alcohology: Craft or science? *American Journal of Psychiatry, 113,* 641–45.

Kirk, W. G., Best, J. B., & Irwin, P. (1986). The perception of empathy in alcoholism counselors. *Journal of Studies on Alcohol, 47,* 82–84.

Lawson, G., Peterson, J., & Lawson, A. (1983). *Alcoholism and the family: A guide to treatment and prevention.* Gaithersburg, MD: Aspen Publishing, Inc.

Leavy, R. L., & Dunlosky, J. T. (1989). Undergraduate student and faculty perceptions of problem drinking. *Journal of Studies on Alcohol, 50,* 107.

Levine, T. (1955). The sexual adjustment of alcoholics: A clinical study of a selected sample. *Quarterly Journal of Studies on Alcohol, 16,* 675–80.

Lindbeck, V. L. (1972). The woman alcoholic: A review of the literature. *The International Journal of the Addictions, 7,* 567–80.

Littrell, J. (1989). *Understanding and treating alcoholism: An empirically based clinician's handbook for the treatment of alcoholism.* Hillsdale, NJ: Lawrence Erlbaum Associates, Inc.

Littrell, J. (1991). *Understanding and treating alcoholism: Vol. 2. Biological, psychological and social aspects of alcohol consumption and abuse.* Hillsdale, NJ: Lawrence Erlbaum Associates, Inc.

McLellen, A. T., Luborsky, L., Woody, G. E., O'Brien, C., & Druely, K. (1983). Predicting response to alcohol and drug abuse treatments. *Archives of General Psychiatry, 40,* 620–25.

Masters, S. H., & Johnson, V. (1970). *Human sexual inadequacy.* Boston: Little, Brown & Co.

Meyer, J., Berman, J., & Rivers, P. C. (1985). Dispositional assessment with alcoholics. *International Journal of Addictions, 20,* 1463–78.

Miller, P. A., & Mastria, M. A. (1977). *Alternatives to alcohol abuse: A social learning model.* Champaign, IL: Research Press.

Murray, R., & Stabenau, J. (1982). Genetic factors in alcoholism predisposition. In E. M. Pattison & E. Kaufman (Eds.), *Encyclopedic handbook of alcoholism* (pp. 135–44). New York: Gardner Press.

Partanen, J., Bruun, K., & Markkaners, T. (1966). *Inheritance of drinking behavior.* New Brunswick, NJ: Rutgers University Center on Alcohol Studies.

Pattison, E. M. (1973). A differential view of manpower resources. In G. Staub & U. Kent (Eds.), *The paraprofessional in the treatment of alcoholism.* Springfield, IL: Charles C Thomas, Publisher.

Rosenberg, C. M. (1974). The responsibility of direct treatment. *Alcohol Health and Research World,* 3–5.

Rosenberg, C. M., Gerrein, J. R., Manohar, V., & Liftik, J. (1976). Evaluation of training of alcohol counselors. *Journal of Studies on Alcohol, 37,* 1236–46.

Rossi, J., & Filstead, W. J. (1976). "Treating" the treatment issues: Some general observations about the treatment of alcoholics. In W. J. Filstead, J. Rossi, & M. Keller (Eds), *Alcohol and alcohol problems: New thinking and new directions.* (pp. 193–227). Cambridge, MA: Ballenger.

Schuckit, M. A., & Morrissey, E. R. (1976). Alcoholism in women: Some clinical and social perspectives with an emphasis on some possible subtypes: In M. Greenblatt, & M. A. Schuckit (Eds.), *Alcoholism problems in women and children* (pp. 5–35). San Diego: Grune & Stratton.

Strachen, G. (1973). Non-alcoholics vs. recovered personnel. In G. Staub, & U. Kent (Eds.), *The paraprofessional in the treatment of alcoholism.* Springfield, IL: Charles C Thomas Publisher.

Tamerin, J. S. (1978). The psychotherapy of alcoholic women. In S. Zimberg, J. Wallace, & S. B. Blume (Eds.), *Practical approaches to alcoholism psychotherapy* (pp. 183–203). New York: Plenum Publishing Corporation.

Vaillant, G. E. (1995). *The natural history of alcoholism revisited.* Cambridge, MA: Harvard University Press.

Wallace, J. (1978). Working with the preferred defense structure of the recovering alcoholic. In S. Zimberg, J. Wallace, & S. Blume (Eds.), *Practical approaches to alcoholism psychotherapy* (pp. 19–29). New York: Plenum Publishing Corporation.

Wilsnack, S. (1982). Alcohol abuse and alcoholism in women. In E. M. Pattison, & E. Kaufman (Eds.), *Encyclopedic handbook of alcoholism* (pp. 718–35). New York: Gardner Press.

Wilson, G. T., & Lawson, D. T. (1976). Effects of alcohol on sexual arousal in women. *Journal of Abnormal Psychology, 85,* 489–97.

Index

371

Credit, assigning of, 32
Criminal behavior, 243–245
Criminal law, 45
Culture
    affiliation, diversity in, 240–242
    appreciation of, by counselor, 6
    values, divergence of, value system of
        counselor, 13

D

Dating, of clients, working in agency and,
    312
Death, right to, value system of counselor,
    14
Decision making, ethical, 42–44
Definitions, in needs assessment, 102
Demands, daily, within agency, 289
Denial, 101
Dependence, defined, 102
Developmental levels, diversity in, 226–227
Developmental stage, diversity in, 223–227
Deviant behavior, 243–245
Diagnosis
    alcoholism, 102–105, 104t-108t
        criteria, 106t-108t
        major criteria for, 104t-105t
    behavior patterns, 122t
    case example, 112–120
    of chemical dependency, 105–110
    class of substance, diagnoses associated
        with, 113t
    as clinical process, 97
    Diagnostic and Statistical Manual of
        American Psychiatric Association,
        110–112
    diagnostic classifications, 97–98
    diagnostic manuals, 110–112, *110–112,*
        113t
    Michigan Alcoholism Screening Test, 102
    Minnesota Multiphasic Personality
        Inventory, 102
    multivariate syndromes, 99
    as social process, 96–97
    substance, class of, diagnoses associated
        with, 113t
    substance abuse, criteria for, *111*
    substance dependence, criteria for, *110–
        111*

    substance intoxication, criteria for, *111*
    substance withdrawal, criteria for, *112*
Diagnostic and Statistical Manual of
    American Psychiatric Association,
    110–112
Diagnostic Levels 1–3, 102–103
Disease, alcoholism as, 350–351
Disease Concept of Alcoholism, 357
Distance, inter-agency communication and,
    309–310
Diversity
    age, 223–227
    Alcoholics Anonymous, 229–230
    chemical dependency development,
        225–226
    criminal behavior, 243–245
    cultural affiliation, 240–242
    developmental levels, 226–227
    developmental stage, 223–227, 225
    deviant behavior, 243–245
    drugs of choice, 248
    employment issues, 239–240
    family
        factors, in development of chemical
            dependency, 228–229
        history, 227–233
    gender, 233–238
    genetics, 227–233
        predispositions, 230–231, 232t
    guilt, sex as source of, 234
    interpersonal needs, 229–230
    medical problems, 242–243
    mental health, 238–239
    overview, 248–249
    personality, 238–239
    psychological factors, 246–248
    psychological family-based risk factors,
        231–233
    racial affiliation, 240–242
    religion, 242
    risk levels, 232t
    self-help groups, 229–230
    sex
        dysfunction, 236–237
        history, 233–238, 234–236
    sex therapist, refering client to, 237–238
    sociological risk factors, family-based,
        231–233
    stress, 245–248, 246–248
    trauma, history of, 245–248

characteristics of, 281–283
research, 277–281
self knowledge, 275
self-regulation, 274
significant others, 276
stabilization, 274
understanding, 274–275
warning sign
  identification, 275
  prevention, 275–276
Religion
  diversity in, 242
  value system of counselor, 11–12
Respect, in counseling, 73–74
Responsibility, issues of, for counselor,
  26–27
Retarded ejaculation, 353
Right to die, value system of counselor, 14
Risk
  factors, chemical dependency, 105
  in group counseling, willingness for, 153
  levels, diversity in, 232t
Roles, in family, family counseling and,
  183–185
Rotating workloads, within agency,
  322–323
Routine tasks, within agency, 297–298
Rumor, inter-agency, 310

S

Screening, by counselor, 62–64
Self awareness, of counselor, 5
Self-disclosing, by counselor, 83–84
Self doubts, working in agency and,
  299–300
Self-help groups, 147–148, 229–230
Self image, enhancement of, 342–345
Self investors, within agency, 328
Self knowledge, relapse prevention and, 275
Self regulation, relapse prevention and, 274
Self respect, of counselor, 5
Sense of humor, of counselor, 6, 17
Sex therapist, refering client to, 237–238
Sexual exploitation of client, 36–38
Sexual history, diversity in, 233–238
Sexual intercourse, with current, former
  clients, working in agency and, 313
Sexuality

difficulties, alcoholic female, 354–355
dysfunction, 236–237
effect of alcohol on, 352
issues, comfort level, in discussing,
  355–356
Significant others, relapse prevention and,
  276
Skills of counselor, 62–69
  clinical evaluation, 62–65
    assessment, 64–65
    screening, 62–64
  referral, 67–68
  treatment planning, 65–67
Social activities, working in agency and,
  326–327
Social symptoms, chemical dependency, 109
Sociological risk factors, family-based,
  231–233
Solicitation of client, for donations, 40–41
Spiritual symptoms, chemical dependency,
  109
Stabilization, relapse prevention and, 274
Staff
  motivation, within agency, 291
  recovering, nonrecovering, conflict,
    within agency, 290–295
  support groups, within agency, 322
Statutory law, 45
Strategic family therapy, 197–203
Stress, 245–248
Structural family therapy, 193–197
Style, of counselor, 5
Substance abuse
  diagnostic criteria, *111. See also* chemical
    dependency
Substance dependence, diagnostic criteria,
  110–111
Substance intoxication, diagnostic criteria,
  111
Substance withdrawal, diagnsotic criteria,
  112
Subsystems, of family, family counseling
  and, 186
Suicide threats, 50–51
Supervision, 87–89
Supervisors, within agency, communicating
  with, 305–306
Support personnel, interacting with, within
  agency, 306
Symptoms, of chemical dependency, 96–99.